THE PTOLEMIES, THE SEA AND THE NILE

With its emphasis on the dynasty's concern for control of the sea – both the Mediterranean and the Red Sea – and the Nile, this book offers a new and multifaceted perspective on Ptolemaic power in a key period of Hellenistic history. Within the developing Aegean empire of the Ptolemies, the role of the navy is examined together with that of its admirals. Egypt's close relationship to Rhodes is subjected to scrutiny, as is the constant threat of piracy to the transport of goods on the Nile and by sea. Along with the trade in grain came the exchange of other products. Ptolemaic kings used their wealth for luxury ships, and the dissemination of royal portraiture was accompanied by royal cult. Alexandria, the new capital of Egypt, attracted poets, scholars and even philosophers; geographical exploration by sea was a feature of the period and observations of the time enjoyed a long afterlife.

KOSTAS BURASELIS is Professor of Ancient History at the University of Athens. His favoured fields of research are in Hellenistic and Roman history. He has written and edited a number of books and numerous articles on related subjects.

MARY STEFANOU is a PhD student at the University of Athens, currently teaching classical philology in a Greek secondary school. She is the author of articles on ancient Greek historical subjects and on the teaching of history. Her main research interests lie in Hellenistic history, the political and institutional history of Ptolemaic Egypt, Hellenistic armies and immigration in the Hellenistic world.

DOROTHY J. THOMPSON, Fellow of Girton College, Cambridge, is an ancient historian with a particular interest in Hellenistic Egypt. She is a Fellow of the British Academy and an Honorary President of the International Society of Papyrologists. The second edition of her prize-winning *Memphis under the Ptolemies* was published in 2012.

THE HEROIC ENTERPRISE ERA

THE PTOLEMIES, THE SEA AND THE NILE

Studies in Waterborne Power

EDITED BY

KOSTAS BURASELIS, MARY STEFANOU AND
DOROTHY J. THOMPSON

CAMBRIDGE
UNIVERSITY PRESS

CAMBRIDGE
UNIVERSITY PRESS

University Printing House, Cambridge CB2 8BS, United Kingdom

Published in the United States of America by Cambridge University Press, New York

Cambridge University Press is part of the University of Cambridge.

It furthers the University's mission by disseminating knowledge in the pursuit of education, learning and research at the highest international levels of excellence.

www.cambridge.org
Information on this title: www.cambridge.org/9781107033351

© Cambridge University Press 2013

First published 2013
Reprinted 2013

Printed and bound in the United Kingdom by Bell and Bain Ltd

A catalogue record for this publication is available from the British Library

Library of Congress Cataloguing in Publication data
The Ptolemies, the sea and the Nile : studies in waterborne power / edited by Kostas Buraselis, Mary Stefanou, Dorothy J. Thompson.
pages cm
Includes bibliographical references and index.
ISBN 978-1-107-03335-1
1. Ptolemaic dynasty, 305–30 B.C. 2. Egypt – History, Naval. 3. Sea-power – Egypt – History – To 1500. 4. Mediterranean Sea – History. 5. Red Sea – History. 6. Nile River – History. 7. Egypt – Relations – Greece – Rhodes. 8. Rhodes (Greece) – Relations – Egypt. 9. Piracy – Egypt – History – To 1500. I. Buraselis, Kostas, 1950– editor of compilation. II. Stefanou, Mary, 1978– editor of compilation. III. Thompson, Dorothy J., 1939– editor of compilation.
DT92.P79 2013
932′.021 – dc23 2012035053

ISBN 978-1-107-03335-1 Hardback

Contents

List of illustrations   *page* vii
   Maps   vii
   Figures   vii
   Tables   viii
Notes on contributors   x
Preface   xiii
List of abbreviations   xv
In memoriam F. W. Walbank   xix
   Christian Habicht

1   Introduction   1
   Dorothy J. Thompson and Kostas Buraselis

2   The Ptolemaic League of Islanders   19
   Andrew Meadows

3   Callicrates of Samos and Patroclus of Macedon,
   champions of Ptolemaic thalassocracy   39
   Hans Hauben

4   Rhodes and the Ptolemaic kingdom: the commercial
   infrastructure   66
   Vincent Gabrielsen

5   Polybius and Ptolemaic sea power   82
   Andrew Erskine

6   Ptolemaic grain, seaways and power   97
   Kostas Buraselis

7   Waterborne recruits: the military settlers of
   Ptolemaic Egypt   108
   Mary Stefanou

8 Our Academic visitor is missing: Posidippus 89 (A–B)
  and 'smart capital' for the thalassocrats   132
  Paul McKechnie

9 Aspects of the diffusion of Ptolemaic portraiture overseas   143
  Olga Palagia

10 Ptolemies and piracy   160
  Lucia Criscuolo

11 The Nile police in the Ptolemaic period   172
  Thomas Kruse

12 Hellenistic royal barges   185
  Dorothy J. Thompson

13 Eudoxus of Cyzicus and Ptolemaic exploration of the sea
   route to India   197
   Christian Habicht

14 Timosthenes and Eratosthenes: sea routes and Hellenistic
   geography   207
   Francesco Prontera

15 Claudius Ptolemy on Egypt and East Africa   218
   Klaus Geus

Bibliography   232
Index   259

Illustrations

MAPS

1.1	Greece and the Ptolemaic Aegean	*page* 5
4.1	The Alexandria–Rhodes route	70
13.1	The Red Sea and Indian Ocean, after Salles 1993: 497	200
13.2	The sea routes to India, after Casson 1989: 225	204
14.1	Seaways in the eastern Mediterranean according to ancient geographers, after Arnaud 2005: 212	216

FIGURES

4.1	Chronological distribution of Rhodian amphora handles in Alexandria (published material), after Lund 2011: 289. By permission of Oxford University Press (www.oup.com)	68
9.1	Marble head of Ptolemy I Soter from Thera, Archaeological Museum. After Hiller von Gaertringen 1899: plate 21	145
9.2	Fragment of inscribed pedestal of portraits of Ptolemy II Philadelphus and Arsinoe II dedicated by Callicrates of Samos at Olympia. Olympia, Archaeological Museum. Photo: German Archaeological Institute, Athens (J. Schumann)	147
9.3	Marble head of Ptolemy III Euergetes probably from Crete. Copenhagen, Ny Carlsberg Glyptothek 573. Photo: Hans R. Goette	149
9.4	Marble head of Berenice II from the Athenian Agora. Athens, Agora S 551. Photo: American School of Classical Studies at Athens, Agora Excavations	150

9.5 Marble head of Berenice II from the Athenian Agora. Athens, Agora S 551. Photo: American School of Classical Studies at Athens, Agora Excavations 151
9.6 Marble head of Ptolemy III Euergetes from Sparta. Sparta, Archaeological Museum 5366. Photo: Olga Palagia 152
9.7 Bronze statue, here identified with Arsinoe III. Calymnos Museum. From the sea near Pserimos. Photo: Olga Palagia 154
9.8 Bronze head of statue in Figure 9.7, here identified with Arsinoe III. Calymnos Museum. After Valavanis 2007: 362, fig. 38 155
9.9 Bronze head of Arsinoe III. Mantua, Palazzo Ducale. After Levi 1931: plate 44 156
9.10 Granite head of Ptolemy VI Philometor probably from a shipwreck near Aegina. Athens, National Museum ANE 108. Photo: Olga Palagia 157
12.1 The royal barge of Ptolemy IV Philopator 191
14.1 The world map of Eratosthenes: a reconstruction, after Aujac 2001: 81 210
14.2 The 'windrose' of Timosthenes: a reconstruction, after Miller 1898: 49, fig. 16 211
15.1 Some eastern Mediterranean coordinates according to Ptolemy 221
15.2 Some eastern Mediterranean coordinates according to Marinus 222
15.3 The upper reaches of the Nile according to Eratosthenes 225
15.4 The upper reaches of the Nile according to 'others' 226
15.5 The upper reaches of the Nile according to Ptolemy 228

TABLES

7.1 Number of cleruchs by ethnic designation (late fourth century–145 BC) 111
7.2 Greek-Macedonian cleruchs (late fourth century–145 BC) 115
7.3 Macedonian cleruchs by period (late fourth century–145 BC) 116
7.4 Cleruchs by main area of origin and period (late fourth century–145 BC) 117
7.5 Surviving documents by reign 119

7.6 Cleruchs from mainland Greece by period (late fourth century–145 BC) 126

7.7 Cleruchs from Cyrenaica by period (late fourth century–145 BC) 128

7.8 Cleruchs from other areas under Ptolemaic control by period (late fourth century–145 BC) 129

Contributors

KOSTAS BURASELIS is Professor of Ancient History at the University of Athens. His favoured fields of research are in Hellenistic and Roman history. He has written and edited a number of books and numerous articles on related subjects.

LUCIA CRISCUOLO is Professor of Greek History and Papyrology at the University of Bologna. Her main field of research is in Hellenistic history. She publishes inscriptions and papyri and has written on Ptolemaic policy and administration, within and outside Egypt, on Ptolemaic relations with Egyptians and on various aspects of Greek rule.

ANDREW ERSKINE is Professor of Ancient History at the University of Edinburgh. His main research interests are in Hellenistic history and Republican Rome. He is the author of *The Hellenistic Stoa* (1990), *Troy between Greece and Rome* (2001), and *Roman Imperialism* (2010) and is the editor of a number of books, including *A Companion to the Hellenistic World* (2003).

VINCENT GABRIELSEN is Professor of Ancient History at the Saxo Institute, University of Copenhagen. He specialises in Greek and Hellenistic history and epigraphy, with research interests including naval and economic history. He recently co-edited *The Economies of Hellenistic Societies, First to Third Centuries* BC (2011) and is Director of the Copenhagen Associations Project, investigating non-public associations of the ancient world.

KLAUS GEUS is an ancient historian and geographer. In 2009 he was appointed full Professor of the Historical Geography of the Ancient World at the Freie Universität Berlin. His fields of specialism are the ancient sciences (geography, astronomy, metrology, mathematics) and historiography (especially Herodotus and Polyaenus). He has published some dozen books and more than one hundred papers and articles.

CHRISTIAN HABICHT studied at Hamburg, Göttingen and Heidelberg, gaining his doctorate in 1952. He held chairs of Ancient History at Marburg and Heidelberg before joining the Institute for Advanced Study at Princeton in 1973. His main fields are Hellenistic history and Greek epigraphy. A member of the Heidelberg and British Academies, the American Philosophical Society and the Academy of Athens, he is now an Emeritus Professor.

HANS HAUBEN, philologist and historian, is Emeritus Professor of Ancient History at the University of Leuven. A student of the late Edmond Van 't Dack, he is particularly interested in the political, military (especially naval) and religious history of the Hellenistic period. His *Studies on the Melitian Schism in Egypt* have recently been published.

THOMAS KRUSE studied in Heidelberg. After research posts at the Universities of Bielefeld and Heidelberg (Institute of Papyrology), where he gained his PhD in 2002, he was appointed Senior Lecturer in Ancient History at Heidelberg. Since 2009 he has been Senior Researcher at the Commission for Ancient Legal History in the Austrian Academy of Sciences, Vienna. His main fields of interest are the history and institutions of Graeco-Roman Egypt.

PAUL MCKECHNIE is an ancient historian whose research interests are in both early Christianity and Hellenistic Egypt. He is Associate Professor (CoRE) in Ancient Cultures at Macquarie University. With Philippe Guillaume, he edited *Ptolemy II Philadelphus and his World* (2008).

ANDREW MEADOWS is Deputy Director of the American Numismatic Society. He has written and edited numerous books and articles on the history, numismatics and epigraphy of the Greek world, including three volumes in the *Sylloge Nummorum Graecorum* series and *Coin Hoards* IX and X, and is Series Editor of the joint ANS–Cambridge University Press Guides to the Coinage of the Ancient World.

OLGA PALAGIA is Professor of Classical Archaeology at the National and Kapodistrian University of Athens. She is a specialist in Greek sculpture and has edited several books, including *Greek Sculpture: Function, Materials and Techniques in the Archaic and Classical Periods* (Cambridge University Press 2006) and *Art in Athens during the Peloponnesian War* (Cambridge University Press 2009). She is currently preparing a monograph on Macedonian painting.

FRANCESCO PRONTERA is Professor of Ancient History at the University of Perugia. In 1992 he founded the journal *Geographia Antiqua* and continues to act as its General Editor. His most recent book is a collection of essays entitled *Geografia e storia nella Grecia antica* (2012).

MARY STEFANOU is a PhD student at the University of Athens, currently teaching classical philology in a Greek secondary school. She is the author of articles on ancient Greek historical subjects and on the teaching of history. Her main research interests lie in Hellenistic history, the political and institutional history of Ptolemaic Egypt, Hellenistic armies and immigration in the Hellenistic world.

DOROTHY J. THOMPSON, Fellow of Girton College, Cambridge, is an ancient historian with a particular interest in Hellenistic Egypt. She is a Fellow of the British Academy and an Honorary President of the International Society of Papyrologists. The second edition of her prize-winning *Memphis under the Ptolemies* was published in 2012.

Preface

This volume owes its conception to the choice by Kostas Buraselis of 'Ptolemaic Waterways and Power' as the subject for the Third International Ptolemaic Colloquium, held in the Peiraeus 18–20 September 2009. At all stages in the organisation of the programme, Mary Stefanou provided invaluable aid. Participants were most generously housed and the meeting sponsored by the Ekaterini Laskaridi Foundation. Sessions in the lively and inspiring atmosphere of the Laskaridis Library were interspersed by visits to the Peiraeus Naval Museum and the Peiraeus Archaeological Museum. A memorable excursion followed to the site of Methana–Arsinoe, where the central importance of the wide-reaching naval power of the Ptolemies in the early–mid Hellenistic period was vividly apparent. All who took part in the proceedings and additional visits not only enjoyed the experience but also acquired a new perspective on the extent of the waterborne power of the Ptolemies, whose role in the Greek world of the Aegean has not always been fully grasped by historians of their Egyptian realm. For this wider focus, all who took part were grateful to the Laskaridis Foundation for generously adopting and variously supporting the realisation of this project.

The transformation of the proceedings of a conference into a coherent volume can be a lengthy process, and one that is not always plain sailing. By this stage Dorothy Thompson had helpfully joined the editorial team. Along the way many debts have been incurred. Together the editors wish to express their thanks to the two (anonymous) Press readers whose thoughtful and penetrating (if at times challenging) reports have certainly helped to improve the final product. Particular thanks are due also to the Classics Editor of the Cambridge University Press, Dr Michael Sharp, for his invaluable guidance, especially on the tricky choice of a title, and for his patience, confidence and imaginative support.

Finally, the editors join in expressing their warm thanks to the Onassis Foundation for a substantial grant towards the costs of publication. This support, generously awarded at a time of tight financial restrictions, is particularly appreciated. As our own small craft takes to the waters, we hope it may make an original contribution to historical understanding worthy of its distinguished sponsors.

Like the initial colloquium, this book is dedicated to the cherished memory of the Hellenistic historian F. W. Walbank (1909–2008).

Athens and Cambridge

Abbreviations

Classical authors are abbreviated as in *The Oxford Classical Dictionary*, ed. S. Hornblower, A. Spawforth and E. Eidinow. 4th edn. Oxford 2012.

Papyrological abbreviations follow *Checklist of Editions of Greek, Latin, Demotic and Coptic Papyri, Ostraca and Tablets*, ed. J. F. Oates, R. S. Bagnall, S. J. Clackson, A. A. O'Brien, J. D. Sosin, T. G. Wilfong and K. A. Worp. 5th edn. *BASP* Suppl. 9. Oakville, Conn. and Oxford 2001, now available in an updated web-based form.

FURTHER ABBREVIATIONS

AAA	Ἀρχαιολογικὰ ἀνάλεκτα ἐξ Ἀθηνῶν/*Athens Annals of Archaeology*. Athens 1968–.
ABAW	Abhandlungen der Preussischen Akademie der Wissenhaften. Philos.-hist. Klasse. Munich 1909–.
ABSA	*Annual of the British School at Athens*. London 1894–.
AC	*L'Antiquité Classique*. Louvain 1932–.
AD	Ἀρχαιολογικὸν Δελτίον. Athens 1915–.
AD Parar.	Ἀρχαιολογικὸν Δελτίον. Παράρτημα.
AJP	*American Journal of Philology*. Baltimore 1880–.
AK	*Antike Kunst*. Olten 1958–.
AncSoc	*Ancient Society*. Leuven 1970–.
Annales HSS	*Annales: histoire, sciences sociales*. Paris 1994–.
Ann. Serv. Ant. Eg.	*Annales du Service des Antiquités de l'Égypte*. Cairo 1900–87.
APF	*Archiv für Papyrusforschung und verwandte Gebiete*. Leipzig 1900–.
ArabA Epigr	*Arabian Archaeology and Epigraphy*. Copenhagen 1990–.

BASP	*Bulletin of the American Society of Papyrologists.* New Haven, Conn. 1963–.
BEFAR	Bibliothèque des écoles françaises d'Athènes et de Rome. Paris 1977–.
BCH	*Bulletin de correspondance hellénique.* Athens and Paris 1877–.
BICS	*Bulletin of the Institute of Classical Studies of the University of London.* London 1954–.
BJb	*Bonner Jahrbücher.* Bonn 1895–.
Bulletin	*Bulletin épigraphique.* Paris 1888–.
CE	*Chronique d'Égypte.* Brussels 1925–.
CID	*Corpus des inscriptions de Delphes.* Paris 1977–.
CIG	*Corpus inscriptionum Graecarum.* 4 vols. Berlin 1828–77.
CQ	*Classical Quarterly.* London 1907–.
CRAI	*Comptes rendus de l'Académie des Inscriptions et Belles-Lettres.* Paris 1857–.
EA	*Egyptian Archaeology.* Bulletin of the Egypt Exploration Society. London 1991–.
EAH	*Το έργον της Αρχαιολογικής Εταιρείας.* Athens 1954–.
Eikasmos	*Eikasmos. Quaderni Bolognesi di Filologia Classica.* Bologna 1990–.
FGrH	F. Jacoby, *Die Fragmente der griechischen Historiker.* Berlin 1923–.
G&R	*Greece and Rome.* Oxford 1931–.
GRBS	*Greek, Roman and Byzantine Studies.* Cambridge, Mass. 1959–.
Hellenica	L. and J. Robert, *Hellenica. Recueil d'épigraphie, de numismatique et d'antiquités grecques.* Limoges 1940–.
I.Beroea	L. Gounaropoulou and M. B. Hatzopoulos, *Inscriptiones Macedoniae Inferioris (inter Bermium montem et Axium flumen repertae)*, vol. 1: *Inscriptiones Beroeae.* Athens 1998.
IC	M. Guarducci, *Inscriptiones Creticae opera et consilio Friederici Halbherr collectae.* 4 vols. Rome 1935–50.

I.Délos	F. Durrbach, P. Roussel, M. Launey, J. Coupry and A. Plassart, *Inscriptions de Délos*. 7 vols. Paris 1926–72.
IG	*Inscriptiones Graecae*. Berlin 1873–.
I.Kition	M. Yon et al., *Kition dans les textes. Testimonia littéraires et épigraphiques et Corpus des inscriptions*. Publications de la Mission Archéologique Française de Kition-Bamboula 5. Paris 2004.
I.Lindos	Ch. Blinkenberg and K. F. Kinch, *Lindos, fouilles et recherches 1902–14*, vol. II: *Inscriptions*. Copenhagen 1941.
I.Paneion	A. Bernand, *Le Paneion d'El-Kanaïs. Les inscriptions grecques*. Leiden 1972.
I.Portes du désert	A. Bernand, *Les portes du désert*. London and Paris 1984.
ISE	L. Moretti (ed.), *Iscrizioni storiche ellenistiche*. 2 vols. Florence 1967–76.
IvO	W. Dittenberger and K. Purgold, *Olympia. Die Ergebnisse der von dem Deutschen Reich veranstalteten Ausgrabung*, vol. V: *Die Inschriften*. Berlin 1896.
JDAI	*Jahrbuch des Deutschen Archäologischen Instituts*. Berlin 1886–.
JHS	*The Journal of Hellenic Studies*. London 1880–.
JJP	*The Journal of Juristic Papyrology*. Warsaw 1946–.
JRS	*The Journal of Roman Studies*. London 1911–.
LGPN	P. M. Fraser and E. Matthews, *Lexicon of Greek Personal Names*. Oxford 1987–.
LSJ	H. G. Liddell, R. Scott and H. S. Jones, with R. McKenzie and revised supplement ed. P. G. W. Glare, *A Greek–English Lexicon*. 9th edn. Oxford 1996.
MDAI(A)	*Mitteilungen des Deutschen Archäologischen Instituts. Athenische Abteilung*. Athens and Berlin 1876–.
Michel, *Recueil*	C. Michel, *Recueil d'inscriptions grecques*. Brussels 1900 (nos. 1–1426); Supplément. Brussels 1912–27.

Milet	Th. Wiegand (ed.), *Milet. Ergebnisse der Ausgrabungen und Untersuchungen seit dem Jahre 1899.* Berlin 1906–.
ML	R. Meiggs and D. Lewis (eds.), *A Selection of Greek Historical Inscriptions to the End of the Fifth Century* BC. 2nd edn. Oxford 1988.
MünchBeitr	*Münchener Beiträge zur Papyrusforschung und antiken Rechtsgeschichte.* Munich 1915–.
OGIS	W. Dittenberger, *Orientis graeci inscriptiones selectae.* 2 vols. Leipzig 1903–5.
OMS	L. Robert, *Opera Minora Selecta. Épigraphie et antiquités grecques.* 7 vols. Amsterdam 1969–90.
Pap. Lugd.-Bat.	Papyrologica Lugduno-Batava. Leiden 1941–.
Pros. Ptol.	W. Peremans and E. Van 't Dack, *Prosopographia Ptolemaica.* Studia Hellenistica 6–. Leuven 1950– and http://prosptol.arts.kuleuven.ac.be
RC	C. B. Welles, *Royal Correspondence in the Hellenistic Period: A Study in Greek Epigraphy.* New Haven, Conn. 1934, reprinted Chicago 1974.
RDAC	*Report of the Department of Antiquities, Cyprus.* Nicosia 1934–.
RE	*Pauly-Wissowa Realencyclopädie der klassischen Altertumswissenschaft.* Stuttgart and Munich 1894–1980.
REA	*Revue des études anciennes.* Paris 1899–.
REG	*Revue des études grecques.* Paris 1888–.
Samothrace	P. M. Fraser, *Samothrace: Excavations Conducted by the Institute of Fine Arts of New York University,* vol. II.1: *The Inscriptions on Stone.* New York 1960.
SEG	*Supplementum Epigraphicum Graecum.* Leiden 1923–.
SIG³	W. Dittenberger, *Sylloge Inscriptionum Graecarum.* 3rd edn. Leipzig 1915–24.
TAPhA	*Transactions of the American Philological Association.* Hartford, Conn. 1870–.
Topoi	*ΤΟΠΟΙ: Orient – Occident.* Lyons 1990–.
ZPE	*Zeitschrift für Papyrologie und Epigraphik.* Bonn 1967–.

In memoriam F. W. Walbank

The following tribute was delivered by Christian Habicht on 18 September 2009 at the Laskaridis Library, Athens (Peiraeus), Greece

This colloquium is dedicated to the memory of Frank Walbank, who passed away on 23 October 2008 at the age of 98. Peter Fraser, author of the monumental *Ptolemaic Alexandria* and the guiding force of the *Lexicon of Greek Personal Names*, had died a little earlier, so that the two pre-eminent historians of the Hellenistic world left the stage within a year.

Kostas Buraselis has asked me to say a few words on Frank Walbank at the opening of our proceedings. Let me begin by saying that Frank and I met only a few times. The first was at the 1968 Symposium on Ancient Macedonia. He was in the chair the afternoon I gave a paper on 'Epigraphic evidence for the history of Thessaly under Macedonian rule', in which I re-dated the first letter of King Philip V to Larisa. When I had finished, he said: 'I am glad to hear that I had the count of Philip's regnal years right, if for the wrong reasons.' It was his polite way of saying that I had come to the same conclusion he had reached long ago. The second time was five years later, at the Second Macedonian Symposium. After that, we met twice in Princeton: when he spoke at the university on ruler cult from Alexander to Augustus, and, again, when he gave a talk on Polybius at the Institute for Advanced Study in Princeton. From these meetings and from his lectures I always came away with the conviction that I had been in the presence of a scholar who was a perfect gentleman (more on this in a minute). It goes without saying that I was in awe of the breadth and depth of his knowledge. His main focus was less than Fraser's on the Ptolemies, since for Polybius they came to life only with Philopator in 220, when the *symplokê*, the intertwining of events in east and west, north and south, began, which is the real starting-point of the historian's narrative. Greece and Macedon were Walbank's main fields, beginning with his monograph on *Aratus of Sicyon*, published when the author was 23 years old, followed by

xix

Philip V in 1940, and culminating in his monumental commentary on Polybius, published between 1957 and 1979, and rounded out by his contribution on the history of Macedon from 301 to the death of Antigonus Doson in 221, in volume III of Hammond's *History of Macedonia* (1988).

I will not comment any further on Frank's work, since it is well known to all of those here, but will instead try to throw a little light on the person he was, the scholar and the perfect gentleman as I have just characterised him. To illustrate my point, let me briefly sketch his debate with Adalberto Giovannini. The two men met at the Macedonian Symposium in 1968, and their debate began the following year. It was not on anything Macedonian, but on the meetings of the Achaean League, a topic vital to Polybius: *synodos, synklêtos, agora*, their composition and competence. In 1969 Giovannini published a paper, 'Polybe et les assemblées achéennes', in *Museum Helveticum*. He challenged the views of Jake Larsen to which Walbank had subscribed. Walbank replied a year later in the same journal with 'The Achaean Assemblies again'. He thoroughly examined Giovannini's arguments and found that they were 'not very compelling'. What I wish to stress is the way he dealt with his opponent, who was not well known at the time and by some thirty years his junior. He called his paper 'lucid and plausible', admitted that he was tempted to accept its substance, and that some of the difficulties he had with it 'had been resolved in the course of a friendly correspondence with its author'. In the end, however, while confessing that he had 'no new solution [of his own] to offer', he once again accepted Larsen's view as the most convincing.

This, however, was not the end. Walbank returned to the subject a decade later in the third volume of his *Commentary on Polybius*, in an appendix of eight pages, 'The Achaean Assemblies'. He had studied the problem further, 'encouraged [as he said] by discussion with G. T. Griffith', and had come 'to a different conclusion, and one nearer to Giovannini's'. He pointed out several difficulties with Larsen's position and accepted some of Giovannini's main conclusions, while still disputing others (the details do not matter here). From beginning to end he had treated the young scholar with respect and as his equal. In his first paper attacking his conclusions, he said in a footnote: 'I should like to take this opportunity to thank Dr Giovannini for his willingness to discuss these problems in a helpful correspondence following the publication of his article.' This debate, to me, is a model of how serious differences of opinion can and ought to be discussed between opponents. Both men deserve credit for how they handled the affair, Walbank in particular as the more senior and much more eminent scholar.

Let me stop here and just add that papers to be read at this Symposium will no doubt once again testify to Frank Walbank's eminence as a historian. What I wanted to bring out in these short remarks is what Peter Garnsey called in his obituary 'an extraordinary generosity of spirit' and 'a rare modesty'. An unnamed colleague from Liverpool, quoted in the obituary of *The Times*, concurs: 'He was a wonderful human being unaffected by his own eminence.'

Christian Habicht

CHAPTER I

Introduction

Dorothy J. Thompson and Kostas Buraselis

Alexandria, founded by Alexander of Macedon on 7 April 331 BC, was to become one of the great cities of the ancient world. This new city on the sea, with its fine double harbour, provided a Mediterranean focus for the country more directly than ever before.[1] As with all sea-ports, Alexandria faced two ways. Like Shanghai or New Orleans later, it also connected the sea to a great river.[2] With canal access developed through to the Nile, Alexandria formed a junction between the main artery of Egypt to the south and the Mediterranean to the north. So when, after Alexander's death, his general Ptolemy son of Lagus took over the country, establishing the rule of the Ptolemies, Egypt depended for its development and success more fundamentally than did any other Hellenistic power on its control of the routes by river and sea. Waterborne traffic was the norm, both at home and abroad, and earlier experience acquired primarily on the Nile was of relevance as the Ptolemies expanded their influence overseas. The city of Alexandria, with its guiding lighthouse, the Pharos, was the centre where many different aspects of this waterborne power may be traced and brought together. In what follows, discussion of the main themes and questions raised in the contributions to this volume comes filtered through an Alexandrian lens.[3]

First the waters themselves, the aquatic dimension – as it were – to the Ptolemaic state.[4] Throughout its recorded history, the fate of Egypt has

[1] On the lay-out of Alexandria's harbours, see Goddio 2011: 129–35.

[2] Cf. Braudel 1972: I, 317–18, double frontage as a feature of important ports. Strabo 17.1.7 (C 793), natural position of Alexandria with double water frontage and harbours, on the coast and on Lake Marea/Mareotis; 17.1.13 (C 798), Alexandria the best port of the inhabited world. Naucratis, in contrast, which had earlier served as the access port for Mediterranean goods, was a river port only.

[3] For Alexandria's foundation, see Bagnall 1979; Krasilnikoff 2009: 24–30; Buraselis 2010: 265–7. On the city more generally, Fraser 1972 remains invaluable. See also A. Bernand 1995; Empereur 1998; Grimm 1998; Hirst and Silk 2004; Harris and Ruffini 2004; McKenzie 2007, on architecture.

[4] The terminology here is difficult; cf. Horden 2005: 179, on 'fluid communications'; Horden and Purcell 2005: 348. *Liquid Continents* is announced as the title for their as yet unpublished sequel to *The Corrupting Sea* (2000).

been inseparable from that of the Nile, which, flowing for 6,825 km, is one of the longest rivers in the world. For 1,200 km of this length, this river runs through Egypt towards the sea. Making its way down through the long central valley of Upper and Middle Egypt, near Heliopolis (now Cairo) the Nile spreads out into several streams and flows through the Delta area towards the Mediterranean. Its course has shifted somewhat over time, but historically the pattern of the river remained much the same until the construction of the first Aswan dam, completed in 1902.[5] With this its annual flood was tamed and, as a result, the rich agricultural produce of Egypt no longer depended on the annual inundation of the land by the silt-rich waters of the Nile. Throughout antiquity, the river formed the main artery along which travelled all manner of people and produce – merchants and military men, officials and travellers, explorers and pirates, the king and his court, and many more, who depended on the river for their way of life. It provided a thoroughfare through the main valley of Egypt, and a series of ports set along its course marked the end of caravan routes reaching out across the western desert to the oases, eastwards to the ports of the Red Sea coast, and to the quarries and mines of the desert to the south. Seas lay both to the north and the east of the country, but the river Nile remained the defining and unifying feature of Egypt.

The foundation of a new urban settlement inevitably affects its environs, both the immediately surrounding area and, as it develops, places further afield. And when, as in the case of Alexandria, that city becomes a capital, the centre of royal and administrative power, then large-scale change in the local ecology, in the political geography and in the economic development of the land is to be expected, with effects on both internal and external relations. With Alexandria as the new capital, the direction and balance of power in Egypt were transformed. The greatest change of all, however, was the involvement – incorporation even – of Egypt in the world of the Mediterranean.[6] With Macedonian kings in control, Egypt now looked out to the north, and for the early Ptolemies the development of naval power became a pressing need.

Earlier Egyptian contacts in the Mediterranean had been of a more limited nature, with the exchange of goods and men rather than strategic concerns as the driving force. The traditional sphere of Egyptian trade lay

---

[5] Willcocks 1904 remains a helpful study. On changes in the course of the Nile, see Jeffreys 2008; Lutley and Bunbury 2008.

[6] Somewhat surprisingly, apart from some discussion of its system of irrigation or its grain, Hellenistic (like Roman) Egypt generally lies outside the bounds of the Mediterranean which forms the subject of Horden and Purcell 2000; see Bagnall 2005: 339–41.

within the eastern Mediterranean, where Cyprus to the north and Phoenicia
to the east formed the most regular points of contact and the source of
crucial imports (see Map 4.1). Some contacts were more distant. Under
Psammetichus I (664–610 BC), for instance, mercenaries had reached Egypt
from as far afield as Ionia and Caria. When the sixth-century BC pharaoh
Amasis invited Greeks to be founder members for his new international
port of trade at Naucratis they too came from the coast of Asia Minor and
the islands.[7] Similarly, from the period of Persian control in 475 BC, the
Aramaic customs record that survives beneath the Ahiqar Romance details
ships reaching Egypt from Ionia and Phoenicia over a period of ten months.
The variety of their incoming cargoes of various metals, oil, wine, empty
jars, clay, wool, planks of wood, oars and other items is hardly matched
by what went out; natron was the only item that left this unnamed port.[8]
Such was the limited nature of Egypt's Mediterranean traffic before the
Ptolemies, and, with the need to import wood, wine and metals, it was
her closer contacts to the east and the west which remained the strongest.
With the foundation of Alexandria all this was changed. Egypt now also
looked north.

It was not, however, just into the Mediterranean that Egypt's connections
now stretched but through the Sea of Marmara into the Black Sea too. The
story Tacitus recounts of the statue of Sarapis brought from Pontic Sinope
may owe its origin to conflation with a district known as Sinopion at
Memphis.[9] Nevertheless, there were now connections with the Pontus.
Sometime under Ptolemy IV a group of young men described as Mares,
from the far south-eastern corner of the Black Sea, are recorded in a list
of expenditure on a voyage from Memphis to Alexandria.[10] Their presence
there is unexplained but is interesting for the light that it sheds on Pontic
connections at this time. The most striking of all such traces is the Egyptian
trireme named Isis found drawn on the walls of a shrine to Aphrodite and
Apollo at Nymphaeum in the Crimea and dating from the second quarter
of the third century BC.[11] There can be no better illustration of Egypt's
entry to the world centred on the Mediterranean but not confined to its

---

[7] Hdt. 2.152, mercenaries; 2.178–9, Naucratis, with Ionians from Chios, Teos, Phocaea and Clazomenae, Dorians from Rhodes, Cnidus, Halicarnassus and Phaselis, Aeolians from Mytilene. Separate
sanctuaries were established by Miletus, Samos and – exceptionally, from further west – Aegina. On
immigrants, see further Vittmann 2003: chaps. 3 (Phoenicians), 6 (Carians), 8 (Greeks).

[8] Porten and Yardeni 1993: C3.7, with Briant 2002: 385. Briant suggests Memphis as the port involved,
but the Delta location of sources of natron (see Lucas 1932) and the sea-going ships detailed in the
account seem to imply a coastal port.

[9] Tac. *Hist.* 4.83; J. Gwyn Griffiths 1970: 395–6.   [10] *UPZ* I 149.4, with editor's note.

[11] Grač 1984; *SEG* 34.756 and 45.997. See Marquaille 2008: 50–1, with n. 52, for further bibliography.

shores. Within a century, therefore, of Alexandria's foundation, Egypt's overseas political, cultural and economic interests grew to range widely, west to Sicily, throughout the Aegean and through to the Black Sea region; for Egypt, gift of the Nile, under the early Ptolemies had now become a maritime power.

With Alexandria as their new capital, the location of both their palace district and administrative headquarters, the vista of the new Greek pharaohs northwards, to the world from which they came, became broader than ever before (Map 1.1). It is the view from Alexandria that this chapter seeks to delineate with the aim of introducing and contextualising the studies that follow. For in the history of Mediterranean powers – and this we should recognise is 'history *in*' rather than 'history *of*' that sea[12] – the arrival on the scene of the kings of Egypt was a new phenomenon, marking something of a rupture with the past.[13]

First comes the development of Ptolemaic naval power, based on the newly protected harbours of Alexandria. Already in his early years, as he sought to establish control, Ptolemy son of Lagus looked seawards. If, taking his cue from Alexander before and concerned to protect his borders, Ptolemy's first foray out of Egypt in 322/321 BC was westwards overland to Cyrene,[14] it was not long afterwards, in 319 BC, that he invaded Syria-Phoenicia, a key source of timber throughout Egypt's history and a territory with important coastal harbours.[15] Cyprus too came within his early sphere of vision, and treaties with four Cypriot dynasts significantly increased his naval power.[16] Overseas involvement in key areas of later Ptolemaic interest was, therefore, under way at the same time as Ptolemy was putting all his military and administrative acumen to work to secure his position at home. With access to timber resources and the support of good allies, especially in the form of kings and local dynasts (like Philocles of Sidon), Egyptian naval strength was growing, and, despite setbacks and reversals of fortune, in this early period Ptolemy I was successful in establishing a Ptolemaic presence in the Mediterranean. Already in 314 BC, at a time when Antigonus was working in Phoenicia to put together a naval force, Ptolemy was reported as enjoying control of the sea. At the same time, in the same area, 100 ships from Egypt under Seleucus' command displayed their strength unimpeded

---

[12] For this distinction, see Horden and Purcell 2000: 2; 2005: 357; cf. Harris 2005: 5.

[13] For 'historical rupture and continuity' involved in the establishment of the Ptolemaic dynasty, see Moyer 2011: 135.

[14] Caroli 2007: 71–83, Cyrene under Ptolemy I.

[15] Hölbl (2001): 14–20; Huß 2001: 97–191; Caroli 2007: 50–70.

[16] Arr. *FGrH* 156 F10.6, Nicocreon of Salamis, Stasicrates of Soli (see *SEG* 36, 331), Nicocles of Paphos and Androcles of Amathus; Ptolemy thereby acquired nearly 200 ships.

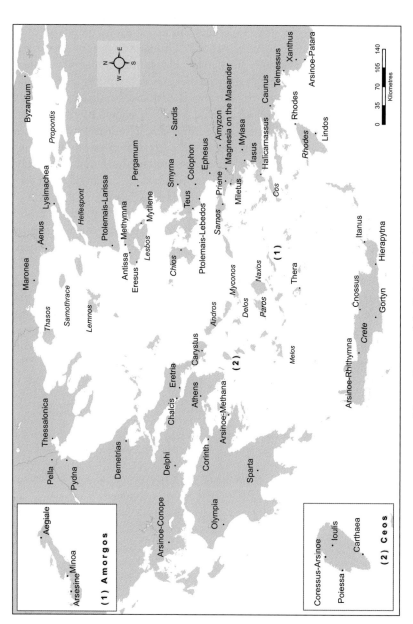

Map 1.1 Greece and the Ptolemaic Aegean

before Antigonid eyes.[17] When later, in 306 BC, Ptolemy sailed up to Cypriot Salamis, soon to be defeated at the hands of Antigonus' son Demetrius, 'his fleet, with the transport ships following, on account of its size appeared from afar an impressive sight to behold'.[18] Some 200 to 210 Ptolemaic fighting ships may have been involved.[19] By no means all his warships will have come from Ptolemy's allies; a massive shipbuilding programme was necessary in these early decades, with Alexandria most probably at its centre.[20] And so, a fine floor mosaic from the Delta city of Thmuis, signed by one Sophilus, portrays Alexandria wearing a naval headdress, a ship's prow on her brow; either side of the portrait flow out long waving ribbons with black and white stripes, tied around her head as though from a diadem. It is hard to imagine a clearer portrayal of Ptolemaic naval and royal power than that combined in this maritime image.[21]

The struggle with the Antigonids for control of Phoenicia and the eastern Mediterranean, in which the navy was involved, continued over many decades. Here its relevance is as a prerequisite for Ptolemaic control of their later League of Islanders (otherwise known as the Nesiotic League). This, Meadows argues in Chapter 2 below, was a league brought into being under Ptolemaic guidance in the very early years of Ptolemy II. With the help of this League and through a mix of Ptolemaic garrisons of occupation and more straightforward alliances, under the first three Ptolemies Egypt pursued her interests over a wide area. Polybius would later sum up the external interests of the early Ptolemies:[22]

ruling over Coele Syria and Cyprus, they loomed over the dynasts of Asia and the [Aegean] islands likewise; under their control were the major cities, strong places and harbours all along the coast from Pamphylia to the Hellespont and in the neighbourhood of Lysimachea. Controlling Aenus, Maronea and other cities even further away, they presided over affairs in Thrace and in Macedonia.

Such, stretching out from Alexandria, was the power of the Ptolemies overseas.

---

[17] Diod. Sic. 19.58, probably from Hieronymus.   [18] Diod. Sic. 20.49.6.

[19] Hauben 1976: 1, plus 200 transport ships carrying infantry; cf. Casson 1991: 136, where the number of 150 Ptolemaic ships does not include the 60 ships from Salamis itself.

[20] On the Ptolemaic navy, see Van 't Dack and Hauben 1978: 69–75; for shipbuilding in Alexandria later, Ath. 5.203e–204d.

[21] Signed by Sophilus and now in the Alexandria Museum. cf. Pollitt 1986: 222, with fig. 235. This portrait, one of two, has also been identified as Berenice II, cf. Empereur 1995: 5, with fig. 3 and inside back cover; Guimiers-Sorbet 2004: 69. In either case, she clearly represents Ptolemaic control of the seas.

[22] Polyb. 5.34.6–9, cf. Marquaille 2008: 39–40.

As in other naval empires, a combination of concerns may be traced on the part of this ruling power. In the area of Ptolemaic control and artistic influence, in later centuries Venice was to establish her maritime empire, in which again strategic and trade considerations reinforced one another in the fashion that A. T. Mahan was to analyse in his classic work *The Influence of Sea Power upon History* (1890). A set of defensive outposts against the westward expansion of the Ottoman empire served also as a gate for the import into Europe of commercial products from the east. Probably the greatest of all such maritime empires was the British, on which in the nineteenth century 'the sun never set'. Queen Victoria too might well have worn a crown of prows. The naval empire of the Ptolemies may be viewed from a broader perspective.

The Ptolemaic navy has been the subject of study before.[23] Here, in Chapter 3, in his discussion of two key individuals under Ptolemy II – Callicrates of Samos and Patroclus of Macedon – Hauben examines the human aspect of Ptolemaic naval policy, which was crucial to the development of the Ptolemaic empire. The extent and nature of the imperial rule of the Ptolemies were carefully delineated in Roger S. Bagnall, *The Administration of the Ptolemaic Possessions outside Egypt* (1976). Subsequent epigraphic discoveries, some of them spectacular, have on the whole served to fill in this picture, although not without some surprises and inevitable debates as to their significance.[24] Whereas, however, the emphasis of Bagnall's work was on structures of government, monetary practice and the administrative officers employed by the Ptolemies in their overseas possessions, the emphasis has more recently moved also to cultural and cultic matters. A related theme of recent work has been the organisation and definition of the imperial space of the Ptolemaic empire, and the role of the king and his family in its cohesion.[25] Thus in the present volume, the importance of Ptolemaic royal cult, which joined the Egyptian gods as a means of binding Ptolemaic allies, is more than once identified as playing an important role.[26]

---

[23] Van 't Dack and Hauben 1978; Casson 1991: 129–42.

[24] For new inscriptions, see, for example, Wörrle 1977, 1978, 1991; Shear 1978; Robert and Robert 1983; Bousquet 1988; Jones and Habicht 1989 (republishing Opelt and Kirsten 1989); Blümel 1992; Gauthier 2003; Wallensten and Pakkanen 2009. For further discussions, see, for example, Gauthier 1979; Chaniotis 1993; Ma, Derow and Meadows 1995; Meadows 2006, 2008, 2012.

[25] The study of royal settlements overseas has been an important element in this. See, for example, Cherry and Davis 1991; Mee and Forbes 1997; Mueller 2006; Gill 2007; Winter 2010.

[26] Abulafia 2005: 91–2 urges consideration of the relationship between trade and cultural or religious influences in a comparative framework (with reference to Japan).

Power, of course, is exercised in very many different forms, and in the case of the Ptolemaic empire the distinction made elsewhere between 'hard' and 'soft' power may be a helpful one.[27] Hard power in this case would be the navy, the garrisons and governors sent around the empire. The 'softer' aspects, in contrast, are the less tangible resources of power, such as are to be found, for instance, in the promulgation of cult or culture. This is where festivals, dynastic cult and the varying images of power become relevant.

The establishment, for instance, of the Alexandrian festival of the *Ptolemaieia* marked an important stage in Ptolemy II's relations with his Aegean allies. Soon after the death of Ptolemy I, his son Ptolemy II formed the plan of instituting a festival in honour of his father, to be celebrated every four years in Alexandria. In honour of Ptolemy Soter and his queen, the Greek states were invited to send their envoys across the seas to Alexandria to take part in an international festival with games, other competitions and much else besides. The invitation to consider this proposal and take part, issued in the joint names of Philocles, king of the Sidonians, and the nesiarch Bacchon, went out to Ptolemy's island allies, who responded with the expected enthusiasm.[28] As nesiarch, Bacchon was in charge of the Islanders and the decree of acceptance from *c.* 280 BC would, on Meadows' argument below, form the first certain evidence for the existence of the Nesiotic League, which, he somewhat controversially suggests, had been recently formed. The survival of a copy of the decree from the small island of Nicuria near Amorgos is indicative of the importance of this central initiative; this was an event to be noted and everywhere recorded by the member cities. The Islanders further decided to set up a record of their response on Delos, next to the altar of Ptolemy Soter.[29] Cult too was an effective way of cementing political relations, and through the institution of this Ptolemaic festival in Alexandria the extension of the cult of Ptolemy I proved particularly powerful in this respect. Attendance at a festival could serve additional ends. Thus Callias, from the Athenian deme of Sphettus, serving as sacred envoy to the Ptolemaea, succeeded in obtaining a royal gift of ropes for the forthcoming Panathenaea back home. Negotiations of this kind formed a common part of such occasions.[30] The case of Eudoxus,

---

[27] Nye 1990: 31–2, for the formulation; cf. 2002: 8–9, on soft power.
[28] *SIG*[3] 390 = M. M. Austin 2006: 450–2, no. 256; on the festival more generally, see Thompson 2000.
[29] *SIG*[3] 390.45–9.
[30] *SEG* 49.113.55–70 = M. M. Austin 2006: 114–16, no. 55; cf. Buraselis 1993: 255.

a later sacred envoy, who came to Alexandria with an invitation to a festival in Cyzicus, had a more surprising outcome, which we shall return to later.

In another example of 'soft power', altars and sanctuaries dedicated to the Ptolemies, either singly or together as a family dynasty, entered the sacred landscape of allied cities and islands. These were often the location of the surviving statues or portraits of Ptolemaic kings and queens. Made in Alexandria and exported around the Ptolemaic empire and beyond, such royal statues are studied by Palagia in Chapter 9. She argues for a degree of central direction in the form that these portraits took in much the same way as has been long accepted in the case of Roman imperial portraiture. In sanctuaries dedicated to the dynastic cult, offerings could be made by Ptolemaic officials or by ambitious locals. In this way loyalty to the regime was put on display, and through the dedications the power of the Ptolemies was paraded and reinforced. So, on the island of Thera one Artemidorus, son of Apollonius from Perge, left his mark on the landscape. He may have held some official position within the Ptolemaic army or the administration, but if he did this remains unknown. Sometime in the reign of Ptolemy III, Artemidorus dedicated the small sanctuary to King Ptolemy and his forebears in an important location, on the main route between the agora and the temple of Apollo Karneios.[31] And Artemidorus was not alone. Many similar dedications were made throughout the Ptolemaic empire.

One particular royal cult was transposed overseas with notable success. This was the cult of Queen Arsinoe II, the sister-wife of Ptolemy II. The initiative may have come from Alexandria, where already during her lifetime the cult of Ptolemy II and his queen as the *Theoi Adelphoi* was added to that of Alexander in 272/271.[32] Arsinoe herself became the brother-loving goddess, as found for instance in the name of the new settlement of Philadelphia in the Arsinoite nome in Egypt, known also as 'the village of (the goddess) Philadelphos'.[33] On the coast close to Alexandria, Arsinoe's cult as the goddess Aphrodite Zephyritis or Euploia was established by the admiral Callicrates. Celebrated in the poetry of Posidippus, Arsinoe was a

[31] *IG* XII.3 464; *IG* XII.3 463/1388 records a further dedication of Artemidorus on behalf of Ptolemy III and his ancestors, probably made to the Egyptian gods Sarapis, Isis and Anubis. Artemidorus is further discussed in the contributions of Meadows and Palagia.
[32] See Hauben below: 39 and 46.
[33] *P.Lond.* VII 1954.1; 1955.1 (257 BC), a letter from farmers *ek kômês tês Philadelphou*; cf. Mueller 2006: 209, *s.v.* Philadelpheia. For a dedication to Arsinoe Philadelphos made during her lifetime, see Wallensten and Pakkanen 2009: 155.

goddess well suited to maritime export.[34] She was worshipped widely in the overseas empire of the Ptolemies and, on one remarkable occasion, her influence was recorded in a matter of policy.[35] The large number of new foundations or refoundations named Arsinoe, both at home and overseas, is a testimony to the popularity of this particular Ptolemaic goddess.[36] In its many forms and different ways, cult of members of the Ptolemaic dynasty joined the garrisons and royal officials in serving to support their empire overseas.

A further aspect of Ptolemaic power may be found in their adoption of the eagle as a dynastic image, both at home and overseas. On the island of Thera, for instance, the same Artemidorus of Perge whose dedication of a sanctuary to dynastic cult we have already noted was active elsewhere in the city. In a further rock-cut sanctuary, at much the same elevation but further round the slope to the north,[37] Artemidorus, who would seem to have been an influential and well-established resident of the island, set up a rock-cut *temenos* with a series of niches dedicated to a range of gods, and with carvings to accompany his inscribed dedications. Here, carved into the rock-face, along with other images, stood an eagle.[38] We know from the adjoining inscription that this was the eagle of Olympian Zeus, but it also closely resembles the Ptolemaic eagle familiar from the image on Ptolemaic coins, for an eagle, with closed wings and standing on a thunderbolt, was the reverse type introduced shortly after 300 BC on all denominations of Ptolemaic gold and silver from the Alexandrian mint.[39] As recognised by Svoronos long ago, what had earlier been the eagle of Zeus was now the eagle of Ptolemy too.[40] That carved in Artemidorus' sanctuary does face in the other direction to the eagle on the coins. Nevertheless, a double reference seems implied. For those who saw just the image in Artemidorus' sanctuary on Thera, this would be Ptolemy's eagle.

So when, in 279/278 BC, the envoys responding to the invitation of Ptolemy II to celebrate his father Soter arrived in Alexandria for the first

---

[34] Posidippus 39, 116, 119 (Austin and Bastianini 2002); cf. Hauben below: 41–2.
[35] For Arsinoe cults, see Marquaille 2008: 58–60; Meadows below: 29–31. On the *prohairesis* of Arsinoe in the Chremonidean War, *SIG*³ 434/5.15–16, with Huß 2001: 273, n. 150; Hauben below: 141, n. 13. In Egypt too Arsinoe's cult was widespread, Thompson 2012: 118–19, 122–3.
[36] Mueller 2006: 35–9, 200–3; cf. Fraser 2009: 342–7; cf. n. 32 above.
[37] For a map of Thera, see Hiller von Gaertringen (1904): plan 2.
[38] See Palagia 1992: 173, with figs. 48b and 52b, providing a clear description of the lay-out of the *temenos* and a new interpretation of the carvings.
[39] Mørkholm 1991: 66, with figs. 97–8; on some Ptolemaic bronze coins the eagle's wings are outspread, see fig. 99 and book cover. Ptolemy's head was the obverse type. See further Panagopoulou 2005–6: 170–1.
[40] Svoronos 1904: νε′–νη′, ρξη′, in turn reporting Furtwängler and Rossbach.

Ptolemaieia, the fine pavilion that they found set up for their entertainment was topped with gilded eagles, which faced one another, with a wing span of some 7.5 m.[41] There may be some exaggeration in Callixeinus' account – the eagles are actually described as 'of gold', while their 'size' (*megethos*) is given as 15 cubits – but in any case the sight will have been an impressive one for all who saw it, even for those who lacked an invitation to join the party within. The eagle of Zeus, now Ptolemy's eagle, was being imprinted on the imagination of those who visited Egypt as a symbol of Ptolemaic rule. In the words of Theocritus, when Ptolemy II was born on the island of Cos:[42]

A great eagle, the bird of fate, screeched out its cry three times from the clouds. This indeed was a sign from Zeus. For awesome kings come under the care of Zeus, son of Cronus, and he stands out above all, the king whom Zeus has loved from the hour of his birth. Great prosperity attends him; he rules over many lands, and many seas.

Theocritus, like others at the time, was well aware how sea power was important to the Ptolemies, and the eagle stood as the ensign of these kings.

The eagle as image of the Ptolemies has a wide circulation both within the Ptolemaic empire and beyond. Somewhat later in the third century, perhaps under Ptolemy IV, when Idumaea still came under Ptolemaic control, a deep rock-cut tomb in Marisa was decorated with fine coloured paintings of Nilotic and other more local (or mythical) animals. And the entry to the tomb's eastern end was guarded by two large eagles painted in red within a black outline.[43] Facing one another with their wings outspread, they stand on trailing wreaths. Whatever the local connotations of this bird,[44] it is hard not also to recognise here some reference to the current rulers of the land. Its first owner could well have been in Ptolemaic service.

Yet a further striking example of the use of this image is to be found in one issue of the bronze coinage of Cleomenes III in Sparta. The obverse carries what appears to be a Ptolemaic eagle standing on a thunderbolt. The coincidence in time with the new subsidy of Ptolemy III to help finance Cleomenes' mercenary army is surely relevant to the eagle's appearance on these coins.[45] Later too, when in 32 BC Antony was in the city accompanied

[41] Ath. 5.197a, from the account of Callixeinus of Rhodes, cf. 5.196a.
[42] Theoc. 17.71–6; cf. Ael. frg. 283, at his birth Soter was protected by an eagle.
[43] Jacobson 2004: 24; 2007: 25, with plates 8–9, eagle or possibly phoenix, cf. 48, for possible date of decoration, but without the eagle connection. Individual burials within the tomb extend late into the second century BC, Peter and Thiersch 1905: 77–80.
[44] The base of a large sculpture of an eagle dedicated to Apollo (Qos in Idumaea) was also found in the area, Jacobson 2004: 26.
[45] Polyb. 2.51.2, support switched from Aratus to Cleomenes; Palagia 2006: 210, for the coinage.

by Cleopatra VII, Athens minted bronze coins featuring the eagle on a thunderbolt; the reference to Egypt again seems clear.[46] Overseas, the generosity and power of Ptolemy could be recognised through his eagle. The imperial bird combined with statues of the royal family and the spread of the dynastic cult to reinforce the power of the Ptolemies across the Mediterranean.

If the fighting ships of the Ptolemaic navy were part of that dynasty's hard power, other forms of vessel belonged to the softer variety. Chapter 12 below considers the ceremonial barges of the Ptolemaic rulers as a feature of their self-presentation both at home and abroad. The wealth and luxury involved in these craft formed part of the Ptolemaic royal image.

The political influence of the Ptolemies within the Aegean and the eastern Mediterranean lasted – in a somewhat diminished form – until the middle of the second century BC, when the death of Ptolemy VI Philometor marked the end to Ptolemaic supremacy overseas. The decline of Ptolemaic sea power as presented by Polybius is the subject of Erskine's contribution to this volume in Chapter 5. However, the economic aspects of Egypt's power, and in particular her expanded trade, continued unabated, for the wealth of the Ptolemies depended on the export through Alexandria of the produce of Egypt's fertile soil, above all the wheat which, besides feeding Egypt's population at home, found a ready market abroad; both aspects of the Ptolemies' supply of grain form the concern of Buraselis in Chapter 6 below. Egypt's involvement in Aegean trade had already received encouragement from the enterprise and somewhat dubious practices of Cleomenes, left in charge by Alexander in 331 BC.[47] From this date onwards Egypt looked out towards Aegean markets and, with the development of the port of Alexandria and its double harbour, Egypt played an increasing role in Mediterranean commerce.

Economic connections naturally led to the extension of Ptolemaic power. For Egypt's island allies and those beyond, commercial links went hand in hand with political ties or the exchange of sacred envoys. And if, as stressed by A. T. Mahan, a major concern of all navies is the protection of commerce,[48] in the ancient world (as sometimes the modern too) with commerce inevitably came piracy.[49] To keep the activities of pirates at a manageable level was the responsibility of any ancient maritime power.

---

[46] Kroll 1993: 105, no. 145.   [47] For details, see Buraselis below: 97–8.
[48] See Crowl 1986: 455, cf. 467, for security and national defence through command of the sea as even more important.
[49] Horden and Purcell 2000: 157, not necessarily leading to the collapse of trade; Horden and Purcell 2005: 351, piracy as an index of 'connectivity'; Harris 2005: 17, on plunder and exchange.

Egypt had long faced a similar problem on the Nile, and that of course continued. Here, in Chapter 11, Kruse looks in detail at how the Ptolemies attempted to deal with piracy on the Nile. Meanwhile, in the ancient Mediterranean pirates played a not insignificant role in the slave trade and other related activities; the question of who was or was not a pirate at any given time depended on the eye of the beholder (see Criscuolo in Chapter 10). As considered below, by Gabrielsen in Chapter 4 as well as by Criscuolo, the right level and approach to control were a problem shared in the early Hellenistic period by Egypt and, especially, Rhodes. Earlier Athens had played the role of protector of the seas, as did Rome later, and piracy of course survived the decline of that empire.[50] It remained and remains an on-going problem for those who sail the seas.

Two of the Seven Wonders of the Ancient World belong to the period covered in this volume. Besides the Lighthouse at Alexandria erected under Ptolemy II and memorialised in a poem of Posidippus,[51] there was the Colossus of Rhodes, a great bronze statue of Helios made by Chares of Lindos. Possibly erected at the end of the long harbour mole, it was said to have been financed from the engines and spoils captured from Demetrius Poliorcetes following his year-long siege of the city (305/304 BC).[52] In this case the Besieger had been ultimately unsuccessful, and crucial to Rhodes' survival was the help of her allies, especially Ptolemy I, who helped with men and food (both grain and beans) to keep the city provisioned. It was in recognition of this help that the Rhodians were credited with first granting Ptolemy I the name of Soter.[53]

This was simply one of many occasions when the closeness of Rhodes and Egypt can be documented. It was a connection built on various factors, but above all on the trading interests of the two states. Throughout this period Rhodes remained the state above all others with which Egypt was commercially connected. In part this resulted from the geography of the area. The location of Rhodes to the north of Alexandria made for relatively easy landfalls in either direction, given the winds and currents of the region.[54] The island lying close to the harbour in Alexandria was, as Gabrielsen notes, named Antirrhodos. Rhodes lay opposite, and the name may be seen to

---

[50] See Braudel 1972: I, 292.   [51] Posidippus 115 (Austin and Bastianini 2002).

[52] Pollitt 1986: 55; Stewart 1990: I, 298–9; Hoepfner 2003: 53, 57–64, for possible location. The date of its erection as *c.* 282 BC depends on Pliny's report (*HN* 34.41) of its destruction by an earthquake fifty-six years later (in 226 BC).

[53] Diod. Sic. 20.100.3–4, also a *temenos* in his name; Hazzard 1992 questions this attribution. The full report of these hostilities in Diod. Sic. 20.91–100 provides an interesting account of the many different types of vessel involved.

[54] Pryor 1988: 6–8 provides a useful introduction; cf. Horden and Purcell 2000: 137–8.

symbolise a close connection between the two states, though in fact their distance apart was 325 nautical miles, which, according to Diodorus, was a four-day passage.[55] Already under Cleomenes, Egypt and Rhodes had been involved together in the racket that Alexander's satrap ran in manipulating the grain trade. Rhodes was where his agents were based.[56] Commercial relations between these two states remained close and flourished. Later, under the Ptolemies, Rhodian merchant vessels were regular and welcome visitors to Alexandria. Rhodian guard ships, their *phylakides*, played a crucial role in countering the pirates of the area. The ubiquity of Rhodian amphora handles surviving in Egypt is testimony to the importance of the direct trade between these partners. Further, Rhodes remained the region's most important entrepôt, lying as it did on the route to Phoenicia, Syria, Asia Minor and Greece (see Map 4.1).

Significant too, as demonstrated by Gabrielsen, was innovation in the organisation of trade, with the development of a new commercial infrastructure in which groups of business partners began to replace the small-scale merchants of earlier times. Benefiting from good credit arrangements in Rhodes and a corporate bearing of risk, networks of traders joined to carry larger cargoes often for named recipients, who themselves might meet the added expense of customs dues. Partners like these, dispersed geographically but working through Rhodes, also shared information on markets and goods; in a world lacking the means of instant communication, information was always at a premium.[57] Sharing information and risk was a winning combination, and the earlier pattern of trade began to change with the growth of more profitable enterprises on a larger scale. Here, at least, the traditional *cabotage* of the Mediterranean world (the equivalent of the role of the more recent tramp steamer), with the small-scale merchant (*emporos*) or pedlar taking on loads from place to place, was giving way to a more developed and internationally based system centred on the port of Rhodes.[58]

If, for at least the first half of the Ptolemaic period, Rhodian ships were the most frequent visitors to sail past Antirrhodos into one of Alexandria's harbours, they were certainly not the only ones. Through Alexandria came a constant traffic of both men and goods. Standing at the link point between the agricultural wealth of Egypt and the Mediterranean markets that consumed their produce, Alexandria was a major centre for

---

[55] Diod. Sic. 3.34.7, Rhodes to Alexandria; cf. Braudel 1972: 358–9, three days in the sixteenth century.
[56] For details, see Gabrielsen below: 78, with nn. 35–6.
[57] On the crucial role of information in traditional markets, see Geertz 1979: 125, 183–5.
[58] Horden and Purcell 2000: 140–5, 150, 365, 565; Bresson 2005: 95–7, with examples.

export. Strabo indeed was later to claim that exports from the city regularly exceeded imports.[59] An impressive variety of products passed through the city, with both Mediterranean and Red Sea trade involved. From the Red Sea, across the desert and down the Nile, came the products of Ethiopia and Africa (though not all of them for export), elephants for the Ptolemaic army, ivory and exotic animals, frankincense and myrrh;[60] and in the last century of Ptolemaic rule, when the monsoons were used for the sailing passage, came products from across the Indian Ocean, spices, cotton and other valuable items. From the south of Egypt, goods came across the desert and down the Nile, Nubian gold and other minerals, and semi-precious stones. Some products were no doubt manufactured for export in Alexandria itself, the well-known perfumes, unguents and drugs, papyrus, textiles, jewellery, metal-work and fine glass. But the richest product of all to pass through the port of Alexandria was without doubt the tax grain (both wheat and barley) levied from the lands that the Ptolemies controlled. As already noted, this was the basis of the wealth on which the new rulers relied as they extended their power into a Mediterranean orbit. At the same time, imports brought the products that their population either needed or sought – as earlier, silver, copper, timber and wine, but also many other goods and comestibles, clothing and carpets, for instance, fine pottery wares, different wines, Greek cheeses, dried figs, honey or garlic.[61] And in the course of the Ptolemaic period, the city of Alexandria became – in the words of P. M. Fraser – the unrivalled centre of world trade.[62]

The variety of products coming through the city was matched by that of the people attracted to visit and often to stay. Immigrants, traders, mercenaries, tourists or those attracted by the prospect of employment or just a better life flooded into Egypt through the port of Alexandria. One group of such men, those who sought employment in the Ptolemaic army, is the subject of Stefanou's study in Chapter 7; here she shows how new evidence has modified the earlier picture.[63]

Meanwhile, in Alexandria the rulers used their wealth to encourage Greek art and artists, literature, culture and cult. In pursuit of influence in other spheres, the Ptolemies extended their support to scholars and many talented individuals in different fields. In Alexandria for much of the

---

[59] Strabo 17.1.7 (C 793).   [60] See Burstein 1996 and 2008.
[61] Fraser 1972: I, 132–88, provides a full survey. See, for example, *P.Cair.Zen.* I 59110.20–9, with IV 59547 and 59548 (mid third century BC), a consignment of salted tunny fish, cheeses from Rhenea and Cythnos, dried figs from Rhodes and Caunus, a winter cloak and vintage sweet wine from Chios, sent up country from Alexandria.
[62] Fraser 1972: I, 133.   [63] See Bagnall 1984.

Ptolemaic period, alongside a lively trade in material goods, royal patronage encouraged the work of artists, scientists and intellectuals attracted to the city for this reason. This continued, perhaps to a lesser degree, despite both the mid second-century BC loss of Egyptian influence in the Aegean and the anti-intellectual stance that is reported for Ptolemy VIII Euergetes II (otherwise known as Kakergetes).[64] The influx of what McKechnie calls 'smart capital' (Chapter 8 below) was important for the Ptolemies in terms of their cultural standing in the competitive world of Hellenistic dynasts.

The most successful period of Ptolemaic rule in terms of its Mediterranean standing was the period of the Ptolemaic empire, and this was effectively over with the death of Ptolemy VI in 145 BC. But the end of the overseas empire did not mean the end of Aegean contacts or of those further to the west, where Ptolemaic kings were to be found taking the journey to Rome with increasing frequency. Egypt was now an established part of the whole Mediterranean world and its concert of powers. At the same time, however, as Ptolemaic seaborne power was active to the north, Egypt continued her age-old contacts with the lands to the east and the south. The Red Sea was the other major body of water that bordered the shores of Egypt, and throughout the Ptolemaic period activities continued to the east of the country in the Red Sea region, along the shores of Arabia opposite, and south round the horn of Africa and along the Somali coast. Most of this was not new territory for rulers of Egypt, but in the Ptolemaic period both trade and exploration there received a definite boost. And in this area, advances in Ptolemaic commerce and in Ptolemaic cultural encouragement go hand in hand.

The first impetus for exploration came from changes in warfare. Following Alexander's experiences in the east and the adoption of elephants in Hellenistic forces, the search for new sources had led the early Ptolemies down along the Red Sea in the search of supplies.[65] For elephants, special craft were constructed; these did not always survive the sudden storms that blow up along the southern stretches of the coast.[66] The other main products of the area, as already noted, were spices from Arabia or the aromatic products from along the Somali coast. From Alexandria a second-century BC loan contract for a voyage along that coast (the Aromata, as it was known) well illustrates the degree to which the different seas and their peoples came together in the city. In this particular contract, a Spartan

---

[64] See Ath. 4.184b–c (from Menecles of Barca) for the positive effects felt elsewhere from expulsion by Ptolemy VIII of professionals and intellectuals from Alexandria. Cf. Buraselis 1993: 262.

[65] Mueller 2006: 150–7, on settlements; Burstein 2008, more generally.

[66] See *P.Petrie* II 40.a.26 (third century BC), a (*naus*) *elephantêgos* swamped by waves.

and a Massaliote are involved; its witnesses include a military leader from Thessalonica, a man from Elaea, another Massaliote, a Carthaginian and a man named Quintus, son of Quintus, who may have come from Italy.[67]

The second major boost to trade from the east came later, as a growing curiosity about the world and its geographical make-up developed. This was an interest developed both within the scholarly confines of the Alexandrian Library and in more practical ways, by those involved in naval activities, in exploration, travel or trade. It represents an important development and a significant result of the expansion in Egypt's maritime power.

Already under Ptolemy II, one of his admirals, Timosthenes of Rhodes, composed a work *On Harbours*. This, Geus argues in Chapter 15 below, was to have a long-lasting influence on geographical studies. It was also in Alexandria that Eratosthenes from Cyrene undertook his most important work. This scholar had been invited by Ptolemy III Euergetes to Alexandria to act as royal tutor, and there he succeeded Apollonius of Rhodes as head of the Alexandrian Library. In addition to work on literary criticism and chronology, Eratosthenes produced mathematical work with a strong geographical flavour. Combining observation with mathematic models, he succeeded in measuring the circumference of the earth to a degree of accuracy not previously achieved. He was a systematic geographer, whose work was used by Strabo later.[68] These two third-century BC geographers, Timosthenes and Eratosthenes, are the subject of Prontera's contribution in the present volume (Chapter 14). Yet another whose geographical work illustrates the growth of interest in the wider world that was now connected with the Mediterranean through Egypt was Agatharchides. Agatharchides himself came from Cnidus but, in the first half of the second century BC, he worked on his study *On the Erythraean Sea* in Alexandria.

Some time later, in the second half of the second century BC, an envoy from Cyzicus visited Alexandria with an invitation to their *Koreia* festival. This was Eudoxus, already referred to above. His visit coincided, so the story went, with the arrival of a shipwrecked Indian sailor, who eventually divulged the route to India across the Indian ocean. An expedition followed, supported, we may note, by the ruling Ptolemy (VIII Euergetes II), and Eudoxus was set on a new life of exploration, which probably only ended in the course of a much later attempt to reach the same destination round the west coast of Africa. The different elements of interest and importance in Posidonius' account of these explorations are discussed in

---

[67] *SB* III 7169. Cf. Rostovtzeff 1953: II, 922, and III, 1555; Casson 1991: 157. Hauben 1985b, stressing the military connection of the witnesses, highlights the need for protection in the area.
[68] Geus 2002.

Habicht's contribution to this volume (Chapter 13).[69] For Eudoxus, royal subsidies for his ventures backfired, as the profits of two of his voyages were confiscated by the crown. Nevertheless, royal patronage was at times important in encouraging both intellectual and physical exploration. Increased geographical knowledge and awareness, cartography and mapping were all products of Ptolemaic interest in the nature of the seas that they sailed – the Mediterranean, the Red Sea and beyond. The visualisation of the world was changing, and travel by sea in the Hellenistic period, with the human encounters that ensued, resulted in a broader appreciation of the make-up of the varied lands that bordered and were linked by these different seas.

What, finally, all this might mean for individuals may be illustrated by two dedications from Egypt. First, from Coptus on the Nile, the port which served the desert routes that ran from the Red Sea coast, comes a dedication made to the great deities of Samothrace (the Cabiri) by a military man from Thera in thanks for his safe return from a Red Sea trip.[70] Then, in a sanctuary of Pan Euodios Soter (Egyptian Min) in the desert of the Thebaid, Melanias son of Apollonius from Perge in Pamphylia set up a dedication to mark his safe return from (the land of) the Troglodytes.[71] Men like these from the empire, working in Egypt on the Red Sea and to the south, illustrate just how far the whole of Egypt now formed part of the wider world of the Mediterranean. This was a truly international world, one that was held together by sea and river routes facilitating long-distance travel.

In all of this, Alexandria, the new capital of Egypt on the coast, formed a crucial point of focus. This was where the Nile met the Mediterranean. Here was the base of Ptolemaic maritime power and the centre that, throughout the period of Ptolemaic rule, acted as a magnet for people, goods and new ideas that crossed the seas to Egypt. Just as the unity of Egypt itself required control along the course of the Nile, so the prosperity of the wider Ptolemaic empire and the political, commercial, human and cultural links that constituted it depended upon mastery of more challenging and turbulent waters. Theirs was truly a waterborne power.[72]

---

[69] The relationship (if any) of Eudoxus to Hippalus, who gave his name to the monsoon, remains unclear; see Habicht below: 201–2 with nn. 13–16; on Hippalus, see now Gorre 2010.

[70] *OGIS* I 69 = *I.Portes du désert* 48 (Ptolemy III?).

[71] *OGIS* I 70 = *I.Paneion* 43 (second century BC).

[72] It should be clear how much this introduction owes to the contributors to this volume. Particular thanks are due to Andrew Meadows and Olga Palagia for their added input. John Thompson has helped immeasurably with discussion and constructive criticism. We wish also to thank Katja Mueller who has prepared Maps 1.1 and 4.1.

CHAPTER 2

The Ptolemaic League of Islanders

Andrew Meadows

To understand the potential significance of a waterway to the Ptolemaic kings, one has only to consider the multifaceted role played by the river Nile within Egypt. Its economic significance was paramount, both as inundator of the Egyptian land and as a means of commercial transport. Its role as a major transportation artery also made it of tremendous significance in military and policing terms. It played a part too in the projection of the figure of the Ptolemaic king throughout the land, both through his role in the traditional religious ceremonies that took place on the river and through his conspicuous display in the new development of royal barges.

This chapter takes as its focus another waterway or, better, series of waterways in the central Aegean. During the third century BC there is evidence for Ptolemaic interaction with and control of a League of Islanders, τὸ κοινὸν τῶν νησιωτῶν. In the three sections that follow I seek first to establish that, contrary to current orthodoxy, this League was a Ptolemaic foundation, second to suggest that the founder was Ptolemy Philadelphus and, though necessarily summarily, to establish how this foundation fits in with broader Ptolemaic policy outside Egypt, and third to suggest the circumstances of the Ptolemaic loss of the League.

In doing so, the implicit conclusion I wish to draw is that the commercial, political and religious approach taken by Philadelphus to this waterway is distinctive and new, and perhaps owes something to lessons learnt on the Nile.

THE PTOLEMAIC FOUNDATION OF THE LEAGUE

Of the inscriptions which form our only evidence for the existence of the Nesiotic League before the Rhodian revival, only one can be dated with absolute certainty to a period of Antigonid control. The remainder, where attribution has been attempted, are generally assigned to the period of Ptolemaic suzerainty and more specifically to the time of Ptolemy

Philadelphus.[1] An accident of survival or discovery perhaps, the effect is nonetheless to throw the spotlight on this oddity. Common sense suggests that the Antigonid should either predate or postdate the run of Ptolemaic stones, but which is it to be?

In 1904 F. Durrbach published the fragmentary decree of the Nesiotic League which provided for the foundation of the festival of the *Demetrieia* to be held in alternate years to the already existing *Antigoneia*.[2] Since there were two occasions on which a Demetrius succeeded an Antigonus on the Macedonian throne (Antigonus Monophthalmus – Demetrius Poliorcetes and Antigonus Gonatas – Demetrius II), two broad date ranges for the decree presented themselves. There are, however, no further internal indications of date on the stone, and Durrbach thus found himself in a quandary:

From examination of the letter forms I do not believe that it is possible to draw any convincing evidence to impose one or the other of the two dates. The engraving is regular, careful, fairly thick and without apices. The M and Σ have slightly and regularly diverging hastas: this is a sign of relative antiquity, but one could not exclude the environs of 240 BC for this feature. On the other hand, the O and the Ω are smaller than the other letters; generally, these smaller forms hardly appear before the beginning of the second third of the 3rd century; but this observation certainly does not hold for Delos, where we sometimes encounter these forms from the beginning of the same century.[3]

Durrbach was thus forced to fall back on inference from contents. Monophthalmus and Poliorcetes assumed the diadem at the same moment, whereas Antigonus Gonatas was king before his son Demetrius. Since the inscription records a staggered introduction of the two festivals, he regarded the latter pair as being the more likely honorands, with a new festival being added for the new king upon the death of the old, and opted for a date around the death of Gonatas in 239 BC. The new stone and the Antigonid control of the Nesiotic League which it evinces would thus follow the Ptolemaic period of control.

During the course of the next three years it was pointed out to Durrbach by Maurice Holleaux that if his restoration of ll. 45–6 as 'alongside the altars

[1] Antigonid: *IG* XI.4 1036. Ptolemaic: *IG* XII.7 506 (*SIG*³ 390); *IG* XI.4 1038; *IG* XII.7 13; *IG* XI.4 1032 (*OGIS* 40); *IG* XI.4 1037; *IG* XI.4 1041; *IG* XI 4.1040; *IG* XI.4 1043; *IG* XI.4 1048; *IG* XI.4 1039; *IG* XI.4 1046; *IG* XI.4 1047; *IG* XII.5 1069; *IG* XI.4 1123–7; Michel, *Recueil* 534 (*CIG* 3655); *IG* XII.5 1004 (*OGIS* 773); *IG* XII.5 1065; *IG* XI.4 559 (*SIG*³ 391); *IG* XII *Suppl.* 169. Uncertain: *IG* XI.4 1044–5. A full list with useful summaries of detail is given by Buraselis 1982: 180–8, who elsewhere (80–1) notes the oddity of distribution. Three of the dedications (all to men in Ptolemaic service: *IG* XI.4 1123, 1126 and 1127) appear as Durrbach 1921–3: nos. 17, 19, 25; three of the decrees (*IG* XI.4 1036, 1038 and 1042) as Durrbach 1921–3: nos. 13, 21, 26 (the last two in honour of Ptolemaic functionaries).
[2] Durrbach 1904: no. 1, later *IG* XI.4 1036, and Durrbach 1921–3: no. 13.
[3] Durrbach 1904: 105 (my translation).

[of the kings]' (παρὰ τὸν βω|[μὸν τῶν βασιλέω]ν) were correct, then the Antigonus and Demetrius concerned really ought to have been rulers at the same time. In fact, even without this restoration, the alternating nature of the two festivals made this assumption more than likely.[4] In the light of this observation Durrbach returned to photographs of the stone and this time concluded:

that the characteristics of the letter forms suggest the end of the 4th century far more than the environs of the year 239: this is suggested notably by certain diagnostic letters: the Π, the M and the Σ with widely spread and diverging hastas . . . The style of lettering, which is that in use in administrative documents around the year 275, presents the most striking analogies with the Nesiotic decree.[5]

For Durrbach, the fact of the joint kingship, together with this new opinion of the letter-forms' significance, now tended to the conclusion that the stone referred to festivals of Monophthalmus and Poliorcetes. Unlike Gonatas and Demetrius II, they were joint kings in the years 306/301 BC, and since Durrbach's *editio princeps* there had been found a Delian inventory apparently mentioning *Antigoneia* dated to the year of the Delian archon Phillis I (296 BC).[6] A trawl through the literary sources yielded a possible occasion for the foundation of the League.[7] All now fitted neatly into place: the *Antigoneia* would have been founded in the wake of Dioscurides' expedition to the islands in 315/314 BC, the festival of Demetrius upon his glorious victory on Cyprus and the joint declaration of the kingship in 306 BC. Furthermore there seemed to be clear confirmation that 314 BC was a year of upheaval in the Cyclades, for it was at this point in time that Delos finally achieved its freedom after close to a century and a half of Athenian control.[8] Thus there was now strong evidence that the Nesiotic League was not a Ptolemaic foundation but rather the creation of Monophthalmus in *c.* 314 BC. Durrbach's reconstruction has received general acceptance

---

[4] Durrbach 1907: 209; cf. Bruneau 1970: 565. Er. Will 1955: 170–2 doubts Durrbach's restoration on topographical grounds and prefers instead παρὰ τὸν βω|[μὸν τῶν Σωτήρω]ν ('alongside the altars of [the Saviour Gods]').

[5] Durrbach 1907: 210–11.

[6] Durrbach 1905: no. 144 (*IG* XI.2 154a) line 42: a bare reference in the accounts of the Delian priests to festival torches for *Antigoneia* (τοῖς Ἀντιγονείοις δᾶιδες εἰς τὸγ χορὸν).

[7] Diod. Sic. 19.62.9: [Antigonus] διελόμενος δὲ τὸν στόλον πεντήκοντα μὲν ναῦς ἐξέπεμψεν εἰς Πελοπόννησον, τῶν δ' ἄλλων ναύαρχον καταστήσας Διοσκουρίδην τὸν ἀδελφιδοῦν προσέταξε περιπλεῖν τοῖς τε συμμάχοις παρεχόμενον τὴν ἀσφάλειαν καὶ τῶν νήσων τὰς μήπω μετεχούσας τῆς συμμαχίας προσαγόμενον.

[8] Habicht 1997: 63. The chronology of these years has been a matter of some debate between proponents of a high chronology, which would see the end of Antigonus' siege of Tyre and his dispatch of Dioscurides in 314 BC, and a low chronology, which places those events in the following year. For a survey of the evidence and a mixed solution compatible with the non-Greek documentary sources, see Boiy 2007: 111–50.

among scholars, and indeed Richard Billows in his study of Antigonus Monophthalmus has integrated the Nesiotic League into a broader pattern of Antigonid interaction with Greek states through leagues.[9]

However, there are problems with such a dating for our decree. To begin with, there is the dissonance of Durrbach's date of 306 BC and his opinion of *c.* 275 BC as providing the best comparanda for the letter forms. Furthermore, Durrbach himself was conscious of the difficulty that the Ptolemaic supremacy in the Aegean of 308/307 BC presented for the apparently continuous celebration of the *Antigoneia* down to 306 BC.[10] Wehrli was troubled enough by this problem to suggest moving the foundation of the *Antigoneia* to 307 BC, after the departure of Ptolemy, but this rearrangement begins to look a little contrived, and it has indeed been criticised by Buraselis.[11] There had been an interlude of Ptolemaic power, and it did not precede the supposed date of foundation of the *Demetrieia* by more than a year or so, and there is no independent evidence for wide-scale Antigonid naval activity in the Aegean in 307 BC. Ptolemy, indeed, was able to maintain his garrison at Sicyon until 303 BC (see further below).

To resolve the problem, new evidence is required. This in fact appeared in 1950, when a stone was published which could have given rise to a re-examination of our Nesiotic decree. Published by M. Andronikos, the famous manumission act from Beroea has made it virtually certain that Antigonus Gonatas and Demetrius II did rule conjointly.[12] The act is dated to the twenty-seventh year of King Demetrius. There were two Macedonian kings named Demetrius. Demetrius Poliorcetes is ruled out, since he died in 284/283 BC having ruled for just twenty-two years. Andronikos suggested that the ruler at the time of the decree must be identified as Demetrius II. Demetrius ruled alone for just ten years, so Andronikos argued that the regnal date of this stone showed that Demetrius had been co-ruler with his father, and subsequently dated his reign from that assumption of the diadem, not from the death of his father. Since Demetrius II died in 229 BC, he must have become co-ruler in 257/256 BC at the latest, and Andronikos argued that the likeliest context for the assumption of the

---

[9] Billows 1990: 217–30. Most recent discussions in L. Gallo 2009 and Hauben 2010.

[10] On the major Ptolemaic offensive in the Aegean of 308 BC, see especially Diod. Sic. 20.37.1: κατὰ δὲ τούτους τοὺς χρόνους Πτολεμαῖος μὲν ἐκ τῆς Μύνδου πλεύσας ἁδρῷ στόλῳ διὰ νήσων ἐν παράπλῳ τὴν Ἄνδρον ἠλευθέρωσε καὶ τὴν φρουρὰν ἐξήγαγε. Κομισθεὶς δ' ἐπὶ τὸν Ἰσθμὸν Σικυῶνα καὶ Κόρινθον παρέλαβεν παρὰ Κρατησιπόλεως. For other sources and prior bibliography, see Buraselis 1982: 49.

[11] Durrbach 1907: 219–22; Wehrli 1968: 116–18; Buraselis 1982: 65–7.

[12] Andronikos 1950: no. 1 (*SEG* 12.314 and *ISE* 109), now republished in an improved version as *I.Beroea* no. 45 ll. 1–3: τύχηι ἀγαθῆι. | βασιλεύοντος Δημητρίου ἑβδόμου καὶ εἴκοσ|τοῦ ἔτους...

co-regency was Demetrius' precocious victory over Alexander of Epirus in *c.* 262/261 BC, although this latter suggestion of course is speculative. Initially, Andronikos' general conclusion was accepted.[13] More recently, it has been called into question, and attempts were made to assign the stone to Poliorcetes, first by Errington (who argued that the stone was dated posthumously)[14] and then by E. Grzybek (who suggested that the regnal years were counted from the death of Philip Arrhidaeus in 317/316 BC).[15] However, the recent re-reading of the text by Hatzopoulos and Gounaropoulou has proved decisive. In lines 27–8, not read by Andronikos, they find the stipulation, προστάτας δὲ ἡγοῦνται καὶ | βασιλέα καὶ βασίλισσαν . . . Since Poliorcetes' wife, Phila, died in 288, there can be no possibility that she was still alive in year 27 of Demetrius Poliorcetes' reign, whatever start-date was used to calculate it.[16] Andronikos was thus correct to date the stone to the reign of Demetrius II and to deduce a period of co-regency for father and son, Antigonus Gonatas and Demetrius.

Durrbach's dating of *IG* XI.4 1036 begins to look vulnerable. The fundamental reason for dating the Nesiotic decree early had been the joint kingship. No other arguments in favour of the early date carry weight without this. The ambiguous epigraphical evidence produces, as we have seen, a tension between the early and mid third century, and Durrbach's second thoughts placed the decree squarely in the middle of this period (though initially he could not exclude a date as late as 239 BC).[17] The mention of *Antigoneia* in 296 (above n. 7) in a Delian, not a League, document proves nothing except that *Antigoneia* of some sort existed in that year. The reference may as well be to a Delian, as opposed to a League, festival.

Other arguments that have subsequently been used to support the case for an Antigonid foundation of the League carry little weight either. Tarn, for example, argued that the apparently pure Ionic make-up of the new League ruled out Ptolemy as a founder since none of the (Dorian) Ptolemaic naval bases are attested as members.[18] Yet there is no sign that, on taking control of the League, Ptolemy imposed Dorian cities upon it: if he could see the advantage of not doing so then, why not in an act of foundation?

---

[13] See, eg., J. and L. Robert, *Bulletin* 1951: 136, at 172–3; Moretti *ad ISE* 109.

[14] Errington 1977. For firm rejection of Errington's arguments, see Walbank in Hammond and Walbank 1988: 317–18.

[15] E. Grzybek 1993.   [16] See Hatzopoulos 1990: 147, n. 51 and *I.Beroea* p. 147.

[17] Cf. Buraselis 1982: 63–4, n. 105: 'Da auch sonst Inschriften, in denen ein (König!) Antigonos erscheint, aufgrund des Schriftcharakters allein immer noch nicht mit Sicherheit Monophthalmos oder Gonatas' (bzw. Dosons) Zeit zugeschrieben werden können.' Buraselis' own examination of the letterforms in 1976 (*ibid.*) led him to accept Durrbach's later decision to rule out the second half of the third century.

[18] Tarn 1913: 436, 77–9.

There are three further inscriptions that have been attributed to relations between Monophthalmus and the Nesiotic League in the late fourth century. The first two (*IG* XI.4 566 from Delos and *IG* XII *Suppl.* 168 from Ios) are fragmentary, but so far as they survive they contain no reference to the Nesiotic League. Both nevertheless mention a King Antigonus, and it is possible that they refer to the same ruler.[19] This ruler, it has been argued, must be Monophthalmus, because in the Delian inscription both an Antigonus and a Demetrius are described as kings (ll. 6 and 15–16),[20] and on one occasion plural kings are mentioned.[21] This, it has been suggested, could only be a reference to the co-regency of Monophthalmus and Poliorcetes. Again, we now know this assumption to be based on a false premise, and in fact there are strong grounds for doubting that the Ietan inscription, with which the Delian one has been paired, could come from the reign of Monophthalmus. The Antigonus concerned is mentioned, after a lacuna, in line 2 of the inscription, in a position suggesting that the previous line ought to have contained mention of benefactions by ancestors of the honorand.[22] If such is the case, then the honorand clearly cannot be Monophthalmus, and if the link is to be maintained between the two inscriptions, then both are presumably to be dated to the joint reign of Gonatas and Demetrius II. But the case for linking the two inscriptions is not strong (see n. 19).

The third, highly fragmentary text comes from Corinth (*SEG* 24.357):

```
[— — — — — — — — — — — — — — — —]
[— — — — —]Ἀκροκορ[ινθ — — — — —]
[— — — — —] πεντακισχιλί[ους — — — — —]
[— — — — —]πεζοὺς ἑπττακ[οσίους — — — —]
[— — — — —] Κεῖοι πεζοὺ[ς — — — — —]          4
[— — — — — ο]υς Κύθνιο[ι — — — — — — —]
[— — — — ου]ς Μυκ[όνιοι — — — — — — —]
```

---

[19] *IG* XI.4 566.5–6: . . . ἐμφανιοῦσῖ τή]ν τε εὔνοιαν καὶ τὴν φιλίαν καὶ [τ]ὴν|[— — — ἣν ἔχει ὁ δῆμος] πρὸς τὸν βασιλέα Ἀν[τίγονον . . .]; *IG* XII *Suppl.* 168 l. 9: . . .]αν βασιλέα Ἀντίγο[νο]ν καὶ παρακατατίθεται [. . . (cf. ll. 4 [restored] and 10 [partially restored]). Billows 1990: 224 argues, on the basis of the presence of the word ὁμονοοῦντες in both decrees, that Monophthalmus is the king in question (Cf. *IG* XI.4 566, l. 13 and *IG* XII *Suppl.* 168 l. 12). The presence of this same word in *IG* XII.5 1065, 4, an inscription clearly to be dated *c.* 280, considerably weakens this position, however. Cf. also the 'Themistocles Decree', ML 23 l. 44, surely from the 260s.

[20] In fact the name Ἀν[τίγονον] is not secure: see Roussel *ad IG* XI.4 566, line 6. Demetrius (line 16) is more secure.

[21] Line 7: though there is no guarantee that these kings are contemporary or from the same house.

[22] The stone reads (ll. 1–2): [. . . . .]δάμαντος εἶπε· πρυτάνεις ἐπεψήφισαν Καλλ[-]|[-]ν αἴτιος γεγένηται τῆι π[ό]λει νῦν τε Ἀντίγονος ὁ βα[-]. *IG* restores [ἐπειδὴ πρότερον Δημήτριος ὁ βασιλεὺς(?) πολλῶν καὶ | μεγάλων ἀγαθῶ]ν αἴτιος γεγένηται κτλ. For discussion, see Habicht 1970: 65–73, revisited 256–7. Fraser 1958: 154 preferred to attribute the stone to the reign of Doson.

Dating this to the late fourth century on the basis of letter-forms, the editor, D. J. Geagan, claimed that 'since the Ptolemies were hardly active militarily in the Peloponnese while the [Nesiotic] league was under their protectorate, the occasion commemorated must have been in the interest of Antigonus and Demetrius'.[23] This occasion, he suggested, was the expedition of Polemaeus (an Antigonid general) in 313/312 BC (Diod. Sic. 19.77.2). There are flaws in this interpretation.[24] First, we must note that there is no mention of the League in the inscription, merely individual islanders. There is thus still no evidence for the League's existence prior to the third century, and nothing to suggest that we should be looking for an occasion during any power's domination of it. Second, as Geagan admits (1968: 383), his explanation is hard-pressed to explain the part played by the Acrocorinth, which occurs nowhere in Diodorus' account of Polemaeus' expedition. Third, once we are free of the need to associate early 'League activities' with the Antigonids, an obvious alternative occasion for the stone's inscription offers itself in the campaign of Ptolemy Soter in 308 BC (above n. 10).

Finally, having brought into question the epigraphic evidence for the early foundation of the League by the Antigonids, it is as well to take a closer look at the supposed literary evidence. The dispatch of Dioscurides (Diod. Sic. 19.62.9) is to be placed in late 314 BC after the termination of the siege of Tyre.[25] He was sent with an unknown number of ships to reassure Antigonus' allies and to try to win over those of the islands who were not yet allies.[26] This raises the question of the state of the Aegean in the period prior to this expedition. Diodorus leaves us in no doubt. In 315 BC Antigonus had been prompted to build his fleet by the dominance of his enemies at sea; Ptolemy, we learn, had in his possession the old Phoenician fleet (Diod. Sic. 19.58.1–2). The despondent reaction of Antigonus' allies in the area of Phoenicia to this thalassocracy is explicitly described.[27]

Antigonus had gone to Phoenicia to muster his fleet and used it there until the fall of Tyre: the Greeks of the Aegean had had no reason to ally themselves to Antigonus in 314 BC, and received little encouragement to do so from the Ptolemaic fleet. What, then, did these islanders make of Dioscurides, and, moreover, which islanders were they? The area of

---

[23] Geagan 1968: 382.　　[24] Noted already by J. and L. Robert, *Bulletin* 1969: 236.
[25] Diod. Sic. 19.61.5. On the chronology of the siege of Tyre and the problems with Diodorus' account of this period, see above n. 18 and Wheatley 1998: 263.
[26] This must refer to the islands of the eastern Aegean: perhaps Rhodes, Samos and Chios (Billows 1990: 118, n. 45).
[27] ἄθυμοι καθειστήκεισαν· πρόδηλον γὰρ ἦν ὅτι θαλασσοκρατοῦντες οἱ πολέμιοι πορθήσουσι τοὺς τοῖς ἐναντίοις κοινοπραγοῦντας ἀπὸ τῆς πρὸς Ἀντίγονον φιλίας (Diod. Sic. 19.58.6).

Dioscurides' activity is left vague. He is to reassure the existing allies, the islands via which he had sailed to Antigonus in the previous year. When next we encounter Dioscurides in the winter of 314/313 BC he is apparently hovering in the north-eastern Aegean (Diod. Sic. 19.68.4), where the predicament of the hapless Lemnians is surely indicative of the forced fluidity of Aegean politics of this period. On the basis of Diodorus' account, which is all we have, Dioscurides interpreted his mission as being to take and secure the eastern Aegean islands. Seen in the light of his activities of the previous year, these can only be the islands on the route he had taken to reach Phoenicia from the Hellespont. To go further and suggest that Dioscurides increased his sphere of operations from the seaboard of Asia Minor to the central Aegean is not warranted by the evidence. From what follows in Diodorus' account, it seems clear that Dioscurides' expedition is preparatory to, perhaps part of, Antigonus' Carian campaign in the following year (313 BC). The notion that the Delians threw off the Athenian yoke and established a festival to Antigonus on the basis of Dioscurides' presence in the area of the Asian coast is seriously to be doubted.

There is simply not the evidence to place the foundation of the Nesiotic League in 314/313 BC, nor to attribute it to the Antigonids. Although there can be little doubt that some of the eastern Aegean islands were under Antigonid control in some form until at least 287 BC, very little evidence in fact survives for this period, and none requires the existence of the League of Islanders. We probably do not have any evidence for what was going on in the Cyclades between the Delian emancipation and the arrival of Ptolemy there in 308 BC.[28] If there were a 'free-for-all' in the course of which some formerly important states (such as Athens) lost their overseas possessions to the cries of 'ἐλευθερία' that were in the air, or to the first big fleet that came along, it should occasion no surprise.

But this is not to return to the old claim that Ptolemy I founded the Nesiotic League in 308. *SEG* 24.357 may well confirm and supplement the extent of the support Ptolemy possessed during his campaigning of 308 BC, but it does not suggest the existence of a League. Moreover, it is not known what happened after his withdrawal from mainland Greece to the island allies Soter had secured in 308 BC. That Ptolemy's interest in the area of operations of 308 BC did not die seems clear from the maintenance of one of the garrisons of this campaign (Sicyon) until it was driven out in 303 BC (Diod. Sic. 20.102.2). Evidence from the islands is sparse: on

---

[28] It is difficult to gauge the significance of the Delian offering made by the Ptolemaic general Leonidas (if it is him) attested by *IG* XI.2 161 B l. 77. See most recently Hauben 2004: 42, n. 91.

Thera, Artemidorus, a man with very close Ptolemaic connections, was present in the reign of Soter (see below); it is tantalising that we hear of a Ptolemaic garrison already present on Andros in 287 BC.[29] But still there is no evidence for the existence of the League.

PTOLEMY PHILADELPHUS AND THE FOUNDATION OF THE NESIOTIC LEAGUE

If not in 314 BC by Antigonus, nor in 308 BC by Ptolemy I, when was the Nesiotic League founded?

At first sight, the earliest evidence for the existence of the League is *IG* XII.5 1004 (*OGIS* 773). This is an honorific decree of Ios for a certain Zenon, 'left in charge by Bacchon the nesiarch' (ὁ καταλειφθεὶς ὑπὸ Βάκχωνος τοῦ νησιάρ[χου]), for intervening with the trierarchs on behalf of ambassadors from the demos concerning slaves who were leaving the island 'on the undecked ships' (ἐπὶ τῶν πλοίων τῶν ἀφράκτων). Since its publication it has been accepted that the decree's honorand is to be identified with that of a decree from Athens dated to the archonship of Diocles (286/285), for 'Ze[non placed] in command of undecked ships by Ptol[emy]' (Ζή[νων καθεστηκ]ὼς ὑπὸ τοῦ | Πτολ[εμαίου ἐπὶ τῶν ἀ]φράκτων).[30] The date of *c.* 286 BC that is thus produced for the Ios decree (and which is now often cited as the beginning of Ptolemaic control of the League)[31] cannot, however, be regarded as anything more than a very rough approximation: while it may be fair to conflate the two Zenons, it is far less easy to assume that the resulting individual only had something to do with undecked ships during one year of his life. Indeed, it is far from clear that the two commands described in the different inscriptions are of the same nature. In the Athenian decree he is plainly a naval officer in charge of deckless ships and has been appointed by King Ptolemy; at Ios he appears to have been left in charge (καταλειφθεὶς) by the nesiarch (note the difference in command structure), the most natural implication being that this was a command with a geographical basis, including responsibility for undecked ships.[32] Whatever the nature of the commands, a margin of error of several years must be allowed in setting a date of *c.* 286 for the Ios decree (and the beginning of Ptolemaic control of the League).

In truth, the earliest date for the League of Islanders is probably provided by another inscription, the famous decree of the Nesiotic League from

[29] *Hesperia* Suppl. 17. l. 20. See Buraselis 1982: 94, n. 229 on Andros as a fetter of the islands.
[30] *IG* II² 650; *SIG*³ 367; Ameling et al. 1995: KNr. 14.   [31] See, e.g., Hölbl 2001: 24.
[32] On the nature of this command, Merker 1970: 150.

Nicuria.[33] The decree is a response to a request from Ptolemy Philadelphus for the Islanders' participation in the preparations for the first *Ptolemaieia* at Alexandria. The date of the first celebration of the *Ptolemaieia* has, to my mind, now been fairly firmly established as the winter of 279/278 on the penteteric anniversary of Soter's death.[34] The decree thus dates to a period shortly before that, that is to say *c.* 281/280 BC. This is the certain date by which the League had been founded. The text of the decree is worth dwelling on for a moment for the acts with which the Islanders credit Ptolemy Soter in lines 13 to 16: 'he freed the cities and gave them back their laws and re-established their ancestral constitution and lightened their tributary payments' (τάς τε π[ό]||[λ]εις ἐλευθερώσας καὶ τοὺς νόμους ἀποδοὺς | [κ]αὶ τὴμ πάτριομ πολιτείαμ πᾶσιγ καταστήσα[ς] | [κ]αὶ τῶν εἰσφορῶγ κουφίσας). The temptation to extrapolate precise details from this formula is probably best resisted: the stated recipients of these benefactions (the entire Greek world) warn us that we are in a realm of generalised propaganda dating back to 312, or perhaps looking forward already to the 260s. Nevertheless, the implication is of a fundamentally different attitude being taken towards the Islanders by the new dominant monarch. This constitutes strong circumstantial evidence that Ptolemy I did not take over the institution of the Nesiotic League from the Antigonids. He seems to have changed, not maintained, the *status quo*.

But did Ptolemy I create the Nesiotic League? This might seem the obvious inference, since it is clear, from *IG* II² 650 and other texts, that he was militarily active in the Aegean in the early 280s, when he took over effective naval control of the area from Demetrius Poliorcetes. Yet, as we have seen, there is no explicit evidence for the existence of the League from the time of Soter. This may be an accident of evidence, but a survey of the evidence for Ptolemy Philadelphus' relationship with the region suggests otherwise. Recent discoveries and re-examination of old evidence in the north-eastern Aegean have thrown an increased emphasis on the early activities of Philadelphus following the upheaval of Lysimachus' death at Corupedion.[35]

---

[33] *IG* XII.7 506; *SIG*³ 390; Kotsidu 2000: KNr. 131 [E1].

[34] The occasion of this first celebration and its relation to the grand procession described by Callixeinus (*apud* Ath. 5.197c–203b = *FGrH* 627 F2) has been one of the more heavily disputed dates in the reign of Philadelphus. For a balanced survey of the evidence and recent scholarship, see Thompson 2000, and Hauben 2004: 41–2 and 2010: 110, for rebuttal of recent attempts to lower the date of the decree to the 260s.

[35] I have argued elsewhere that the creation of administered provinces in Caria and Lycia was the work of Philadelphus, not Soter: Meadows 2006 and 2008.

On Samothrace there seems now to be early evidence of Ptolemaic appropriation of the sanctuary, advertised by two monumental edifices. The Rotunda of Arsinoe is now dated in the publication of the site to the period following Arsinoe's flight from Cassandrea to Samothrace and thence to her brother Ptolemy (c. 279–275).[36] The Propylon of Ptolemy is dated on architectural grounds slightly later.[37] The earliest known personal dedication to the Samothracian gods was made by the Ptolemaic officer Artemidorus of Perge in his *temenos* on Thera. Artemidorus himself seems to have been a Samothracian initiate.[38] *IG* XI.4 1044, the remains of a decree of the Nesiotic League in honour of a Samothracian, is unfortunately too fragmentary to shed light on the relations between these two institutions. This swift movement on Samothrace into the vacuum created by the death of Lysimachus seems to have been mirrored on nearby Lesbos, where an Arsinoe Philadelphos altar plaque points to Ptolemaic influence on the island in perhaps the 270s.[39] The mention of royal revenues deriving from the island in a papyrus dating to the reign of Philopator is testimony to direct administration of the island at that date, but when this started is uncertain.[40] For the decree from Methymna in honour of Damus, the priest of King Ptolemy son of Ptolemy and Ptolemy, a date in the 260s has been proposed by P. Brun, although the reign of Philopator remains a more probable context.[41] A garrison is also now known at Antissa in the reign of Philopator: it is uncertain how much earlier it was installed.[42]

The establishment and spread of the cult of Arsinoe with its curious altars is itself informative of the new turn Ptolemaic policy was taking under Philadelphus. In a classic study, L. Robert has shown these altar plaques to be integral to the cult of Arsinoe–Aphrodite Euploia–Zephyritis

---

[36] Roux in McCredie, Roux and Shaw 1992: 231–9, on the basis of Arsinoe's declared pedigree in the inscribed dedication of the building (*IG* XII.8 227; *OGIS* 23; *Samothrace* 10: [βασ]ίλισσα Ἀρ[σινόη βασιλέως Πτολε]μαίου θυγά[τηρ]), dates the building to the period of her marriage to Philadelphus, suggesting the sanctuary she received at Samothrace as the reason for her personal dedication. For the latter: Just. *Epit.* 24.3.9; Longega 1968: 40–2.

[37] Frazer 1990: 231–3, noting that the separation in date between the two buildings is very short, suggests a date on stylistic grounds of around the turn from the first to the second quarter of the third century. The formulation of the dedication (*IG* XII.8 228; *OGIS* 23; *Samothrace* 11; Ameling et al. 1995: KNr. 237) seems to suggest a date later than the rotunda.

[38] *IG* XII.3 *Suppl.* 1337; Cole 1984: 61–4. On Artemidorus' status, see 36 below.

[39] *IG* XII.2, 513; Brun 1991: 101–2, 107. Note also the probable reference to relations between Methymna and Alexandria in Posidippus 37 (A–B): Bing 2003: 260–4.

[40] *P. Tebt.* I 8, with Bagnall 1976: 162.

[41] *IG* XII *Suppl.* 115. For the redating of the inscription see Brun 1991: 105–8. The later date was favoured by Habicht 1970: 109, n. 1 and Bagnall 1976: 162. Brun's proposal has now been strongly rejected by Labarre 1996: 54–6.

[42] See Stefanou, Chapter 7 in this volume: 127, n. 149.

(Εὔπλοια–Ζεφυρῖτις).[43] The foundation of this cult was due, according to Posidippus, to the Ptolemaic admiral Callicrates of Samos.[44] Altar plaques of the type found at Methymna have also been found at Delos, Paros, Ios, Amorgos, Thera, Miletus, Samos, Caunus, Eretria and Cyprus, as well as in Egypt.[45] Clearly, the cult was as widespread throughout the Aegean as it was celebrated at Alexandria. On the one hand this cult must have had its straightforward purpose: '[Arsinoe–Aphrodite] assumait la garde non seulement des marins et des militaires, mais encore des voyageurs et du personnel de la marine marchande.'[46] It was no doubt comforting for any sailor who put to sea anywhere in the Greek Mediterranean to have a consistent goddess to whom to pray for safety. But she already existed. The assumption of this role by Arsinoe, the Ptolemaic queen, is new and requires further explanation. The propagation of this hybrid cult went further than assuaging fear of the sea, it asserted the fact and the extent of the new Ptolemaic empire: 'the deification of Arsinoe was a political act'.[47] It declared the medium of domination to be the sea, while, by placing the queen on a level with Aphrodite, it stressed the need to pray as much to the Ptolemaic house as to the goddess for safety on the sea. As the brother and sister dominated a sanctuary at Samothrace, so they appropriated the cult of Εὔπλοια. Nor can it have been merely a question of Ptolemaic garrison troops bringing their own cult for their own use. There is no evidence for Ptolemaic garrisons on Delos, Paros, Ios or Amorgos. This private cult was adopted by 'free' Greeks within the sphere of Ptolemaic influence, undoubtedly under the example of Greek officers such as Callicrates in the Ptolemaic fleet.[48]

To this evidence for cult we may add Robert's observation that Arsinoe also 'devint l'éponyme nouvelle d'un bon nombre de villes refondées qui

---

[43] Robert 1966a: esp. 199–208 (= OMS VII 623–32).

[44] Posidippus 39 A–B; 119 A–B (13 G–P); 116 A–B (12 G–P). Further discussion on Callicrates in Posidippus in Bing 2003 (cf. also Hauben's contribution to this volume) and on Arsinoe in Stephens 2004; Bing associates two further epigrams with the cult of the queen: 36 and 37 A–B.

[45] IG XI.4 1303 (Delos); IG XII.5 264, 265+266 (Paros); IG XII.5 16 (Ios); IG XII.7 99, 263, 264, EAH (1989) 112 = SEG 40.739 (Amorgos); IG XII.3 462+1386 + IG XII Suppl. 156 (Thera); Milet I.7 288–289 (Miletus); AD Parar. 11 1927–8: 31 no. 4 (Samos); Marek 2006: no. 54 = SEG 44.895 (Caunus); AK 33 1990: 113–14 = SEG 40.763 (Eretria). Some seven altars and seventeen plaques are known from Cyprus: Anastassiades 1998: 132–3 with the addition of SEG 53.1755 and 54.1531. For Egypt: Ann. Serv. Ant. Eg. 6 1905: 190 no. II, SEG 20.691, SEG 24.1229–1230.

[46] Hauben 1983: 111–12.

[47] Thompson 2012: 118, of Arsinoe's cult in Egypt.

[48] Note Obbink's reading of Posidippus' epigrams on the foundation of the cult: 'the focus is on safety . . . cult . . . Ptolemaic celebrity . . . and most importantly on Greekness'. See Obbink 2004: quotation at 22, and 2005: 106, and especially Bing 2003 on the role of Callicrates; see further Hauben, Chapter 3 in this volume.

étaient toutes ou presque toutes d'excellents ports et des bases navales'. Indeed, in Epigram 5 (Pf.) of Callimachus, we find the town of Arsinoe and the cult of the queen linked on the island of Ceos.[49] The refoundations at Coresia on Ceos and Methana in the Peloponnese have generally been assigned to the time of the Chremonidean War, essentially because this was the main known event involving Ptolemaic naval forces in what appeared to be the correct period,[50] but a date in the 270s cannot be ruled out.

Such appropriation of cult and civic names served both to unify the *disiecta membra* of the Ptolemaic dominions and to stamp the royal authority upon them. These far-flung areas of the Ptolemaic empire were further tied to Alexandria by the shrewd creation of a new cult and festival, that of the *Ptolemaieia* in honour of Ptolemy I, with their games and procession at Alexandria. Whereas the private cult of Arsinoe Euploia worked as a unifying force within the dominions, the new celebrations of the deified Ptolemy Soter served to focus the attention of the Greek world on the splendour of the dynasty and its capital. The isolympic nature of this festival was stressed from the very beginning. Embassies were sent around the Greek world inviting states to send *theôroi* to witness the spectacle. Of the two fragmentary records of this diplomatic offensive that survive, one records the response of the Nesiotic League.[51] It is the Nicuria decree discussed above (*IG* XII.7 506; *SIG*³ 390), wherein the Islanders find themselves ready to comply with Philadelphus' request, 'since in fact they had already honoured Soter as a god': Προ|[σήκ]ει πᾶσι τοῖς νησιώταις τετιμηκόσιμ πρ[ότε]||[ρον τ]ὸν σωτῆρα Πτολεμαῖον ἰσοθέοις τιμαῖ[ς] (ll. 26–8).

The Nicuria decree is, as we have seen, probably to be dated to *c.* 280 BC. By this point the Islanders had made the decision to found a cult in honour of Ptolemy I, whom they regarded as their Soter. The League then had existed by at least *c.* 280 and had found it desirable to found *Ptolemaieia*. But when and why, precisely? The one hint perhaps comes in an honorific decree of the League providing for the announcement of the honours at the first *Ptolemaieia* in Delos ([τοῖς] πρώτοις Πτολεμαιείοις ἐν Δήλωι), where 'the Islanders sacrifice in Delos to the other gods and to

[49] Robert 1966a: 202, cf. Robert 1960a: 153–5; Bagnall 1976: 142–3; Cherry and Davis 1991: 12, n. 5. For a collection of the evidence for the Arsinoe foundations, see now Fraser 2009: 342–7.

[50] For the pedigree of this view, see Robert 1960: 155, n. 1. That Arsinoe on Ceos existed by the time of the Chremonidean War seems a fair inference from *IG* XII.5 1061. The foundation of Methana–Arsinoe has now been confirmed as belonging to the reign of Philadelphus: see Wallensten and Pakkanen (2009).

[51] The other is the reply of the Delphic amphictyony (*CID* IV.40) published perhaps in 262/261 or 266/265. For the problems of dating this decree (the archonship of Pleiston), see the editor's note with pp. 26–8. For the claim that this stone nevertheless records the reply to the original invitation to the first *Ptolemaieia*, see Fraser 1961.

Ptolemy Soter and King Ptolemy' (θύ|ουσιν οἱ νησιῶται ἐν Δήλωι τοῖς τε ἄλλοις θεοῖς καὶ| Σωτῆρι Πτολεμαίωι καὶ βασιλεῖ Πτολεμαίωι).[52]

'Ptolémée Philadelphe était donc alors associé au culte que les Insulaires rendaient à son père . . . Les Insulaires, qui, à une date inconnue, avaient érigé à Délos deux statues de Ptolémée II [*IG* XI.4 1123 and 1124], honoraient donc le roi à l'égal d'un dieu dès la première décennie de son règne.'[53] There seem then to be good grounds for associating this federal celebration of *Ptolemaieia* with Philadelphus too. Again we are pushed into the last two to three years of the 280s. This should come as little surprise, for it was at this period, in the year 280 BC, that Philadelphus decided to found a Delian festival in honour of his father.[54] He was squeezing the memory of his father for all that it was worth, and the islanders of the Aegean, whether through gratitude or fear, knew to play along.

The evidence for the existence of the Nesiotic League is thus to be pushed back to 280 or very shortly before. We can perhaps go some way towards confirming this picture by focusing on that uniquely League official, the nesiarch. Bacchon at first glance is no more easily datable than the League itself: he is nesiarch in the Nicuria decree, and thus *c.* 280 BC, but no other inscription is so readily datable.[55] The Delian temple accounts mention two *phialai* given by Bacchon, which may perhaps prove slightly more helpful. One was given before 279 BC, the other in 278 BC or 277 BC.[56] Again we note that there is no evidence that requires the extension of Bacchon's career back before the period *c.* 280–275 BC. The evidence of Bacchon's dedications combined with those of Apollodorus son of Apollonius allows us to extend the evidence for the nesiarchate, however, for one line later in the accounts for 279 BC follows an entry of 'two *phialai* on plinths, the dedication of [Apol]lodorus', φιάλαι δύο ἐμ πλ[ιν]θεί|ο[ις, Ἀπολ]λοδώρου ἀνάθημα (*IG* XI.2 161.B14–15). That Apollodorus was also nesiarch is certain from

[52] *IG* XI.4 1038 ll. 16–17 and 23–5. See Kotsidu 2000: KNr. 131 [E2], at p. 207 for a date for this decree in the period 279–274 BC.

[53] Bruneau 1970: 532. The federal *Ptolemaieia* are known otherwise only from *IG* XI.4 1043 ll. 14–16.

[54] The first *phialê* of the Delian *Ptolemaieia* dates to 279 BC. Bruneau 1970: 520–2: in theory the first *phialê* of a Delian foundation was paid for with the interest on a sum of money deposited in the previous year. This being the case, envoys were sent with foundation money to Delos probably in the same year as envoys were sent around the Greek world regarding the Alexandrian *Ptolemaieia*.

[55] *IG* XI.4 1038 (*OGIS* 67) appears to come in the period between the Nicuria decree and the marriage of Philadelphus to Arsinoe II (275 at the latest). The others are: *IG* XI.4 1039a+b; *IG* XI.5 1004 (*OGIS* 773); *IG* XII.5 1065; *IG* XI.4 559 (*SIG*³ 391); *IG* XI.4 1125 + 1126; *IG* XII.5(2) 1310 (*OGIS* I 43 + *add*. II p. 539); *IG* XI.4 551. On Bacchon's career, see Hennig 1989: 177–9.

[56] *IG* XI.2 161 B12–13 and 162 B9–10 (279–8 BC) for the first; *IG* XI.2 164 A54–56 (276 BC), 199 B38–39 (274 BC), *I.Délos* 298 A170–172 (240 BC) and 300 B18–20 (? late third century) for both. The last two give Bacchon his title. For correction to the texts of *IG* and *I.Délos* and the numbers of *phialai*, see Rigsby 1980.

a decree from Cyzicus describing him as such (Michel, *Recueil* 534. 7–8) and, since the bowls are described in inventory lists of the later third century as the dedication of '[Apol]lodorus the nesiarch' (Ἀπολ]λοδώρου νησιάρχου),[57] it is clear that we are dealing with the same man.[58] There are thus three *phialai* donated by Ptolemaic nesiarchs prior to 279, suggesting that the Nesiotic League goes back at least to 282 BC. The case for 282 BC as the foundation date is further bolstered by the appearance in this year for the first time of Coan *theôroi* to Delos.[59]

One further piece of evidence may be brought to bear on the problem, and suggests another way in which the Aegean waterways of the Nesiotic League were conceived by the Ptolemaic power. In 288/287, as is now well known from the famous Callias decree, Ptolemaic help to Athens in her struggle against the Antigonids came in the form of troops with whom Callias 'protected the harvest, making every effort to bring as much grain as possible into the city': προ|εκάθητο τῆς τοῦ σίτου συγκομιδῆς πᾶσαν ποιούμενος | σπουδὴν ὅπως ἂν εἰς τὴν πόλιν σῖτος ὡς πλεῖστος εἰσκ|ομισθεῖ· (*Hesperia* Suppl. 17 24–7). At about the same time, the Ptolemaic naval commander Zenon (discussed above) was busy securing the delivery of grain to Athens, probably from a number of overseas sources.[60] This is the sort of help that a royal power can give on the basis of military presence. On the other hand, when hardship fell upon Athens in the reign of Philadelphus, 'Callias sailed personally to Cyprus, met the king there, and on behalf of the city generously secured as a gift to the People 50 talents of silver and 20,000 *medimnoi* of wheat which were measured out from Delos to the representatives sent by the People' (*ibid.* ll. 50–5).[61]

This latter episode clearly belongs to the early years of Philadelphus' sole reign, probably in 282 BC. The implication is that Delos is now established as an important node in a transportation network stretching to Greece, if not as a Ptolemaic granary, or 'clearing house'.[62] This is the sort of aid that a royal power can give with the benefit of a secure commercial network.

---

[57] *I.Délos* 338 Bb24 (224 BC), cf. *I.Délos* 300 B22 and Durrbach's note there. That the title of Apollodorus should be given only in the late third-century accounts is not a cause for concern. The same pattern applies to dedications of, for example, Bacchon, whose title first appears in *I.Délos* 298 (240 BC).

[58] See most recently Paschidis 2008: 532–4.

[59] *IG* XI.2 158A l. 74; Sherwin-White 1978: 91, with n. 50.

[60] *IG* II.2 682 ll. 28–30. On the circumstances, see Oliver 2007: 123–4.

[61] ἀναπλεύσα[ς] αὐτὸς ἰδί<α>ι Καλλίας | εἰς Κύπρον καὶ ἐντυχὼν ἐκεῖ τῶ[ι β]ασιλεῖ φιλοτίμως ὑ|πὲρ τῆς πόλεως ἐκόμισεν τῶι δήμωι ἀργυρίου μὲν τάλαν|τα πεντήκοντα, πυρῶν δὲ δισ-μυρίους μεδίμνους δωρεὰν | οἳ παραμετρήθησαν ἐγ Δήλου τοῖς ἀποσταλεῖσιν ὑπὸ τ[ο]|ῦ δήμου.

[62] The episode is introduced 'when the younger King Ptolemy received the kingship': παραλαβόντος τὴν βασιλε[ί]αν Πτολεμαίου τοῦ νεωτ|έρου βασιλέως (*Hesp.* Suppl. 17 ll. 44–5). On the implications of this introduction, see Shear 1978: 25–6, placing the embassy in 282; on Delos as Ptolemaic

As in the world of religious practice, so in the sphere of military aid and commercial transportation the Aegean waterway looks very different under Philadelphus. The Nesiotic League, I would suggest, made that difference. To see how it did so it is worth taking a closer look at the nature of the League. It was a curious institution. As Rhodes and Lewis put it, 'It is noticeable that the third-century League of Islanders is prepared to award to an honorand citizenship and proxeny in all the cities of the League as if it were a federal state capable of awarding federal citizenship and proxenies.' Yet at the same time, 'It grants honorands . . . access . . . "to the *boulê* and *dêmos*", not "to the *synedrion*", because the reference is to the decision-making bodies of the individual states.'[63] The League is a superstructure, over and above the individual member *poleis*, which assumes some of the sovereign powers of those states. But it does not completely absorb those states, nor is it self-contained in the way of a true federal state, such as the Achaean League. For the chief official of the League – the nesiarch – seems not to be appointed from within but rather by Ptolemy.[64] And this is the crucial point: the structure of the Nesiotic League as we see it in the inscriptions is the product of royal initiative and subject to continuing royal intervention.[65]

Once more, comparison with Ptolemaic practice elsewhere, and particularly under Philadelphus, is instructive. In Caria the Chrysaoric League, which like the Nesiotic served a useful, unified administrative purpose, is first attested in the reign of Philadelphus, and it has been suggested by P. Debord that it may have been a Ptolemaic creation. In Lycia, the Lycian League is first attested, most probably, under Ptolemaic rule, although the office of the Lyciarch is not attested before the Roman period.[66]

It is, I believe, no coincidence that our evidence for the Ptolemaic Nesiotic League comes principally, perhaps entirely, from the reign of Philadelphus, not Soter. Bruneau, in his comprehensive survey of royal

'clearing house', 30. Further arguments for the date in Oliver 2007: 243 and discussion of the role of Delos at 245–6, n. 81. On the connection between Ptolemaic naval power and grain supply, see also Buraselis, Chapter 6 in this volume.

[63] Rhodes and Lewis 1997: 298.   [64] See Bagnall 1976: 156–7, with n. 145, and Gallotta 2009: 342.

[65] The relationship of the Ptolemaic *oikonomos* of the islands, if such he is, attested on Ios in *IG Suppl.* 169, remains tantalisingly opaque. See Bagnall 1976: 146–7; Gallotta 2009: 342.

[66] Caria: Debord 1994; Lycia: discussions in Bagnall 1976: 217–18 and Domingo Gygax 2001: 81–3. Robert 1966b: 53–8 published a fragmentary honorific inscription from Termessos, dated to Audnaios year 5 of Philadelphus (Sept/Oct 281) for one Philip, son of Alexander, Macedonian, whom he restored as κατασταθεὶς παμφυλι[άρχης, on analogy with the nesiarch. However, his restoration is almost certainly wrong.

cult on Delos, has noted a basic difference between the behaviours of the
first two Ptolemies:

> The precious offerings number seven in total... Of these seven, four and per-
> haps five were made by Ptolemy I, and the sixth by his wife Berenice; the sev-
> enth was made by Arsinoe Philadelphos; it is not that Ptolemy Philadelphus was
> less generous than his father, but rather, instead of isolated offerings, he pre-
> ferred the foundation of annual festivals. Thereafter, there is no sign of Ptolemaic
> munificence.[67]

While the approach of Soter was essentially ad hoc, that of Philadelphus
was to organise and establish. The latter's foundation of *Ptolemaieia* on
Delos mirrors his organised and organising approach to the memories
and cults of other members of his family. The Alexandrian and Delian
Ptolemaieia (and perhaps the Nesiotic festival at his instigation too) are
part of a larger pattern. They form part of Philadelphus' establishment of
himself in the role of successor to his father, in much the same way that
his remarkable marriage to his full sister did at the same period.[68]

Again, it seems to me to be no coincidence that our evidence for the
restoration of the Delian amphictyony in the form of the Nesiotic League
belongs to the period at the beginning of Philadelphus' reign, when such
organisation of cult was demonstrably taking place in other areas. The
strongly Ionian nature of this new foundation was stressed by Tarn.[69]
For him, the purpose behind such a make-up was backward-looking: an
attempt to avoid the resonances of the previous two island confederacies.
This may in part be true, but there must also have been a positive reason. A
new League with an internal religious cohesion was a stronger entity than
one thrown together merely on geographical preconceptions. Ptolemy did
not need to make Thera (or Samos) members of this League, since garrisons
did the work for him there. But for all but one of the islands of the League,
Andros, Naxos, Cythnos, Amorgos, Myconos, Ceos, Tenos, Paros, Ios,
Syros (?) and Siphnos (?), Heraclea (?), Icaros (?), Cimolos (?), Melos (?),
Nisyros (?), Rhenea (?) and Seriphos (?),[70] there is no evidence for garrisons
at all. Ionic amphictyony, the restoration of 'the ancestral constitution' and
a roving Ptolemaic official took up the slack. The initiative behind this

---

[67] Bruneau 1970: 516 (my translation).
[68] See, e.g., Burstein 1982 and Carney 1987: 430–1; Buraselis 2008.   [69] Tarn 1913: 76–8.
[70] For membership of the Ptolemaic League, see Fraser and Bean 1954: 156–7, n. 2, supplemented by
    the exhaustive treatment of Huß 1976: 213–37, summarised on 238. For Tenos, Étienne 1990: 93
    suggests membership on the basis of *prostatai* in the *c.* mid third century: *IG* XII.5 802. Cf. Palagia
    1992 for the possibility that Artemidorus of Perge may have been involved there.

restoration, apparently with old Ionic resonance, was that of Philadelphus, following thoughtfully in the wake of his father's last actions in the Aegean.

The human instruments of this policy are worth some consideration too. It was not Philadelphus himself who wrote to the League of Islanders with his request, but rather Philocles, king of the Sidonians, and Bacchon the nesiarch (*IG* XII.7 506.1–3). It was not Philadelphus who gave the obvious leads in the propagation of the cults both of himself and his sister, but his nauarch Callicrates.[71] Rather than the complete absence of one-time offerings by the Ptolemaic house under Philadelphus noted by Bruneau above, it may not be going too far to suggest that the offerings made by Apollodorus and Bacchon as nesiarchs were in fact Philadelphus' by proxy. Certainly in the case of the dedication of another known nesiarch, Hermias, it is difficult to resist this conclusion. In this last case it was not a question of a single *phialê*, but rather the deposit of 3,300 drachmas as the foundation sum for the cult of Arsinoe Philadelphos, the *Philadelpheia*, in 268 BC.[72] Comparable perhaps is the extraordinary series of dedications by Artemidorus son of Apollonius on Thera. The exact position of Artemidorus, an *émigré* from Perge, is uncertain, but the best evidence for the length of his stay on the island also proves his close association with the first three Ptolemies. The conclusion is inevitable that he must have been a Ptolemaic official of some sort, and in this light the dedications in his *temenos* become significant, particularly that to *Homonoia* (Ὁμόνοια). Artemidorus himself clearly envisioned 'his *temenos* as of value not only to himself, but to the city of Thera and all resident foreigners'. Private cult is surely out of the question. In this light the goddess *Homonoia* takes on an extra significance, when combined with the dedicator's known Ptolemaic sympathies, and the temptation to link the cult on Thera with another with Ptolemaic connections on the mainland has not been resisted.[73]

---

[71] See above for the temple of Aphrodite–Arsinoe. Cf. *IvO* 306 and 307 (= *OGIS* 26 and 27) with Merker 1970: 154 and Hauben 1970: 24–36 for statues of the royal couple set up by Callicrates at Olympia. It was apparently also in the year of Callicrates' tenure of the eponymous priesthood of the dynastic cult at Alexandria (272/271 BC) that the *Theoi Adelphoi* were added to it: *P.Hib.* II 199.11–17. Hauben 1970: 41–6, and Chapter 3 in this volume; Merker 1970: 155; Fraser 1972: II, 364, n. 208.

[72] Bruneau 1970: 533–4, 543–5. As Tarn 1913: 292 noted, 'Arsinoe's name comes first of all, taking precedence even of Apollo himself.'

[73] Artemidorus and the Ptolemies: *IG* XII.3 464. *Pros. Ptol.* 15188 lists him as 'officier?'. Cf. Bagnall 1976: 133–4 and Palagia 1992. The dedications in his *temenos*: *IG* XII.3 421–2 *Suppl.* 1333–1350, 1388, of which 1336 and 1342 to Ὁμόνοια. Illustrations and descriptions in Hiller von Gaertringen 1904: 90–102 with Palagia 1992, for amplification and corrections. Function of the *temenos*: *IG* XII.3 *Suppl.* 1335d; Cole 1984: 64. Private cult: West 1977: 308, with n. 3. Link with mainland cult of the *koinon* of the Greeks at Plataea: Étienne 1985: 260.

THE END OF PTOLEMAIC CONTROL OF THE LEAGUE

Homonoia, of course, was a key theme in the rhetoric as the Greeks struggled with Macedon in the Chremonidean War.[74] The strenuous efforts made by the Ptolemaic house to insert itself within this movement make it all the more intriguing to discover what went wrong, and how the Nesiotic League ceased to be Ptolemaic. Having detached *IG* XI.4 1036 and its Antigonid festivals from Monophthalmus and his son and given them to Gonatas and his son, what occasions can we propose for these two foundations? Let us start with the creation of the second festival, the *Demetrieia*. We are looking for a time at which the *Antigoneia* are already in place and when something of sufficient importance has happened to place Demetrius on the same level as his father. Durrbach's initial instinct must surely have been correct: the appropriate occasion for the establishment of such a festival is the coronation of Demetrius II. The date, however, is not 239 but rather somewhat closer to the period 262/261–257 suggested by Andronikos. Durrbach's second instinct was also correct, the provision of alternating festivals is a sign that two kings shared the throne, and this decree marks the point at which the son achieved equality with the father.

But can we go a step further? The festivals involved are not straightforward vase-festivals such as were set up by a variety of Hellenistic monarchs on the island, and which continued to be celebrated, no matter who the current sovereign of the island was, as long as the money deposited on foundation lasted. Rather, these festivals, certainly in the case of the *Demetrieia*, and most probably in the case of the earlier *Antigoneia*, were founded by the League of Islanders in honour of the monarchs: 'ici les Insulaires accordent des honneurs divins à celui qu'ils reconnaissent comme leur souverain ou leur protecteur', and as such these festivals can only have survived as long as did that suzerainty.[75] Unfortunately, we have no firm date for the (joint) accession of Demetrius II, but, as we have seen, the period *c.* 262–257 most probably includes it. If Demetrius was born *c.* 275 BC, then he would have reached the age of 18 in *c.* 257 BC:[76] the latest date allowed by the Beroea inscription may thus be closest to the truth. Certainly, then, the Nesiotic League was under Antigonid 'protection' by 257 BC. At this point in time the *Antigoneia* already existed, and, if it is correct to see the *Antigoneia* as a League-instituted festival, then the League must have come under Antigonid control before 257 BC. It is a fair guess that the moment

---

[74] See the discussion in Erskine 1990: 90–5.   [75] Bruneau 1970: 566.
[76] Date of birth: Hammond and Walbank 1988: 317; majority: 160, n. 2.

of establishment of Antigonid control coincided with the foundation of the festival in honour of Gonatas. If this must predate 257, the obvious context for this acquisition is the end of the Chremonidean War with the fall of Athens in 263/262 BC.[77] Here is not the place to enter into prolonged discussion of the date of the battle of Cos by which Antigonid control was established over the Aegean. Suffice it to note that, if the proposed redating of *IG* XI.4 1036 is accepted, it almost certainly follows that the battle of Cos predates the promulgation of this decree and must be placed at the end of the 260s, not the mid 250s.[78] Ptolemaic control over the League would never be re-established.

CONCLUSION

The third-century Nesiotic League was, I have suggested, a Ptolemaic construct that cannot be divorced from the broader religious, commercial and political organisation of the Aegean attempted by Ptolemy Philadelphus. It failed. Partly, perhaps, this was because the lines of communication to Alexandria were too long, and partly because the ambition of Macedonian kings could not tolerate such an entity in their backyard. But also it was because the religious innovation Philadelphus attempted to introduce was part of a broader policy towards Greece that the Ptolemies could not or would not pursue after their defeat in the Chremonidean War.[79] The response of the League of Islanders when taken over by the Antigonid house was initially to honour the kings – as they had the Ptolemies – with eponymous festivals. But it cannot be coincidence that the decree that provided for the second of these festivals seems to constitute the last evidence for existence of this League. In fact, irrespective of when we date *IG* XI.4 1036, the disappearance of the League from the epigraphic record after the flurry of its activity in the reign of Philadelphus leaves no doubt that it faltered after the rise of Macedonian power in the Aegean in the mid third century BC. The Antigonid approach to this waterway would be quite different.[80]

---

[77] On the precise chronology of the fall of Athens, see Dorandi 1991: 24–6.

[78] For a summary of the previous debate, see Walbank in Hammond and Walbank 1988: 587–600. Against the date of 255 proposed by Buraselis 1982: 147–51, see also Reger 1985 and 1994a: 40–1.

[79] The opportunity never presented itself to Philadelphus and, I shall argue elsewhere, Euergetes' conception of empire was substantially different. On the political vicissitudes of the Cyclades after 260 BC, see in general Reger 1994a.

[80] My thanks are due to Christian Habicht, Lucia Criscuolo and the late Peter Derow, as well as to audiences in Oxford, Durham and Athens for their comments on earlier versions of this chapter.

CHAPTER 3

Callicrates of Samos and Patroclus of Macedon, champions of Ptolemaic thalassocracy

Hans Hauben

This chapter aims to reinvestigate and compare the careers, tasks and competences of two high officers who served during the golden age of the Ptolemaic maritime empire, i.e. from the mid 70s to the early 50s of the third century BC, when political hegemony, military expansion and economic prosperity are reflected in the early papyri of the Zenon archive.

Still during the lifetime of Arsinoe II, Callicrates of Samos and Patroclus of Macedon were the first eponymous priests of Alexander and the Brother/Sister Gods (272/271 and 271/270 BC respectively), already suggesting a particular bond with the queen and the royal family. Whereas Callicrates, the true courtier of the two, was involved in establishing the (maritime) cult of Arsinoe–Aphrodite at Cape Zephyrium, Patroclus, first and foremost a soldier, was the supreme commander of the expeditionary force sent to Greece at the start of the Chremonidean War, the (late) queen's war against Antigonus II Gonatas.

In most sources Patroclus is styled, and acts, as *stratêgos*, recalling in part the famous Sidonian king, Philocles. Callicrates, whose actual duties remain obscure, is largely known as *nauarchos*. Both officers, with the network they established over the Aegean and eastern Mediterranean, may be regarded as pillars of the Ptolemaic thalassocracy in its heyday.

More than two millennia before Muhammad Ali (1805–48) managed to free his adoptive country from centuries of Mamluk and Ottoman lethargy, Ptolemy I resolutely opened up the tired old land of the pharaohs. He transformed it into an internationally respected, expansionist and multi-ethnic power that would soon dominate a substantial part of the eastern Mediterranean and Aegean world.[1] After having acted as satrap answerable to an increasingly fictitious central government (323–306 BC), somewhat

[1] The many aspects of the striking analogy were established and perceptively commented on by Fraser 1981, whereas the atmosphere in Egypt on the eve of the modern era has recently been evoked by Strathern 2007.

like his nineteenth-century counterpart, he had himself proclaimed king in his own right (306–283/282 BC).[2] Already recognised during his lifetime as Saviour God by various Greek city-states over which he had spread his wings of liberation, he was posthumously given a similar, this time empire-wide, cult by his son.[3] Centred in Alexandria and associated with that of Alexander, this put him in the wake of the world conqueror.

Focused from the very outset on the sea, the empire founded by Ptolemy I Soter was essentially maritime. It continued to prosper – with the inevitable ups and downs – under Ptolemy II Philadelphus and III Euergetes, when it attained its largest extent.[4] It was still flourishing under Ptolemy IV Philopator when, with all due respect to Polybius, decay was only slow to set in.[5] It is clear that the Ptolemaic empire's soundness was intimately connected with the strength of its thalassocracy.

In order to establish and preserve such a thalassocracy, a number of requirements had to be fulfilled. It was necessary to control a sufficient number of well-situated islands and coastal areas, with advantageous factors like geographical spread, strategic value and economic strength prevailing over territorial size. It was essential to maintain a series of naval bases and to have access to vital harbours, often belonging to renowned and thriving Greek or Phoenician *poleis*. Large, costly and technically advanced war fleets helped enforce a protagonist's claims. So, apart from the necessary funds and engineering skills, the Ptolemies needed sufficient manpower as well as suitable timber supplies. Manpower was in principle no problem in Egypt, though the country was in want of specialised personnel. Timber was more difficult to find, which obliged them to look elsewhere.[6]

That is not to say that the first Ptolemies' thalassocracy was never disputed. On the contrary. Often they had to yield naval supremacy to their Antigonid and Seleucid opponents to the point that for short periods it might vanish almost completely. Such was the case between 306 and 301, particularly in 303/302, when Antigonus and Demetrius came to dominate the seas.[7] But even in its heyday, Ptolemaic thalassocracy – like every ancient thalassocracy – was a relative notion. Omnipresence at sea was impossible as naval communications were difficult.[8]

[2] For the date of the first Ptolemy's death, late 283 or early 282, see Hauben 1992: 159; Huß 2001: 250.
[3] Hauben 2010.   [4] See the map in Baines and Málek 1980: 54.
[5] As was convincingly shown by Huß 1976: esp. 265–70. See now also Erskine, Chapter 5 in this volume.
[6] These different aspects were discussed by Hauben 1987a.   [7] Hauben 1974: 106, 113.
[8] Communication at sea was a major problem until recent times: Strathern 2007: 55 (on Napoleon's fleet).

Yet, even allowing that absolute dominance at sea was illusory and that the Ptolemies were not able to safeguard each and every traveller or merchant against political enemies or pirates, we may say that the Ptolemies came nearest to that ideal in the early years of the second monarch of their dynasty, particularly in the 270s and early 260s. The acme of their sea power coincided with what might be called 'the age of Arsinoe II'. It lasted for some ten years, from her 'divinely incestuous' marriage[9] (contracted between 279 and 274 BC),[10] beyond her untimely death on 9 July 270 or 1 or 2 July 268 BC,[11] until the first years of the Chremonidean War (268–262).[12] Waged at least in part to satisfy the late queen's Macedonian ambitions, the war started in the (immediate) aftermath of her reign, when her presence at the Alexandrian court was still tangible.[13] During that relatively short time span Ptolemaic thalassocracy seemed as little challenged as was Arsinoe's ascendancy. It was in those years – Arsinoe was still alive – that Theocritus wrote his seventeenth idyll in praise of King Ptolemy II.[14] Outweighing other sovereigns in wealth and by the quality of his ships, the king 'ruled the waves', just as he held sway over 'the land and the roaring rivers' (17.86–95). According to Callixeinus, his navy surpassed in numbers and strength all contemporaneous fleets, (theoretically) numbering up to 336 warships.[15] Identified with Aphrodite, queen Arsinoe became the patron deity of the

---

[9] The most direct reinterpretation of this incest as a divine union on the model of Zeus and Hera was provided by Theocritus' seventeenth idyll: 126–34 (cf. Gow 1965: II, 345–6). On the unheard-of character of such a union among the Greeks up to that time, see Mélèze Modrzejewski 1998: 152 ('Sans doute la tradition grecque n'est-elle pas étrangère aux pratiques endogames . . . Mais le mariage avec une soeur ayant le même père et la même mère (ὁμογνήσιος) était un fait sans précédent'); cf. 154, 156–9 and 167–9 (Greek tradition and following centuries); Ager 2005: 4–5 ('the first full-sibling marriage of the dynasty'), 17–18 (also pointing to an Egyptian association with Osiris-Isis); Hardie 2006: 37–8. The Egyptian aspect has recently been stressed and developed by Buraselis 2008.

[10] Hauben 1983: 99, with n. 1. Many scholars date the marriage to 278.

[11] Cf. Hauben 1992: 160–2; Bing 2003: 245, n. 6, 257 (endorsing Grzybek's new dating). In the meantime many scholars continue to reckon with 270. For a current *status quaestionis* with the most recent bibliography, see Collombert 2008: 83, n. 1; also O'Neil 2008: 68 (268) versus Marquaille 2008: 63 (270).

[12] On the chronological limits of the war, see Hauben 1992: 162; Huß 2001: 271, 279; O'Neil 2008: 68–71, 85–6. Whereas Heinen 1972: 182–9 and O'Neil date the end of the war to 261 (though the latter's demonstration is slightly confusing (86)), other scholars nowadays seem to prefer 262 (Huß; Knoepfler 1995: 'la fin de la guerre de Chrémonidès doit dater au plus tard du début de l'été 262, non pas du printemps 261').

[13] Cf. Hauben 1983: 114–19; 1992: 162; Huß 2001: 273, esp. with n. 150. On the circumstances of the Chremonidean War and Arsinoe's debated role, see now the balanced discussion in Paschidis 2008: 164–70.

[14] Gow 1965: I, 130–9; II, 325–47. Cf. Hauben 1989: 448, n. 44 (cf. 451, n. 66).

[15] Ath. 5.203d. Cf. Van 't Dack and Hauben 1978: 72–3; for the (more or less theoretical, because in part deduced) number of warships, see n. 119 there.

maritime empire.[16] Though standing firm in the next decades, Ptolemaic supremacy at sea would be increasingly undermined by both Antigonus Gonatas and his successive Seleucid counterparts, Antiochus I, Antiochus II and Seleucus II.

Epigraphical and papyrological sources confirm Callixeinus' catalogue of ships in several respects. They reveal that highly respected naval engineers, especially on Cyprus, designed for Ptolemy II the most advanced warships: the *eikosêrês* and *triakontêrês* were typically Hellenistic monstrosities.[17] The ambitious construction programme was financed by means of a sophisticated system functioning empire-wide, a 'liturgic trierarchy', in which the highest officials were involved.[18] We know from one of the Zenon papyri, the most important archive from Graeco-Roman Egypt, that at the time of the Second Syrian War the cost of an *ennêrês* in the port of Halicarnassus was borne by a certain Xanthippus. For a short time during the Third Syrian War that Xanthippus was to become governor of the provinces beyond the Euphrates.[19] There was also the *trierarchêma*, a heavy tax for the upkeep of the navy, levied – once again – upon the members of the highest circles. The admiral himself seems to have been responsible for its collection, as we may infer from a document more or less contemporaneous with the Xanthippus papyrus. The letter was addressed by a tax collector to Apollonius, the well-known *dioikêtês*,[20] who had to pay 570 drachmas a year.[21]

Going back to the period just after the said decade and coinciding in part with the Second and Third Syrian Wars, the Zenon papyri reflect the material prosperity of the time, a direct consequence of Ptolemaic expansion. The variety of origins of the products dealt with in the documents gives an idea of the extensive commercial network the *dioikêtês* had managed to build up throughout the eastern Mediterranean.[22] On the other hand, daily life in Egypt as reflected in the papyri appears to have been barely affected by the not always happy events on the wider

[16] Hauben 1970: 42–8, 66–7; 1983: 111–14, 124–7; 1989: 458, 461; Barbantani 2005; Marquaille 2008: 58–60. Bing 2003: 256–7 rightly points to the fact that in one of the new Posidippus epigrams the new goddess is directly addressed as Arsinoe, without adding *theos* or mentioning the 'host divinity'. For this type of cult, see Hauben 1989: 451, with n. 65 ('dieu intégral').

[17] *OGIS* I 39. Cf. Rice 1983: 152–4; Hauben 1987a: 220–2, with further references; Chaffin 1991–3: esp. 215, 224–5; Leonard and Hohlfelder 1993: 368–9. The basic publication on the Hellenistic naval arms race is Tarn 1930: 122–52; cf. Casson 1971: 97–123, 137–40.

[18] For that institution, see Hauben 1990b: esp. 127–8, 132–9.

[19] *P.Cair.Zen.* I 59036, 1 February 257. Hauben 1990b: 120, 124, 132–9; cf. 1990a: 37, with n. 68; 2006: 195–6.

[20] *Pros. Ptol.* I+VIII 16, II+VIII 1844, IV 10064, V 12725, 13497, 13588, 14055.

[21] *P.Mich.* I 100, *c.* 257. For other (rarely recorded and far from certain) cases of *trierarchêma*, see Clarysse and Thompson 2009: 253–4; 2011: 38.

[22] See Peremans 1931–2.

scene. Though scholars like Peremans and, more recently, Winnicki have attempted to exploit the documents from that perspective, it seems that military operations and maritime setbacks had no serious repercussions upon the commercial activities and international connections of Apollonius and his circle,[23] nor – unless perhaps only to a small degree – on their inland travels by boat.[24] We must bear in mind, however, that the potentially most informative period in the archive is rather limited, being that between late 261 and April/May 256, when Zenon acted as the minister's commercial agent and private secretary. After that he became the manager of his employer's large Fayum estate near Philadelphia and, from 248 or 247 on, a private businessman and small entrepreneur in that same area: a drastic change of horizon which inevitably entailed a narrowing of his field of interest.[25]

That Zenon came from Caunus in Caria,[26] and that Apollonius and other members of the circle also seem to have been Carians – Rostovtzeff even spoke of a 'Carian nest' in Alexandria[27] – is no accident: the Caunian connection goes back to the early days of Ptolemaic expansion, when the city had come under their sway. That happened for the first time in 309, during 'Ptolemy's Grand Tour' of 309–308[28] (Ptolemaic control apparently lasting until the debacle off Cyprian Salamis in 306),[29] and for a second time in or shortly after 286/285, when Caunus, at that time a major naval base for the routed Demetrius Poliorcetes, fell into Ptolemaic hands again.[30] Although the second period of control is not completely to be excluded, it was probably on the former occasion, in 309, that the city was taken by the well-known dynast Philocles.[31] For, as Polyaenus reports, unfortunately without any specific chronological indication, Philocles achieved his goal

---

[23] Apollonius' presumed sister Doris returned to her homeland in the middle of winter (258/257) during the Second Syrian War (lasting from *c.* 260 or 259 (Huß 2001: 281–2) until 253): see Clarysse 2009: 35–6. Cf. Hauben 1985a: 105–6; Zimmermann 1992.

[24] Peremans 1933 and 1939, using the Zenon papyri to establish the date of the sea battle off Cos; Winnicki 1991, trying to interpret the busy activities of Apollonius' travelling party in the Delta in the light of military preparations in connection with the Second Syrian War, whereas the traditional interpretation holds that the travels were basically inspection tours also made for economic purposes (cf. Hauben 2006: 190, 195–6, 199, 211–12).

[25] Cf. Pestman et al. 1981: 220–44, 264–8; Clarysse and Vandorpe 1995: 22–31.

[26] See now Marek 2006: 53–62 (Testimonia 120–38).

[27] Rostovtzeff 1922: 178, 182–3. On Zenon's and Apollonius' Carian connections, and on the 'Carian nest', see now Clarysse 2009: 33–6. On Zenon's father Agreophon and his 'little brother' Epharmostus, see Hauben 1985a.

[28] Huß 2001: 173–8.

[29] Ptolemy's catastrophic defeat off Salamis (306) is a decisive element which Marek (2006; see next note) failed to take into account in his otherwise meticulous discussions.

[30] See the detailed analysis in Marek 2006: 97–8, 131, 134–6, 265–7.   [31] *Pros. Ptol.* VI 15085.

thanks to a stratagem.[32] Diodorus, for his part (whose account for the mid 280s is unfortunately lacking), explicitly deals with the city's capture in 309 but is silent about Philocles' role.[33] The fact, however, that he adds several peculiar details about the conquest points to the importance or spectacular character attributed to the event. As the same can be inferred from Polyaenus' story, both versions should preferably be linked to one and the same action, that of 309.[34] Other sources confirm that Philocles, just like general Leonides,[35] took part in the 309–308 expedition.[36] On the other hand, Philocles was still very active in the region during the 280s. Whatever the case, the allegation that Demetrius' fleet by 286/285 stationed in Caunus[37] fell into Ptolemaic hands by the desertion of that very commander, supposed to have been in Antigonid service until then, transferring by his treason (another stratagem, as it were) Antigonid thalassocracy to Ptolemy, is a tough myth to dispel, a 'factoid' gradually elaborated by modern scholarship, yet plainly contradicted by Philocles' actual life and accomplishments.[38]

The discussion concerning the fate of Caunus is enlightening for various reasons. First of all, it shows how important this unhealthy but favourably situated city was in the Ptolemaic naval, strategic and human resources system. Secondly, it reminds us of the central role played by Philocles of Sidon, a traditional Phoenician city king acting as a Ptolemaic

---

[32] Polyaenus, *Strat.* 3.16; Marek 2006: 22 (Testimonium 43).

[33] Diod. Sic. 20.27.1–2; Marek 2006: 20 (Testimonium 39).

[34] The unfinished state of the recently discovered Caunian statue base commissioned by two brothers for 'Philocles, King of the Sidonians' (Marek 2006: no. 82) in my opinion links that Ptolemaic general with the events of 309 rather than with those of 286/285: after 285 Ptolemaic control seems to have remained undisputed for a long while, whereas after 309 Ptolemy lost his maritime prevalence very soon to the advantage of Antigonus because of the Salamis disaster. Moreover, it is probable that the recapture of 286/285 happened without a struggle, taking into account Demetrius' desperate situation compared with the Aegean triumphs of his opponent. Of course, it is not impossible that further switches occurred between 309 and 286/285, but concrete indications are lacking. The fact that two Caunian citizens acted as Ptolemaic officials in Lycia in 288/287 (Marek 2006: 53, Testimonium 119) does not necessarily imply that their *polis* was under Ptolemaic control at that time: Marek 2006: 97, 135, with n. 324. (There is, in my opinion, also insufficient proof for a short Antigonid intermezzo *c.* 269/268: see the detailed discussion in Marek 2006: 135–6; cf. 267!; and, whatever the case, for chronological reasons Philocles can no longer have been involved in a supposed Ptolemaic reconquest in the early 260s.)

[35] On Leonides, see Hauben 1975: 51–4, no. 19.   [36] See Hauben 1987b: 419, n. 30; 2004: 34, 43–4.

[37] Plut. *Demetr.* 49.3 = Marek 2006: 21 (Testimonium 40: 'an die dortige Küste . . . wo [Demetrius] die Flotte zu finden hoffte'); cf. 97, 135. Unfortunately, we do not know how long Demetrius' fleet had been stationed there: cf. 131.

[38] Hauben 1987b: 416–17, with n. 19; 2004: 29, with nn. 8–9. That Philocles had once been Demetrius' admiral is still to be found in O'Neil 2003: 512, 521.

stratêgos,[39] in this case a kind of plenipotentiary viceroy of the north. For more than thirty years, from about 310 until the early 270s, he was one of the closest and most respected collaborators of the first two Ptolemies,[40] enjoying the confidence of both father and son, a remarkable fact in the light of their strained relationship. It is Philocles who should probably be considered the main architect, or at least one of the main architects, of early Ptolemaic expansion in the Mediterranean,[41] an achievement on which the next Ptolemies would continue to rely.

After the disappearance of the grand old man, the main pillars of Ptolemaic thalassocracy manifestly became the Samian *nauarchos* Callicrates, the son of Boiscus, and the Macedonian *stratêgos* Patroclus, the son of Patron.[42] Names of other high naval officers under Ptolemy II are virtually lacking, the meagre evidence being often obscure and ambiguous.[43] A noticeable exception is the admiral Timosthenes of Rhodes, an intriguing and versatile personage, who probably also flourished at the time of Queen Arsinoe.[44] His activities, however, seem mainly concentrated on western (Roman and Carthaginian) waters and in the far south, not on the more 'usual' areas of Ptolemaic intervention.

So let us focus on Callicrates and Patroclus, the high (naval) commanders who dominated the late 270s and early 260s (and even beyond), witnessing the golden age of Ptolemaic sea power. Though comparatively well documented, their records fell victim to the significant third-century 'historiographical shipwreck',[45] so that we have to go through much puzzling and guesswork. In the following pages we shall try to analyse and compare their respective personalities, titles, duties and competences, basically distinct yet hardly separable aspects of their careers.

---

[39] And not *nauarchos*, as has too often been contended: see Hauben 1987b: 420–1, with n. 36; 2004: 27–9, with n. 6. The most recent case where Philocles is styled as such is a list of Phoenicians in Egypt in Jan K. Winnicki's posthumous work (2009: 281).

[40] Hauben 1987b and 2004. On the Coan Diotimus inscription (Hauben 2004: 29–34), see now also Habicht 2007: 125–7.

[41] Cf. Hauben 1987b: 419.

[42] Callicrates: *Pros. Ptol.* III+IX 5164 = VI 14607; Mooren 1975: no. 010; Paschidis 2008: 393–6, no. D35 (links with Samos). Patroclus: *Pros. Ptol.* III+IX 5225 = VI 15063; Tréheux 1992: 70 (offering a *phialê* on Delos); Tataki 1998: 398–9, nos. 25 (Patroclus, with bibliography) and 30 (Patron).

[43] A (somewhat younger) case in point is Ptolemaeus (*epiklêsin*) Andromachou, nowadays generally associated with the battle off Andros (*Pros. Ptol.* III+IX 5237 = V 13786 = VI 14544). On this mysterious figure, see Buraselis 1982: 124–41, 173–4 (cf. Marek 2006: 136, n. 336); Huß 1998: 242–4; Domingo Gygax 2000; Tunny 2000: 87–8, 90; Domingo Gygax 2002: 55–6.

[44] *Pros. Ptol.* V 13794 = VI 16313; Hauben 1996: 221–34; Prontera, Chapter 14 in this volume.

[45] On this ruin, see Préaux 1975–6.

We can imagine that both must often have been involved in the same actions, but in the preserved sources they 'meet' each other only twice.

Their first 'rendezvous' was in Alexandria in March 271, when Patroclus succeeded Callicrates as eponymous priest of Alexander and the *Theoi Adelphoi*, the highest sacral office in the Ptolemaic realm. What is peculiar is that they were the first to officiate in honour of the recently deified royal couple (272/271 (C) and 271/270 (P)), whose cult was closely associated with that of the founder of the Macedonian empire.[46] As they exercised their priesthood still during the lifetime of Arsinoe II,[47] we may guess that both were appointed, if not on her orders, at least with her consent. At that moment they must already have proved their (military? political? administrative?) skills as well as an unconditional attachment to the royal house, including the specific cause of the queen. Under no circumstances can this most prestigious priesthood be seen as the mere start of their respective careers.[48]

The second and last time they were associated in the sources was when they were honoured with *proxenia* and the title of benefactor by the city of Olus in eastern Crete, a place of strategic importance that could serve as an ideal naval base, close to the notorious isle of Spinalonga and the present-day port of Ayios Nikolaos.[49] As I have tried to show elsewhere, they were the leaders (Patroclus coming first, obviously being the chief, and Callicrates, the second in the hierarchy if not in actual command) of an impressive Ptolemaic delegation of nine representatives, of different nationalities, among them two of Callicrates' brothers (Perigenes and Aristonicus). These possibly constituted a group of high officers, whose arrival is generally associated with the early days of the Chremonidean War in the (early) spring of 267. They may have been (among) the commanders of the expeditionary force sent to Attica.[50] From the fact that Patroclus is also spotted in Itanus, another strategic but more isolated maritime bastion

[46] Clarysse and Van der Veken 1983: nos. 14–15. Cf. Ijsewijn 1961: nos. 14–15.

[47] As the new – sixteenth – Macedonian year already started on 24 March 270, Patroclus at any rate left office before the queen's decease. The names of their immediate successors (270–265) are still unknown.

[48] It would be interesting to know whether their predecessor for the year 273/272 (still merely the priest of Alexander), a certain Nearchus or Neomedes, son of Neocles or Philocles, was or was not a son of the Sidonian king. The evidence is too uncertain to allow any conclusion. Cf. Ijsewijn 1961: no. 13; Clarysse and Van der Veken 1983: no. 18; Hauben 1987b: 425 n. 67.

[49] *IC* I xxii.4A ll. 35–42.

[50] On this group, see Hauben 1970: 49–52; Heinen 1972: 146–7; Marek 1984: 319–20; Hauben 1996: 234–6. One of them, Antiochus of Aptera (Crete), would follow in Callicrates' and Patroclus' footsteps by becoming eponymous priest in 248/247. The same honour was granted in 261/260 (just after the Chremonidean War) to a certain Ptolemaeus, brother of Aristander of Rhodes, another member of the delegation.

further to the east, we can deduce that the Ptolemies were trying to gain a sufficiently firm foothold on the island by establishing control over a few key ports.

That is seemingly all Callicrates and Patroclus had or did in common. For the rest it looks as if their careers developed completely apart.

Callicrates is mentioned in a series of inscriptions spread over the Aegean and eastern Mediterranean, as well as in several epigrams of Posidippus. In a number of cases he is styled *nauarchos*, but nowhere is there any trace of specific military activities, nor of concrete interventions in local, social or political conflicts. The admiral seemed more involved in religious, diplomatic, sporting and cultural matters. The study we wrote four decades ago is in need of a thorough revision, as it has become obsolete in many respects; the basic conclusions, however, remain valid.[51] An authoritative article by Peter Bing, mainly focusing on the newly discovered Posidippus epigrams,[52] deepens the more ideological aspects of Callicrates' personality as well as his privileged relationship[53] with the royal family.[54]

The admiral's most prestigious achievement was the institution of a cult[55] and the building of a temple in honour of the goddess Arsinoe–Aphrodite Euploia Zephyritis, protectress of seafarers,[56] at Cape Zephyrium near Canopus.[57] By doing so he promoted the (late?)[58] queen to the status of

---

[51] Hauben 1970; cf., most recently, Marquaille 2008: esp. 43–4 and 58–60, with n. 86.

[52] C. Austin and Bastianini 2002: esp. nos. 39 and 74; 116 and 119 were already known.

[53] Referring to a poet like Callimachus, Anna Świderek (1974: 304) contends that 'Callicrates was by no means an exception at the Alexandrian court' as far as his almost pious sentiments toward Ptolemy and Arsinoe were concerned. But court poets are a category apart. So I think that, compared with other officials of his social and professional level, Callicrates was really showing an exceptional attitude in that respect.

[54] Bing 2003. On the epigrams of Posidippus in the light of Ptolemaic court ideology, see Thompson 2005a (271: the role of Callicrates).

[55] Hauben 1970: 43, with n. 1.

[56] On Aphrodite Euploia, see Pirenne-Delforge 1994: 433–7. On the differences between Callimachus' and Posidippus' poetic perceptions of the cults of Arsinoe II, see Stephens 2005: 243–8, also questioning to a certain extent the real bearing and significance of that of Arsinoe–Aphrodite, given the fact that Posidippus is practically our only source.

[57] That a son of Callicrates officiated as priest of the new goddess is far from certain: Hauben 1970: 80; Wehrli 1970: 404.

[58] At any rate, as the cult of Arsinoe–Aphrodite was intimately linked to that of Arsinoe Philadelphos (which is demonstrated by the new Posidippus epigrams: Bing 2003: 257–61, but can no longer be deduced from the Satyrus papyrus: Schorn 2001: 210–20, against Robert 1966a: 197–202), they must have come into being more or less simultaneously. The cult of the queen as Philadelphos was instituted shortly after her death: cf. Hauben 1970: 44–6 and 80; 1983: 112–13. On the other hand, it is certain (an *argumentum e silentio*) that at the time Theocritus wrote his seventeenth idyll (during or shortly after the First Syrian War: cf. Gow 1965: II, 326 and 339) the identification had not yet been introduced: Aphrodite is associated rather with the deceased and divinised Berenice I. An analogous reasoning holds for Idyll 15 (*Syrakosiai*) (about 272: Gow 1965: II, 265), where the queen (vv. 24, 110–11) is in no respect identified with the Cypriot goddess (vv. 100–44).

divine patroness of the Ptolemaic maritime empire. The initiative (whether his own or at the court's instigation)[59] was completely in line with both his admiralship and his pioneer priesthood. That he was obviously the queen's favourite fuels speculation about his role at the time of the come-back of Ptolemy's elder sister in the early 270s.[60] In a certain way, he might be regarded as 'the maritime empire's patroness's patron'. As far as we can see, the new cult was a success, apparently meeting popular expectations[61] and giving a serious boost to Ptolemaic propaganda.

That Callicrates continued to be held in high esteem by the throne long after Arsinoe's death is proved by the events of 262–260: in obviously delicate conditions, evoked in a long inscription, he had been sent to Miletus at the head of a group of royal 'Friends' in support of Ptolemy the Son.[62] Could these friends (or some of them) have been the same as the officers mentioned in the Itanus document about half a decade before? Miletus had just overcome a protracted period of grave internal crisis (266–263).[63] It seems that the city's (and the Son's) allegiance towards Alexandria currently stood under pressure – there had even been attacks from outside. If the Son, Ptolemy II's co-regent, was indeed the son of Arsinoe II and Lysimachus, as some now believe,[64] we can understand that the whole set of circumstances was a result of the frustrations produced by the setbacks of the Chremonidean War. The Milesian inscription suggests that Callicrates was the prince's personal supervisor, though the brave young man must already have been in his early 40s.[65] But had not the same Callicrates once been the prince's mother's protector? Clearly acting here as diplomat and at the same time high commander, he was now involved in a conflict that, from the Ptolemaic point of view, might just as rightly have been called 'Arsinoe's War' if one considers how the queen had fostered her son's Macedonian ambitions. Once more this confirms Callicrates' continuous loyalty towards Arsinoe and her family, even after her death. Unfortunately, the mission was not crowned with success.

On occasions which cannot always be dated with certainty, Callicrates turns up in different Aegean and eastern Mediterranean places as the dedicator or recipient of honours.[66]

---

[59] Cf. Stephens 2005: 247–8.   [60] Cf. Hauben 1970: 67.
[61] Cf. Hauben 1983: 111–12, with n. 50; 1989: 460.
[62] *Milet* I.3 with VI.1 139; cf. *RC* 14. See Marquaille 2008: 55; O'Neil 2008: 84.
[63] Cf. *Milet* I.3 with VI.1 123 ll. 53–6 (Apollo as *stephanêphoros*). In 262/261 and 261/260 the Milesian government was pro-Ptolemaic: ll. 57–8.
[64] For a thorough discussion, see Huß 1998: esp. 237–8, 240. Among scholars who reject this identification, we might mention, e.g., Heinen 1972: 97–100; Tunny 2000: 86–9; Domingo Gygax 2002; Buraselis 2005: 96–9.
[65] See the clear survey by Huß 1998: 247–8.   [66] Hauben 1970: 34–41, 46–57; Bing 2003.

First of all, there was a particular bond with his Samian homeland.[67] After some short interruption(s) around the mid century, the island was to remain a major Ptolemaic naval base until after the reign of Ptolemy IV.[68] The Samians knew how to express their appreciation for Callicrates' (pretended or real) high level of protection. As can be deduced from a very mutilated inscription set up by a private individual, he was honoured together with and on the same footing as the royal couple: an exceptional sign of profound esteem.[69] He also received a statue,[70] in all probability from the people, in the sanctuary where the Saviour Gods, clearly the king and queen's deified parents, were worshipped.[71] And a long time after his death as it seems, the Samians erected another statue to Callicrates as their Benefactor.[72] For his part, Callicrates dedicated a statue of a certain Tinnis, a relative or friend of his, the daughter of Dionysodorus. The statue was set up in the Heraeum, the most famous sanctuary on the island and one of the most renowned throughout the Greek world.[73]

No wonder that a man of Callicrates' stature is also documented in other great (Pan)hellenic sanctuaries, like those of Delos, Cyprus and Olympia. On Delos, the members of the League of Islanders honoured him as admiral.[74] As for Cyprus, a statue was erected in the much-frequented age-old *temenos* of Paphian Aphrodite.[75] That was possibly also the case in the sanctuary of Apollo (Hylates) near Curium,[76] where he also seems to have made a dedication to the god.[77] Both native pre-Hellenic deities had long since become hellenised, taking on an international appeal. In Olympia, Callicrates set up two huge Ionic columns on a monumental pedestal dedicated to Zeus, with the statues of Ptolemy II and Arsinoe II.[78]

---

[67] Paschidis 2008: 393–6. On possible Samian relatives, see 396, n. 1.

[68] Shipley 1987: 185–201; cf. Huß 1976: 233.

[69] *OGIS* I 29 + *add.* II p. 539, now *IG* XII.6 588 (on the problematic restorations, see Paschidis 2008: 395, n. 2). Cf. Paschidis 2008: 395: 'Kallikrates was not only honoured as an intermediary between Samos and the Ptolemaic court, but as an agent of Ptolemaic benefactions himself, on a par with the king and the queen.'

[70] *IG* XII.6 282, the inscription originally published by Günter Dunst in Hauben 1970: 83–4, for which different restitutions have since been proposed.

[71] See the commentary referring to *IG* XII.6 4, a mutilated text from the time of the third Ptolemy, where in l. 12 a *hieron* (of the Ptolemaic kings) seems to be mentioned.

[72] *IG* XII.6 283. In line with Hallof's commentary, Gauthier's statement (1985: 59, with n. 172) that this seems to be the earliest example of a statue base for a private benefactor ('grand évergète citoyen') must now be revised. The inscription *IG* XII.6 316 is too mutilated to be taken into account here.

[73] *IG* XII.6 446.   [74] Durrbach 1921–3: no. 25.   [75] Mitford 1961: no. 18.

[76] Mitford 1971: no. 40; cf. Bagnall and Drew Bear 1973: 110–11, pointing to the relative uncertainty of the restitutions and interpretations of Mitford, who supposed without positive evidence that the city of Curium had dedicated the statue to Apollo.

[77] Mitford 1971: no. 58.

[78] *OGIS* I 26–7 (wrongly attributed to Ptolemy I and Berenice I by Paschidis 2008: 258).

This took place still during the queen's lifetime, and it is Bing's merit to have demonstrated what made the splendid monument in that specific location so striking, facing the great temples of Zeus and Hera.[79] Like Theocritus, Callicrates presented his royal protectors 'in terms evoking divinity, specifically as a couple like Zeus and Hera'.[80] It is possible that the monument was erected on the occasion of the royal sibling marriage or, rather perhaps, at the institution of the cult of the Brother/Sister Gods.

One of the new Posidippus epigrams speaks of a victory at the Pythian games (in all probability those of August/September 274) in Delphi, another Panhellenic sanctuary, where Callicrates' colts won the chariot-race.[81] In memory of that victory Callicrates had a bronze statuary group set up, representing a chariot with its team and charioteer. As Bing has convincingly suggested, that must have happened in Egypt, in honour of the *Theoi Adelphoi* on the occasion of his eponymous priesthood (272/271).

That Callicrates was not only interested in the Graeco-Macedonian world but in the religion of his new homeland as well, may be inferred from his building of a shrine at Canopus 'on behalf of King Ptolemy and queen Arsinoe' for the typically Egyptian gods Isis and Anubis.[82]

Bing offers an extremely positive and fascinating image of the Samian nauarch,[83] to the point of presenting him as a prototype of the ideal Hellenistic personality: a man who integrated old and new, deeply rooted in tradition yet open to the concepts of a new age. He felt as much at ease at the Macedonian court in Alexandria as in his beloved Greek mother *polis*, lavishly spending money to honour his sovereigns, though never renouncing his origins and relatives at home. He was a bridge-builder between Greek culture and Egyptian religion. A worshipper of the most *Hellenic* among goddesses in his city of origin and a participant in the most genuine of sacred sports festivals in Greece, he nevertheless promoted the most *Hellenistic* of new cult forms: that of the living royals. Outspokenly attached to power and glory, he remained modest if required.[84] He was cherished by poets as well as respected by the common people, even long after his death. Callicrates was a typically integrating figure, a man who stood for inclusiveness. Patroclus, as we shall see, was quite the opposite.

[79] Bing 2003: 244, 252–4.   [80] Bing 2003: 253.
[81] C. Austin and Bastianini 2002: no. 74; Bing 2003: 244, 246–52. Cf. Bingen 2002, on which see Bing 2003: 250, n. 17. According to the latter, the female colt, who made the decision on the final victory by drawing one of the judges' rods to herself, symbolised Callicrates, who also invoked divine blessing upon himself. I cannot escape the feeling that that 'wondrous female amongst the males' (v. 9) is a subtle reference to Queen Arsinoe II, the strongest character among the Ptolemaic leaders.
[82] Breccia 1926: 51–2, no. 1 = *SB* I 429.   [83] Bing 2003.   [84] Bing 2003: 254–5.

Hardly could two persons be found working at the same level in the same sector showing more divergent profiles.

Apart from Callicrates' priesthood, only one official title is known relating to a specific function, that of *nauarchos*, admiral. The wording of the Milesian inscription, on the other hand, implies that he actually belonged to the narrow circle of the king's friends. At that time *philos* was not yet an honorific title linked to well-defined offices, as it would become in the reign of the fifth Ptolemy. It was just a designation pointing to an informal yet real court position, implying a close and confidential, often influential, relationship with the monarch.[85]

At first glance, it seems strange that Callicrates' *nauarchia*, apart from in three of the four Posidippus epigrams in question,[86] is only mentioned (or preserved) in a few inscriptions.[87] Sometimes the text is so mutilated that every attempt at restoration seems futile; in other instances the title was simply omitted. But on further consideration this non-occurrence does not seem particularly unusual, as Callicrates often appears simply as a courtier or private individual. So the lack of a title is not relevant to the real position of the man at a given time and does not necessarily mean that he was not yet or no longer in post as admiral.[88] Combined with the impossibility of attributing a precise date to most inscriptions (Arsinoe's death being the crucial – yet not undisputed – chronological marker), this makes it very difficult to present a reliable chronological overview of Callicrates' career. Thus probably the earliest reference to him, the poem almost certainly relating to the Pythian games of 274,[89] does not mention any title. It was Anna Świderek who rightly observed that the duration of Callicrates' admiralship cannot possibly be determined 'since neither the beginning nor the end of this period are dated definitely'.[90]

There is scarcely any information on Callicrates' specific duties or activities as a fleet commander. We do not know whether he participated in any sea battle or whether he had combat troops under his command. Only the international state of affairs and the political and military situation in Olus and Miletus at the beginning and, respectively, the end of the Chremonidean War can give us any idea of the reasons and circumstances necessitating his presence (though the title of admiral is lacking in the

---

[85] See Mooren 1975: 1–7.
[86] C. Austin and Bastianini 2002: nos. 39, 116, 119. In no. 74 no title is given.
[87] Samos: *IG* XII.6 282 (restored; uncertain); *IG* XII.6 446; *IG* XII.6 588 (restored); Delos (League of Islanders): Durrbach 1921–3: no. 25; Palaepaphos: Mitford 1961: no. 18; Canopus: Breccia 1926: 51–2, no. 1 = *SB* I 429.
[88] Cf. Hauben 1970: 34–59, *passim*.   [89] C. Austin and Bastianini 2002: no. 74.
[90] Świderek 1974: 304.

documents concerned). And we know that about 257, during the Second
Syrian War, he was ultimately responsible for the financial resources of the
Ptolemaic war fleet, at least if he was the same person as the Callicrates
mentioned (again without title) in the Michigan Zenon papyrus.[91]

However, given the fact that he was honoured in a wide range of places,
covering a variety of areas of the Ptolemaic empire and beyond; that he
received accolades as nauarch without further specification or motivation,[92]
particularly from the Islanders on Delos (their political and religious headquarters) as well as from the Cypriots (or a comparable official local body)
at their main shrine;[93] in view, moreover, of the expressly maritime character of the cult he founded for Arsinoe, it has been concluded that he was,
for a relatively extended (though not further definable) time the overall
chief of the Ptolemaic fleet, 'the' – i.e. highest and permanent – admiral of
the Ptolemaic empire.[94] 'Highest' implies that the simultaneous existence
of subordinate admirals remains possible; 'permanent' that his assignment
was not confined to a particular expedition or war.

On the other hand, there is nothing that points to explicit administrative, political or military powers over the islands and coastal areas like those
of Philocles or Patroclus. But even then Callicrates' authority, whatever it
entailed, must have been strongly felt in the Aegean and eastern Mediterranean. Otherwise some of the statues set up for him – for example, those
in Delos and Palaepaphos – cannot be explained.

At any rate, we may assume that his *nauarchia* must have involved
the general and technical responsibility for the Ptolemaic navy. It is also
probable that he helped determine the empire's overall maritime policy and
that he advised the king on the establishment of naval bases all over the
realm. Considering his privileged relationship with the (late) queen it is not
at all absurd to suppose that he took an active – not necessarily exclusive –
part in refounding a network of strategic ports into as many 'Arsinoes'.[95]
It is also conceivable that he helped spread the cult of Arsinoe: consider,

[91] *P.Mich.* I 100; cf. above, p. 142, with earlier discussion.
[92] For this kind of reasoning, see Mitford 1959: 126–7, n. 111; 1961: 9, no. 18, commentary; cf. Hauben 1970: 46, no. 1; 47–8, no. 3; cf. 67–9. As for the inscriptions from Curium (46–7, no. 2), which have been published since, they do not include Callicrates' title, as perhaps mistakenly suggested.
[93] Just as he received, analogously, a statue from the people of Samos simply because he had been their benefactor (*IG* XII.6 283). The motivation is implied in the title given to the honoured person.
[94] Cf. Świderek 1974: 304: 'we can now take it as proved that he was the supreme commander of the Ptolemaic navy'.
[95] On this phenomenon, see Robert 1960: 156–60; Longega 1968: 114–18; Barbantani 2005: 146–7; Clarysse 2009: 35 (in southern Asia Minor).

for instance, the small *Arsinoês Philadelphou* altar plaques found in many different places where the influence of the Ptolemaic fleet was strong.[96]

As suggested above, Macedonian Patroclus, the son of Patron, must already have won his spurs in royal service (court, administration, army) before being awarded his eponymous priesthood in 271/270. There *may* have been a direct link with the execution of Sotades, the priesthood being a reward, or, conversely, a stimulus. Unfortunately, many things about the incident remain obscure, in particular its chronology. At any rate the sacerdotal office is unmistakable evidence for Patroclus' adherence to the royal family.

The basic studies on Patroclus are still those of Marcel Launey and Heinz Heinen. Launey's brief but innovative article was published around the end of the Second World War. In Heinen's thorough analysis from the early 1970s, made within the framework of a study on the Chremonidean War, recent archaeological discoveries in Attica were already incorporated. More recent contributions are the *Untersuchungen* of Boris Dreyer, an up-to-date article by Walter Ameling in *Der Neue Pauly* and the 'Re-examination' of James O'Neil.[97]

Contrary to Callicrates' Samian nationality, Patroclus' Macedonian descent spontaneously evokes a (prominent) position in the army rather than a specifically naval career. Indeed, although Pausanias, in a maritime context, calls him *nauarchos*,[98] it is clear that Patroclus' official title was *stratêgos*, as was convincingly established by Launey;[99] this is how he is

---

[96] Cf. Mitford 1939: 30–2; Robert 1966a: 192–210, esp. 206–8; Hauben 1970: 66–7. An altar plaque from Caunus found recently was republished by Marek 2006: no. 54, with commentary 246–7 (cf. 97 and 135): 'Fundorte außerhalb Ägyptens sind Zypern, Lesbos, Delos, Paros, Ios, Amorgos, Thera, Milet . . . Eretria auf Euboia.'

[97] Launey 1945; Heinen 1972: 95–213, esp. 142–52 ('Der Flottenzug des Patroklos'), 152–9 ('Das Ehrendekret für den Strategen Epichares'), 159–67 ('Militärische Anlagen in Attika'), 167–81 ('Zum Verlauf der Landkriegsoperationen'), 189–97 ('Die Flottenoperationen des Chremonideischen Krieges'); Dreyer 1999: 283–375 (very detailed), *passim*; Ameling 2000; O'Neil 2008: 71–87.

[98] Paus. 1.1.1.

[99] Launey 1945: 36–8. Like Philocles, Patroclus is often – strictly speaking incorrectly – styled *nauarchos* or admiral in modern studies: see Launey 1945: 35, n. 5. This 'mistake' also appears in more recent publications such as *Bulletin* 1968: 247; Tréheux 1992: 70; Weber 1993: 425; Cohen 1995: 125 (correct: 137); Petrakos 1997a: 616, 626; Mélèze Modrzejewski 1998: 153 and 155 (cf. also, more correctly, 153: 'stratège militaire, commandant de flotte'); *IG* XII.6 343 (2000), commentary; Jacoby 2004: 196, n. 11; Ager 2005: 5; O'Neil 2008: 65, 71, 74; Paschidis 2008: 427, 433. Very peculiar is the reasoning of Tracy 1990: 68, n. 22: 'It is highly probable that Patroklos did serve as nauarch earlier in his career [i.e. at the time of the Samian inscription *IG* XII.6 343, before becoming *stratêgos*], but we have no certain record of it.' So implicitly the author is thinking of a form of *cursus*, in which the *nauarchia* was subordinate to the *stratêgia*; at least the latter idea could be right, as is probably implied by the Olus inscription.

styled in official inscriptions, at least whenever a title is mentioned (as in the decrees of Itanus and Carthaea), as well as in some literary texts.[100]

Launey believes that 'tout ce que nous savons de Patroklos se rattache ou peut se rattacher au début de la guerre chrémonidéenne'.[101] According to the now generally accepted chronology, that war started in August 268 (Chremonides decree),[102] the first campaigns being launched in the spring of 267. Apart from the fact that 'tout' seems definitely too much,[103] Launey's thesis looks most attractive and could be largely true.

Let us start with Crete. Patroclus' mission to the island – he was, according to the Itanus decree, officially 'sent off by King Ptolemy as *stratêgos* to Crete' – cannot be more sensibly interpreted than in the light of a militarily underscored diplomatic offensive at the start of the war. At that very time Ptolemy had an undeniable interest in gaining a foothold on that rich, populated, yet troublesome and somewhat out-of-the-way territory. Itanus and Olus, the only places where Patroclus is attested, were excellent bases that were easy to defend.[104] Did he leave garrisons in one or both of these cities?[105] We do not know for sure. In Itanus, where he interfered or arbitrated in the city's internal affairs,[106] Patroclus received *proxenia* as well as citizenship – a particularly distinguished honour – and the title of benefactor, for himself and his descendants; in Olus, where he was honoured together with Callicrates and seven other officers (and/or diplomats), whose chief he obviously was, only *proxenia* with the title of benefactor. Such a large and distinguished group visiting that port is an additional argument for the thesis that the activities had something to do with impending hostilities. By establishing (a measure of) Ptolemaic control over Crete, probably also including cities like Aptera and Rhithymna, as can be inferred from the officers' list,[107] Patroclus hoped to secure his rear when leaving for Attica.

Launey wanted to link Sotades' ruthless execution by Patroclus to the latter's expedition of 267 as well. At the same time he emended 'the island of *Kaunos*' (geographically meaningless according to him) into 'the island

[100] Itanus: *IC* III iv.2–3; Carthaea: *IG* XII.5 1061; literary texts: Phylarchus (Ath. 8.334a–b) and Hegesander (Ath. 14.621a). The sources are listed in Launey 1945: 36–7 and *Pros. Ptol.* VI 15063. In the very mutilated, recently (re)published Samian inscription on a statue base found in the Heraeum (*IG* XII.6 343 = Tracy 1990: 67–8, no. 2; to be dated relatively early, i.e. *c.* 280–270 as discussed further below) Patroclus is simply honoured by the people of Samos, obviously without any title or even motivation.
[101] Launey 1945: 38.   [102] Schmitt 1969: no. 476.   [103] Cf. Ameling 2000: 419.
[104] *IC* III iv.2–3, the one being a copy of the other (Itanus), and I xxii.4A ll. 35–42 (Olus).
[105] This is more or less surmised for Itanus: Bagnall 1976: 121; Marek 1984: 319.
[106] See Paschidis 2008: 459–61.   [107] Marek 1984: 320.

of *Kaudos'* in Athenaeus (Hegesander) and Eustathius.[108] That interpretation, the text emendation included, has been accepted by the majority of scholars.[109] Only recently has it been expressly rejected by Christian Marek.[110]

The story of Sotades of Maronea is most revealing:[111] not only does it tell us a lot about the relationship of Hellenistic monarchs with their intellectual detractors and the way in which the Ptolemies reacted to critical voices in particular,[112] but it may also say something about Patroclus' disposition and confirm his feelings of unconditional loyalty towards the kings. Sotades had, among other slanders, written some vilifying verses about the incestuous marriage of the Brother/Sister rulers.[113] After having been imprisoned for a long time in Alexandria, he had managed to escape to 'the island of *Kaunos/Kaudos'*, where he was traced and sadistically put to death by Patroclus, who 'stuck his feet in a jar full of lead, took him out to sea, and drowned him'.[114]

The contrast is surely striking. Callicrates, on the one hand, was joyfully praised and celebrated by a compliant poet, while Patroclus grimly persecuted one of the latter's less submissive fellow intellectuals. We should, however, beware of hasty conclusions, since this gruesome act may have represented the execution of a royal sentence, rather than the general's personal vengeance.[115]

The brief reconstruction of the poet's end as presented here was elaborated by Launey[116] before being expounded, especially from a juridical point of view, by Mélèze Modrzejewski.[117] It results from the harmonisation of two different versions: imprisonment of many years

---

[108] Hegesander: Ath. 14.621a; Eustathius: *Commentarii ad Homeri Iliadem* P 432, p. 1069, ed. van der Valk III 879, quoted by Marek 2006: 21–2.

[109] E.g. Ameling 2000: 420.   [110] Marek 2006: 21.   [111] *Pros. Ptol.* VI 16717.

[112] On this topic, see the fundamental study of Weber 1998/9: esp. (on Sotades) 150, 162–5, 172–3 ('able to cause a good deal of unrest in the frail structure of the court society'). Cf. Völcker-Janssen 1993: 84; Weber 1993: 425; Furley 2001; Jacoby 2004: 195–6, with n. 11; Ager 2005: 5; Touloumakos 2006: 123–4.

[113] According to Mélèze Modrzejewski (1998: 152), 'un délit qui tenait, en termes de catégories modernes, à la fois de la lèse-majesté et du blasphème', as Sotades offended (strictly speaking from 272/271 on) a divine couple. On the legal character of the offence (traditional *kakêgoria* having become in a Macedonian and monarchic context a case of lèse majesté): 159–69.

[114] Hegesander: Ath. 14.621a–b, trans. S. Douglas Olson, Loeb Classical Library 2011.

[115] Thus Mélèze Modrzejewski 1998: 155–6, with n. 17 (on the sacred character of drowning as death penalty); see also Mélèze Modrzejewski 2008: 163–6 (among the 'châtiments exceptionnels', comparable to the classical *apotympanismos* and the later *damnatio ad bestias*). Cf. Launey 1945: 44 (putting the problem).

[116] Launey 1945.

[117] Mélèze Modrzejewski 1998. According to the author, the imprisonment in Alexandria was a 'détention préventive' (154–5).

(Plutarch),[118] as against brutal execution (Hegesander-Eustathius). As for the geographical and chronological setting of this sensational story, the pros and cons seem to keep each other in balance, rendering a definitive solution impossible.[119]

As Launey suggests, two other inscriptions, this time from the central and western Aegean respectively (Thera, Patroclus being in Iulis on Ceos, and Carthaea on Ceos),[120] can also be attributed to Patroclus' expedition on his way to Attica, the more so as they make it clear that he visited (and probably also garrisoned) Thera before setting sail for Ceos.[121]

Thera, with its impressive acropolis, being the post-eruption settlement dating from the ninth century BC, situated on the south-east of the island about 350 m above sea level,[122] was apparently tormented by social troubles (the extant part of the inscription gives no details), as took place on several other Aegean islands in the time of Philocles. Patroclus was honoured by the people of Thera because he had sent the *epistatês* Apollodotus from Iulis,[123] as well as a board of five judges, to put an end to their conflicts. Iulis was Patroclus' headquarters on Ceos,[124] a comparatively large island comprising four *poleis* (see Map. 1.1). After having successfully accomplished their mission according to the customary procedures, the judges,[125] without any doubt Iulian citizens, had returned home.

The position of Apollodotus is somewhat ambiguous. His citizenship is unclear, his relation to the visiting judges obscure, his title, borne by different kinds of official, open to more than one interpretation.[126] According to Heinen (inspired by Holleaux), Apollodotus was only entrusted with a temporary ad hoc mission: to help settle the internal troubles, together (working independently?) or in collaboration (as a kind of president or supervisor?) with the tribunal. After having accomplished his task he would have returned home together with the judges.[127] Bagnall, on the other hand, sees a clear parallelism with the *epistatês* Hieron of Syracuse,[128] who, 'established in Arsinoe' on Ceos, was obviously its permanent garrison commander.[129] Emphasising that the simultaneous appointments of judges and *epistatês* were not necessarily interconnected, Paschidis too appears to

---

[118] Plut. *Mor.* 11A (*De liber. educ.* 14).
[119] On this problem, see the Appendix at the end of this chapter.
[120] *IG* XII.3 320 = *OGIS* I 44 (Thera); see Paschidis 2008: 433–4, no. D74–8 (Iulian judges sent to Thera); *IG* XII.5 1061 (Carthaea).
[121] Launey 1945: 38–9.   [122] E.g. Chilton et al. 2004: 199–200.   [123] *Pros. Ptol.* VI 15139.
[124] Cf. Cherry and Davis 1991: 14, 16, 26.   [125] On this institution, see e.g., Lonis 2000: 220–1.
[126] For an overview of the different possibilities and interpretations, as well as the *epistatai* at the time of Patroclus' expedition, see Peremans and Van 't Dack 1968: 94 and 95.
[127] Heinen 1972: 148–9.   [128] *Pros. Ptol.* VI 15148.   [129] Bagnall 1976: 124, 141–2; cf. below.

view Apollodotus as a garrison commander.[130] The basic question, in other words, is whether or not Apollodotus' *epistasia* in Thera and Hieron's on Ceos implied the same competences.[131]

Let us consider the situation on Ceos first. The man who is generously honoured by the people of Carthaea is not the general, as in Thera, but the *epistatês*. 'Appointed by King Ptolemy', Hieron, the son of Timocrates, 'had come to the island together with general Patroclus.' Does this mean that he had already been nominated in Alexandria? Or was it the general who, in the name of the king, had assigned him to the job after their arrival? As Paschidis has shown, the phrase τεταγμένος ὑπὸ τὸμ βασιλέα (accusative) denotes a royal officer in general rather than an official appointed by the king to a specific job as is implied by the same phrase with 'king' in the genitive.[132]

Arsinoe was the new name of Coressus/Coresia, situated on the bay of Ayios Nikolaos on the north-western coast of Ceos. It was the main port of the island, with an outstanding harbour, a typical feature of every city receiving the (late) queen's name. Fronting Attica and capable of controlling naval communications in the area, it would be an excellent base, especially in view of the operations to come.[133] The refounding of the city, whose new name makes its first appearance here, must have been the work of Patroclus.[134] It seems that Arsinoe received a Ptolemaic garrison,[135] and that Hieron was indeed its first commander.[136] It is striking that he was honoured by the people of Carthaea for having intervened in favour of a certain Epiteles in an obscure and seemingly trivial matter concerning personal property rights.[137] Does this imply that his authority over the Coresia base extended to (the) other parts of the island?[138] Probably, like Apollodotus in Thera, he was at least expected to set things right and keep peace among its inhabitants, who had now come under direct Ptolemaic sway.

[130] Paschidis 2008: 433.
[131] It is clear that in Heinen's view (1972: 149–50) Apollodotus' *epistasia* was fundamentally different from that of Hieron.
[132] Paschidis 2008: 430–1, with 431, n. 1.
[133] Cf. Robert 1960: 144–56; Cherry and Davis 1991. See already Graindor 1906: 97: 'Koressos avait l'avantage de posséder un port de premier ordre, le plus spacieux et le plus sûr peut-être de toutes les Cyclades.'
[134] Launey 1945: 39; Cherry and Davis 1991: 12, 13, 16; Cohen 1995: 137–9. Of course, admiral Callicrates should not be completely excluded, but concrete information is lacking here.
[135] Cherry and Davis 1991: 12, 13, 16–17, 26. See also Bagnall 1976: 141–3, 157; 1980: 246.
[136] Also Heinen 1972: 150 sees in him a 'permanent' royal military official, at least for the duration of the war.
[137] See the clarifying comments of Graindor 1906: 98.
[138] Cf. reflections of Bagnall 1976: 143 and Paschidis 2008: 427–8.

By its geopolitical and geological situation alone, Thera was predestined also to become a garrison place. Who else but Apollodotus, in the light of our available sources, could have been its commander? As he received, almost simultaneously with Hieron, the same title in comparable circumstances, it is indeed tempting, with Bagnall, to consider him a royal military official – with a range of civilian competences – of the same rank as the Syracusan.[139] Nevertheless, some doubts remain. According to the decrees, Apollodotus was simply sent by Patroclus, whereas Hieron is explicitly called a royal official. Another difference is that Hieron, in contrast to Apollodotus, appears with his full nomenclature, *patronymikon* as well as *politikon*. Especially the absence of Apollodotus' *politikon/ethnikon* seems strange, but the fact that his *patronymikon* is also lacking, like those of the judges, makes it less so. The judges' *politika* were superfluous, as they all came from Iulis. Does this mean, then, that Apollodotus was also a Iulian, as suggested by Heinen? Probably yes. But would a real garrison commander not have been chosen from among the members of the general's retinue? Of course we would expect this, but given the fact that the Ptolemies had already been present in Nesiotic waters for some twenty years, they must have known a sufficient number of reliable persons there. The crucial condition was that the appointee did not originate from the island where he had to serve. Even so, if Apollodotus' mission actually included the command of a Ptolemaic garrison installed by Patroclus, why was he only (appointed and) sent when the main expeditionary force had already landed in Ceos? So it means that in this case too, we have to reckon with a few uncertainties.

Thera and Ceos were probably not Patroclus' only stops. On this occasion (or at any rate during the campaign) Methana in the Argolid is also likely to have been garrisoned and renamed after Queen Arsinoe.[140] In addition to an excellent peninsular location, it could also serve as an important base and harbour. The topographical setting with its peculiar strategic advantages was strikingly similar to that of Koroni, another of Patroclus' war bases.[141]

[139] Bagnall 1976: 124, 142.
[140] Launey 1945: 44; Heinen, 1972: 131 (very cautious on the chronology: 'der Chremonideische Krieg ist nur eine von mehreren Möglichkeiten, wenngleich eine durchaus wahrscheinliche'); Bagnall 1976: 135 ('a logical part of Patroklos' ring around Attica in this war'); Habicht 1994: 162; Cohen 1995: 124–6 ('strategically located on the peninsula extending out from the Argolid, Arsinoe was an important base for controlling naval traffic in the Saronic Gulf' (125)). Cf. now the dedication of the 'Arsinoeis of the Peloponnese' from Poseidon's sanctuary at Calaureia for Ptolemy II and Arsinoe II: Wallensten and Pakkanen 2009.
[141] A fact brought to my attention by Kostas Buraselis during a visit to Methana–Arsinoe at the end of the colloquium. Cf. O'Neil 2008: 74: the fort of Koroni 'provides little access to the mainland,

The result of Patroclus' expedition was that the Ptolemies, who had already established their supremacy over the Aegean from 288 to 286 and strengthened their position in the following years thanks to the interventions of Philocles and the nesiarch Bacchon,[142] were now, at the start of the Chremonidean War, tightening their grip on the Cyclades after having expanded their control to Crete.

Itanus, Thera and Methana–Arsinoe would survive as the last Ptolemaic naval bases in the Aegean until after the death of Ptolemy VI (June/July 145), when they had to be evacuated. As a consequence, between 144 and 139 the *nauarchia* would be added to the competences of the governor of Cyprus.[143]

Meanwhile Patroclus consecrated a bowl (*phialê*) on Delos. It turns up in the inventories from 257 on,[144] a year that can only be used as a *terminus ante quem* for the offering. In itself it does not prove that the general was still in office at that time. 'L'offrande *pourrait* [my italics] dater de l'époque où Patroclos est actif dans les îles, vers 265 [meaning: at the start of the Chremonidean War]', writes Tréheux. Impossible to say more.

Similar considerations hold for the statue in the Samian Heraeum with which Patroclus was honoured in Callicrates' homeland. No title or motive is given. Nor is it possible to assign a precise date to the base or to sketch the context of its dedication. On palaeographical grounds Tracy would give it a relatively early date: '275', 'shortly after 280', 'the first decade after Philadelphos' assumption of power', 'within ten years of 280'. The hand belongs to a cutter who is dated to *c.* 305–*c.* 270.[145] So, 267 is not far away and perhaps it is not impossible (albeit purely hypothetical) that the statue was erected on the occasion of the famous trip through the islands.

About this time – probably during the Chremonidean War – the Samians honoured a Ptolemaic high officer, who must have belonged to the same social and military class as Patroclus and Callicrates. Pelops, the son of Alexander,[146] was also a Macedonian and a commander of an intervention force (τεταγμένος ἐπὶ δυνάμεως), and, like Callicrates, a 'friend of the king'. In 264/263, when the war was still going on, he acceded to the

its entrances largely face the sea'. The same can be said of Methana, a maritime and Aegean, rather than a land-army and Peloponnesian, base: see the detailed description of this 'petit Gibraltar' in Robert 1960: 157–9. Both fortified emplacements bear the same signature.
[142] *Pros. Ptol.* VI 15038.
[143] Hauben 1996: 236–8, where the chronology once established by T. B. Mitford has been slightly adjusted.
[144] The references are listed in *Pros. Ptol.* VI 15063 and Tréheux 1992: 70.
[145] Tracy 1990: 64, 67–8, no. 2; cf. *SEG* 40.730: '*c.* 275 B.C.'; *IG* XII.6 343: 'c.a. 280–270 a.'.
[146] *IG* XII.6 119; *Pros. Ptol.* III+IX 5227 = VI 14618.

eponymous priesthood.[147] According to Bagnall, he cannot have been the commander of the Samian garrison. His task must have covered a larger area. As the 'islets of Pelops' (off the Peloponnesos, near Methana) were apparently called after him, he was probably involved in the same operations as was Patroclus.[148] In that case he must have been the latter's subordinate, for, according to the Samian inscription (the only one, to be sure, yet carefully drawn up), he did not bear the title of *stratêgos*.

In several places where he disembarked, such as Itanus, Thera, Methana and Coresia, Patroclus, as we saw, must have stationed a number of soldiers.[149] It is difficult to say how many, but as a rule such garrisons were quite small. According to Bagnall, 'naval power plus diplomacy was the principal means of control', the number of garrisons remaining rather restricted.[150] So we are not entitled to argue, with Launey,[151] that this was why after his arrival in Attica, according to a notorious passage in Pausanias,[152] Patroclus made it clear that he had no, or not sufficient, trained soldiers (left) at his disposal. Until half a century ago Pausanias was the only source explicitly linking Patroclus to the Chremonidean War.

A close study of the evidence, especially the relatively recently published Rhamnusian decree for the Athenian *stratêgos* Epichares,[153] has shown that the hostilities in Attica against Antigonus Gonatas started relatively early, already in the spring of 267.[154] 'The soldiers who, with Patroclus, had come to [the Athenians', viz. Rhamnusians'] rescue' (ll. 23–4), and for whom shelters had been built, were anything but efficient. They had not been able to dispel the Antigonid army, already present in the *chôra*, nor even to fight the pirates who were collaborating with the invaders and seriously harassed the population,[155] a situation which 'severely disrupted the economy' of the deme.[156]

This new inscription seems to confirm, be it only in part, the Pausanias passage. For, according to the Periegete, Patroclus, loosely called *nauarchos* in this context, declared himself incapable of taking the offensive against

[147] Mooren 1975: no. 11; Clarysse and Van der Veken 1983: no. 27.
[148] Bagnall 1976: 83–4. Cf. Habicht 1994: 162; Rodriguez 2000: 27–8 (but that Pelops would have been the commander of the Ptolemaic fleet in the eastern Aegean is merely hypothetical).
[149] Think of Napoleon, who, on his way to Egypt, after having expelled the burnt-out Knights from Malta, left behind a garrison of some 4,000 troops (about 10 per cent of the total) under general Vaubois. The drain was compensated in part by local recruitment: Strathern 2007: 51.
[150] Bagnall 1980: 246; cf. 1976: 157.   [151] Launey 1945: 39.   [152] Paus. 3.6.4–6; cf. 1.1.1.
[153] *SEG* 24.154. The *editio princeps* is in Petrakos 1967; cf. *Bulletin* 1968: 247; Heinen 1972: 152–4; *SEG* 40.135. On Rhamnus (including the events of the Chremonidean War), see Petrakos 1997a; Oliver 2001: 142–8.
[154] For a detailed chronology, see the important study of Knoepfler 1993; cf. O'Neil 2008: 75–6.
[155] Cf. Heinen 1972: 157–8, 209.   [156] Oliver 2001: 148.

the Macedonian invaders. The reason, so he said, was that his men were (without doubt native)[157] Egyptians and sailors (*nautai*). To a certain extent, the text remains a *crux*. For, as we saw, it is inconceivable in the given circumstances that the general would not have had any military contingent under his command, even after his different stops and garrisoning of the islands. Moreover, the Rhamnus inscription shows that his men, no matter how deficient, *were* soldiers, *stratiôtai*. So Patroclus' *nautai* are probably to be understood as Egyptian *epibatai*, marines, not just (or not all) as sailors.[158] But were they exclusively Egyptian and only marines? Or did Patroclus lie to his Spartan allies or exaggerate his problems?

Even if apocryphal, the pronouncement is revealing for a certain Macedonian (and Greek) milieu.[159] It shows a visceral contempt for native Egyptians, still the majority of the population in the new African homeland. Here again we see a contrast between the sophisticated Samian courtier with his keen interest in matters Egyptian, and the old-fashioned Macedonian fire-eater of the 'Philip and Antipater' line, distrusting all that seemed in contradiction to the home-made prejudices.

Patroclus' army may have suffered from a lack of commitment. The fact, however, that he fortified an uninhabited island near Cape Sunium, present-day Gaïdaronisi, then given the general's name (*Patroklou Nêsos* or *Charax*), seems to suggest that it was at least his initial intention to put in a good deal of effort.[160] There is also an impressive series of defensive structures in Attica that – combined with pottery and numismatic finds – may or may not be linked to the Chremonidean War: the interpretation is not always certain and remains for a large part under discussion.[161] Yet, as O'Neil has pointed out,[162] the fortifications, camps, watch-posts of Atene, Koroni, Vouliagmeni, Heliupolis (on the foothills of Mt Hymettus) were surely used by Patroclus' troops, showing that he pushed them 'further into Attica than Pausanias realised'. But in contrast to the bases on the islands, the forts in Attica were soon abandoned. It seems that in the last years of the war Ptolemaic support was seriously cut back.[163] All in all, the situation remains ambiguous.

---

[157] See Van 't Dack and Hauben 1978: 87–9; Hauben 1990a: 33, n. 34. Cf. Rodriguez 2004: 112, n. 38, 118.

[158] Van 't Dack and Hauben 1978: 88; Rodriguez 2000: 25–6.

[159] For these (sometimes ethnically inspired) feelings of superiority and disdain, see Rodriguez 2004.

[160] Paus. 1.1.1; cf. Strabo 9.1.21; Steph. Byz., *s.v.* Πατρόκλου νῆσος.

[161] Literature abounds. A good overview with critical discussion was already provided by Heinen 1972: 159–67. Cf., e.g., *Bulletin* 1964: 168–9a; Ameling 2000: 420. See now O'Neil 2008: 74–8.

[162] O'Neil 2008: 74–5. Cf. also Rodriguez 2000: 23–8.

[163] See the analysis by O'Neil 2008: 83–9, stressing Ptolemy's 'unwillingness to commit all his resources'.

It is not my intention to reopen that file here – it would be a study in itself – nor to reopen discussion on the battle of Cos. Many scholars still think that this naval clash took place about 262 or 261, thus concluding the war between Antigonus Gonatas and the second Ptolemy.[164] In that case, the *stratêgos* Patroclus is supposed to have been the commander of the Ptolemaic sea forces. So, the famous Phylarchus fragment with the large-fishes-and-green-figs joke[165] refers either to the Chremonidean War or the battle of Cos, or both. It is interesting to see how, according to that fragment, both Antigonus and Patroclus (all in all, not as humourless as the Sotades incident might suggest) were plainly conscious of the fact that nothing less than the *thalassokratia* (the corresponding verb is used) was at stake.

Whatever the case, it is clear that now that the queen was dead, 'her' war was not fought with the vigour or conviction one might have expected. The truth is, as Heinen says, that, whether or not the battle of Cos belonged to the Chremonidean War, the final losers were Patroclus and Ptolemy II.[166] Although it was far from being the end of Ptolemaic sea power, for Alexandria the time of 'absolute' thalassocracy was over, once and for all.[167] The general who initially seemed to be one of its champions may in the end have become one of its unintentional gravediggers.

If it has proved impossible to reconstruct Callicrates' career, an attempt to define the chronological termini of Patroclus' active life is an equally hopeless task.[168] It is clear, however, that his *floruit* belongs to the late 270s and the 260s, with a probable peak in (the first episode of) the Chremonidean War.

Ever since the Patroclus inscriptions have been known, there has been controversy over his exact competence. In the days of W. W. Tarn he was seen as one of the great Ptolemaic admirals, who, endowed with extensive powers, were thought to hold their office for a period of ten years each.[169] This surely original but artificial construction was soon

---

[164] Cf. Reger 1985. Others prefer a setting in the Second Syrian War: thus, Dreyer 1999: 416–19 (detailed discussion with bibliographical references); cf. Marek 2006: 135 (255 BC).

[165] Ath. 8.334a–b.

[166] Heinen 1972: 209: 'Wie man auch über die Chronologie [of the battle of Cos] urteilen mag, Ptolemaios II. war gescheitert.'

[167] Heinen 1972: 211: 'Allerdings hat Kos – auch wenn man diese Schlacht in den 2. Syrischen Krieg setzt – nicht den totalen Zusammenbruch der ptolemäischen Seeherrschaft in der Ägäis zur Folge gehabt... Doch die absolute ägyptische Vormachtstellung in der Ägäis war für immer gebrochen.' Cf. Buraselis 1982: 160–70.

[168] Cf. Ameling 2000: 419, giving in my opinion a questionable chronological framework (between 275 and 257) for the general's career.

[169] Tarn 1911: 256–8; 1933: 61–8 ('The Duration of the Ptolemaic Nauarchate'). Cf. Launey's comments (1945: 35–6). Recently, Tarn's theory has again briefly surfaced: Dreyer 1999: 231.

abandoned, especially once Launey had demonstrated that Patroclus was in fact a general, not a nauarch. Nowadays, most scholars seem to agree with Launey, although their actual terminology (often hesitating between *stratêgos*/general and *nauarchos*/admiral) is not always consistent. But if he was a general, what kind of a general was he? A super-general with comprehensive authority, like Philocles, or simply a military *stratêgos*, as many scholars seem to admit today?[170] The problem is that *stratêgos* is a generic term, with different and fluctuating meanings, especially in these still formative decades of Ptolemaic imperial organisation. Even 'military *stratêgos*' without further specification is ambiguous and misleading, so that we need to define what we mean when using the term. But trying to make such neat distinctions is, to a certain degree, a false problem, because everything was determined by the actual circumstances and the concrete assignment given by the king.

In the present case, we see Patroclus intervening in the domestic affairs of the islands, where he had to take important initiatives and drastic decisions in the name of a monarch residing far away in Alexandria. We can imagine that his appointment was the result of careful screening. His eponymous priesthood alone implies that his *stratêgia* cannot have been an ordinary commandership. Moreover, it looks as if, at least during his mission, he even ranked above the admiral Callicrates, an individual who, as we saw, counted among the most prominent and closest collaborators of the king.

In my view Patroclus is basically to be put on the same level as Philocles,[171] the 'viceroy of the north',[172] Patroclus being a 'viceroy of the Aegean' or something like that. Of course, Patroclus held his office for a shorter time, but nobody could predict how the war would run its course. Just like Philocles, he served in the context of critical international developments. The difference is that the king of the Sidonians had a prestigious home base and a still more prestigious title that conferred upon him a relatively relaxed freedom of action, while living at a time when everything had still to be built up and much seemed possible. So, if in certain respects circumstances

---

[170] Launey 1945: 37–8: 'Ce serait une erreur de voir en Patroklos un de ces stratèges aux attributions autant administratives que militaires, qui représentaient l'autorité royale dans les possessions extérieures des Lagides.' I agree that we should not see him as a form of territorial governor. But the Aegean inscriptions prove that he had, at least indirectly, via his *epistatai*, some civilian competence. Cf. Weber 1998–9: 163, n. 70: 'important military strategos'.

[171] In this respect I am of the same opinion as Tarn 1911: 257–8. To a large extent, I can also endorse the view of Bengtson 1967: 184–7, who thinks in terms of a temporary military command, but one which resulted in a series of 'Vollmachten'. Comparing one to the other he is absolutely right when he writes that 'von einer regelrechten "Provinzialstatthalterschaft" des Philokles und des Patroklos... keine Rede sein [kann]' (187). Less happy is his description of Philocles as a 'ptolemäischer Admiral' (186).

[172] Hauben 1987b: 418–20.

had changed, fundamentally they remained similar. The 'full powers' given to Patroclus were in principle the same as those with which the Sidonian king – in fact also a Ptolemaic *stratêgos*[173] – had been entrusted. There is, of course, the intriguing case of Pelops, who seems to have participated in the Chremonidean War and may have shared some part of his responsibilities with Patroclus, intervening on both sides of the Aegean. However, as far as we can estimate, he must have held a lower military rank.

The official titles in the epigraphical documents show that Patroclus' *stratêgia* and Callicrates' *nauarchia* did not overlap. But in many other respects our sources are defective, leaving room for speculation.

With regard to Callicrates, we can only guess at his specific duties as nauarch. There are no contemporary nauarchs on the same level, and although Patroclus crossed his path several times, we have virtually no information about any (in itself very probable) concrete interaction between the two.

We know a lot about Philocles' lofty position because on several occasions he had to deal with the nesiarch Bacchon, the governor of the League of Islanders, who was definitely his subordinate. No such interaction with a nesiarch is explicitly attested for the *nauarchos* Callicrates or the *stratêgos* Patroclus. Nor was there a nauarch like Callicrates in the days of Philocles: their (hypothetical) interaction could have taught us something about the Callicrates–Patroclus relationship.

In other words, both Callicrates and Patroclus stand on their own: no interaction between them, nor between them and any nesiarch. There is only an analogy between Philocles and Patroclus. The exact difference between the *stratêgia* of the latter two and the *nauarchia* of Callicrates seems doomed to remain a mystery.

APPENDIX

The geographical and chronological setting of Sotades'
execution: Kaunos *or* Kaudos?

For geographical reasons, opting for *Kaunos* excludes a link with the 267 expedition, whereas opting for *Kaudos* makes that link practically unavoidable. Moreover, if we reject the *Kaudos* hypothesis, any date between the wedding of the *Adelphoi* and the (indeterminate) end of Patroclus' career

---

[173] Hauben 1987b: 421.

remains possible: in the first place, because the king's (and Patroclus') intervention was not necessarily an immediate response to Sotades' obscenity,
which means that the execution did not necessarily follow soon after the
wedding; secondly, because Belistiche (Philadelphus' mistress on whom
Sotades also wrote a poem) was perhaps already dwelling at court before
Arsinoe's death, implying that there is no objection to an execution long
before the start of the war; and, thirdly, because the duration of Sotades'
'long' imprisonment is not specified.[174]

For reasons of security *Kaudos* was preferable, of course. Think of
Harpalus, another hunted man, who had tried to find refuge in Crete
before being killed by his subordinate Thibron.[175] As for the isle of Gau-
dos/Caudos, it was the southernmost point of Europe, one of the most
remote places of the Aegean, though probably more densely populated in
antiquity than Gávdhos is today (some fifty inhabitants, making up six
families).[176] Isolated as they were, Crete, and a fortiori Gaudos, must have
had the allure (and given the illusion) of being really safe havens.[177]

Nevertheless, *Kaunos* also makes sense, the more so as it is the reading
transmitted by the textual tradition and – a fact overlooked by Launey –
since in antiquity Caunus was in fact sometimes called a *nêsos*.[178] Of course,
taking refuge in a city like Caunus was risky, as Launey rightly contends,
but what could a man like Sotades, constantly looking for publicity by
offending royals, achieve if he hid on an insignificant islet situated about
50 km off the south-western coast of Crete?

So we have to accept that in the final analysis the question remains open.

---

[174] For these intricate questions, see the different arguments in Weber 1998–9: 162–5 (mistakenly
attributing to Launey the view that Plutarch's version was more reasonable and should therefore be
preferred (163, n. 71); in fact Launey (1945: 33) found that this was the common opinion, against
which he wanted to react – on the problem of the poem on Belistiche, compare 164 with n. 79
there!); Jacoby 2004: 195–6, n. 11; Marek 2006: 21.

[175] Cf. Badian 1961: 32.

[176] Gaudos (rather than Gozo) was also the isle of C(l)auda past the south coast of which Paul's ship
coming from Kaloí Liménes was blown off course and off which there was a short stop-over: Acts
27:8–16; cf. Baslez 2008: 268–70, 420 n. 93; Meijer 2000: 116–22; cf. 112. On (modern) Gávdhos,
see, among others, Fisher and Garvey 2001: 372–80.

[177] An additional argument could be that Sotades possibly came from Crete (Suda, *s.v.* 'Sotades' (Adler
871); cf. Weber 1993: 425; 1998–9: 162) and so knew the region. However, Professor Habicht has been
so kind as to inform me that in his view the poet must have originated from Maronea in Thrace (cf.
LGPN IV: 325), the existence of a *polis* with that name in Crete being somewhat problematic. The
quite famous (pseudo-Ephesian) Cretan Sotades, twice victorious in the long race in Olympia (384
and 380 BC; Paus. 6.18.6), may have caused the error. I prefer to leave the question open, although
Sotades' early contacts with Lysimachus may argue in favour of the Thracian thesis.

[178] See Marek 2006: 21–2.

CHAPTER 4

Rhodes and the Ptolemaic kingdom: the commercial infrastructure

Vincent Gabrielsen

INTRODUCTION

The Lindian Temple Chronicle, now in the National Museum in Copenhagen, records the dedications made by the Pharaoh Amasis (570–526 BC) to the prestigious temple of Athene in Lindos; the source cited in the Chronicle for this item of information is, in fact, Herodotus.[1] A Lindian inscription from before 411 BC – that is, from the time when Lindos was still a separate city-state – awards *proxenia* and other honours to one Damoxenus, a resident of Egypt. Then, further, a decree passed by the newly unified city-state of Rhodes shortly after 408 BC grants *proxenia* to a citizen of Aegina who had provided – no doubt to the Rhodians – his services as a translator (*hermeneus*) at a renowned port of trade, Naucratis.[2] For Lindos, like the other two Rhodian *poleis*, Ialysus and Camirus, was among the founder states of the Hellenion at Naucratis (Hdt. 2.178).

These are some of the testimonies attesting to the long history of contacts between Egypt and the city-states on the island of Rhodes, especially Lindos.[3] From about the middle of the fourth century these contacts, now formally applying to the unified city-state of the whole island, were strengthened further. Control of access to Black Sea grain and other commodities by Philip II of Macedon turned Egypt into an even better (and nearer) alternative source of supply for many Aegean cities,[4] especially for Rhodes. A strong political and economic cooperation was to develop. At the level of personal relations, moreover, it may be remembered that it was Mentor, a Rhodian in the service of the Great King, who in the

---

[1] *I.Lindos* no. 2, XXIX. Cf. Hdt. 2.182.
[2] *I.Lindos* no. 16 Appendix, and no. 16. On the *synoikismos* of the three *poleis* Ialysus, Camirus and Lindos, leading to the formation of a federal state, the *polis* of Rhodes, see Gabrielsen 2000.
[3] On the early history of Lindos, see Konstantinopoulos 1972: esp. 49.
[4] Didymus' *Commentary on Demosthenes* 11.1, cols. 10.34–11.5: *FGrH* 328: Philoch. *FGrH* 328 F162, cf. Theopomp. *FGrH* 115, F292, with Bresson 2000: 131–49 (chap. 7: 'L'attentat d'Hieron et le commerce grec'), and Gabrielsen 2007: 306–7.

340s brought Egypt again under Persian rule, while his brother Memnon, also in Persian service, was fiercely fighting Philip.[5] Thus, although the links between Rhodes and Egypt did indeed become very close under the Ptolemies, they had roots going further back in time. As will shortly be seen, we have reasons to believe that these roots were quite deep already at the time of Cleomenes of Naucratis, Alexander's governor in Egypt.

Describing the city-state of Rhodes in the year it was besieged by Demetrius Poliorcetes (305–304 BC), Diodorus (20.81) writes the following:

> Rhodes had reached such a peak of power that it took upon its own, on behalf of the Greeks, the war against the pirates and cleared the sea of that scourge . . . The Rhodians, then, by establishing friendship with all the dynasts, kept themselves immune of any justifiable complaint, but their sympathies inclined mostly towards Ptolemy. For it so happened that they derived the majority of their revenues from the merchants sailing to Egypt and that in general their city was sustained by that kingdom [*trephesthai tên polin apo tautês tês basileias*] (trans. Austin 2006: no. 47).

Diodorus' words are echoed in a recently discovered papyrus fragment of a historical work (from the late second or early first century BC) which emphasises the diplomatic support offered by the Rhodians to Ptolemy on his assumption of the title of king (*P.Köln* VI 247, cf. Plut. *Demetr.* 18). In their alliance with Antigonus at the end of the siege (304 BC), the Rhodians added a clause of non-aggression against Egypt (Diod. Sic. 20.99.3), and honoured Ptolemy with the construction of the Ptolemaion and the establishment of a cult bearing the name of the ruler (Diod. Sic. 20.100.3–4).[6] Politically, Hellenistic Rhodes enjoyed a privileged position vis-à-vis the Hellenistic powers: militarily it possessed a first-rate navy, while economically it had won acclaim as an important commercial centre in the eastern Mediterranean. Except for a brief period of political hostilities between them around the mid third century,[7] Rhodes and the Ptolemaic kingdom stayed close friends. A top naval power and also a famed commercial centre had forged a special relationship with one of the greatest Hellenistic monarchies and a major food producer.

'Special' here refers to two features. One is the complementarity existing between the two states, as each provided what the other needed (Fraser 1972: I, 162–9). The other feature is the sheer quantities involved in their

---

[5] Berthold 1984: 33; cf. Hiller von Gaertringen 1931.

[6] Ptolemaion: Filimonos 1989. Cult: Habicht 1970: 109; Hazzard 1992 expresses scepticism about Pausanias' claim (1.8.6) that Ptolemy I received the epiklesis *Sôtêr* at that time. Political relations *c.* 330–304 BC: Hauben 1977; Wiemer 2002: 71–96.

[7] Polyaenus, *Strat.* 5.18 (battle of Ephesus); *I.Lindos* no. 2 2 C.XXXVII (war between Rhodes and Ptolemy II Philadelphus). The date and causes are unknown, cf. Wiemer 2002: 98–101.

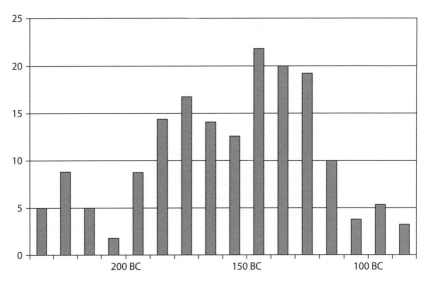

Figure 4.1 Chronological distribution of Rhodian amphora handles in Alexandria (published material), after Lund 2011: 289

commercial exchanges, which are exemplified by the thousands of tons of Egyptian grain shipped to Rhodes, and by the thousands of Rhodian ceramic containers, the amphorae, that came by ship to Alexandria and other Egyptian locales.[8] These privately organised, day-to-day exchanges were sometimes supplemented by lavish royal gifts of money, naval materials and especially grain. During Demetrius' siege (305–304 BC) Ptolemy sent about 600,000 artabas, or 17.5 million litres, of grain (Diod. Sic. 20.88.9, 96.1, 98.1, with 99.2). Again, in 227/226, when Rhodes was hit by a catastrophic earthquake, Ptolemy III Euergetes was one of the rulers who rushed to help Rhodes. He donated 1 million artabas of grain, accompanied by two further consignments of 12,000 and 20,000 artabas each, i.e. a total of some 30 million litres of grain, one of the largest shipments known from the ancient world (Polyb. 5.88.1–90.4). The movement of goods from Rhodes to Egypt and the quantities involved can also be illustrated by modern statistics relating to the chronological distribution of Rhodian amphorae. A recent estimate, which is based on *published* material from Alexandria only, shows that Alexandrian imports of Rhodian amphorae

---

[8] Grain trade: Casson 1954; Bresson 2007, 2008. Rhodian amphorae at Alexandria: Empereur 1982; Lund 1999.

reach very high levels in the second century, particularly in periods when Rhodian exports to other places seem in decline (Figure 4.1). Egypt and Rhodes remained close and loyal partners.

On this evidence alone, the long stretch of water – 325 sea-miles – between Egypt and Rhodes can justifiably be regarded as one of the 'golden sea routes' of the Mediterranean (Map 4.1).[9] Given the certainty that these commercial exchanges – both the ordinary ones and those triggered by royal donations – were conducted by private economic actors, our sea route was indisputably the source of enormous prosperity as well as a sure indicator of marked economic growth, primarily in the two places it connected, but also amongst their commercial partners. Inevitably, too, that trade route made up – in both a notional and in a physical sense – the lifeline of the relationship between the two states. Emblematic of their nearness is perhaps the fact that the small island right before the entrance to Alexandria's artificial harbour carried the name of Antirrhodos.[10]

Nearly all of this was noted by Rostovtzeff in his 1937 article 'Alexandrien und Rhodos' and by subsequent scholarship.[11] Much less, however, is known about the specific factors – institutional, economic or other – which combined to make this particular sea route an exceptionally profitable one. Accordingly, my aim in this chapter is to treat two interconnected factors, each of which, we shall see, not only made our route a source of prosperity, but also enriched overseas trade at large with a new, more profitable and efficient organisational base. One of these factors is the function of the Rhodes–Alexandria route also as a 'protection route'. The other consists of a significant innovation in the way the Rhodes–Alexandria trade was conducted. Both of these factors relate to one, very crucial constraint of seaborne commerce: the transaction costs of merchants.

THE MERCHANT'S TRANSACTION COSTS

'Transaction costs', as a component of economic analysis, has been revitalised by New Institutional Economics. This treats the character of constraints on economic transactions, constraints that hamper the conduct,

---

[9] Casson 1971: 287, table 3.

[10] Strabo 17.1.9 (C 794). The island of Antirrhodos had a palace and small moles. Strabo says that 'they called it by this name as if it was a rival to Rhodes', but parallels from elsewhere in the Greek world (e.g. Anticythera; cf. also the pair Aradus–Antaradus on the Syrian coast) support an explanation that emphasises connectivity rather than rivalry.

[11] Rostovtzeff 1937; Fraser 1972: I, esp. 160–9; Gabrielsen 1997: 64–84; Wiemer 2002: 25–8, 78–9, 86–8.

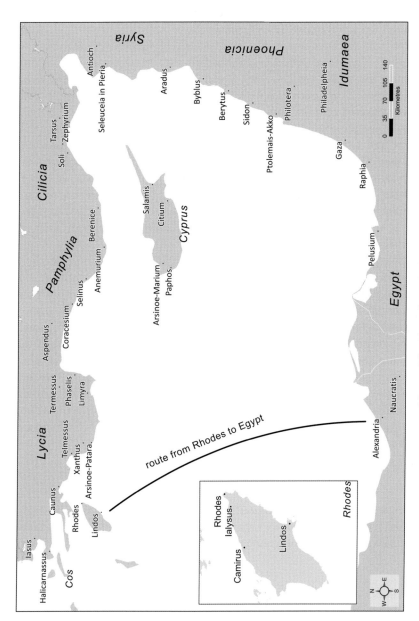

Map 4.1 The Alexandria–Rhodes route

profitability and even the further growth of such transactions; and also the ways in which the impact of these constraints can be minimised or neutralised. Principal variables are, for instance, the ability to obtain timely, cheap and reliable information and to access a system that is able to enforce contracts efficiently. But in reality anything that produces friction, uncertainty and generally extra expense comes under the heading of transaction costs. In discussions of the impact-minimising factors a key role is attributed to institutions, primarily to those of the state, but also to others.[12] Here, it is the expenses directly influencing a trader's expected profits that will receive special attention, particularly two fairly weighty items: (a) the taxes (*telê*) to be paid on entering and exiting the Rhodian and Alexandrian harbours;[13] and (b) the expenses accruing from sea raiding, or piracy. The combined demands of these two items appear to have been so heavy that one wonders whether partaking in the Rhodes–Alexandria trade was a paying proposition at all. I start with the taxes.

One of the taxes to be paid by merchantmen which put in at the harbours of Rhodes was the *ellimenion* (Polyb. 30.31.12). This charge has been understood in different ways. Most scholars identify it with the *pentêkostê*, a 2 per cent charge on the value of the merchandise.[14] However, from a thorough re-examination of the evidence, Véronique Chankowski has questioned this identification. She argues, in my view convincingly, that *ellimenion* (in the singular) refers specifically to the charge paid for using the harbour, i.e. harbour dues, which in some cases, too, was reckoned as a percentage of the value of the goods on board the ship.[15] It thus seems probable that merchants putting in at Rhodes paid both the *pentêkostê* and the *ellimenion* – in Alexandria, as we shall see, the two duties existed side by side. In addition to these, merchants had also to pay a variety of market dues (*agoraia telê*). Before 166 BC, the Rhodian state reportedly earned 1 million drachmas a year from the harbour dues (*ellimenion*) alone; that amount almost certainly relates to the price at which tax farmers (*telônai*) ordinarily bought the right to collect the tax, which means that the sum collected from traders in a year was higher. On this evidence, then, the 'golden sea route' between Rhodes and Egypt was indeed golden, but much more so for the Rhodian treasury and the tax farmers than for the merchant. What about the other end of our sea route, Alexandria and Pelusium?

---

[12] See Frier and Kehoe 2009; and, more generally, Ricketts 2002: esp. chap. 2. [13] Purcell 2005.

[14] Walbank 1957: 459–60; Vélissaropoulos 1980: 218–22; Berthold 1984: 206, n. 28; Gabrielsen 1997: 68–9; Wiemer 2002: 335–6.

[15] Chankowski 2007: esp. 310–19. Evidence from Cimolos suggests that the *ellimenion*, too, could be an *ad valorem* tax of possibly 2 per cent: T. W. Jacobsen and Smith 1968: lines 30–2.

The clearest evidence we possess about the taxes paid by merchants arriving in Egypt is a papyrus from the Zenon archive dated to the year 259 BC. This lists the charges paid at Pelusium for goods imported on two ships, that of Patron and that of Heracleides.[16] Each ship carried a variety of commodities that originated from different places: expensive wines from Chios and Thasos, honey from Theangela, Rhodes and Attica, nuts and fish from the Pontus, a variety of choice meats from elsewhere, etc. The charges paid fall into four kinds. By far the most onerous ones are the customs dues, which, depending on the individual commodity, amount to 20, 25, $33\frac{1}{3}$ and finally 50 per cent of the value of the goods. The $33\frac{1}{3}$ per cent is, for instance, paid on olive oil, while on wine the charge is 50 per cent. Claire Préaux noted long ago that these are the highest rates known from the entire ancient Mediterranean world.[17] The remaining kinds of taxes paid on imported goods consist of a lesser amount ($1\frac{1}{2}$ obol) for the upkeep of the navy (*triêrarchêma*); a transport tax for moving the goods from Pelusium inland (*diapylion*); and finally, a 1 per cent tax for using the harbour, i.e. what is elsewhere called *ellimenion*.

The total charges paid on the mixed cargoes of these two ships totalled 3,712 drachmas – which exceeds the amount (3,000 drachmas) that fourth-century merchants from Athens usually borrowed in order to *buy* a whole shipload of merchandise (Dem. 35.9–10; [Dem.] 56.6). In the case of an Alexandria-bound ship that carried only wine, a main export of Rhodes and a commodity taxed at 50 per cent at Alexandria, the customs dues would have amounted to about 6,000 drachmas (i.e. double the price of a cargo bought at Athens).[18] Taxes at 3,000 to 6,000 drachmas per ship, depending on the cargo, are indeed substantial. And what we actually have details for might only be half the actual expense. Speaking of Alexandria in Roman times, Strabo (17.1.13 (C 798)) mentions the imposition of both import and export taxes. It is generally supposed that both of these go back to Ptolemaic times.[19] Be that as it may, there is already enough evidence to suggest that

---

[16] *P. Cair. Zen.* I 59012; M. M. Austin 2006: no. 298. The great care given to the collection of customs dues is shown by *P. Tebt.* I 5.22–7; M. M. Austin 2006: no. 290. See further Préaux 1939: 372–9; Orrieux 1983: 56–8.

[17] Préaux 1939: 375, cf. Orrieux 1983: 58; Bresson 2002.

[18] My calculation is based on the following: (1) the Serçe Liman wreck from Hellenistic times is reported to have carried 1,000 amphorae from Cnidus: Bass 2005; note also that the newly discovered shipwreck off Cyprus seems to have been able to carry 800–900 amphorae: www.reuters.com/article/lifestyleMolt/idUSL3090532320080530; A. Wilson 2011: 214–15, table 14.1; (2) in the Pelusium customs document the most expensive wines are valued at 18–20 drachmas per amphora, the cheapest ones at 3 drachmas per amphora and those in between at 12 drachmas per amphora. A ship carrying 1,000 amphorae of medium-quality wine (12 drachmas per amphora) would thus be worth 12,000 drachmas, 50 per cent of which is 6,000 drachmas or 1 talent.

[19] Préaux 1939: 77, 372: Fraser 1972: I, 150, with nn. 151–2.

our 'golden sea route' made a considerable contribution to the Ptolemaic treasury but put a heavy strain on the purse of the merchant. To sum up, the ports of Rhodes and Alexandria were, in fiscal terms, prohibitively expensive. They both were meant to feed some very demanding public treasuries.

On top of all this came the charges demanded by the unofficial – but heavily armed – tax claimer, the sea raider. It is perhaps an irony of history that the pirate should experience a revival in our own day, harassing trade along the Somali waters and putting powerful states (and shipping companies) in a very awkward position. Here, I shall not go into details about the *modus operandi* of this figure in antiquity, especially since this is the subject of Lucia Criscuolo's chapter (10) in this volume. I shall merely note three things. First, that in his business the proceeds from extortion often exceeded the profits from selling a catch: families and cities preferred to ransom their own people at prices higher than the going market rates for slaves. Secondly, that even though the pirate was to be found almost everywhere, his preferred hangout was heavily trafficked routes such as our 'golden sea route'. And thirdly, that precisely on the Rhodes–Alexandria leg the pressures generated by the seaborne raider had a western origin, Crete, as well as an eastern origin, primarily Cilicia, Pamphylia and sometimes Cyprus too (Strabo 14.5.2 (C 669)).[20] It is impossible to say exactly how expensive the merchant's meeting with the pirate could become: a merchantman from Naucratis heading for Caria had to surrender cargo worth 57,000 drachmas to its captor on the high seas, actually an Athenian naval vessel acting unofficially (Dem. 24.11–12), though others could certainly get off with less than that. Yet there is no doubt that when added to the economic demands of the official tax claimers such extra costs would make the merchant's budget explode.

To sum up, we are apparently faced with a paradox. With such high transaction costs, imposed by taxes and sea raiding, one would have expected the merchants to abandon the Rhodes–Alexandria run for more profitable routes, with a decline in the trade between the two states as the unavoidable result. However, our written and archaeological sources make it crystal clear that that was *not* the case. Why? In the remainder of this chapter, I shall briefly suggest two complementary answers to this question.

THE PROTECTION ROUTE

The first answer is that, primarily thanks to the services provided by the Rhodian navy, the merchant could make the Rhodes–Alexandria voyage

---

[20] De Souza 1999; Gabrielsen 2003.

relatively safe from intercepting pirates and so at substantially reduced transaction costs. As a major naval power, Hellenistic Rhodes had surpassed its predecessor, Classical Athens, in an important area. Its navy had attained a strong and highly publicised dimension by way of making the offer of protection (*phylakê*) against pirates its main specialism. Diodorus, in the passage cited above (see p. 67), emphasises the fact that Rhodes had taken upon itself the war against the pirates on behalf of the Greeks. Similarly, Strabo (14.2.5 (C 562–3)) praises Rhodes' 'good order' (*eunomia*) and the special care it devotes to naval matters; 'as a result', he says, 'it controlled the seas for a long time and destroyed piracy'.

Emblematic of Rhodes' specialism in providing protection is her possession of a dedicated class of exceptionally fast-sailing craft known as 'protection ships' (*phylakides nêes*).[21] In this area, the complementarity between Egypt and Rhodes is neatly illustrated by the fact that the Ptolemies had their own *phylakides* to police, not the Aegean but the Nile (see Kruse, Chapter 11 in this volume).[22] In 306 BC, when merchantmen carrying grain from Egypt to Rhodes were about to be intercepted by Antigonus' warships, they were rescued by a squadron of Rhodian ships, no doubt *phylakides*, which 'happened' to be on the spot (Diod. Sic. 20.82.2; for the tactics, see also Lycurg. *Leoc.* 18). By that time, it seems, the Rhodian protection system was already operative on the Alexandria–Rhodes route. The lavish donations by Hellenistic rulers to Rhodes after the earthquake of 227/226 BC ought to be seen in this light as well: all givers were interested in maintaining Rhodes' ability to provide its *phylakê* services at sea. Accordingly, their donations consisted of cash, grain and naval materials. Ptolemy III Euergetes was, of course, the biggest giver of all (Polyb. 5.88–90).

From about 200 BC, the Rhodians expanded the infrastructure of their protection system with the acquisition of naval bases in eastern

---

[21] Diod. Sic. 20.93.5 (304 BC): ἐκπλευσάντων δὲ τούτων καὶ τριχῇ διαιρεθέντων Δαμόφιλος μὲν ἔχων ναῦς τὰς καλουμένας παρὰ Ῥοδίων φυλακίδας ἔπλευσεν εἰς Κάρπαθον καὶ πολλὰ μὲν πλοῖα τῶν Δημητρίου καταλαβών (And after these [sc. nine ships] had sailed out and had been divided in groups of three, Damophilus, who had in his charge ships of the kind called by the Rhodians 'protection ships', sailed to Carpathos and seized many of Demetrius' ships). See also Segrè 1932: 452 (Rhodian decree, mid third century BC): Rhodian force of *phylakides* stationed at Aegila/Aegilia (mod. Anticythera); *Syll.*³ 1225 (= Segrè 1932: 459): Rhodian *phylakides* fighting Tyrrhenian pirates, cf. *I.Lindos* no. 88; *IG* XI.4 751 ll. 3–16; Ael. Arist. *Or.* 25 (43).4; *IG* XII.1 45 (Rhodes, first century BC?). Cf. Robert 1946; Gabrielsen 1997: 43–5, 108–11.

[22] *UPZ* I 110, col. I, 20–31 (of 164 BC). I thank Thomas Kruse for drawing my attention to this piece of evidence. Moreover, *trihêmioliai*, a Rhodian invention (Robert 1946: 126), were also used in the Ptolemaic navy: *UPZ* II 151.1–4 (259 BC), *P.Hamb.* 58 (160 BC), cf. Kruse 2011. On the degree of naval complementarity between Ptolemaic Egypt and Rhodes, cf. also Buraselis, Chapter 6 in this volume.

Crete.[23] The crucial document here is the treaty with Hierapytna (*Syll.*[3] 581; *IC* I vii.1). But we know that at about the same time almost identical treaties, seeking to ensure the same kind of military advantages for the Rhodians, were struck with Olus and Chersonesus.[24] All this evidence suggests the conception and pursuance by the Rhodians of a larger plan, whose aim was to enhance considerably their radius of action and striking capabilities along the westward swathe of the Rhodes–Alexandria route, and probably on the eastward one as well. Essentially, the Cretan signatories came under an obligation to put their cities, manpower, harbours and naval bases at the disposal of Rhodes; and also to cooperate with the Rhodians in regularly organised anti-pirate campaigns. Inasmuch as Hierapytna, Olus and Chersonesus previously counted amongst those who had made it their business to harass shipping on the Rhodes–Alexandria route,[25] they were now obliged by treaty to use their naval resources for the furtherance of the Rhodian-led protection business. And, it may be remembered, it was allegedly assaults on the shipping by Cretan pirates that prompted Rhodes to start the Second Cretan War in 155 BC.[26] Merchants working the Rhodes–Alexandria route were the prime beneficiaries of the protection services offered by the Rhodians. This seems to be the meaning of Diodorus' statement that the Rhodians *katharan parechesthai tôn kakourgôn tên thalattan* (literally, 'provided the sea [sc. to seafarers] clear of evil-doers') (20.81.3).

What it meant for the sea trader to be shuttled back and forth by a major naval power is demonstrated also by fourth-century Athenian evidence. Sometimes, Athenian warships convoyed merchantmen sailing from the Black Sea to the Piraeus and other Aegean destinations. Hieron, a place right at the northern entrance to the Black Sea straits, functioned as the point of rendezvous at which the Athenian naval squadrons picked up the merchantmen in order to escort them through the straits and thence to the Aegean.[27] In 325/324 BC, a new such point was established somewhere

---

[23] The last concrete indication of the Ptolemaic presence in Itanus, *IC* III iv.14, is agreed to date from the reign of Epiphanes, but the approximate date of a withdrawal from Crete is difficult to establish. Bagnall (1976: 122) proposes between 195 and 165, roughly.

[24] Rhodes and Olus: *SEG* 23.547. Rhodes and Chersonesus: Chaniotis 1991. In addition, *IC* I xvi.35 attests to the presence of a Rhodian naval squadron in Lato probably in the early second century BC: Gabrielsen 1997: 54–5.

[25] See Chaniotis 2005: 132.

[26] Polyb. 33.4 (with Diod. Sic. 31.37–8, 43–5) and 33.15.3–4; Trog. *Prol.* 35; possibly also *I.Lindos* cols. 1007–9 (inscription from Carpathos), lines 11–14. *Pace* Berthold (1984: 223) and Brulé (1978: 63–4), pirate raids may have been mentioned (by the Rhodians) as one of the formal causes of the war: see Gabrielsen 1997: 55–6; similar conclusion in Wiemer 2002: 351.

[27] Moreno 2008; Gabrielsen 2007.

in the Adriatic.[28] Whenever this system was at work, the leg from and to Hieron, like certain other routes, was also a 'protection route'. At other times, however, no such services were provided to the merchant by the state. The Athenian Grain Tax Law of 374/373 BC, for instance, specifies that any merchant who wishes to convey grain from Scyros, Lemnos and Imbros to Athens is to do so 'at his own risk' (*kindynôi tôi heauto*).[29] In reality, this meant 'at his own expense', since on that occasion the merchant had to pay from his own means any extra costs likely to accrue from his meeting with pirates.

As Classical Athens' heir in the field of sea power, Hellenistic Rhodes not only continued the practice of offering *phylakê* at sea, but also refined further her techniques in that area through organisational, infrastructural and tactical improvements – the latter, as we have seen, having a clear rub-off effect on Ptolemaic policing of the Nile. Rhodian 'protection ships' (*phylakides nêes*) operated along our seaway already in 306–304 BC (Diod. Sic. 20.93.5, with 20.82.2), but their function may go back at least to the 330s.[30] So from the later fourth century, our 'golden sea route' seems to have been a 'transaction-costs protected' route, since one of the most pre-eminent naval powers of the Hellenistic world worked actively towards keeping the Rhodes–Alexandria merchant unburdened by pirates. The Ptolemies, for their part, cost-protected merchants in their own way. Included in the lavish gifts of Ptolemy III to Rhodes in 227 (see p. 68 above) were 300 talents in silver coinage and 1,000 talents in bronze coinage (Polyb. 5.89.1). To assess the real value of this one must take into account the fact that Egypt was a closed monetary zone; on entering it foreign traders normally had to exchange their own currencies with local coins of an often lesser intrinsic (i.e. metal) value, a fiscal device that benefited the crown but meant some economic loss for the trader. Thus by adding coinage to his gifts, particularly the bronze issues that were common in day-to-day transactions, Ptolemy III was sparing traders operating from Rhodes an extra expense. This, in sum, is one of the reasons traders, in spite of the high taxes, still showed a strong preference for the Rhodes–Alexandria route.

---

[28] *IG* II² 1629 (of 325/324 BC) ll. 165–278, esp. 217–30, with Gabrielsen 2007: 307.

[29] Stroud 1998: lines 10–11.

[30] Lycurg. *Leoc.* 18: οὕτω δὲ σφόδρα ταῦτ᾽ ἐπίστευσαν οἱ Ῥόδιοι ὥστε τριήρεις πληρώσαντες τὰ πλοῖα κατῆγον, καὶ τῶν ἐμπόρων καὶ τῶν ναυκλήρων οἱ παρεσκευασμένοι δεῦρο πλεῖν αὐτοῦ τὸν σῖτον ἐξείλοντο καὶ τἄλλα χρήματα διὰ τοῦτον (The Rhodians placed so much faith in his [sc. Leocrates'] news that they manned *triêreis* and forced the merchant ships into [the Rhodian] harbour; and the merchants and shipowners who had arranged for their bottoms to sail here [to Athens], unloaded their grain there [sc. at Rhodes], and their other merchandise too) (author's trans).

THE MODALITIES OF SEA TRADE: A FOURTH-CENTURY INNOVATION

Perhaps even more important is the other reason, which seems to have resulted from innovative thinking about how sea trade could be conducted in a more profitable way. A basic asset exploited here was Rhodes' favourable geographical position in relation to Alexandria.

Several sources report that towards the late 330s to early 320s merchants of different nationalities began coming to Rhodes, whence, to quote Lycurgus, they 'sailed for trade all over the inhabited earth'.[31] A good number of these merchants took care of the trade with Egypt. Two factors especially had attracted them to settle at Rhodes and to work the Rhodes–Alexandria route.

First of all, not only could merchant ships make the Rhodes–Alexandria run in only three and a half days,[32] but this route, in contrast to most others, was open to shipping all year round ([*Dem.*] 56.30), a factor that increased Rhodes' commercial nearness to a major supplier of grain. This had a positive chain effect: (a) suppliers of the high-interest-yielding maritime loans were able to put the same amount of money to work two or three times a year (*ibid.*); (b) Rhodes-based merchants were offered relatively cheap credit;[33] and, as a consequence, (c) they were able to undertake more return voyages within a year than those who worked other routes. In combination, these features offset markedly the heavy taxes at the Rhodian *emporion*, thus increasing the margin of the merchant's net profit. So, exploitation of the favourable geography and climatic factors had the result of enhancing Rhodes' renown as a major trading centre and with it the renown of our route as a profitable one. One can only agree with M. Rostovtzeff and C. Préaux that still in the mid third century Rhodes, not Alexandria, was the great entrepôt in the trade with Phoenicia, Syria, Asia Minor and Greece.[34]

Secondly, it appears that around 325 BC Rhodes was becoming widely known as an attractive trading centre because a new, more successful way of organising trading was getting off the ground there. Everywhere, the

---

[31] Lycurg. *Leoc.* 15: πρός τε τὴν πόλιν τὴν τῶν Ῥοδίων, καὶ τῶν ἐμπόρων τοῖς ἐπιδημοῦσιν ἐκεῖ, οἳ πᾶσαν τὴν οἰκουμένην περιπλέοντες δι' ἐργασίαν (both to the city-state of Rhodes and to those merchants who have taken residence there; merchants who sail around the inhabited word for trade). See also Polyaenus, *Strat.* 4.6.16 (Rhodian merchants in the ports of Syria, Phoenicia, Cilicia and Pamphylia in 305 BC).

[32] Casson 1971: 287, with n. 76.

[33] [*Dem.*] 56.12: the rate of interest demanded for the Egypt–Rhodes voyage (τοὺς εἰς Ῥόδον τόκους) is lower than that which lender and borrowers have agreed on for the Piraeus–Egypt voyage (τοὺς μὲν τόκους τοὺς ἐν τῇ συγγραφῇ γεγραμμένους).

[34] Rostovtzeff 1937: 76; Préaux 1939: 378.

prevailing mode had hitherto been represented by the pedlar (*emporos*) who, alone or with a partner (*koinônos*), purchased his merchandise at one *emporion* to sell it at another *emporion*, and then to bring a return cargo to his port of origin. This type of merchant persisted. But by the early 320s he had attained a rival who operated in a different way and who, by virtue of this, turned the profession into a much less uncertain and considerably more profitable business. Having established himself at Rhodes, this new type attracted many others there.

Parmeniscus, a grain merchant from Athens and partner to one Dionysodorus, was obliged by contract to make the round trip Athens–Egypt–Athens. What he did, instead, is detailed by [Dem.] 56 (*Against Dionysodorus*). On his way back from Egypt, Parmeniscus put in at Rhodes, sold the shipment of grain there – thus breaching his contract – and decided to make Rhodes the base of his commercial operations. In addition to moving goods between Egypt and Rhodes, he set himself up as a supplier of maritime loans (17). More importantly, Parmeniscus now did business as a member of a larger group of associates.

The activities of that group are reported by Pseudo-Aristotle's *Oeconomica* and by [Dem.] 56 (*Against Dionysodorus*). Headed by Cleomenes of Naucratis, Alexander's governor in Egypt, this allegedly mafia-like network speculated on the price of grain.[35] Briefly, it operated in the following manner. Cleomenes was amassing and monopolising Egyptian grain. Then, (a) some of his associates would dispatch the grain from Egypt; (b) others would sail in charge of the shipments to a few select destinations, a main one being Rhodes; (c) still others, who were posted at these commercial centres, would receive the shipments and then redistribute them to further destinations; and finally, (d), yet another group of associates, who were dispersed abroad, would send letters with information about at which *emporia* grain was being sold at the highest price so that it could be shipped there. We should note that, rather than being formed by a principal and his agents, the network consisted of a functionally differentiated group of 'collaborators' (*synergoi*).[36] Moreover, communications between them were conducted through letters (*epistolai, grammata*), which was not unusual for traders ([Dem.] 56.10), even though sometimes messengers might be used (9).[37] By entering this network, Parmeniscus not only exchanged Athens

[35] Arist. [*Oec.*] II, 33a, 1352a 16–23, 33b, 1352b 15–19; [Dem.] 56.7–8.
[36] At [Dem.] 56.7, Cleomenes' collaborators are also called *hypêretai*, but this is probably used pejoratively.
[37] Commercial letters: P. J. Wilson 1997–8 (Archaic and Classical lead letters).

for Rhodes, he also exchanged his pedlar status for that of a well-connected business associate.

Ancient commentators regard the way Cleomenes' network operated as morally questionable, to which modern scholars add that it was also highly exceptional.[38] Both opinions are misleading, if relevant at all. For one thing, merchants are not put on earth to defend the high moral ground, nor do powerholders – whether Cleomenes or others – always follow the prescriptions of their own ideology, especially its derogatory view of commerce.[39] For another, this way of doing business does not seem exceptional in the post-Alexander period. The basic pattern – i.e. close collaboration between *dispatchers*, *redistributors* and *recipients* of shipments – re-emerges in a papyrus from the Zenon archive, dated to about 258 BC. This text informs us that goods sent from Sidon (in Phoenicia) to Apollonius the *dioikêtês* and his people have arrived in Egypt, not via the direct route along the Phoenician and Palestinian coast, but via Rhodes.[40] The *dispatcher* of goods, which include gifts to Apollonius, is one Abdemoun of Sidon. The one who took care of the *re-shipment* of the goods from Rhodes is Abdemoun's brother, who carries the Greek name Zenon. Finally, those *receiving* the shipment at Alexandria are Apollonius and his staff.

Corroborative evidence for the same pattern seems to be provided by a fairly large number of inscribed sherds (*ostraca*) that have been found in a single tomb in the south-western sector of the necropolis of Rhodes, and which are preliminarily dated to the later second–early first century BC. They appear to be letters addressed to the 'master' (*kyrios*) or the 'masters' (*kyrioi*) of agricultural establishments, and they contain lists of agricultural produce.[41] Definite conclusions must await the proper publication of this material. But it seems probable that the letters are purchase orders sent to merchants or producers at Rhodes by their overseas business associates (*synergoi*, *koinônoi*). If so, they, too, hint at the conduct of commercial operations by geographically dispersed networks of business associates whose centre of operations was Rhodes. Two general points are indicated by this evidence.

---

[38] Van Groningen 1933: 183–93; Bresson 2000: 286; cf. Le Rider 1997. Moreno (2007: 231–3, 297–8) brings out nicely the ways in which [Dem.] 56 depicts Cleomenes' network as a highly immoral enterprise.

[39] Examples in Gabrielsen 2011.

[40] *P.Ryl.* IV 554: ἥκει σοι μετὰ τῶν / Ἀπολλωνίου ξενίων / παρὰ Ἀβδημοὺν Σιδωνίου / ἃ ἀπέστειλεν Ζήνων / ὁ ἀδελφὸς αὐτοῦ ἐγ Ῥόδου / ὧν τὰ τέλη καταβέβληκε Ἀριστεύς. Cf. Rostovtzeff 1937; Fraser 1972: I, 168, with n. 287.

[41] Gabrielsen 1997: 107. My warmest thanks to Drs Anastasia Dreliossi-Herakleidou and I. Chr. Papachristodoulou for kind permission to mention this invaluable but as yet unpublished material.

The first concerns the overly pessimistic view of modern scholarship on the transmission of information regarding prices and other trade-related matters, and consequently on the degree of integration characteristic of ancient markets. Our evidence shows pessimism to be rather exaggerated, if warranted at all – typically, it one-sidedly underlines the constraints themselves, at the expense of an enquiry into how economic actors might try to overcome these constraints. Two examples will suffice. Money-lenders at Athens are shown to have been perfectly able to receive from abroad, timely and efficiently, information that was absolutely crucial for determining the rate of interest payable by merchants trading in the Black Sea.[42] Moreover, it looks very much as if a system capable of transmitting information widely was available to merchants even before *c.* 330 BC (e.g. Xen. *Oec.* 20.27–8). Business networks, as the case of Cleomenes attests, brought further improvement in this area. Speed, which is the variable emphasised by the pessimists, did indeed make information a costly commodity. But the variable (so far a neglected one) that heightened considerably the quality of information, making it even more costly, was reliability. Its prerequisite, trust, is what groups of business associates were able to generate, share and disseminate over a wider area. The more trust in circulation, the higher the quality of information, and so the lesser its cost amongst those who share it. Such trust-spreading synergies tended to render markets less imperfect and more integrated.

The second point is that, in contrast to the pedlar, this novel way of trading through networks of merchants and informants, dispatchers and receivers, offered two significant advantages. One was that a particular cargo could leave its place of origin and reach the foreign importer without being broken up into smaller portions. The latter is, for instance, precisely what Parmeniscus did while still a mere pedlar: he unloaded the Egyptian grain at Rhodes and then sent the remaining merchandise to Piraeus in separate consignments carried by several chartered ships ([Dem.] 56.21, 24). But that was not the most profitable way of conducting trade. For, as an ancient author writes, merchants find it advantageous to sell their cargoes whole (*athroa ta phortia peprasthai*) at one place without breaking bulk (*mê kotylizein*: Arist. (*Oec.*) II, 2, 8 1347b 7–9).

The other advantage was that the cargo had a *named addressee* or *addressees* to receive it at its final destination. In most – if not all – such cases, the merchandise had already been bought and probably also paid for either at the port of origin or at the port of reshipment – in our case,

---

[42] Dem. 35.10, with Gabrielsen 2007: 304.

Rhodes. If our Rhodian *ostraca* are indeed purchase orders, they would tend to confirm this pattern as well. Now, a particular feature of almost all the surviving customs duty documents from Ptolemaic Egypt is that the goods imported are cleared through customs by the *importer and named addressee* of these goods himself (who sometimes also pays for the freight), rather than by the merchants who bring them to Alexandria. This is, for instance, the case with the two ships captained by Patron and Heracleides, and also with the goods sent by Abdemoun to Apollonius and his staff (*hôn ta telê katabeblêke Aristeus*: see p. 79 above). The same practice, moreover, is seen in another papyrus from the Zenon archive, which concerns a shipment of goods (including oil in Samian and Milesian jars) imported by Apollonius. It records the nominal value of the goods after payment by the importer of customs duty, freight and some other taxes.[43] Thus, in reality, the merchant putting in at Ptolemaic Egypt was wholly exempt from the heavy taxes usually demanded, provided of course that he was one of those well-connected businessmen who conveyed goods to specific importers, and not a pedlar who brought his merchandise for sale in the Alexandrian *emporion*.[44]

I conclude my brief treatment of the connections between Rhodes and Alexandria with two remarks. First, such partnerships as those discussed above seem to have challenged existing norms, since they transgressed almost every single boundary we know of. For instance, the ethno-cultural boundary marked by the Abdemoun–Zenon pair of brothers; or the social and juridical chasm separating Cleomenes – a top member of the new Greek aristocracy – and Parmeniscus, probably only an Athenian metic. Secondly, Cleomenes' network makes widely endorsed dichotomies break down. Here, the command economy and the market economy do not battle each other but cooperate, inasmuch as powerholder and professional merchants are united as collaborators in a single economic expedient. Furthermore, any attempt to dissociate these individuals from the group of dependable, upright and honest businessmen, putting them into the supposedly aberrant group of unscrupulous kleptocrats – tight-fisted practitioners of *chrêmatistikê* – would be totally misguided. They were simply both things at the same time.

[43] *P.Cair.Zen.* I 59015 recto.
[44] Strabo 17.1.9 (C 794). Fraser 1972: I, 24–5: 'The place at which goods imported from abroad were checked and subjected to customs dues, and was no doubt also a general centre for trading in merchandise, as at Athens', with n. 165: *P.Tebt.* I 5.33–5: ὁμοίως δὲ περὶ τῶν εἰσαγόντων διὰ τοῦ ξενικοῦ ἐμπορίου.

CHAPTER 5

Polybius and Ptolemaic sea power

Andrew Erskine

The Ptolemies feature quite prominently in Polybius' history, prominently at least for a state that never went to war with Rome. The Achaean historian recounts, among other things, the Fourth Syrian War and the battle of Raphia, the turmoil in Alexandria at the death of Ptolemy IV, Antiochus IV's invasion of Egypt and the dynastic quarrels of the Ptolemies in the mid second century. But, to be blunt, he does not have a lot to say about Ptolemaic sea power. When F. W. Walbank wrote his fundamental essay on Antigonid sea power he was able to draw heavily on Polybius, but one would be hard-pushed to do the same for the Ptolemies.[1] There is little in Polybius that would lead anyone to think that Ptolemaic Egypt had once been the dominant naval power in the eastern Mediterranean. Only one chapter suggests otherwise, and that chapter will be the starting-point for my discussion here.

Nonetheless, Ptolemaic sea power is taken for granted by most scholars writing on Egypt in the first half of the third century BC; terms such as 'thalassocracy' and 'maritime empire' are regularly used to define the Ptolemies' relationship with their extensive overseas possessions.[2] Nor is it unreasonable to think that a significant naval presence would have been necessary to sustain all the military and naval bases that were scattered around the eastern Mediterranean and the Aegean. Modern scholars are not alone in attributing significant naval resources to the Ptolemies. The Alexandrian historian Appian, perhaps with a certain patriotic gloss, looks

I am very grateful to Kostas Buraselis and Mary Stefanou, not only for inviting me to such a stimulating conference (see the Preface to this volume) but also for a memorable lunch at the Ptolemaic naval base of Methana. Particular thanks are also owed to Philip de Souza who generously helped me with advice on Hellenistic navies. The writing of the chapter was supported by a Leverhulme Trust Research Fellowship.
[1] Walbank 1982; it is primarily the second half of the essay with its focus on Philip V that draws on Polybius.
[2] For instance, Heinen 1984: 441 (maritime empire); Hauben 1987a: 217 (maritime empire), 225 (thalassocracy); Cohen 1995: 35 (thalassocracy). Ptolemaic thalassocracy in its heyday is the focus of Hauben, Chapter 3 in this volume.

back from the Roman empire to the great days of Egypt under Ptolemy II Philadelphus. Listing the king's military forces, he gives him at least 1,500 warships with fittings for twice that many.[3] This was a considerable military power, although possessing a fleet is not in itself sufficient; to be viable, it must be maintained and manned. More cautious modern estimates give Ptolemy II the capacity to launch 400 ships.[4] This is a less dramatic figure but still the largest fleet in the eastern Mediterranean; even this may be a little on the high side.[5]

To some extent the gulf between these two images is chronological, reflecting a contrast between the early and late third century. Scholars often see a weakening in Ptolemaic authority at sea, especially in the Aegean, from around the middle of the century. Support for this is found in the Ptolemies' loss of control over the League of Islanders and defeats in two elusive battles, Andros and Cos, elusive because no one is quite sure when they happened or what their significance was.[6] But the influence of Polybius may also be a factor here. Whereas the Antigonid and Seleucid kingdoms are resurgent at the beginning of his narrative, their Ptolemaic counterpart is about to begin its decline. This interpretation of Ptolemaic history is outlined in book 5 chapter 34, which will be the focus of the first part of this chapter before turning to his evidence for Ptolemaic naval activity in the second part.

STRUCTURING A NARRATIVE OF DECLINE

Polyb. 5.34 is a passage of particular importance for our understanding of the Ptolemies' overseas empire and therefore its power at sea. Here Polybius succinctly analyses the nature of what we might loosely call Ptolemaic

---

[3] App. *Praef.* 10; Morrison and Coates 1996: 37–8. A more poetic appreciation of Ptolemy II's naval power is provided by Theoc. 17.86–92, on which see Hunter 2003: 159–69.

[4] Rauh 2003: 82–3; Préaux 1939: 39–40, who cites Ath. 5.203d for the figure of 400. Athenaeus' text here is a strange mix of precision and hyperbole, and it is not clear where Préaux draws the 400 from; Athenaeus details all the warships from *trihēmioliai* upwards to the number of 336 (based on official figures, argues Van 't Dack 1988: 27), then adds that the number of ships the Ptolemies 'sent to the islands and the other cities over which he ruled was more than 4,000'.

[5] Van 't Dack 1988: 22–34 offers a useful review of the Ptolemaic navy. In addition to their Mediterranean fleet, the Ptolemies also had a smaller number of ships in the Red Sea and operating along the Nile: Van 't Dack and Hauben 1978: esp. 60–4; Kruse (on the Nile fleet), Chapter 11 in this volume.

[6] The issues are nicely summed up by Ager 2003: 44; for the League of Islanders, see Merker 1970; Bagnall 1976: esp. 136–41; and Meadows, Chapter 2 in this volume; for later Ptolemaic involvement in the Cyclades, Reger 1994a; for Andros and Cos, Buraselis 1982: 119–51; Reger 1985; Hammond and Walbank 1988: 587–600, with bibliography and a list of proposed dates at 599–600.

foreign policy in the eastern Mediterranean.[7] This passage occurs in the
context of the accession of Ptolemy IV Philopator in 221 BC. This king,
says Polybius, thought that with no rivals at court and with new, young
kings on the Seleucid and Antigonid thrones he had nothing to fear either
at home or abroad. As a result:

he showed himself to be inattentive and unpleasant in his relations with those
at court and with those who administered matters within Egypt and he treated
with contempt or indifference those in charge of affairs abroad, to which his
predecessors had devoted even more attention than they had to the administration
of Egypt itself. As a result they used to threaten the kings of Syria by both land
and sea, since they controlled Coele Syria and Cyprus. At the same time they
put pressure on the minor rulers in Asia and on the islands, as they were masters
of the chief cities, places and harbours along the whole coast from Pamphylia to
the Hellespont and the region around Lysimachea. Furthermore, they kept watch
over the situation in Thrace and in Macedon through their occupancy of Aenus,
Maronea and other cities even further afield. In this way, with such a long reach
and such a far-flung system of client states to protect them, they never worried
about their rule in Egypt. For this reason they naturally gave great attention to
foreign affairs.

Polybius thus tells us that the Ptolemaic kings had extensive possessions
outside Egypt, and as a result they were able to keep their Egyptian territory
secure. It is an impressive range of overseas territories: Cyprus and Coele
Syria relatively close at hand, then the islands of the Aegean and the coast of
Asia Minor reaching as far as the Hellespont, and with Maronea and Aenus
on the north coast of the Aegean pressing right up against the Antigonid
kingdom.[8] All these possessions are presented as a kind of defensive shield,
notwithstanding how they may have been acquired.[9] This, at least, was
the case until the accession of Ptolemy IV Philopator, who neglected the
interests of the state in favour of sex and alcohol – or so says Polybius
anyway.

This passage is the starting-point for many discussions of Ptolemaic
policy outside Egypt. Polybius' defensive interpretation is variously questioned, supported or rejected. Perhaps, some suggest, Polybius is imposing
a second-century understanding on third-century material, in other words
that is how it was in the second century BC but Ptolemaic Egypt was much

---

[7] For the use of the phrase 'Ptolemaic foreign policy' here, see the cautionary remarks of Marquaille
2008: 39–42.
[8] For a good sense of how extensive the Ptolemies' possessions overseas were, see Bagnall 1976. Ma
1999: 39–43 gives a vivid picture of the depth of their holdings in Asia Minor, while Hauben 1987a
is a fundamental study of the importance of Cyprus to the Ptolemies.
[9] For Pédech 1964: 551–2, Polybius conceives their aim as 'à la fois offensif et défensif'.

more aggressive earlier.[10] Or the Ptolemies are credited with a policy of defensive imperialism, extending their rule but with a view to improving their own security.[11] Others question whether Polybius is right to pinpoint Philopator's reign as a time of decline. Ptolemaic possessions at the end of his reign, it is argued, are not much different from what they were at the beginning.[12] Polybius provides a useful outline of the Ptolemaic empire in the third century, but, as these differing opinions suggest, we are not obliged to accept his interpretation.

It may be that all that can be said about this much-discussed chapter of Polybius has been said, but here I want to try what I hope is a new direction. What I think has not been done, or at least not sufficiently, is to place this passage explaining Ptolemaic policy fully within the context of Polybius' history, in particular within his treatment of the Ptolemies more generally. Discussion tends to separate the chapter from the narrative and treat it in isolation, concentrating on it as a statement about Ptolemaic overseas strategy. Yet, for once, we have a passage of Polybius which is not a fragment, so there is a context in which to interpret it. Moreover, Polybius was a historian who took great care over how he shaped his narrative, producing 'a narrative of carefully contrived design', as Brian McGing has put it.[13] The aim of this part of my chapter, then, is to consider the chapter's place and significance in the Polybian narrative. Once the chapter is understood in its broader context it will be seen that Polybius offers a deeper and more nuanced interpretation of later Ptolemaic history than is often assumed.[14]

Polybius' analysis of Ptolemaic foreign policy occurs as part of the prelude to his account of the Fourth Syrian War (219–217 BC), which he describes as the war between Antiochus and Ptolemy for Coele Syria. He is concerned to lay out what is happening throughout the world in the 140th Olympiad (220–216 BC), the period when the affairs of the inhabited world start to come together and which marks the beginning of his history proper, an account of the fifty-three years in which the Romans came to world empire.

---

[10] Bekker-Nielsen 2004: 50–1 ('anachronistic').

[11] Ed. Will 1979: 153–208, with Polybius' position termed 'impérialisme défensif' (160); Hölbl 2001: 28 ('a kind of defensive imperialism'). Diod. Sic. 18.43.1 offers a similar interpretation of Ptolemy I's seizure of Coele Syria.

[12] Huß 1976; Bagnall 1976, to be read with 214, n. 1. Turner 1984: 159 takes it further back and blames Philadelphus. Will 1979: 207–8 accepts the contrast between the first three Ptolemies and Philopator but explains Philopator's neglect as also prompted by a feeling of inviolability that had developed under his predecessors.

[13] McGing 2010: 95–128 examines the narrative of books 4 and 5 (quote from 96). For a more general narratological account of Polybius, Rood 2004.

[14] Contrast Walbank 1979b: 183–6, especially his criticism of Polybius' treatment at 185.

After covering events in Europe he moves on to Asia and the Fourth Syrian War.[15] But Polybius, being Polybius, does not want to start with this. It is necessary, he says, to go back to the beginning, which is the beginning of the reign of each king. It is not, however, simply for narrative completeness that he does this, for he stresses at some length the importance of beginnings for the understanding of the whole. In making this point he seems to have in mind not merely that the historian should pay attention to beginnings in understanding what happened but that the readers of history should pay particular attention to how historians open their narrative. Here is what he writes:

For the ancients, by saying that the beginning is half of the whole, were advising that in every matter one should take the greatest care to make a good beginning. Although they may seem to be exaggerating, it appears to me that this falls short of the truth. For one may confidently say that the beginning is not half of the whole but even reaches to the end. For how can one begin something well without grasping in one's mind the conclusion of the project and without knowing where, with reference to what and for what object the task is being undertaken? Furthermore, how can one sum up events satisfactorily without referring to the beginning, and indicating from where, in what way and for what reason things ended up as they did? Therefore thinking that beginnings reach not to the middle but to the end, those writing or reading about things in their entirety should pay the greatest attention to them. This is something that I will now try to do.[16]

I have given this passage at length (in spite of its rather rambling quality) because it comes almost immediately before his account of the beginning of the reign of Ptolemy IV Philopator and signals that what he is about to say there has far-reaching significance. Clearly he feels it is important for understanding Philopator's reign, but whether it is also important for the subsequent history of the Ptolemies is something that must be considered. Beforehand, however, it is necessary to examine Polybius' treatment of the reign of Philopator.

The two protagonists in the Fourth Syrian War, one Ptolemaic, the other Seleucid, came to power within two years of each other, Ptolemy IV in 221 BC and Antiochus III not long before in 223 BC. Yet it is Ptolemy that Polybius begins with. His account of Philopator opens with the famous chapter on Ptolemaic overseas possessions, noting the new king's neglect

---

[15] Polyb. 5.30.8–31.1.
[16] Polyb. 5.32, a chapter that has been rather neglected; it is treated very briefly by Walbank 1957: 562–3, who notes only the proverb that opens it, while Pédech 1964, whose subject is Polybius' historical method, surprisingly appears to have almost nothing to say about it (37). For the importance of beginnings to Polybius, see Derow 1994.

of them in contrast to his predecessors; then it moves on to treat two conspiracies, one by the Spartan Cleomenes and a second by the Aetolian Theodotus, but the controlling presence is not the king but his adviser Sosibius.[17] In the case of Antiochus it is different; there is no analogous account of Seleucid territories, but Antiochus too is faced with men who do not recognise his authority, a satrap in revolt, and a devious and malign adviser, Hermeias. Antiochus, however, exerts his power and takes control. Molon's revolt is crushed, and Hermeias is taken on a casual stroll to some isolated spot and stabbed to death.[18] If we consider the beginnings of these two reigns together, and Polybius clearly structured them so we should, we can say that Ptolemy can assert his authority over neither his territory nor his court, whereas Antiochus can do both.[19]

But that opening passage, 5.34, about Egyptian possessions overseas has a greater significance than this. First, it is noticeable that Polybius stresses defence: these possessions and the maintenance of them are crucial to the security of Egypt, and that is why the Ptolemaic kings paid, as he put it, 'great attention to foreign affairs'. This is rather a questionable interpretation of early Ptolemaic policy, which sidesteps the acquisition of these territories in the first place. In fact, it is an odd explanation for Polybius himself, who is usually not slow in crediting states with expansionist ambitions,[20] but in practice he is not here really concerned about the early Ptolemies. He has very little to say about either the Ptolemies or the Seleucids prior to the accession of these two kings, and, when he does, it is often in the context of later kings using their predecessors to justify claims to territory.[21] His narrative of the Ptolemies begins with Philopator. By highlighting the defensive aspects of the Ptolemaic approach to foreign

[17] Cleomenes: Polyb. 5.35–9; Theodotus: 5.40, 5.61.3–62.3. Sosibius: 5.35–8, 5.63–5, 5.66.8–67.4, 5.87.5. For the events, see Ed. Will 1982: 26–37; Hölbl 2001: 127–9; Errington 2008: 165–8; for Sosibius: Huß 1976: 242–51.
[18] Crushing of Molon: Polyb. 5.51–5; death of Hermeias: 5.56. For the events, see Schmitt 1964: 116–58; Will 1982: 15–23; Errington 2008: 171–3.
[19] For structural similarities (and with the accession of Philip V as well), see Ager 2003: 47–8; McGing 2010: 117 (with 117–18 on Philopator).
[20] Famously Rome: 1.3.6; Philip V and Macedon: 5.102.1 (on which see Walbank 1993), 15.24.6. Eckstein 2008: 145 argues on the basis of 11.34.14–16 (printed as chapter 39 in Loeb Classical Library 2011) that Polybius credited Antiochus III with 'ambitions for unlimited, world-wide rule', but although the passage shows him as ambitious, there is no explicit statement of universal ambition. Interestingly, however, Antiochus' campaigns are interpreted by Polybius here as making safe his kingdom, which might suggest that, had Polybius written a history of the early Ptolemies, he might have used aggression to underpin defence, as for example Errington 2008: 148.
[21] For example, arguments over Coele Syria (5.67, 28.20.6–9) or Thrace (18.51.3–6); Ptolemy III Euergetes does enter the narrative but largely through his involvement with Cleomenes, 2.47.1–2, 51.2, 63, and it is noted that it was he who captured Seleuceia in Pieria, shortly to be lost by his successor, 2.58.10 (see below).

affairs, Polybius draws attention to the failings of a king incapable not only
of expansion but even of protecting what he has. The subject of 5.34 is
really Philopator and only indirectly the early Ptolemies – it is a mistake
therefore to look here for any kind of in-depth treatment of early Ptolemaic
policy. What Polybius does is to choose those aspects of the early Ptolemies
that are most relevant to his interpretation of the failure of Philopator.

Challenges to a state's security can come from outside and from within.
Antiochus III was a very obvious external threat, but it is internal dissent
which Polybius prioritises. Significantly, the discussion of overseas possessions leads directly to the problem of conspiracy, which is raised in the last
sentence of chapter 34:

But the aforementioned king [Philopator] neglected all these matters due to his
unbecoming love affairs and senseless and continuous drunkenness. Unsurprisingly
he soon found that there were a number of plots against both his life and his throne,
the first of which was that of the Spartan Cleomenes.

The conspiracy of the Spartan king Cleomenes is described at length, even
though it does not seem to have had any noticeable impact: Cleomenes and
his supporters had found the Alexandrian people completely indifferent
to their attempts to stir them to revolution.[22] But it does allow for the
analysis of 5.34 to be developed a little further in the following chapter,
5.35. Cleomenes had arrived in Alexandria during the last years of Ptolemy
III Euergetes' reign after his defeat at the hands of the Macedonian ruler
Antigonus Doson. He had hoped that the Ptolemies would sponsor an
expedition back to the Peloponnese so that he could reclaim his throne.
With the accession of Philopator all that changed. Sosibius and his friends
who were, according to Polybius, effectively running the administration felt
it would be unwise to allow Cleomenes to return because his knowledge
of Egypt might enable him to become a threat to Ptolemaic interests.[23]
This may seem implausible, but it is the justification for these fears that is
noteworthy:

With Antigonus now gone and none of those remaining being a match for
Cleomenes, they were worried that he would quickly and easily bring Greece
under his control and so make himself a serious and formidable opponent for
themselves. Not only had he seen for himself the affairs of Egypt and come to
view the king with contempt but he knew that the kingdom had many parts that
were only loosely attached and were far removed from the centre and consequently

[22] Polyb. 5.35–9, Plut. *Cleom.* 31–9; for Cleomenes' career in Sparta, see Cartledge and Spawforth 2002:
48–58; Erskine 1990: 123–49.
[23] Polyb. 5.35.7; for Sosibius and his friends, see Huß 2001: 458–64.

offered plenty of opportunity for revolutionary intrigue. For there were not a few ships at Samos and a substantial force of soldiers at Ephesus.[24]

This offers another perspective on those extensive overseas possessions of the Ptolemies. In chapter 34 a network of bases and clients had relieved the Ptolemaic kings of anxiety that anything might threaten their rule in Egypt, but now in chapter 35 that situation is reversed. It is the far-flung and disparate character of the Ptolemaic empire that makes it vulnerable – it is exactly this that is causing Sosibius anxiety. For Polybius, therefore, Ptolemaic strength is also its weakness. The fleet and naval bases scattered over the eastern Mediterranean gave a strong king control over the islands and coast, and ensured the security of Egypt itself, but their dispersed locations, distant from Egypt, meant that with a less active king they could become focal points for dissent – or be picked off by enemies. The fragmented character of the Ptolemaic empire would have been all the more apparent to Polybius when contrasted with the geographical unity of his own Achaean League, which occupied a substantial part of the Peloponnese.

Cleomenes may have posed no real threat, but others would show that these fears were justified. The first Ptolemaic loss was Seleuceia in Pieria, an isolated Ptolemaic enclave on the Syrian coast, which had been captured in the 240s by Ptolemy III Euergetes during the Third Syrian War. It was now seized by Antiochus III in a coordinated land and sea assault, aided by treachery from within.[25] Shortly afterwards a disgruntled Ptolemaic commander, the Aetolian Theodotus, who was in charge of Coele Syria, would offer to hand the territory over to Antiochus.[26] This allowed the Seleucid king to occupy the important coastal cities of Tyre and Ptolemais along with the ships that were stationed there. Primary among Theodotus' motivations, we are told, was his unhappiness over the behaviour of the king and those close to him. Significantly, too, his betrayal also involves him secretly entering Ptolemy's camp in an attempt to assassinate the king, one of the threats to the king's life that Polybius had alluded to earlier at the end of chapter 34.[27] The territorial losses were to some extent rectified

[24] Polyb. 5.35.9–11. On the Ptolemaic bases at Samos and Ephesus, see Bagnall 1976: 80–8 and 170–1.
[25] Polyb. 5.58–61.2, with treachery at 60.2 and 60.9–10. For its original capture by Euergetes, 5.58.10–11, with Beyer-Rotthoff 1993: 48–54 on its significance for the Ptolemies and Cohen 2006: 126–35 on the history of the city.
[26] Polyb. 5.40.1 describes him as τεταγμένος ἐπὶ Κοίλης Συρίας, but how broadly this should be understood is unclear, Bagnall 1976: 15–16.
[27] Polyb. 5.40.1, 61.3–62.3, 67.9; the assassination attempt is also described in 3 Macc. 1.2–3 but with a different slant, Gera 1998: 13–15. There may be some allusion to Theodotus' betrayal in the demotic

by Ptolemy's victory at Raphia shortly afterwards, which restored Egyptian
authority over Coele Syria.

Chapter 34 introduced two themes, the scattered nature of Ptolemaic
possessions and the tension between the interests of the state and court
life, especially in the depraved form practised by Philopator. These are
developed further in chapter 35 through the example of Cleomenes and
then observed in practice in the attitudes and actions of Theodotus. The
two themes are not unrelated. The dissolute life of Philopator leads not
only to the neglect of the empire abroad but also to the alienation of those
who are best able to defend it. To what extent these themes continue to
underpin Polybius' treatment of later Egyptian history is unclear because
of the fragmented nature of the text after book 6. In contrast to the fullness
of Polybius' treatment of the beginning of Philopator's reign, his extended
account of the king's last years in book 14 is now lost. It covered Philopator's
increasingly dissolute life and included the start of the native Egyptian
revolts, but any information on it is sketchy at best.[28] In what remains of
Ptolemaic history after Philopator's death the court, intrigue and plots do
figure prominently, but that is in part at least because such stories appealed
especially to the later excerptors, familiar as they were with the Byzantine
court; indeed, when Constantine Porphyrogenitus made a collection of
excerpts from the Greek historians, 'On Plots' (*De insidiis*) was one of the
categories.[29] Nonetheless, I think we can see that Polybius continued to
bear in mind these two themes that he had used to open his account of
Ptolemaic history. The reign of Philopator gave us a debauched king, that
of his successor Ptolemy V Epiphanes gives us a child king. In both cases the
king for different reasons is incapable of rule (leaving aside modern attempts
to rehabilitate Philopator), and power is held instead by unscrupulous
advisers. Combined with the dispersed character of Ptolemaic possessions,
this meant a kingdom at risk.

In what survives of book 15 two events relevant to Egypt stand out.
First, there is the notorious pact between Antiochus and Philip in which
they 'tear to pieces the kingdom of the boy'.[30] Secondly, there is a bloody
dispute in Alexandria as one of the leading figures at the court, Agathocles,

text of the Raphia stele of 217, which refers to 'the acts of treachery which the leaders of the troops
had committed', Walbank 1957: 587, translated in Austin 2006: no. 276, lines 25ff.
[28] Polyb. 14.11–12, on which see Walbank 1967: 434–9 and 1979a: 183–4. For native revolts, see McGing
1997 and Veïsse 2004.
[29] Moore 1965: 127–8. Polyb. 15.25.3–37, for example, on Agathocles' intrigues and the death of
Philopator is from the *De insidiis*.
[30] Pact: 15.20; the historicity of the pact has been a major cause of debate among scholars, see recently
Eckstein 2008: 121–80 (in favour) with a review of the debate at 129–31; the court: 15.25–34.

seeks to monopolise power for himself. So a kingdom that is vulnerable when the king is incapable becomes even more vulnerable, and Antiochus and Philip are able to pick off the parts they want.

Polybius' narrative of their predatory moves is lacking, but it is clear from Livy that among the places captured or threatened are all those listed in book 5 chapter 34. Philip seized Maronea and Aenus, and moved towards the Hellespont, his way smoothed by a certain amount of treachery. Antiochus occupied Coele Syria and then seized much of the coast of Asia Minor right up as far as Lysimachea, which he began rebuilding; he even made an unsuccessful attempt on Cyprus.[31] It is hard to avoid the conclusion that Polybius had these later events in mind when he outlined early Ptolemaic policy in 5.34 and that he was not thinking of Philopator alone in that passage. Significantly, the Ptolemaic losses in these years also included Samos and Ephesus, which were the two bases singled out by the anxious Sosibius in the next chapter, 5.35.[32] That Polybius' presentation of Ptolemaic possessions in these two chapters is shaped in part by the events that followed the death of Philopator is suggested also by the fact that he did not include those places which continued to be held well into the second century. For example, it was Thera rather than Samos that was the main Ptolemaic naval base in the Aegean at the time of Philopator's accession, and that island remained in Ptolemaic hands until around 145.[33]

Fortune, Polybius observed (15.20.8), soon punished the Antigonid and Seleucid dynasties for their conduct while taking care to restore the kingdom of the Ptolemies – although that kingdom never did recover all the territories it lost so rapidly after the death of Philopator. Nonetheless, in spite of the Ptolemaic dynasty regaining the favour of fortune, Polybius may well have kept that initial analysis of the strengths and weaknesses of the Ptolemaic empire in mind (albeit a shrinking empire). In the 160s there was a series of dynastic disputes between the two sons of Ptolemy V which led in 163 to the division of the kingdom. At this stage the elder brother Ptolemy VI Philometor held Egypt itself, while his younger brother Ptolemy VIII Euergetes II held Cyrene, but the two continued to quarrel about Cyprus, the younger seeking Roman support for his claim to it.

---

[31] Philip's conquests between Maronea and Hellespont in 200: Livy 31.16; Antiochus takes Coele Syria in the Fifth Syrian War: Livy 33.19.8; his occupation of the coast of Asia Minor: Livy 33.38.

[32] Samos, lost to Philip in 201: App. *Mac.* 4.1, Polyb. 16.2.9, with Shipley 1987: 190–6 on the island's complex history in the decade following, which involves a brief and nominal return to the Ptolemaic fold; Ephesus, lost to Antiochus in 197 or 196: Polyb. 18.41a; Jerome, *Comm. on Daniel* 11.15; Livy 33.38.1, with Walbank 1967: 603.

[33] Bagnall 1976: 133–4 on Thera as 'the headquarters of the Ptolemaic Aegean fleet after the reign of Philadelphos', cf. Shipley 1987: 190.

Polybius' coverage of this long-running dispute only survives in fragments, but his comments on this appeal to Rome make interesting reading. The Romans, he wrote (31.10.8), gave the younger brother support because they saw how great the power of the Egyptian kingdom was and feared the consequences if it ever acquired a competent leader. This repeats the theme of 5.34: a competent ruler and territory overseas make Egypt strong, but it is possible to divide and so diminish and weaken it. This passage falls after the original termination date of the history – the fifty-three years end with Pydna in 168 – so when Polybius was composing the beginning of the reign of Philopator, he may not have intended to go as far as these dynastic disputes. He could, nevertheless, have had the division in mind when he thought about earlier Ptolemaic history; it may even have helped to shape his ideas, since this was the Egypt with which he was familiar. Nor does the theme of the corrupting influence of the court disappear. Two of the governors of Cyprus, Polycrates and Ptolemaeus, men who worked hard in that position to keep the kingdom secure and financially viable, succumbed to a life of depravity once they returned to Alexandria.[34]

Polybius' interpretation of Ptolemaic foreign policy in the third century as outlined in 5.34–5 is closely tied to his understanding of subsequent Ptolemaic decline, not only in the reign of Philopator but also under his successors. This perspective means that the emphasis is on the early Ptolemies as bringers of security rather than as exponents of aggressive expansionism. Yet that security was dependent on a strong centre. The combination of a weak centre and dispersed possessions brought not security but decline.

PTOLEMAIC NAVAL ACTIVITY IN POLYBIUS

Ptolemaic naval activity is more notable by its absence in Polybius than its presence, and this is the case even where his text is not fragmentary. If we look again the key passage in this chapter, 5.34, we can see that Polybius talks of the Ptolemies threatening the kings of Syria by land and sea through their possession of Coele Syria and Cyprus; the parallel phrasing makes clear that Cyprus had special significance for their command of the sea, but it is implicit rather than explicit.[35] He goes on to mention their control over islands and cities and harbours along the coast. But what he does not say anything about is a fleet. It could be that he takes the presence of a fleet for granted, but it may also be that it is the diffuse and scattered

---

[34] Polyb. 18.55, 27.13.   [35] For Cyprus, see Hauben 1987a.

character of Ptolemaic rule that interests him more, and it is there that he sees weakness lying.

Nonetheless, a neglectful king will neglect his navy. Polybius himself was certainly not unaware of the importance of sea power and of maintaining a fleet.[36] They are crucial to his treatment of the First Punic War, for example, and it is the failure of the Carthaginians to maintain their fleet later in the war that contributes to their final defeat. The reason for not emphasising the Ptolemaic fleet may be fairly prosaic: Polybius does not treat the fleet as important in the maintenance of the Ptolemaic empire of the late third and early second centuries for the simple reason that the Ptolemies did not treat it as important.[37] So long as their rivals were not maintaining big fleets, there was no need for the Ptolemies to do so either – they could still get access to their overseas possessions, and those possessions would be protected by garrisons and perhaps a small quota of ships. Moreover, their rivals, especially at sea, would have included not only the other Hellenistic kingdoms but also the Carthaginians, whose own power in the Mediterranean was considerably weakened after its defeat by Rome in 241.[38]

We can return to the Fourth Syrian War, because here we can benefit from Polybius' continuous narrative in his fifth book. Naval warfare plays a fairly small role in this. It is at its most effective when Antiochus captures Seleuceia in an assault by land and sea. There is, however, no mention of any naval resistance by the besieged, nor of any Ptolemaic naval forces coming to assist. This could be because the Ptolemies did not have sufficient warships fitted and ready for action, but it could also be because the city fell fairly quickly due to treachery.[39] Whether Antiochus captured any ships on this occasion is not said, but it would be surprising if a port city with a Ptolemaic commander had no ships. Nonetheless, when the coastal cities of Tyre and Ptolemais are handed over to him not long afterwards, Antiochus does get the ships that are stationed there – forty ships, twenty of which are fully fitted warships, *kataphraktoi*, while the rest are varieties of lesser ships.[40] This may not appear to be a substantial fleet, but in the context of the naval forces deployed in the Fourth Syrian War it is not an insignificant number. Antiochus invades Coele Syria by land and sea, the fleet staying level with the army. In his account of the war Polybius records one naval battle, fought

---

[36] See Pédech and Marsden in Gabba 1974: 300–1, together with the forthcoming paper by P. de Souza, 'Polybius on naval warfare'.

[37] Cf. Van 't Dack 1988: 28–32 on the reduced capacity of the Ptolemaic fleet from the late third century onwards.

[38] On the Carthaginian navy, see now Rawlings 2010.   [39] Polyb. 5.58–61.2, with n. 24 above.

[40] Polyb. 5.61–2, on which Morrison and Coates 1996: 57.

alongside a land battle in 218. The Ptolemaic admiral Perigenes is said to have had 30 warships and 400 transports, although it can be assumed that only the warships were used in the battle. As the two sides are described as evenly matched in both number and armament, the Seleucid admiral Diognetus must have had a similar number. These are fairly small numbers for Hellenistic kingdoms to be deploying.[41] Ptolemaic Egypt is considered a major naval power, yet when faced with an invasion it dispatched a fleet of only thirty warships. Perhaps this was because it did not expect the Seleucid fleet to be any larger, but it may also be that Ptolemaic plans were upset by the loss of Tyre and Ptolemais, which depleted their immediate resources while augmenting those of the Seleucids. Certainly, prior to this the two fleets would have been much less evenly balanced.[42]

These forces are meagre when compared with the fleets put into action by the city-states of the fifth century BC or earlier in the Hellenistic period. The Athenians alone were said to have supplied 127 ships to the battle of Artemisium in the Second Persian War; at Aegospotami at the end of the Peloponnesian War the Athenians lost 171 ships, with 9 escaping.[43] The ships may have been smaller in the fifth century, but this was still a significant number. It has been calculated that manning a fleet of 100 triremes required 17,000 rowers.[44] Substantial fleets were regularly in action in the wars of the successors. At the battle of Salamis off Cyprus in 306 Ptolemy I mustered some 140 or 150 ships against the slightly greater forces of Demetrius Poliorcetes.[45] In the case of the third-century west, Polybius himself describes the battles that took place between the Romans and the Carthaginians during the First Punic War. Both sides, he writes, were operating with fleets that numbered over 300 ships each, figures that suggest he would hardly have been impressed by the Ptolemaic fleet that sailed under Diognetus in 218.[46]

[41] Number deployed and number possessed may be very different; Beyer-Rotthoff, in a review of Ptolemaic naval forces, suggests that Ptolemy IV had at least 110 ships at the start of his reign (1993: 249); see also n. 4 above.
[42] Polyb. 5.62.3 notes that the ships from Seleuceia were handed over to Diognetus, who went on to lead the Seleucid forces in the sea battle.
[43] Hdt. 8.1.
[44] Artemisium: Hdt. 8.1; Aegospotami: Xen. Hell. 2.1.28; manning triremes and larger ships: Casson 1995: 302–5; Lee 2006: 503; Hunt 2007: 124–5.
[45] Diod. Sic. 20.49–52; Plut. Demetr. 15–16; Hauben 1976; Morrison and Coates 1996: 19–30. At the time of his removal from the kingship of Macedon Demetrius was said to have had some 500 ships under construction, Plut. Demetr. 43. See Billows 1990: 357–8 on the naval resources of Antigonus and Demetrius.
[46] Polyb. 1.25.7–9; Polybius' figures are often thought to be too high by as much as a hundred, cf. the summary of the arguments in Walbank 1957: 82–5, although they are defended by Tipps 1985:

One reason states did not consistently maintain large fleets was the expense: to keep a substantial fleet at the ready required considerable resources in both money and manpower.[47] It is noticeable that Ptolemy Philopator had to put great effort into gathering together sufficient land troops for the army that was to be victorious at Raphia.[48] The lack of a sizeable fleet is the maritime equivalent, but it would require that much more time to rectify. Polybius does in fact represent Sosibius and Philopator's advisers early in his reign as being wary of spending money on military adventures abroad; this is one of their reasons for not supporting an expedition by Cleomenes, but a similar fiscal prudence could apply to other aspects of state expenditure. Interestingly too in the case of Cleomenes expenditure is related to how the enemy is perceived; as the Macedonian king Antigonus Doson had recently died there was little purpose in funding anti-Macedonian activities at this point (Polyb. 5.35.8). Polybius observes this way of thinking elsewhere too: in the later stages of the First Punic War the Carthaginians, thinking that the Romans were no longer likely to challenge their mastery of the sea, neglected their fleet, with the result that when the Romans took to the sea again the Carthaginians were defeated (Polyb. 1.61). Moreover possessing ships and having ships in a suitable state for warfare were two very different things. When Philip V seized Samos shortly after the death of Philopator he took possession of the ships there, but the majority of them had not been fitted out and so were initially unusable.[49] This does not suggest a very active navy in the last years of Philopator's reign. What the Egyptian king perhaps preferred were grand gestures; he famously built the largest ship yet known, albeit one almost impossible to manoeuvre.[50] The construction of such a ship advertised naval power without requiring him to build and man a whole fleet.

Polybius provides only very limited evidence for the Ptolemaic navy in the late third and early second centuries, but the evidence he does provide suggests that the Ptolemies themselves in this period were not so committed to naval warfare as their predecessors had been. They were not prepared to put the necessary resources into this highly expensive branch of ancient warfare, although, like the Carthaginians, they may have continued to believe in their own mastery of the sea. Given the character

---

437–45. For the Roman navy at this time, see Thiel 1954 and Steinby 2007, with contrasting views on Roman naval experience prior to the First Punic War.

[47] Cf. De Souza 2007: 361–3 and Van 't Dack 1988: 22–4 on the construction and manpower of Hellenistic fleets.

[48] Polyb. 5.63–7.   [49] Polyb. 16.2.9, on which Walbank 1967: 505–6.

[50] Ath. 5.203e–d, cf. Thompson, Chapter 12 in this volume. For Hauben 1981, however, the construction of the ship was a complete waste of resources and symptomatic of the problems of Philopator's reign.

of the Ptolemaic empire it might seem strange that Polybius does not comment on this failure more explicitly, because it would render them unable to defend their widespread possessions. But for Polybius it was the very structure of the Ptolemaic kingdom that contributed to its decline, the scattered and often remote nature of its overseas possessions and the tension that existed between the interests of the state and those of the court. If anything, neglect of the fleet was a symptom, not a cause. With a strong king, these problems would have been resolved. But without one the Egypt of Polybius was a land of conspiracy, intrigue and division. There was not a lot of room for naval supremacy here.

CHAPTER 6

Ptolemaic grain, seaways and power

Kostas Buraselis

EGYPTIAN GRAIN EXPORTS BEFORE THE PTOLEMIES

Egypt was in ancient perception the gift of the Nile,[1] and grain may be seen as a significant expression of this relationship. The land was traditionally thought of as blessed by nature,[2] and a potential source of food for other countries too.[3] In Trajanic times Pliny characteristically highlighted the temporary and highly unexpected reversal of the natural order when that 'most productive country'[4] (*fecundissima gens*) had to be aided by Rome with the dispatch of grain, instead of its usual provision of the food-supply for the imperial capital.

Although Egyptian grain had been neither unknown nor, of course, unappreciated in the Greek world before Alexander,[5] it seems that the 'golden age' of this particular export from Egypt to various destinations in the eastern Mediterranean came only after the Macedonian conquest of Egypt,[6] and especially under the early Ptolemies. The latter point has been well borne out in an analysis of the available evidence by D. W. Rathbone.[7] However, already under that pre-Ptolemaic founder of Hellenistic Egypt,

---

[1] The basic idea is already in Hdt. 2.5; cf. Arr. *Anab.* 5.6.5.

[2] A fine expression of this view: Theoc. 17.79–80.

[3] Thus, for example, we already find Ramses II directing a grain donation to the Hittites during a famine, see Grimal 1988: 330.

[4] In his *Panegyricus* of the *optimus princeps*, 31.6: *actum erat de fecundissima gente, si libera fuisset* ('It would have been the end of that most productive country, had she been free', trans. B. Radice, Loeb Classical Library 1969).

[5] As an example one may note that the Spartans in 396 received a big gift of grain from their ally Pharaoh Nephereus (Nepherites): Diod. Sic. 14.79.4.

[6] Cf. Garnsey 1988: 152–64.

[7] Rathbone 1983: esp. 50–3. His main relevant conclusions:

> It would thus seem that it was under the early Ptolemies that Egypt became a major regular exporter of grain to the Greek cities . . . All these [things needed by the Ptolemies as 'one of the most powerful successor-dynasties of Alexander'] had to be acquired from outside Egypt, and the single largest commodity which the Ptolemies could export in return was precisely grain. Of necessity the Ptolemies had to export grain, whether a favourable market for it existed or not (51).

Cleomenes of Naucratis,[8] the problem appears of safeguarding at the same time both Egyptian self-sufficiency in grain and a regular flow of grain export to secure state revenues, that is, the exploitation of local production desirable for the land's foreign administration. Thus, in the Ps.-Aristotelian *Oeconomica* we find Alexander's governor trying to limit the extent of that export in a period of shortage of grain in Egypt itself while a proper famine was pressing other Mediterranean areas (probably in 330/329 BC):[9]

When Cleomenes of Alexandria was serving as satrap of Egypt, a famine occurred, assuming an acute form in other areas but a moderate one in Egypt itself. Cleomenes thereupon ordered a prohibition of grain export. However, as the nomarchs stated that they would be unable to pay in the tributes [foreseen] because of the ban on grain export, he permitted the latter [again], but imposed a high tax on it. Thus he managed to gain much from a limited export, and he deprived the nomarchs of the [claimed] excuse that they made.

In a further passage of the same treatise we see Cleomenes' effort to increase the amounts of grain available in the internal market of Egypt during a similar crisis, mirrored in unusually high prices of grain, by establishing a form of direct contact between his administration and the local producers and thus forcing grain merchants to accept his own, even higher prices. As the text itself presents it:[10]

In a period when grain had reached the price of 10 drachmas [a measure] in the country, he invited those involved in the grain production to himself and asked them under which conditions they would accept to work for him [alone]. These answered that they would provide him with grain at lower prices than those for the grain merchants. Nevertheless, he asked them to deliver him the grain at the price offered to the others [the merchants], while he set up the [market] price of grain at 32 drachmas, and thus began his [own] sale of grain.

---

[8] On his policy and personality: Le Rider 1997 (cf. esp. 78 on the relation of high prices in Egypt itself and the export of grain).

[9] 2.33a (1352 a16–23):

Κλεομένης Ἀλεξανδρεὺς Αἰγύπτου σατραπεύων, λιμοῦ γενομένου ἐν μὲν τοῖς ἄλλοις τόποις σφόδρα, ἐν Αἰγύπτῳ δὲ μετρίως, ἀπέκλεισε τὴν ἐξαγωγὴν τοῦ σίτου. Τῶν δὲ νομαρχῶν φασκόντων οὐ δυνήσεσθαι τοὺς φόρους ἀποδοῦναι τῷ μὴ ἐξάγεσθαι τὸν σῖτον, ἐξαγωγὴν μὲν ἐποίησε, τέλος δὲ πολὺ τῷ σίτῳ ἐπέβαλεν, ὥστε συνέβαινεν αὐτῷ εἰ μὴ < ... > ἐξαγομένου ὀλίγου πολὺ τέλος λαμβάνειν, αὐτούς τε [νομάρχας] πεπαῦσθαι τῆς προφάσεως.

[10] Ib. 33e (1352 b14–20):

Τοῦ τε σίτου πωλουμένου ἐν τῇ χώρᾳ δεκαδράχμου, καλέσας τοὺς ἐργαζομένους ἠρώτησε πῶς βούλονται αὐτῷ ἐργάζεσθαι· οἳ δ' ἔφασαν ἐλάττονος ἢ ὅσου ἂν τοῖς ἐμπόροις ἐπώλουν. Ὁ δ' ἐκείνους μὲν ἐκέλευσεν αὐτῷ παραδιδόναι ὅσουπερ ἐπώλουν τοῖς ἄλλοις, αὐτὸς δὲ τάξας τριάκοντα καὶ δύο δραχμὰς τοῦ σίτου τιμὴν οὕτως ἐπώλει.

To complete the context, one should also take note of the well-known inscription from Cyrene listing grain quantities directed to cities and individuals in old Greece during a period of famine *c.* 330 BC, an aid sometimes even brought into connection with Macedonian policies.[11]

One basic conclusion from the examination of this evidence may be the appearance of grain export already in the early Hellenistic period from what was to become Ptolemaic Africa to Mediterranean destinations suffering shortages or famine. At the same time, in two of the relevant cases the self-sufficiency of Egypt seems to have been also under stress. The Ptolemies needed to keep these data in mind when later drawing up the overall plan for the administration of their kingdom.

PRODUCTION AND EXPORT OF GRAIN IN PTOLEMAIC EGYPT

The crucial difference, and difficulty, of that administration in comparison with Pharaonic practice was, of course, its main characteristic as representing a foreign rule over the land, and its effort to strengthen and preserve itself by demographic infusions of Greek and Hellenised, military and civil employees attracted to Egypt by royal generosity. These Greeks had further to be offered a minimum of Greek life there, allowing them the enjoyment of some non-Egyptian commodities like wine or olive oil (also necessary for the proper working of a Greek *gymnasion*). Furthermore, the whole concept of the grand defensive strategy of the Ptolemies and the material upkeep of their army and navy to protect their extensive and often outlying dominions imposed on them an energetic search for revenues, well beyond Pharaonic preoccupations. It is well known and long established that the dynasty was therefore heavily dependent on a flourishing export trade for their products to balance their import and other needs.

Now, while these Ptolemaic *conditiones sine quibus non* have always received the attention they deserve, one often tends to overestimate Egyptian productivity and, especially, to underestimate the uncertainties that the grain harvests so crucial to that production might entail. For it is equally well known that grain shortages could affect Egypt itself even under the careful organisation of the Ptolemies (as later that of the Roman emperors),[12] very probably also because of the increased and systematised

---

[11] Commented text and discussion of the relevant literature: Rhodes and Osborne 2003: 486–93 (no. 96). They tend, however, to separate the Cyrenean initiative from Macedonian directives (490–3).

[12] Apart from the case under Trajan (Plin. *Pan.* 30–2) already mentioned, we also know of similar problems in the period of Tiberius/Germanicus (Tac. *Ann.* 2.59; Suet. *Tib.* 52.2; Joseph. *Ap.* 2.5) and possibly Hadrian (Wörrle 1971, Hadrian's(?) letter to Ephesus).

range of their export trade outlined above. Simply stated, the Nile was not always as collaborative as Ptolemaic vital interests would have liked it to be.

Literary evidence for a serious shortage of grain in Egypt under either Philadelphus or Euergetes[13] is included in Moschion's report on the famous *Syrakosia / Alexandris*,[14] the supership built by Hieron II at Syracuse and sent as a gift laden with 60,000 *medimnoi* (?) of grain and further goods to his royal colleague at Alexandria as 'there was a shortage of grain in Egypt' (καὶ γὰρ ἦν σπάνις σίτου κατὰ τὴν Αἴγυπτον).[15] The propagandistic effect of such a gift from Sicily to Egypt is easy to grasp: only fellow giants can help each other in times of need.

A second eloquent testimony to similar difficulties and their parameters is included in the Canopus decree of the Egyptian priests for Ptolemy III Euergetes and Berenice II (*OGIS* 56, 239/238 BC), which can now be better studied with the help of the valuable edition and commentary of its three versions (Greek, hieroglyphic and demotic) by Stefan Pfeiffer.[16] One of the benefactions of Euergetes towards his subjects emphasised in that document is his decisive intervention to save Egypt from the menacing consequences of a bad Nile flood. According to the Greek version of the decree (13–19):[17]

at a time when the river had reached a lower level [than normal], and all the inhabitants of the country were very anxious because of this and recalled the disaster that had occurred [in similar conditions] under some of the previous kings, during the reign of which the country had experienced periods of drought, they [Ptolemy III and his wife] stood up to their role as caring masters... showed their ample providence in the measures they took, and often overlooked their fiscal interest for the sake of saving the people, had grain brought to the country from

---

[13] The regnal years of Hieron II (269–215 BC) do not allow us to know which Ptolemy was the recipient, and Jacoby's view (*FGrH* III B, p. 606) that the long Romano-Carthaginian peace after 241 should be seen as a *terminus post quem* is not decisive. Casson 1971: 185 and Hauben 1981: 399 identified the Ptolemy in question as Euergetes I. Lehmler 2005: 229 accepts the same identification on the basis of the Canopus decree (see below) but this is also not certain. Rostovtzeff 1953: 1250 preferred to date the incident under Philadelphus, while Huß 2001: 368 (with n. 108) would not exclude either date.

[14] *FGrH* 575 F1–6 (= Ath. 5.206d–209e).   [15] *Medimnoi* are more probable: Duncan-Jones 1977.

[16] S. Pfeiffer 2004.

[17] τοῦ τε ποταμοῦ ποτε ἐνλιπέστερον ἀναβάντος καὶ πάντων τῶν ἐν τῆι χώραι καταπε-πληγμένων ἐπὶ τῶι συμβεβηκότι καὶ ἐνθυμουμένων τὴν γενομένην καταφθορὰν ἐπί τινων τῶν πρότερον βεβασιλευκότων, ἐφ᾽ ὧν συνέβη ἀβροχίαις περιπεπτωκέναι τοὺς τὴν χώραν κατοικοῦντας, προστάντες κηδεμονικῶς... πολλὰ μὲν προνοηθέντες, οὐκ ὀλίγα δὲ τῶν προσόδων ὑπεριδόντες ἕνεκα τῆς τῶν ἀνθρώπων σωτηρίας, ἔκ τε Συρίας καὶ Φοινίκης καὶ Κύπρου καὶ ἐξ ἄλλων πλειόνων τόπων σῖτον μεταπεμψάμενοι εἰς τὴν χώραν τιμῶν μειζόνων διέσωισαν τοὺς τὴν Αἴγυπτον κατοικοῦντας...

Syria, Phoenicia and Cyprus and many other places at higher prices, and thus saved the population of Egypt . . .

We may note first that the decree alludes to past problems of the same sort, probably not faced with equal efficiency (a 'disaster' or 'ruination', καταφθορά, of the country had not been avoided!) by the ruler(s) of the times. That these unhappy experiences should be referred as far back as the Pharaonic period is rather improbable.[18] I think that we should recognise here additional evidence for such problems in the more recent past of Egypt since Alexander. The counter-measures of Ptolemy III to avert a famine are also worth analysing. He is credited with implementing a large project for the import of grain into Egypt from Syria, Phoenicia, Cyprus and many other places at great expense. We cannot know where these 'many other places' were, but the three specified sources of import seem all to be Ptolemaic dominions:[19] Cyprus and Phoenicia certainly, 'Syria' probably also, if Coele Syria or the (by that time) Ptolemaic port of Seleuceia in Pieria[20] is meant here. Another aspect, also noted by Pfeiffer,[21] is worth consideration: this royal action, without known Pharaonic precedent, corresponds closely to the code of benefaction (*euergesia*) in the Greek world, especially in regard to securing food for the people at reasonable cost or for free. Thus not only did Euergetes seem once more to deserve his by-name, but in this case he was demonstrating a wider concept of grain provision and circulation than had been traditional in Egypt. He appears not simply as a ruler interested in the welfare of his Egyptian subjects within a narrow local context but as a Mediterranean crisis manager in the interest also of his Egyptian subjects. To succeed in this role it was highly important for the king to have easy access to alternative areas of grain procurement. If at least some of these happened to be royal dominions or allied/friendly states (as certainly in the case discussed above), so much the better for the royal administration: access to the product needed was easier, and the prices might be high but could probably be better negotiated by the sovereign of the country of transaction.

[18] Contra Bonneau 1971: 127, who seems to me to make too much of the plural ἀβροχίαις in the text. Cf. S. Pfeiffer 2004: 96.
[19] Thus already S. Pfeiffer 2004: esp. 97 ('Von Interesse sind die drei Gegenden, aus denen das Königspaar für teures Geld Getreide hat einführen lassen. Es handelt sich bei allen um ptolemäische Besitzungen') and 219 (import of the grain necessary 'aus anderen Gegenden ihres [: des Ptolemäer-] Reiches'.
[20] Euergetes' longer-standing gain after the Third Syrian War. Cf. Huß 2001: 351.
[21] S. Pfeiffer 2004: 223: 'Die gesamte Aktion der beiden Regenten wirkt auch deshalb im höchsten Masse griechisch, weil das Einführen von Getreide in pharaonischer Zeit von seiten eines Pharaos kaum bzw. überhaupt nicht belegt ist. Auch finanzielle Aufwendungen von Pharaonen für die Bevölkerung finden sich in den Quellen pharaonischer Zeit nicht erwähnt.'

How far more difficult the situation in Egypt itself could become in an age when similar royal means and such a wider network of mobilisation during a grain crisis apparently failed to exist or to work may be seen in two further relevant Ptolemaic examples from a later period, under Cleopatra VII. In the earlier case,[22] we have Cleopatra's strict prohibition (under penalty of death!) on the forwarding of grain and lentils to destinations other than Alexandria, in order to protect the capital from a present or clearly imminent famine. As her (and her brother's) *prostagma* has it: 'Nobody in the nomes beyond Memphis should buy and forward grain or lentils to Lower Egypt, also not to the Thebaid under any pretext whatsoever. All should bring [these commodities] without any official obstacle to Alexandria, otherwise those found guilty of neglecting this order will be sentenced to death.'[23] Thus a difficulty that could possibly have been solved through royal expenditure and coordinated import in a better period of Ptolemaic rule had now to be met by sacrificing the really vital interests of the larger part of the country to the benefit mainly of those in the capital. The second case, the decree of the priests of Amon at Thebes for the Ptolemaic general and dignitary Callimachus in 39 BC[24] refers expressly to a famine (preceding, perhaps in 41–40 BC).[25] Of course, in these later years the whole situation of Ptolemaic agriculture had seriously deteriorated, but the scope of royal or other remedies was also much more limited. Natural production might seriously fluctuate at any time, but the possibilities of the state to react were each time quite different.

THE WIDER FRAMEWORK OF PTOLEMAIC FOREIGN POLICY AND GRAIN

This wider concept of a regular flow of grain under their rule need not apply only to the Ptolemies' heartland. Reasonable and effective coordination would demand involving the whole area of Ptolemaic dominion and interests. This point may be illustrated by two important documents concerning Ptolemaic policy towards the not-subjected but certainly allied

---

[22] *C.Ord.Ptol.* 73 (50 BC). Cf. Thompson 1983: 74–5.

[23] *C.Ord. Ptol.* 73.2–8: Μηδένα τῶν ὑπὲρ Μέμφιν νομῶν/ ἀγοράζοντα πυρὸν ἢ ὄσπριον κατά/γειν εἰς τὴν κάτω χώραν, ἀλλὰ μη/δ' εἰς τὴν Θηβαΐδα ἀνάγειν παρευ/ρέσει μηδεμιᾶι. Πάντας δ' ἀνυφοράτους/ ὄντας εἰς Ἀλεξάνδρειαν παρακο[μ]ίζειν,/ ἢ ὁ φωραθεὶς θανάτωι ἔνοχος ἔσται.

[24] *OGIS* 194 ≈ *SEG* 24.1217 ≈ A. Bernand 1992: no 46 (I.106–9+II.109–15). Cf. Burstein 1985: no. 111.

[25] σιτοδεία (ll. 10, 14). The same difficulties seem to be referred to also in: App. *B Civ.* 4.63, τετρυμένην (sc. τὴν Αἴγυπτον) τε ὑπὸ λιμοῦ. Joseph. *Ap.* 2.60, *Putasne gloriandum nobis non esse, si quemadmodum dicit Apion famis tempore Iudaeis triticum non est mensa?*

city of Samothrace. The island city honoured two representatives of the Ptolemaic administration in Thrace under Ptolemy III (Ptolemaic rule in this area started around the beginning of his reign)[26] with two honorary decrees:[27] respectively for the governor of the whole Thracian Ptolemaic 'province', Hippomedon the Lacedaemonian, and for the governor of Maronea, Epinicus. We owe to a lucid study of Ph. Gauthier[28] the clarification of the exact historical background of these texts in contrast to previous misconceptions: what Samothrace asked for and achieved here was (a) the permission of Hippomedon that the city might export grain (and need not pay harbour dues for this) from the Ptolemaic zone in Thrace and (b) a loan without interest from Epinicus to create a special fund for grain purchase in times of need. The second case is only indirectly connected to the Ptolemaic administration in Thrace and its management of grain involving Samothracian interests. In the case of Hippomedon, however, we have his clear agreement to include Samothrace, even temporarily, in the system of provisioning the kingdom as a whole.[29] This was obviously not a question of merchants alone but first of all a royal prerogative. The 'channelling' of grain from Ptolemaic territory should give priority to Ptolemaic needs, the needs, that is, of Egypt and its dependencies of all sorts and degrees. Thrace was also a grain-producing area: the quantities of grain produced or stored in some way in its Ptolemaic zone of control were, perhaps mainly in times of crisis, regulated to flow internally towards the kingdom and its dependencies.[30] These included Alexandria and Egypt, if needs be, or any other point on the map of Ptolemaic interests.

Another expression of the same Ptolemaic policy of securing and controlling on their own behalf the grain flow of the Mediterranean against the background of a naturally wider grain market may be discerned in the dynasty's activities as far north as the Propontis and the Black Sea. Our fragmentary evidence shows that, at least under Philadelphus, Alexandria played an important role in these areas: Philadelphus' involvement in the

---

[26] Basic testimonies are: *OGIS* 54 l. 14 and *P.Haun.* 6, frg. 1.7. Cf. Buraselis 1982: 124–34, 173–5; Huß 2001: 433.

[27] Fraser 1960: 39–40; Gauthier 1979: 88–9. Both inscriptions are now re-edited in Loukopoulou et al. 2005: *TE* 63–4.

[28] Gauthier 1979.   [29] Cf. Buraselis 1993: 256.

[30] Evidence for grain as a form of Ptolemaic income in Thrace appears also in *P. Tebt.* I 8 = *Chrest. Wilck.* 2: . . . χρημάτων καὶ σίτου καὶ τῶν ἄλλων φό(ρων) τῶν ὑπαρξάντων ἐν τοῖς κατὰ Λέσβον καὶ κατὰ Θράικην τόποις διασαφῆ(σαι) εἰ μετείληφεν. Cf. the re-edition by Bagnall 1975 (with a useful discussion of the date of the document: probably under Philopator). New evidence for Ptolemaic trade, i.e. export activity (linen articles), in Asia Minor and the Aegean islands: Scholl 1997. On the circulation of Ptolemaic coins in the Aegean and its significance: Chryssanthaki 2005.

Bosporus was so weighty that he donated land in Asia Minor to Byzantium and received cult honours from that city.[31] He is, further, one of the rulers instituted as guarantor of his will by Nicomedes I of Bithynia.[32] One should also neither overemphasise nor underestimate the importance of diplomatic contacts between the Bosporan Kingdom and Alexandria in the age of Paerisades II, based on the evidence of an embassy of the latter in Egypt.[33] After all, the great northern granary of the Black Sea that was so long established was similarly subject to changing conditions of production and on occasion also dependent on imports of grain.[34]

Of course, the royal policy of allowing and regulating the flow of grain to its allies was no Ptolemaic invention but an old political expedient: it had been practised by none other than the Bosporan kings in the classical period,[35] and we find it essentially present in Antigonus Monophthalmus' remarks on supplying the unified Teos/Lebedos with grain from his adjacent royal tributary land in Asia.[36] Even later we find it, for example, in the special (and successful) request of the local governor of the Hellespontine region to Eumenes II to provide Apollonia-on-the-Rhyndacus (?) with grain, for sowing and food.[37] Relevant non-royal measures are also known from the Hellenistic world: the Achaean Confederacy issued a ban on grain export from its area in a period of crisis, from which only friends could be excepted; the case specified here is that of the Elateians, who had previously resided as refugees at Stymphalus within the confederacy.[38]

However, the big difference in the case of the Ptolemies consists in their unrivalled position to develop such a policy because of their regular and

---

[31] Dionysius of Byzantium, XLI (p. 17 Wescher) = Ameling et al. 1995: 271 (no. 239). There is also a tradition (Apollonius of Aphrodisias, third century BC?) of a Ptolemaic expedition along the northern coast of Asia Minor under Philadelphus preserved in Steph. Byz., *s.v.* Ἄγκυρα. Cf. Habicht 1970: 116–17.

[32] Memnon, *FGrH* 434 F14 (c. 255–253 BC). Cf. Huß 1976: 98.

[33] *SB* III 7263 (also *c.* mid third century BC). Cf. Fraser 1972: I, 172 and II, 291 (n. 313).

[34] Polyb. 4.38.5 certainly depicts the realities of both the third and the second centuries BC: Σίτῳ δ' ἀμείβονται (sc. οἱ κατὰ τὸν Πόντον τόποι), ποτὲ μὲν εὐκαίρως διδόντες, ποτὲ δὲ λαμβάνοντες. Cf. Walbank 1970: 486–7.

[35] The evidence has been collected and cited by Gauthier 1979: 85.

[36] Welles 1934: no. 3 (Antigonus' I letter to Teos on the synoecism with Lebedos), 80–5:

Ἡμεῖς δὲ πρότερον μὲν οὐ[κ ἐβουλόμεθα μηδεμιᾶι πό]/λει δίδοσθαι τὰ σιτηγήσια μηδὲ σίτου γίνεσθαι παράθε[σιν, οὐ θέλοντες τὰς]/ [π]όλεις εἰς ταῦτα ἀναλίσκειν χρήματα συχνὰ οὐκ ἀναγκαῖα [ὄντα, ἐβουλόμεθα δὲ]/ [ο]ὐδὲ νῦν ποεῖν τοῦτο, πλησίον οὔσης τῆς φορολογουμέ[νης χώρας ὥστε ἐὰν χρεία]/ [γ]ίνηται σίτου, εὐχερῶς οἰόμεθα εἶναι μεταπέμπεσθαι ἐκ [ταύτης ὁπόσ]/[ο]ν ἄν τις βούληται.

[37] Ameling et al. 1995: no. 242, 17–18: τῶι βασιλεῖ μνησθεὶς ἐξεπορίσατο σῖτον εἰς σπέρμα καὶ διατροφήν; cf. Holleaux (1938–68): II, 103.

[38] Moretti, *ISE* I.55, 15–6 + *BCH* 93 (1969): 159–60: οὐκ οὔσας σίτου ἐξαγωγᾶς τοῖς Ἀχαιοῖς διὰ τὸν περιεσ[τῶτα καιρὸν? καὶ τὰν σι]τοδείαν. Cf. Gauthier 1979: 86; Chaniotis 2005: 129.

extensive possibilities of grain export, often also in the form of well-targeted donations. One may recall Ptolemy I's repeated grain transports to Rhodes during its siege by Demetrius I,[39] but also Ptolemy III's later gift of grain to Rhodes, the largest of this sort on that occasion, after the well-known earthquake of 227 BC.[40] Athens too had repeatedly depended on imports and donations of Egyptian grain, as for example when through Callias' mediation Athenian representatives received 20,000 *medimnoi* of grain on Delos,[41] obviously a convenient trading point and at that time possibly also the seat of a royal granary. The symbol of the filled horn or double horn (*cornucopia*) on Ptolemaic coins[42] may be seen to symbolise not only the prosperity of the Ptolemies but also the favourable prospects for their satellites.

CONDITIONS OF SAFETY FOR GRAIN TRANSPORT

To transport grain, their basic asset, from and on occasion to Egypt, the Ptolemies had to ensure a system of regular, extensive and safe communications by sea.[43] The connection becomes clear, for example, in the case of Athens besieged by Demetrius I during the tyranny of Lachares (295): the merchant and captain of a ship trying to import grain to Athens were exemplarily hanged by Demetrius.[44] The consequent shortage of food (and thus high prices) in the city were only temporarily alleviated by the appearance of a strong Ptolemaic fleet off the coast of Aegina opposite, and they deteriorated even further after the arrival of naval reinforcements to Demetrius, which finally dissuaded Ptolemy's admirals from any thought of a sea battle.[45] Even more explicit is the relation between the presence of warships and the safe transportation of grain to Athens in the later Athenian

---

[39] Ameling et al. 1995: no. 203 (one planned and two realised grain transports to Rhodes during the island's siege by Demetrius). Cf. *ibid.* no. 205 (donation of Ptolemy II to Rhodes). Similar Ptolemaic donations to other cities: no. 224 (Ptolemy I/II to Cos); no. 239 (Ptolemy II to Byzantium); no. 243 (to Heraclea of Pontus); no. 244 (to Sinope). The historicity of a donation of grain by a Ptolemy to Seleuceia in Pieria reported by Isidorus (in Athenodorus of Tarsus, *FGrH* 746 F4.3), and connected with the transport of Sarapis' statue to Egypt, is at least dubious.

[40] Polyb. 5.89.1–5. Cf. Walbank 1970: 619–20.

[41] *SEG* 28.60, 53–5: (ἐκόμισε Καλλίας) πυρῶν δὲ δισμυρίους μεδίμνους δωρεὰν οἳ παρεμετρήθησαν ἐκ Δήλου τοῖς ἀποσταλεῖσιν ὑπὸ τ[ο]ῦ δήμου. Cf. Ameling et al. 1995: no. 16, and the similar testimony of the Phaedrus decree (*SIG³* 409 = Ameling et al. 1995: no. 15). On the relevant role of Delos: Reger 1994b: 116–19; on Ptolemaic grain for Athens: Oliver 2007: 249–52.

[42] Not only on the reverse of queens' (starting with Arsinoe II) but also of kings' coins, e.g. accompanying the portrait of Euergetes under Philopator: Mørkholm 1991: no. 316.

[43] Not in the sense, of course, that the relevant trade would be operated exclusively or even extensively by the state itself: cf. the still valid remarks of Préaux 1939: esp. 150–1.

[44] Plut. *Demetr.* 33.   [45] *Ibid.*

decree for the Ptolemaic admiral Zenon: as commander of a squadron of *aphrakta* he escorted grain transports to the city, probably in July 286, i.e. in the still difficult period following Demetrius' last siege of Athens in the previous year.[46] One should also not forget in this respect the ever-present problem of Hellenistic piracy, which exposed cargo ships to frequent danger. Protecting grain transports must have then been a serious concern of those forwarding quantities of grain, as either traders or donors.[47]

This function of the Ptolemaic navy is usually assumed to have been fully undertaken by the Rhodians at a later date. Certainly, the Rhodians did play this role of 'sea police' especially in the Aegean; this is particularly the case of the part of their fleet known as *phylakides* (guard ships), the role of which has been studied in detail by Gabrielsen and Wiemer.[48] I think, however, that the extent of Ptolemaic dominions combined with the attested, even if temporary, difficulties in Ptolemaic–Rhodian relations at some point around the middle of the third century BC[49] render a complete dependence of the Ptolemies on Rhodian 'sea police' rather improbable, at least as long as the rulers of Egypt took their role as a naval power seriously.

CONCLUSIONS

We are thus coming to realise that the capital value of seaways as 'grainways' for the Ptolemies, both to ensure Egyptian self-sufficiency and to channel such critical cargoes to their dispersed dominions and allies in the Mediterranean, was not a detail but a crucial element in the whole context of Ptolemaic policy. The view elaborating on Polybius' old picture of the Ptolemaic 'long hands' extended as a form of military protection far beyond Egypt's direct borders,[50] that is, the interpretation of a Ptolemaic

---

[46] *IG* II² 650 = *SIG*³ 367 ll. 14–17: ἐπιμελεῖται δὲ/ [καὶ τῆς κομιδῆς το]ῦ σίτου τῶι δήμωι ὅπως ἀ/[ν ἀσφαλέστατα δια]κομίζηται συναγωνιζό/[μενος τῆι τοῦ δήμ]ου σωτηρίαι. Cf. Habicht 1995: 132. On Zenon as Ptolemaic admiral *epi tôn aphraktôn*: *IG* XII.5 1004, from Ios; on *aphrakta*: Casson 1995: esp. 134–5.

[47] An early example in case is *OGIS* 9, a Clazomenian decree for a general of Poliorcetes who τῆι πόλει τὰ πλοῖα τὰ σιτ[αγωγὰ] διέσωσε. De Souza 1999: 53–4 tends to minimise this activity in regard to the Ptolemies. However, even much later at least an official Ptolemaic dispatch of grain seems to have been escorted by a royal representative: thus in *OGIS* 760 Ariston son of Heracleides from Soli, ἐκπεμφθεὶς δὲ καὶ ὑπὸ τοῦ βασιλέως Πτολεμαίου τοῦ πρεσβυτέρου ἐπὶ τῆς σιτικῆς δωρεᾶς τῆς ἀποσταλείσης Ῥωμαίοις (4–5), is honoured by Chalcis during the war with Perseus (c. 169 BC).

[48] Gabrielsen 1997: 108–9 (and Chapter 4 in this volume); Wiemer 2002: 23–6.

[49] This is the essence of the otherwise still mysterious battle of Ephesus (Polyaenus, *Strat.* 5.18). Cf. most recently Wiemer 2002: 98–100 (with earlier bibliography).

[50] Polyb. 5.34.5–9 (contrasting Philopator's policy to that of his predecessors; here, 9, the vivid expression μακρὰν ἐκτετακότες τὰς χεῖρας, καὶ προβεβλημένοι πρὸ αὐτῶν ἐκ πολλοῦ τὰς δυναστείας). Cf. Walbank 1970: 564–5, and Erskine, Chapter 5 in this volume.

defensive strategy as the main force behind their often leading naval role in the eastern Mediterranean of the third century BC needs to be essentially supplemented. Ptolemaic Egypt would not be content either in regard to its inner stability or its outer relations simply with military protection, of whatever sort and strength. The kingdom could much more effectively pursue its basic strategic needs through establishing and securing a firm network of commercial activities, grain being both the prime and a multiple instrument of policy in the dynasty's hands. When Theocritus in his *Encomium* of Philadelphus spoke of '[the king's] best ships sailing the sea' and his rule (in this order) over 'the whole sea, land and sounding rivers',[51] he knew how to emphasise the importance of sea- and riverways as arteries of Ptolemaic rule. Therefore we may now appreciate even better how insufficient the old dilemma (or even trilemma) once neatly expressed by Edouard Will in his penetrating analysis of Ptolemaic foreign policy vs economy[52] actually was: 'être riches pour être puissants ou être puissants pour être riches? Ou les deux?' Ultimately, that relation proves to be a question of balance between various factors, and ones not always easily coordinated, such as inland production and self-sufficiency in basic goods vs commerce and enrichment, economic and political security in Egypt itself vs the pursuit of an international place of eminence, especially in the age of the early Ptolemies. Egyptian grain never ceased to be the foundation of the dynasty's power until their last years, but by then the seaways, the arteries of their great organism, were not theirs any more in the same way as earlier, nor was Ptolemaic blood pulsing throughout the eastern Mediterranean as it had done before.

---

[51] Theoc. 17.90–2: . . . οἱ νᾶες ἄρισται/ πόντον ἐπιπλώοντι, θάλασσα δὲ πᾶσα καὶ αἶα/ καὶ ποτα-μοὶ κελάδοντες ἀνάσσονται Πτολεμαίῳ.
[52] Cf. the whole 'essai d'analyse' of Ed. Will 1979: 153–200 (quotation: 200).

CHAPTER 7

Waterborne recruits: the military settlers of Ptolemaic Egypt

Mary Stefanou

GENERAL INTRODUCTION

In his well-known fourteenth idyll, Theocritus presents two friends, Aeschinas and Thyonichus, who are meeting after a long time. Aeschinas is desperately in love with Cynisca: because she does not respond to his feelings, he is heartbroken and thinks of going abroad to serve as a soldier in order to forget her. Thyonichus sympathises with him and advises him to go off to Egypt, as 'Ptolemy [i.e. Ptolemy II Philadelphus] is the best paymaster a free man could have'.[1]

It is hardly surprising that Theocritus praises King Ptolemy. These verses, though, reveal in a way the mentality of many in 'Old Greece' during the Hellenistic period. The decision of Aeschinas to leave his homeland suggests that men of his era would not hesitate to join a Hellenistic army when they came up against difficulties or in order to seek a better life; the Ptolemaic army was being 'advertised' as the best option for whoever was willing to emigrate. In fact, we do not know whether the Ptolemies actually were 'the best paymasters', at least in the sense of paying higher wages to their mercenaries than did other Hellenistic rulers. However, the practice of settling soldiers as cleruchs in Egypt by granting them plots of land would probably seem quite appealing to someone willing to emigrate to a really promising land.[2]

Given the on-going military needs of the Ptolemies, those settled as cleruchs in Egypt formed an important sector of immigrants to this Hellenistic state. The aim of this chapter is to consider the origin of these cleruchs in the light of new documentation and to question the significance

---

[1] Theoc. 14.59.

[2] The practice was probably introduced by Ptolemy I, although perhaps not systematically. This is deduced mainly from Diod. Sic. 19.85.4; Joseph. *AJ* 12.7; Aristeas, *Ep.* 12–4. However, the oldest known royal ordinance on cleruchs dates from year 10 of Ptolemy II Philadelphus (12 October 276 BC) and refers to billets (*stathmoi*), *P.Petr.* III 20V.ii.1–9 = *SB* VI 9454.3: after 10 February 245 BC – Arsinoite.

of their origin. The main focus will be on those recruits who originated in 'Old Greece', coming, that is, from mainland Greece, from the Aegean and from the coastal areas of Asia Minor.

The origin of Ptolemaic cleruchs more generally was the subject of an important study by R. S. Bagnall published over twenty-five years ago. Bagnall's conclusions were themselves based on figures derived from the prosopography compiled by F. Uebel almost forty-five years ago.[3] Bagnall's database comprised a total of 453 men, under one-third of the total list of cleruchs in Uebel, since for the remainder of cases no ethnic designation is known. Bagnall suggested that since 'two-thirds of the cleruchs . . . come from areas that the Ptolemies did not control . . . it is quite impossible that any significant number of these people entered Ptolemaic service after the time of Ptolemy I'. In his view, Ptolemaic cleruchs were 'the descendants of those soldiers in the army formed by Ptolemy I Soter during his first couple of decades of satrapal rule'.[4] His main contention follows:

One need not go so far as to assert that the Ptolemies . . . created no new cleruchs . . . But fundamentally, the cleruchs seem to have been almost a closed class, the founding fathers of the Ptolemaic state, after a fashion, and their descendants . . . If this is so, it is evident that becoming a military settler was not a very realistic expectation for a third- or second-century Ptolemaic mercenary.[5]

Such mercenaries, he suggests, were recruited by the Ptolemies primarily from their empire; this was not the case for their military settlers.[6]

The large number of papyrological documents published since Uebel's prosopography calls for a fresh treatment of the subject. The discussion in this chapter is based on a new prosopography of all cleruchs bearing an ethnic, which has been compiled taking into account all new data up to the present. New statistics have also been prepared on the same basis. My updated prosopography contains 752 individuals bearing about 100 different ethnics, constituting a larger and, thus, more representative sample than the one that Bagnall had to work on.[7] The statistics obtained from this new dataset prompt us to reconsider Bagnall's conclusions and to re-evaluate the character of this group of immigrants. Many points of interest emerge from such a re-evaluation, but above all it brings into question the claim that cleruchs formed an 'almost closed class'.

---

[3] Bagnall 1984; Uebel 1968. [4] Bagnall 1984: 15–16. [5] Bagnall 1984: 18. [6] Bagnall 1984: 16.
[7] The updated prosopography of Ptolemaic cleruchs formed part of my MA thesis (Stefanou 2008). It will now form the basis of a more general treatment of Ptolemaic cleruchs and their importance for the social and economic history of Ptolemaic Egypt in my PhD dissertation.

The first aim of this chapter is, on the basis of this same enlarged dataset, to re-examine more generally the areas of provenance of Ptolemaic cleruchs. Then we shall focus more specifically on the men that originated from the area of the Aegean. Discussion will not be confined to a general treatment of the subject; instead, each ethnic group will be considered individually in order to determine the time frame of their immigration and settlement in the kingdom, as well as the possible circumstances in which this took place.

We have confined our research up to the end of the reign of Ptolemy VI Philometor, in 145 BC, since from that point on the use of ethnics seems to have decreased.[8] Some ethnic terms appear to have degenerated into fictitious designations, pointing rather to people of a certain occupation or status (i.e. belonging to a specific military unit or a special legal category).[9] The same period saw significant reforms in the Ptolemaic army and also developments in the institution of the cleruchy.[10]

THE ORIGIN OF PTOLEMAIC CLERUCHS

Based on the new enlarged prosopography, we can present an updated picture of the different areas that Ptolemaic cleruchs came from. Table 7.1 shows the number of all cleruchs attested according to their ethnic designations. A note of caution is needed in the use of the following tables. Despite the enlargement of the sample, by nearly 300 men in comparison with that of Bagnall, those cases attested still constitute just a part – though a now more indicative part – of the actual (still unknown) number of those settled as cleruchs by the Ptolemies. Keeping also in mind the fact that we may not fairly compare the population of a single Greek *polis* with the total population of Macedon or of the Thracian tribes,[11] we have first grouped the ethnic designations into separate geographical areas, depending on the specific city-state or area to which they refer.

---

[8] So La'da 1996: 90–2.
[9] Vandorpe 2008: 87–8 (with previous bibliography); La'da 1996: 64–9 and 79–81. See also Mélèze Modrzejewski 1983: 250, who argues that, apart from certain cases, ethnics are in general used to designate the real ethnic origin of individuals up to the end of the third century.
[10] Van 't Dack 1988: 9–16. For the use of the same time limit, see Uebel 1968: 4–5. See also the comment of Bagnall 1984: 9 n. 6 on the meaning of ethnics after the middle of the second century BC.
[11] See also Launey 1987: 366–7, on the comparison between armies of Thracian kings and Greek military forces. Strabo (7 frag. 47 (48)) also testifies that in his time Thrace could provide 200,000 infantry soldiers and 15,000 cavalry.

Table 7.1 *Number of cleruchs by ethnic designation
(late fourth century–145 BC)*

Ethnics	Number of cleruchs	Percentage
Peloponnese		
Argeios	5	0.66
Korinthios	7	0.93
Megareus	3	0.40
Sikyônios	1	0.13
Trozênios	1	0.13
Élios	2	0.26
Asinaios	1	0.13
Arkas	8	1.06
Achaios	15	1.99
Lakôn	1	0.13
Central Greece – Thessaly		
Athênaios	17	2.25
Thêbaios	1	0.13
Chalkideus	10	1.32
Lokros[a]	2	0.26
Ainian	7	0.93
Boiôtios	5	0.66
Oitaios	2	0.26
Phôkeus	1	0.13
Akarnan	7	0.93
Kephallên	3	0.40
Dolops	1	0.13
Larisaios	3	0.40
Magnês ?[b]	2	0.26
Thessalos	22	2.91
Aegean Islands		
Naxios	1	0.13
Thêraios	1	0.13
Kôios	4	0.53
Samios	3	0.40
Chios	2	0.26
Mêthymnaios	1	0.13
Mytilênaios	1	0.13
Lesbios	1	0.13
Krês	11	1.46
Northern Greece		
Êpeirôtês	2	0.26
Pharios	1	0.13
Olynthios	1	0.13
Amphipolitês	5	0.66
Pellaios	2	0.26
Ainios	5	0.66

(*cont.*)

Table 7.1 *(cont.)*

Ethnics	Number of cleruchs	Percentage
Lysimacheus	2	0.26
Kardianos	4	0.53
Propontis		
Perinthios	4	0.53
Sêlymbrianos	1	0.13
Byzantios	2	0.26
Chalkêdonios/Kalchêdonios[c]	2	0.26
Kianos	1	0.13
Kyzikênos	1	0.13
Pontus		
Sinôpeus	1	0.13
Tianos	1	0.13
Krômnitês	1	0.13
Hêrakleôtês ?[d]	19	2.52
Bosporitês	1	0.13
Mes[êm]brianos	1	0.13
Asia Minor: city-states		
Pergamênos ?[e]	2	0.26
Ephesios	1	0.13
Priêneus	2	0.26
Milêsios	2	0.26
Halikarnasseus	2	0.26
Kaunios	1	0.13
Arsinoeitês apo Lykias	1	0.13
Magnês ?[f]	1	0.13
Myêsios	2	0.26
Aspendios	6	0.79
Pergaios[g]	2	0.26
Selgeus	1	0.13
Nagideus	1	0.13
Soleus	2	0.26
Cyprus		
Salaminios	2	0.26
Asia Minor: ethnic regions		
Paphlagôn	2	0.26
Bithynos	2	0.26
Mysos	10	1.32
Pisidês	5	0.66
Lykios	3	0.40
Kar	2	0.26
Galatês	1	0.13
Balkans		
Illyrios	2	0.26
Agrian	1	0.13

Table 7.1 *(cont.)*

Ethnics	Number of cleruchs	Percentage
Paiôn	5	0.66
Thraix	127	16.82
East		
Sidônios	1	0.13
Ask[alônitês] ?[b]	1	0.13
Antiocheus ?[i]	1	0.13
Ioudaios	37	4.90
Idoumaios	1	0.13
Araps	2	0.26
Mêdos (translation of *Mdy ms n Kmy*?)[j]	1	0.13
Kardouchos	1	0.13
Cyrenaica		
Barkaios/Barkaieus	6	0.79
Ptolemaieus apo Barkês	2	0.26
Kyrênaios	84	11.13
Hespereitês/Hesperitês	4	0.53
Libys	5	0.66
Italy – Sicily		
Syrakosios	10	1.32
Tarantinos	2	0.26
Kampanos	1	0.13
Iapyx	1	0.13
South Italy ?[k]	1	0.13
Macedon		
Makedôn	181	23.97
Unidentified city-states[l]		
Erythraios	1	0.13
Apollôniatês	5	0.66
Unknown[m]	7	0.93
Total	**752**	**100**

[a] This ethnic could refer to any of the three homonymous city-states in central Greece, the *Ozolai*, the *Opountioi* or the *Epiknêmidioi Lokroi* (Talbert 2000: *s.v. Locris*); see also Launey 1987: 166.
[b] These two cleruchs (Uebel 1968: no. 538 = La'da 2002: E1378, and Uebel 1968: no. 136 = La'da 2002: E1381) have, with reservations, been attributed to the area of Magnesia in Thessaly, rather than one of the two other homonymous cities in Asia Minor (Magnesia ad Sipiyum in Lydia and ad Maeandrum in Caria: Talbert 2000: *s.v. Magnesia*), following Launey 1987: 225 and 1144–5; see also La'da 2002: 164–6. On the problematic identification of the ethnic *Magnês*, see Launey 1987: 223–6.
[c] One of these cases (Uebel 1968: no. 105 = La'da 2002: E2557) is uncertain, because the ethnic is fragmentary and can be supplemented as either *Cha[lkêdonios]* or *Cha[lkideus]* (*P.Petr.* II 47.27: 210/209 BC – Arsinoite; for the supplement, see La'da 2002: 302).

(cont.)

table notes continued

^{d} The attribution of the ethnic designation *Hêrakleôtês* to Heraclea Pontica is based mainly on the number of cleruchs originating from other city-states of the area of Pontus and Propontis, as well as the relations, well attested in the literary sources, of the Ptolemies with Heraclea Pontica (see, for example, Memnon, *FGrH* 434 F17); the attribution remains uncertain. Given the number of ancient cities called Heraclea (nineteen, according to Talbert 2000: *s.v. Heraclea* and *Herakleia;* see also Launey 1987: 609–10), these men could come from different cities; see also Launey 1987: 612.

^{e} These two cases (Uebel 1968: no. 382 = La'da 2002: E1953 and La'da 2002: E2712) are not certain, because the ethnic is fragmentary and can be supplemented, in the first case as either *Perga[ios]* or *Perga[mênos]* (*P.Petr.* III 112Rf.13–4: 221–220 BC – Arsinoite; for the supplement, see La'da 2002: 227–8) and in the second as *Per[sês]*, *Per[gaios]*, *Per[gamênos]* or *Per[inthios]* (*CPR* XVIII 27.86–8: 232 or 206 BC – Theogonis, Arsinoite; for the supplement, see La'da 2002: 328).

^{f} In this particular case the ethnic has, with some reservation, been attributed to the city of Magnesia ad Maeandrum (Uebel 1968: no. 258 = La'da 2002: E1370), following the identification in Pap. Lugd.-Bat. XXI: 491; see also La'da 2002: 164. For the identification of the ethnic *Magnês*, see also n. *b* above.

^{g} Two more cases could be added in which the ethnic is fragmentary and can be supplemented only with some reservation: see above n. *e*.

^{h} This term, attested in *P.Petr.*^{2} I 9.3–4 (238/237 BC – Krokodilopolis, Arsinoite), is probably an ethnic rather than a patronymic, according to La'da 2002: 325, who made the supplement; see also the comment of Uebel 1968: 223 n. 3.

^{i} Given the number of ancient cities called *Antiocheia* (eighteen different cities, according to Talbert 2000: *s.v. Antiocheia* and *Antiochia;* see also Launey 1987: 612–13), the connection of this ethnic with a specific city is not possible in the absence of further information. Since only one cleruch is involved (Uebel 1968: no. 525), it seems more sensible just to place this person among the cleruchs coming from the broader area of the east.

^{j} Uebel 1968: no. 365; for the interpretation of the ethnic, see La'da 1994: 183–9.

^{k} This involves a person named *Mara[ios] Ptolemaiou* (Uebel 1968: no. 73) mentioned in *P.Petr.* III 57b.2–3 (3 February 201 BC – Arsinoite) who, based on his name (one quite common among Greeks of southern Italy), could have originated from that area, cf. Uebel 1968: 54 n. 4; *LGPN* III A: *s.v.* Μαραῖος.

^{l} Within this category we have placed the cleruchs carrying the ethnics *Erythraios* and *Apolloniatês*, which cannot safely be attributed to any particular city-state. There are five different cities named *Erythrai* (Talbert 2000: *s.v. Erythrai*) and seventeen named *Apollonia* (Talbert 2000: *s.v. Apollonia*); cf. also Launey 1987: 430, 798 and 1207, who attributes the ethnic Ἐρυθραῖος only with some reservation to the homonymous city in Asia Minor.

^{m} We have placed in this category: (a) three cleruchs carrying the ethnic *Magnês*, who could not be assigned to one of the three homonymous cities or areas: La'da 2002: E1382 (*BGU* XIV 2423.A.i.11 + *BGU* X 1938: *c.* 150 BC – provenance unknown), La'da 2002: E1383 (*BGU* XIV 2423.A.i.7 + *BGU* X 1938: *c.* 150 BC – provenance unknown) and the father of the individual recorded as La'da 2002: E1385 (*BGU* XIV 2391.10–1: *c.* 250 BC – Heracleopolite?); for the ethnic, cf. also La'da 2002: 164–6 and above nn. *b* and *f* ; (b) three cases where the ethnic designation is not preserved and the origin of the cleruchs is deduced from their name or other information: Uebel 1968: no. 1279 = La'da 2002: E2792 (*SB* XII 11053.A.2–3: 22 March 267 BC? – Tholthis, Oxyrhynchite; for the ethnic, see Uebel 1968: 95), Uebel 1968: no. 1333 = La'da 2002: E2803 (*SB* III 6303.10–11: 216/215 BC – Tholthis, Oxyrhynchite; for the ethnic, see Uebel 1968: 316 n. 3) and Uebel 1968: no. 220 (*P.Cair.Zen.* IV 59719.11 and 15: mid third century BC – provenance unknown and *P.Cair.Zen.* IV 59787.83: mid third century BC – Philadelphia (?), Arsinoite; for the ethnic, see Uebel 1968: 93 n. 1); (c) one further case where the ethnic is so fragmentary that it can be supplemented as *M[akedôn]* only with many reservations: Uebel 1968: no. 573 = La'da 2002: E2644 (*P.Petr.*^{2} I 18.19–20: 236/235 BC – Theogonis, Arsinoite; for the ethnic, see the editor's note.

Table 7.2 *Greek-Macedonian cleruchs (late fourth century–145 BC)*

Ethnic origin	Number of cleruchs	Percentage[a]
Mainland Greece	127	**16.87**
Peloponnese	44	5.84
Central Greece – Thessaly	83	11.03
Northern Greece	22	**2.92**
Greek cities of Propontis	11	**1.46**
Aegean islands	25	**3.32**
Cyprus (*Salaminios*)	2	**0.26**
Greek cities of Asia Minor	26	**3.44**
Greek cities of Pontus	24	**3.18**
Greek cities of Italy and Sicily	13	**1.73**
Unidentified Greek cities	6	**0.79**
Cyrene	84	**11.16**
Barca	8	**1.07**
Euhesperides	4	**0.53**
Macedonians	181	**24.04**
Total	**531**	**70.77**

[a] The percentages presented are based on the total number of cleruchs.

The first general conclusion to be drawn from these data is that the majority of cleruchs had a Greek origin. Specifically, 127 cleruchs came from mainland Greece, i.e. the Peloponnese, central Greece and Thessaly (see Table 7.2). If we add those from northern Greece (22), the cities of Propontis (11), Pontus (24) and Asia Minor (26), the islands of the Aegean (25), Cyprus (2), the Greek cities of Italy and Sicily (13), the cities of Cyrenaica (96), some unidentified Greek cities (6) and, finally, the Macedonian cleruchs (181), it is clear that more than two-thirds of the total, nearly 71 per cent, were cleruchs of Graeco-Macedonian origin (see Table 7:2). Furthermore, as Bagnall already observed,[12] the real percentage would probably be higher, since there is a substantial further number of cleruchs attested in the documents whose ethnics do not survive or are not mentioned, but who have Greek names; many of these too are likely to have been of Greek origin.[13]

This preponderance of Greeks (including Macedonians) is quite telling of the royal will to strengthen the Greek population of Egypt by means

[12] Bagnall 1984: 13–14. [13] See also Bagnall 1984: 13.

Table 7.3 *Macedonian cleruchs by period (late fourth century–145 BC)*[a]

	Late fourth century–246 BC		246–205 BC		205–145 BC		Total (late fourth century–145 BC)	
Macedonians	**21**	15.11%	**75**	18.56%	**85**	40.48%	**181**	24.04%
Total number of cleruchs	138		404		210		752	

[a] Next to the number of cleruchs attested in each period, the percentage figure represents this in relation to the total number of cleruchs attested in each period. In the last column, the percentages are based on the total number of cleruchs of all periods.

of the institution of the cleruchy. Furthermore, this supports the idea that the Ptolemies tried to staff their military forces mainly with Greeks, for Greeks, apparently, were regarded as soldiers of considerable military ability.[14] Ptolemy I, and his successors, aimed both to keep existing Greek and Macedonian soldiers permanently in Egypt and to attract more soldiers from the Greek world; settling them as cleruchs in the Egyptian *chôra* was an effective method of implementing this policy.[15]

It may also be noted that besides cleruchs of Greek origin, we also find a significant number of Thracians (127), representing nearly 17 per cent of the total, and a considerable number of Jews (37), representing about 5 per cent (Table 7.1). In each case we have to do with areas under strong Greek influence in the Hellenistic age.

MACEDONIAN CLERUCHS

Macedonians, as already noted, constituted the most numerous group from a single area (see Table 7.3); nearly a quarter of the total sample (just over 24 per cent) appears to have been of Macedonian origin. Certainly, the occurrence of a high proportion of Macedonian cleruchs in a kingdom established by a Macedonian is not in itself surprising. Still, in order to determine the time of their possible arrival and settlement in Egypt, we have divided the references to these cleruchs into three periods: the first runs down to the end of Ptolemy II Philadelphus' reign (246 BC) and the

---

[14] Winnicki 1985: 48. On the reputed quality of Greek troops, cf. Polyb. 5.36: Cleomenes III, the Spartan king exiled in Alexandria, considers the mercenaries from Greece to be definitely superior, and is quite contemptuous of soldiers from Syria and Caria. See also Griffith 1935: 127; Walbank 1957: 567–8; Launey 1987: 538; Buraselis 1993: 259.

[15] Van 't Dack 1988: 7.

Table 7.4 *Cleruchs by main area of origin and period (late fourth century–145 BC)*[a]

	Late fourth century–246 BC		246–205 BC		205–145 BC		Total (late fourth century–145 BC)	
Macedonians	21	15.11%	75	18.56%	85	40.48%	181	24.04%
Mainland Greece	31	22.3%	68	16.82%	28	13.33%	127	16.87%
Cyrenaica	30	21.58%	59	14.61%	7	3.33%	96	12.76%
Thracians	22	15.83%	67	16.58%	38	18.10%	127	16.87%
Jews	1	0.72%	15	3.71%	21	10.00%	37	4.91%
All cleruchs	138		404		210		752	

[a] See above, Table 7.3, n. *a*.

second to the end of the reign of Ptolemy IV Philopator (205/204 BC), while the third spans the first half of the second century until the end of Ptolemy VI Philometor's reign (145 BC) (Table 7.3).

Accordingly, until the middle of the third century, twenty-one Macedonians are attested as cleruchs. Their percentage in this period is quite significant (15.11 per cent) but not so high as the number of cleruchs from mainland Greece or Cyrenaica, and comparable only to the number of Thracian cleruchs as recorded in Table 7.4. In the second half of the third century, the number of Macedonian cleruchs nearly quadrupled (75 men compared with 21 in the previous period); this increase is in line with the general increase in the number of cleruchs after the middle of the third century (404 cleruchs with ethnics are attested, as against 138 in the previous period; see Table 7.3). During the first half of the second century, the number of Macedonian cleruchs remains at the same high level; in fact, it shows a slight increase (85 men compared with 75 in the previous period; see Table 7.3).

The first observation to be made is that the new documents published over the last forty years since Uebel's prosopography somewhat alter the picture presented by Bagnall in the case of Macedonian cleruchs. For the first two periods, figures then (in brackets) and now (see Table 7.3) are reasonably comparable: until 242 BC, 21 (17); 242–205 BC, 75 (60). By the first half of the second century, however, the picture has changed. The number of Macedonian settlers recorded by Bagnall showed a sharp (50 per cent) decrease from the previous period (30 compared to 60 earlier). This stands in stark contrast to the small increase noticed for the same period in our figures. This is not of minor importance, as we shall shortly see.

According to Bagnall, as already noted, all these Macedonian settlers would have consisted simply of soldiers of Ptolemy I Soter and their descendants, since it would be impossible for the Ptolemies to recruit new Macedonians from the rival kingdom of the Antigonids. This, in his view, resulted in a situation whereby Ptolemaic cleruchs came to form an 'almost closed class'.[16] The documented increase, however, in the number of Macedonian cleruchs after the middle of the third century calls this conclusion into question.

The increase in the number of Macedonians, and cleruchs in general, was attributed by Bagnall to the survival of so many papyri dating to the second half of the third century, many of which concern cleruchs.[17] However, a survey of all surviving papyrological documents by reign clearly shows that this is not the case (see Table 7.5). The documents dating to the first half of the third century, most of them during the reign of Philadelphus, are far more numerous than those dating to the second half of the third century, as well as to the first half of the second (2,240 documents as against 1,594 and 1,513 respectively).

On the other hand, the type and content of the documents – which cannot be presented in a table – could certainly affect our sample to a degree, but it seems somewhat implausible to regard these as the only reason for the near quadruplication of the number of cleruchs after the middle of the third century. Indeed, the fact that the number of Macedonian cleruchs remains at the same high level – even with a slight increase – during the first half of the second century renders the attribution of this increase only to chance even less plausible. This changed picture is, of course, the result of new texts published since Uebel's basic study in 1968.

Then there is the question of the wider picture in this period. Although we must accept that the existence of the kingdom of the Antigonids would have prevented the Ptolemies from a massive and organised recruitment of soldiers from Macedon, nevertheless cases of Macedonians emigrating to Egypt on their own initiative cannot be excluded. In the ancient world there were no borders, in the modern sense, to restrict the movement of people. Therefore, Macedonians on friendly terms with the Ptolemies or who were seeking a better life in a welcoming kingdom could, possibly,

[16] Bagnall 1984: 15, 18. For a similar view, see also Griffith 1935: 114; Launey 1987: 90–1.
[17] Bagnall 1984: 9 and 12–14.

Table 7.5 *Surviving documents by reign*[a]

Period	Number of surviving papyri	Percentage
Ptolemy I (late fourth century–285 BC)[b]	8	0.1
Ptolemy II (285–246 BC)[c]	2,232	34
Total: first half of third century BC	**2,240**	**34.1**
Ptolemy III (246–221 BC)	862	13.2
Ptolemy IV (221–205 BC)	530	8.1
Second half of third century BC	202	3.1
Total: second half of third century BC	**1,594**	**24.4**
Third century BC (undetermined)	336	5.1
Total: third century BC	**4,170**	**63.6**
Ptolemy V (205–180 BC)[d]	406	6.2
Ptolemy VI (180–145 BC)	984	15
First half of second century BC	123	1.8
Second century BC (undetermined)	377	5.8
Total: first half of second century BC	**1,890**	**28.8**
Undetermined (fourth to first century BC)[e]	495	7.6
Total	**6,555**	**100**

[a] The data of this table derive from a search of the web-based Heidelberger Gesamt-verzeichnis der griechischen Papyrusurkunden Ägyptens (HGV) made in 2009.
[b] The limit taken for the reign of Ptolemy I was not the year of his death, 283/2 BC, but 285 BC, when Ptolemy II became co-regent; see Skeat 1969: 10 and 29–31; Hazzard 1987; E. Grzybek 1990: 131, 171 and 175.
[c] In cases attributed to the reign of Ptolemy II, we have also included 820 documents dated to the first half or *c.* the middle of the third century BC.
[d] In the entry for Ptolemy V we have also included sixty-nine documents dated to the first half of the second century BC.
[e] This category includes 245 documents dated between the fourth and the first centuries BC, 97 dated between the third and second centuries BC, and 153 documents dated between the second and first centuries BC.

decide to join the Ptolemaic army and might then have been settled as cleruchs in Egypt. The Antigonids could not have held them back.

Others too might choose to emigrate to Egypt, men ill-disposed towards or on bad terms with the kings of Macedon, mostly men who had themselves suffered persecution under the Antigonids or who had others in their entourage who had done so. In fact, the revolt of Alexander, regent of Antigonus II Gonatas in Greece, indicates that the dynasty of Macedon could encounter internal opposition – sometimes, quite strong opposition. Philip V is also known to have persecuted, imprisoned or put to death some of his generals and friends on various occasions.[18] The idyll of Theocritus with which we started indicates that emigration was indeed regarded as a solution for those looking for a way out of their problems.

Furthermore, the fact that the few cleruchs coming from Pella and Amphipolis (see Table 7.1) are attested only after the middle of the third century,[19] the occurrence of Macedonian mercenaries in the Ptolemaic army throughout the third and second centuries,[20] the cases of a 'leader of foreign troops' (*hegemôn exô taxeôn*) designated as *Thessalonikeus*[21] and a *Kassandreus* 'set in charge of the city by the king' (*kathestamenos hypo tou basileôs epi tês poleôs*), who was honoured by the Ptolemaic garrison stationed at Antissa on Lesbos,[22] all indicate that individual Macedonians might render their services to the Ptolemies, regardless of Ptolemaic relations with the Antigonids.

Moreover, after Alexander's campaign, Macedonians were settled throughout the Hellenistic world in military settlements (*katoikiai*) founded by himself or his successors,[23] especially in Asia Minor, Syria and Palestine, from where the Ptolemies could easily recruit manpower. Some, therefore, of the Macedonian cleruchs may have come not from Macedon directly but from Asia Minor also. Finally, the many wars fought during the third century provided further opportunities to obtain new soldiers; so

---

[18] For the case of Megaleas, Crinon, Apelles and Leontius, see Polyb. 5.14.11–16.10; 5.25; 5.27–9; Hammond-Walbank 1988: 381–4. Philip's general in Lychnis was also persecuted (Livy 27.32.9), and five more of his *philoi* were executed in 205 or 204 BC (Diod. Sic. 28.2). Finally, in 183 BC, three men and some of their associates were executed (Polyb. 23.10.9), and at the same time Philip ordered the imprisonment of the sons and daughters of the Macedonians who had been executed (Polyb. 23.10.4–7); for all these, see Hammond and Walbank 1988: 485.

[19] Five cleruchs bearing the ethnic *Amphipolitês/Amphipoleitês* are attested in documents all dated from 237 to 209–207 BC: (a) La'da 2002: E0131 (*BGU* XIV 2397.21: 214/213 BC – Tholthis, Oxyrhynchite); (b) Uebel 1968: no. 880 = La'da 2002: E0133 (*P.Petr.*² I 3.3–4: 238–7 – Krokodilopolis, Arsinoite); (c) Uebel 1968: no. 905 = La'da 2002: E0134 (*P.Petr.*² I 17.20–1: 236/235 BC – Krokodilopolis, Arsinoite); (d) Uebel 1968: no. 106 = La'da 2002: E0135 (*P.Petr.* II 47.28–9: 210/209 BC – Arsinoite; *P.Petr.* III 74a.1: 209–207 BC – Hiera Nesos, Arsinoite); (e) Uebel 1968: no. 523 (*P.Tebt.* III.1 815.fr.8.R2.3–4: *c.* 223/222 BC – Tebtynis, Arsinoite). Two further individuals from Pella, from the same family, are attested in a single document dated 231 or 206 BC (*CPR* XVIII 21.436–8: Theogonis, Arsinoite; see also La'da 2002: E1943 and E1944).

[20] See La'da 2002: E1585 (135/134 BC), E1493 (244–242 BC), E1610 (173 BC), E1569 (173 BC), E1565 (173 BC), E1507 (173 BC), E1452 (113 BC); also the case of a Macedonian Ptolemaic mercenary on the coast of Syria (*SEG* 27.973 bis. 20: second half of the third century BC).

[21] La'da 2002: E0689 (*SB* III 7169: second century BC – provenance unknown).

[22] An inscription from Antissa presented by A. Matthaiou at a symposium held in the Epigraphical Museum of Athens in 2005 records (ll. 3–5): Δημήτριος Ὀρέστου Κασσαν[δρ]εὺς ὁ καθεσταμένος ὑπὸ τοῦ βασιλέως [i.e. Ptolemy IV, from the context] ἐπὶ τῆς πόλεως.

[23] See Launey 1987: 331–53.

why not Macedonians as well, namely men who were captured or who even
defected voluntarily from the opposing camp? The occurrence of such cases
of defection or capture renders this assumption plausible.[24] Therefore, the
arrival and settlement of new Macedonian cleruchs throughout the third
century can by no means be excluded.

Consequently, the view that all these cleruchs were simply soldiers
recruited by Ptolemy I Soter and their descendants, and that these were just
under-represented in the documents of the first period, seems implausible.
It would on balance seem more likely that the arrival of new immigrants
was the main reason for the significant increase in the number of Macedonian cleruchs after the middle of the third century. Thus the notion that
the cleruchs formed an 'almost closed class' does not stand.

The immigration and settlement of new cleruchs was, we have argued,
possible even at a later date. We can now turn to consider in greater detail
the Macedonians attested for each of the three periods in order to determine
the possible time of their arrival and settlement in Egypt. In the first period
(see Table 7.3), twenty-one Macedonians are attested as cleruchs, men who,
therefore, may indeed have been soldiers in the army of Ptolemy I Soter
or the descendants of these; equally well they may have arrived in Egypt
during the reign of Philadelphus.

The full number of Macedonians in the army of Ptolemy I is not
known. He may have obtained Macedonian soldiers on various occasions:
from the military forces left in Egypt by Alexander,[25] at the agreement in
Babylon in 323 BC[26] or from the royal guard (c. 1,000 men) that probably
escorted Alexander's corpse.[27] Furthermore, during Perdiccas' campaign
and especially after his assassination, Macedonians from his army deserted

---

[24] See, e.g., Diod. Sic. 19.85.4, 8,000 captured at the battle of Gaza in 312 BC; 20.19.4, defection
of soldiers from the army of Antigonus Monophthalmus in 305 BC due to bribery by Ptolemy I.
For the possibility that some soldiers were captured during the Second Syrian War, see *P.Petr.* II
13.3.9–10 (middle third century BC – Arsinoite); cf. Winnicki 1991: 102 with n. 85, *desmôtai* refers to
war-captives, possibly settled as cleruchs. Captives and soldiers from Asia Minor during the third
century: τῶν ἀπὸ τῆς [Ἀ]σίας/ αἰχμαλ[ώ]των (*P.Petr.* III 104.3: 244/3 BC – Arsinoite); τῶν ἀπὸ
τῆς Ἀσίας στρατιωτῶν (*P.Enteux.* 54 recto.2: 11 May 218 BC – Bakchias, Arsinoite).

[25] These forces must have become the core of Ptolemy's army when he took over the satrapy of Egypt.
According to Arrian (*Anab.* 3.5.3), a part of that army consisted of mercenaries, but it is quite possible
that at least a number of Macedonians were included; see Lesquier 1911: 2. In contrast, Griffith 1935:
29–30 and 109 claims they were all mercenaries. On these forces, see also Q. Curtius Rufus (4.8.4),
with a different version from Arrian, especially regarding the leading officers. See also Hammond
1996: 104.

[26] Bagnall 1984: 16–18 and n. 19. For this view, see Welles 1970: 52. For the view that Ptolemy, arriving
in Egypt without military forces recruited there with the cash he found in the country, see Lesquier
1911: 1 and Griffith 1935: 109.

[27] Hammond 1996: 107–8.

to Ptolemy.[28] In any case, the latter is known to have had a number of Macedonian soldiers in his army at the battle of Gaza in 312 BC.[29] In the same battle Ptolemy I managed to capture 8,000 men from Demetrius' army, among them quite probably some of the 2,000 Macedonians that staffed his phalanx.[30]

These captives were, according to Diodorus,[31] settled in Egypt, perhaps as cleruchs. Given that Macedonians were in high demand by Hellenistic monarchs,[32] it is quite reasonable to imagine that Ptolemy I would try to keep in Egypt those Macedonians already in his service by settling them as cleruchs. He could use them to staff the phalanx and the elite corps and at the same time enhance the Macedonian character of his newly founded kingdom. However, having no other testimony apart from the reference of Diodorus, and mainly owing to the lack of papyri from Soter's reign, it is impossible to verify these assumptions. Since the area of the Fayum was not properly drained until the reign of Philadelphus,[33] Soter would probably have settled his soldiers in the valley of the Nile or the Delta, but we simply cannot know more on this subject.

The first cases of Macedonian cleruchs attested actually date from the period 282–274 BC and involve two men[34] who could easily have been soldiers of Soter or their sons. The majority of Macedonians, however – and of cleruchs in general – appear after 260 BC, and, since their age is not known, it is not possible to estimate the moment of their arrival and of their settlement in Egypt. Still, this fact, together with the probable drainage of 'The Marsh' (the Fayum) in the same period, which provided

---

[28] Diod. Sic. 18.33–6.

[29] According to Diodorus (19.80.4), at Gaza Ptolemy had 18,000 infantry and 4,000 cavalrymen, ὧν ἦσαν οἱ μὲν Μακεδόνες, οἱ δὲ μισθοφόροι. For the interpretation of this passage, see Griffith 1935: 109–10 and n. 1.

[30] See Griffith 1935: 114 and n. 1.   [31] Diod. Sic. 19.85.3.

[32] For Macedonians in the army of Alexander and their quality, see Berve 1926: 103–33; Hammond 1984: 51–4. We do not know how many Macedonian soldiers were in the army of Alexander when he died, nor is it possible to follow their fortunes during the turbulent period that followed his death. Hammond 1984: 58 n. 21 estimates the number of Macedonians that Alexander kept in Babylon in 323 BC at around 13,000 infantry soldiers (6,700 for the new phalanx and 6,000 in the elite corps of *argyraspides* and *hypaspistes*). These numbers, assuming they are for Macedonians only, are in accordance with those recorded in Q. Curtius Rufus (10.2.8; i.e. 13,000 infantry and 2,000 cavalry) for troops staying in Asia Minor when Alexander sent back Macedonian veterans under the command of Craterus (10,000 men, according to Arr. *Anab.* 7.12.1s). For Macedonians in the armies of the Successors up to the battle of Ipsus, see Launey 1987: 293–305; for Macedonian veterans of Alexander after his death in general, see Hammond 1984.

[33] Lesquier 1911: 46; Thompson 2003: 118–19. For works involved in the drainage of Lake Moeris, see Thompson 2005b: 305–6.

[34] La'da 2002: E1715 (*P.Hib.* I 30fr.a.2: 282–274 BC – Heracleopolite) and La'da 2002: E2819 (*P.Hib.* I 30fr.d.12–14: 282–274 BC – Heracleopolite).

Philadelphus with vast areas of arable land, indicates that the settlement of cleruchs in general must have become intense after 260 BC and around the middle of the third century. Ptolemy II would settle on the new land of the Arsinoite nome all new Macedonian immigrants who joined the Ptolemaic army, as well as the descendants of soldiers recruited by his father.

In the second half of the third century, as we have already seen, the number of Macedonians nearly quadrupled (seventy-five men, compared with twenty-one), in line with the general increase in the number of cleruchs (Table 7.3). It seems only reasonable to assume that at least a number of these men arrived in Egypt after the reign of Ptolemy I. The policy, then, of Ptolemy II Philadelphus seems to have been followed by his successors, since the ethnic *Makedôn* continued to be highly prestigious throughout the Hellenistic period. However, the increase in the number of Macedonian settlers in the first half of the second century, even if by only 10 men (85 men, compared with 75), is more difficult to explain as the result of the arrival of newcomers or the settlement of more cleruchs, because it stands in contrast to a significant drop in the total number of cleruchs (210 men, compared with 404 in the preceding period). Macedonians now accounted for 40.48 per cent of cleruchs (Table 7.3).

The decrease in the total number of cleruchs cannot be attributed to an insufficiency of relevant sources,[35] since, 1,513 documents are dated in this period, and there are 377 more to be dated generally in the second century, compared with 1,594 in the previous period (see Table 7.5). Rather, in my view, it indicates a decline in immigration into Egypt after the end of the third century,[36] together with a degree of restraint in the settlement of new cleruchs of non-Egyptian origin. This is indeed in accordance with the transformation of the *klêros* into a hereditary possession during the second century, as well as the grant of *klêroi* to more Egyptian *machimoi* and to men serving in the Ptolemaic police. Thus the majority of cleruchs attested in documents of this period should rather be regarded as descendants of men already settled sometime in the third century, but by no means excluding the possibility of a few individual cases of newcomers.

The same conclusion must stand for Macedonians as well. The slight increase in their number in the first half of the second century may then

---

[35] This decrease in the number of cleruchs is shown not only by our statistics, which take into account only those cleruchs with an ethnic designation attested, but also by those based on Uebel's prosopography of all attested cleruchs (Uebel 1968, with 381 in the first half of the second century, compared with 672 in the second half of the third century, and only 367 in the earliest period).

[36] See also La'da 1996: 91–2, who reached the same conclusion on examining all ethnic designations preserved in the sources.

quite plausibly be attributed to the particular status of this particular ethnic. For the ethnic *Makedôn* was invested with high status and prestige, and those so designated held a privileged position in the Ptolemaic kingdom. The descendants of old Macedonian immigrants were, therefore, keen to preserve their ethnic designation, combined with the consciousness of their 'Macedonian' descent, while the use of other ethnics was gradually being discontinued by other long-term immigrant settlers.[37] Furthermore, the special status of this designation led gradually to its degeneration into a fictitious ethnic, designating also non-Macedonians – those, for example, who served in 'Macedonian' military units. Although, according to La'da, there is no certain proof that this degeneration took place before the middle of the second century,[38] there are certain indications suggesting the possible fictitious use of the ethnic already from the beginning of the second century.[39] Accordingly, this small increase in the number of Macedonian cleruchs could in fact result from the more frequent use of the designation *Makedôn* in comparison with other ethnics after the end of the third century, especially by men belonging to military units. Besides, this increase might also mean that men of 'Macedonian' descent were more eager to join the class of cleruchs, inheriting their father's *klêros* and following in his footsteps, in contrast to descendants of immigrants of other ethnic origins who may well have sought different careers. For the Ptolemies, *Makedones* (even of non-'Macedonian' origin) would still be preferable as cleruchic settlers. In any case, this slight increase in connection with the considerable decrease in the number of cleruchs from elsewhere certainly reflects the fact that Macedonian cleruchs as a group are more easily traced in the sources than others.

CLERUCHS FROM MAINLAND GREECE

Turning next to the cleruchs from the rest of mainland Greece, namely the Peloponnese, central Greece and Thessaly, we find 127 cases attested in

[37] See La'da 1996: 89–92 for the gradual discontinuance of the use of foreign ethnics after the end of the third century.

[38] La'da 1996: 123–6; see also Tataki 1998: 34. The ethnic *Makedôn* when used in conjunction with the term *triakontarouros* may be considered a fictitious designation already during the third century, referring to the specific military unit of *triakontarouroi* (La'da 1996: 122), perhaps the Ptolemaic Macedonian phalanx (Uebel 1968: 40 nn. 3 and 381). For this reason, we have excluded all those carrying this designation, namely fifty-eight cases, from both our prosopography and statistics.

[39] Based mainly on two cases of Macedonians with Iranian names: La'da 2002: E1441 (*CPR* XVIII 19.392–3: 231 or 206 BC – Theogonis, Arsinoite) and E1440 (*P.Heid.* VIII 417.19–20: 190/89 BC – Heracleopolis). See also La'da 1996: 120–2.

total (see Table 7.2). More specifically, forty-four cleruchs come from ten different cities in the Peloponnese, and among these the most numerous group is that of those called Achaeans (see Table 7.1). The ethnic *Achaios* would appear to be a generic (and comfortably abbreviated) reference to citizens of any member-city of the Achaean League; such members could apparently designate themselves as *Achaioi* instead of using their own separate ethnics.[40] In any case, the occurrence of a number of Achaean cleruchs is not surprising, since friendly relations between the Achaean League and the Ptolemies are well documented. Plutarch refers to the contacts between Aratus and Philadelphus, the visit of the former to Alexandria and the grant of significant financial aid to the Achaeans by the latter,[41] as well as to the award to Ptolemy III of the leadership (*hêgemonia*) over the Achaeans by land and sea.[42] Moreover, according to Polybius, there were many treaties of alliance between the Ptolemaic kingdom and the Achaean League.[43] The Ptolemies would, therefore, seek to recruit soldiers from an ally. In fact, Polybius records that Ptolemy VI Philometor and Ptolemy VIII Euergetes II sent envoys in 169/168 BC requesting, in this case unsuccessfully, 1,000 infantry soldiers and 200 cavalrymen from the Achaeans for their war against Antiochus IV.[44]

As far as the area of central Greece and Thessaly is concerned, eighty-three cases of cleruchs are attested (see Table 7.2). Among them, the largest group are the Thessalians, to whom we may also add three men from Larissa and two Magnesians, if these do indeed come from the homonymous area in Thessaly (see Table 7.1).[45] The occurrence of a number of Thessalian cleruchs, which is also affirmed by the reference in the papyri to a hipparchy named that 'of the Thessalians and the other Greeks' (*tôn Thessalôn kai tôn allôn Hellênôn*),[46] is not surprising, since Thessalians were famous for their cavalry. Alexander had a significant number of Thessalian cavalry soldiers in his army.[47] The Ptolemies too would try to keep Thessalians serving in their army by settling them as cleruchs.

During the first half of the third century, the percentage of cleruchs from mainland Greece reaches 22.3% (31 men; see Table 7.6); this constitutes the largest group in this period, followed closely by Cyrenean cleruchs (21.58%) and, lagging behind, Macedonians (15.11%) and Thracians (15.83%)

---

[40] See also Bingen 2007: 96.   [41] Plut. *Arat.* 11–13.   [42] Plut. *Arat.* 24.4.   [43] Polyb. 22.9.
[44] Polyb. 29.23–5. For the Achaean diaspora in Ptolemaic Egypt, see also Bingen 2007: 94–103.
[45] See above, Table 7.1, n. *b*.
[46] See, e.g., *P.Enteux.* 15 recto.3–4: 13 January 218 BC – Magdola, Arsinoite; see also Winnicki 1989: 222–4.
[47] For more details, see Launey 1987: 221–3.

Table 7.6 *Cleruchs from mainland Greece by period*
(late fourth century–145 BC)[a]

	Late fourth century–246 BC		246–205 BC		205–145 BC		Total (late fourth century–145 BC)	
Mainland Greece	31	22.3%	68	16.82%	28	13.33%	127	16.87%
Peloponnese	12	8.63%	24	5.94%	8	3.81%	44	5.84%
Central Greece – Thessaly	19	13.67%	44	10.88%	20	9.52%	83	11.03%
Total number of cleruchs	138		404		210		752	

[a] See above, Table 7.3, n. *a*.

(see Table 7.4). This is indicative of the composition of the class of cleruchs up to the middle of the third century and, to a certain extent, of the Ptolemaic army also.

In the second half of the third century the number of cleruchs from mainland Greece more than doubled (sixty-eight men, compared with thirty-one in the previous period: see Table 7.6). As in the case of the Macedonians, it seems improbable that these cleruchs were simply descendants of soldiers in Soter's army who were under-represented in the documents of the first period. Besides, the simultaneous decrease in their percentage in relation to the overall number of cleruchs is to be mainly explained by the even higher increase in the number of Macedonians. We may conclude that the arrival and settlement in Egypt of military immigrants from mainland Greece continued at least until the end of the third century.

In the first half of the second century, however, their number shows a significant drop, to a level lower than in the first period (only 28 men, *c.* 13 per cent: see Table 7.6), which implies in turn that the immigration of these men was in decline, in accordance with the overall pattern, as shown above. This does indeed suggest that most of these individuals are likely to have been descendants of cleruchs settled in the third century rather than newcomers; the latter possibility is not, however, to be completely excluded. On the whole, mainland Greece seems to have played an important role as a human-resource pool for the Ptolemaic army, at least until the end of the third century.

CLERUCHS FROM AREAS UNDER PTOLEMAIC CONTROL

In comparison with those from Macedon and the rest of mainland Greece, cleruchs coming from the Aegean area are quite limited in number: only twenty-five, eleven of whom are Cretans; the rest of this group is designated by eight different ethnics (see Table 7.1). The scarcity here of Islanders is striking, given that the Ptolemies had many of the Aegean islands under their control in addition, for a period of time, to the League of Islanders.[48] Specifically, there is only one cleruch from Thera, perhaps the longest-held Ptolemaic possession in the Aegean; three cleruchs from the island of Lesbos, despite the strong Ptolemaic presence there at least during the reign of Philopator;[49] and four more coming from Cos, which is even more surprising, considering the close relations of the Ptolemies with the island where Philadelphus was born (see Table 7.1).[50]

Moreover, the fact that only eleven Cretan cleruchs are attested is in contrast both to their acknowledged skill as light-armed troops, mainly as archers,[51] and to other evidence of Cretan soldiers in the Ptolemaic army: Polybius, for instance, mentions that at the battle of Raphia the army of Ptolemy IV Philopator included a corps of 3,000 Cretans.[52] Furthermore, the Ptolemies kept a garrison at Itanus.[53] One possible explanation for the small number of Cretans among the cleruchs could be, as already proposed by Launey, that Cretan soldiers preferred to serve as mercenaries for a short period of time, returning afterwards to their homeland, rather than becoming permanently settled in a foreign area.[54]

A similar picture can be drawn for cleruchs coming from the North Aegean and the Propontis (see Table 7.2). Specifically, only eleven men come from Thracian cities (Aenus and Cardia–Lysimachea) (see Table 7.1), despite the fact that parts of Thrace and the Hellespont were under Ptolemaic control, at least from the reign of Ptolemy III Euergetes, according to the inscription of Adoulis[55] and that of Hippomedon, the Ptolemaic

[48] For Ptolemaic possessions in the Aegean, see Bagnall 1976: 103–5 (Cos–Calymnos), 123–58 (central Aegean–League of Islanders), 161–2 (Lesbos) and 168–9 (Chios). For the League of Islanders, see Meadows, Chapter 2 in this volume, proposing a Ptolemaic foundation for the League.
[49] See Bagnall 1976: 161–2. A Ptolemaic garrison at Antissa is now known from the inscription presented by Matthaiou in 2005 (see above, n. 22). For Ptolemaic influence on Lesbos, see also Meadows, Chapter 2 in this volume.
[50] *FGrH* 239 B F19; see also Theoc. 17.58–65.   [51] See Launey 1987: 280–6.   [52] Polyb. 5.65.7.
[53] For relations between the Ptolemies and Crete, see Bagnall 1976: 117–23; Chaniotis 1996: esp. 16–18, 30–49.
[54] See Launey 1987: 276–80.   [55] *OGIS* 54.14–15.

Table 7.7 *Cleruchs from Cyrenaica by period (late fourth century–145 BC)*[a]

	Late fourth century–246 BC		246–205 BC		205–145 BC		Total (late fourth century–145 BC)	
Cyrenaica	30	**21.58%**	59	**14.61%**	7	**3.33%**	96	**12.76**
Cyrene	24	17.27%	53	13.12%	7	3.33%	84	11.16%
Barca	4	2.88%	4	0.99%	0	–	8	1.07%
Euhesperides	2	1.44%	2	0.50%	0	–	4	0.53%
Total number of cleruchs	138		404		210		752	

[a] See above, Table 7.3, n. *a*.

governor (*stratêgos*) of Thrace and areas of the Hellespont;[56] garrisons are also known to have been placed at Aenus and Maronea.[57] Particularly low too is the number of cleruchs coming from the Greek cities of Asia Minor, from Aeolis to Cilicia (twenty-six men; see Table 7.1), despite the fact that part of Asia Minor was already under Ptolemaic control during the reign of Philadelphus.[58]

In sum, the number of cleruchs coming from areas that were at least for a period under Ptolemaic control appears unexpectedly low. This is also the case with the number of those from long-standing Ptolemaic possessions, such as Coele Syria and Cyprus (see Table 7.1).[59] The only exception seems to be the area of Cyrenaica; the number of cleruchs from Cyrene is quite significant throughout the third century (seventy-seven men), but it sees a sharp drop in the second century (when only seven cleruchs are attested; see Table 7.7).

As a result of this survey, we may conclude that, in the main, Bagnall was right in supposing that the Ptolemies recruited mainly mercenaries from their possessions outside Egypt, as opposed to members of regular army units, who would then be settled in Egypt as cleruchs. This may indeed be regarded as one of the main reasons for keeping these areas under

[56] *IG* XII.8 156 = *Syll*[3] 502; see also Bagnall 1976: 160 and n. 4; Gauthier 1979: 76–89. Polybius (5.34.7–8) also mentions that at Philopator's accession the Ptolemies held various points on the Hellespont and the *topoi* around Lysimachea, as well as Aenus, Maronea and πορρώτερον ἔτι πόλεων. See further Bagnall 1976: 159–61 and n. 6; for the conquest of this area, see Buraselis 1982: 132–41 and 172–3.

[57] Livy 31.16.4; see also the Epinicus decree in Gauthier 1979: 80 n. 10 and 88–9; for previous bibliography, see Bagnall 1976: 160 and n. 4.

[58] For Ptolemaic possessions in Asia Minor, see Bagnall 1976: 89–102 and 105–16.

[59] For Cyprus under Ptolemaic rule, see Bagnall 1976: 38–79.

Table 7.8 *Cleruchs from other areas under Ptolemaic control by period (late fourth century–145 BC)[a]*

	Late fourth century–246 BC		246–205 BC		205–145 BC		Total (late fourth century–145 BC)	
Aegean islands	3	2.16%	17	4.21%	5	2.38%	25	3.32%
North Aegean	2	1.44%	16	3.94%	1	0.48%	19	2.53%
Propontis	2	1.44%	6	1.49%	3	1.42%	11	1.46%
Asia Minor	4	2.88%	15	3.71%	7	3.33%	26	3.44%
Total number of cleruchs	138		404		210		752	

[a] See above, Table 7.3, n. *a*.

their control.[60] However, a more specific explanation could be added: the kings needed manpower to staff the garrisons stationed locally and would probably try to avoid the demographic enfeeblement of their possessions. It is also possible that, apart from royal preference, the men themselves were unwilling to leave their homelands, since the establishment of Ptolemaic control in these areas offered more prospects for a reasonable standard of living without the need to emigrate, through service, for instance, as mercenaries in local garrisons. In the case of Cyrene, its special status as the first foreign possession of Ptolemy I Soter and one which remained in Ptolemaic hands for over two centuries (until 96 BC), as well as its position in close proximity to Egypt and possibly also its very similar climatic conditions, can perhaps explain the high number of Cyrenean cleruchs.

Moreover, we should note that in the first half of the third century there are very few cleruchs from any of the other areas that were, at least for a period, under Ptolemaic control (eleven men in total). However, in the second half of the third century, these numbers do show some small increase (fifty-four men in total), in line with the general tendency (see Table 7.8). The fact that the majority of such cleruchs are attested only after the middle of the third century indicates that Ptolemaic expansion must have played a role at least in the immigration of the few whose names survive. Although Ptolemaic possessions provided very few cleruchs in all, the men from these regions who are known must have arrived in Egypt after, and perhaps even because of, the conquests of Philadelphus in parts of the Aegean and along the coast of Asia Minor, as is clear from Theocritus'

[60] Bagnall 1984: 16; see also Buraselis 1993: 258–9.

encomium to Ptolemy II.[61] The main period of immigration from these regions would, however, seem to have followed the expansion of Ptolemaic control under Ptolemy III Euergetes over Cilicia, Pamphylia, Ionia, the Hellespont and Thrace.[62] Some weight is thus given to the view that, until the end of the third century, men continued to arrive in Egypt and were settled there as cleruchs by the Ptolemies.

In the first half of the second century the number of cleruchs from these areas is significantly reduced (sixteen men in total; see Table 7.8). This decrease must have been the consequence of the overall decline in immigration into Egypt, as well as the loss of Ptolemaic possessions in the areas under discussion. In the case of Cyrene, the establishment by Ptolemy VIII Euergetes II of a separate rule in the area from 163 until 145 BC can only partly explain the sudden drop in the number of cleruchs coming from this area (see Table 7.7).

CONCLUSIONS

The immigration of military men into Egypt and their later settlement as cleruchs may be attributed to two different factors: to royal incentives as well as to the private initiative of individuals. The relations and possible alliances between the Ptolemaic kingdom and certain areas (such as the Achaean League, mentioned above) certainly provided the kings with opportunities for the recruitment of soldiers and, further, favoured immigration into Egypt. However, these relations and alliances do not seem to have played the key role either in the movement of people or in the granting of *klêroi*. The Ptolemies preferred to settle as cleruchs a large number of soldiers from Macedonia and from the cities of mainland Greece, since these men were considered particularly valuable. The majority of cleruchs, as we have clearly seen, had a Greek–Macedonian origin. Contrary to what has been argued in the past, it seems that Macedonians and men from mainland Greece may often have decided to settle as cleruchs in Egypt on their own initiative and for reasons of their own, regardless of relations between their homelands and the Ptolemaic kingdom.

On the other hand, many of the areas under Ptolemaic control, including the Aegean islands, cities in Thrace, the Hellespont and Asia Minor, were only used by the kings to a limited degree as sources of manpower for their regular army. For the reasons we have suggested, possession of these areas by the Ptolemies seems to have encouraged just a few men to emigrate

[61] Theoc. 17.87–90. [62] For these Ptolemaic possessions, see above nn. 55–8.

and settle in Egypt. However, the establishment of a seaborne empire, controlling a considerable part of the Aegean during a significant period of Ptolemaic rule, certainly facilitated the movement of people and in general favoured their emigration towards Egypt. As the Ptolemaic kingdom grew into a powerful and wealthy empire, Egypt would definitely appear to provide a desirable and most promising destination to whoever sought the chance of a better life.

Turning finally to the institution of the cleruchy itself, the view that Ptolemaic cleruchs formed an 'almost closed class', as earlier argued by Bagnall, must be revised. The large number of cleruchs attested in the second half of the third century (a significant number of Macedonians among them) cannot, as we have seen, be convincingly attributed to the pattern of surviving documentation. Such attestations, rather, imply that immigration into Egypt and the settlement of new cleruchs by the Ptolemies continued at least until the end of that century. Hostile relations and rivalry between the Hellenistic states did not inhibit military men from immigration into Egypt on their own initiative. And here they were settled as cleruchs by Ptolemaic kings.

CHAPTER 8

Our Academic visitor is missing: Posidippus 89 (A–B) and 'smart capital' for the thalassocrats

Paul McKechnie

Naphtali Lewis called Ptolemaic Egypt 'Eldorado on the Nile'.[1] For its rulers, however, this was true but not sufficient as a description. Creating a powerful and sustainable settler society was a matter of investing, not only of finding treasure; and a vital element in the programme of investment was attracting human capital to the enterprise. Human capital in the modern world is equally pivotal. In 2012 in New Zealand, 242 years after Captain Cook anchored in Poverty Bay, Immigration New Zealand, a service of the Department of Labour, said that:[2]

New Zealand's business migration categories are designed to contribute to economic growth, attracting 'smart' capital and business expertise to New Zealand, and enabling experienced business people to buy or establish businesses in New Zealand.

In the context of policy in the Department of Labour, the goal of attracting 'smart capital' makes it important to define and measure human capital; and the method of calculation is described in *Labour Market Outcomes for Immigrants and the New Zealand-born 1997–2009*,[3] where (to simplify) years in education plus years in the labour market add up to an individual's human capital.

Without recourse to these survey tools for policy analysis, the Ptolemies, too, were in the market for 'smart capital'. Their success in attracting it

---

[1] Lewis 1986: 8–34.
[2] In 'Investing and Doing Business in New Zealand' www.immigration.govt.nz/migrant/stream/invest/default.htm.
[3] New Zealand Government Department of Labour 2011: 3–4:

> The NZIS collects data on qualifications earned at both the school and post-school level. We use this information to estimate the number of total years spent by each individual in school and post-school education. We then calculate the number of years of potential labour market experience for each individual as their age minus their total years spent in education minus 5 (that is, the school starting age). This is a necessary approximation for actual labour market experience that is not collected in the NZIS.

in many fields is self-evident: Demetrius of Phalerum, Euclid, Herophilus, Callimachus – a list which could be expanded almost indefinitely. And yet it is notorious that philosophy was not pursued in Alexandria at the same level of endeavour which characterised the work of the smartest practitioners of other fields. So P. M. Fraser in *Ptolemaic Alexandria* wrote:[4]

After the great achievements of the Alexandrian scholars and scientists, Alexandrian philosophy in the Ptolemaic period cuts a poor figure, for it is a feature of intellectual life which only took root in the city at the very end of the Ptolemaic period, and then in an uncreative, though influential form.

This chapter seeks to interrogate the paradox of apparently disappointing philosophical work against the background of the Ptolemaic thalassocracy. How was it, I want to ask, that 'smart capital', abundant in other fields, was apparently not at the rulers' disposal in philosophy?

The 'uncreative, though influential' philosophy referred to by Fraser is the teaching of Antiochus of Ascalon (*c*. 130–68 BC), who rejected scepticism for dogmatism.[5] Antiochus was an Academic, and his decision at an advanced age to reassert what he took to be authentic Academic doctrines lies behind the classification in Sextus Empiricus of his school as the 'Fifth Academy'.[6] Antiochus was Alexandria's most famous Academic, but he is not the Academic to whom the title of this chapter refers. That is a man who, until the 'new Posidippus' appeared relatively recently, one might have thought scarcely counted as an Academic. Posidippus, however, describes Lysicles as the 'first voice of the Academy'. *De mortuis nil nisi bonum* – and Posidippus was moved to write of this 'first voice of the Academy' by his death in a shipwreck. The epigram in question is no. 89:

Λυσικλέους κεφαλὴν ὁ κενὸς τάφος οὗτος ἀπαιτεῖ
δάκρυ χέων, καὶ θεοῖς μέμφεται οἷ᾽ ἔπαθεν
τοὖξ Ἀκαδημείας πρῶτ[ον σ]τόμα, τὸν δέ που ἤδη
ἀκταὶ καὶ πολιὸν κῦμα [θανόντ᾽ ἔλαχον.]

The published English translations are not all in agreement on how this should be read. Frank Nisetich and Margherita Maria Di Nino reach the same meaning as Austin and Bastianini:

This empty tomb calls in mourning for beloved Lysicles
and blames the gods for what he suffered, the first
voice of the Academy, but by now the shores
and sounding seas [have claimed him for their own].
Translated by Frank Nisetich[7]

---

[4] Fraser 1972: I, 480.   [5] Cic. *Acad.* 22.69.   [6] Sext. Emp. *Pyr.* 1.220.   [7] In Nisetich 2005: 37.

Shedding tears, this empty tomb demands Lysicles' body back, and blames the
gods for what suffering the first voice of the Academy had to endure; him now the
shores and the grey wave possess, no one knows where (translated by Margherita
Maria Di Nino).[8]

> 'Dearest Lysicles' is requested by this cenotaph
>   as it sheds tears and blames the gods for what
> the Academy's first voice has suffered. But him, no doubt,
>   already the shores and grey wave [have gained in death as their own].
>   Translated by C. Austin and G. Bastianini[9]

But Richard Thomas has a different understanding, particularly of line 3:

> This empty tomb shedding a tear demands back the head of Lysicles and blames
> the gods for what the first voice of the Academy (Polemon)
>   suffered [and the first voice of the Academy blames the gods for what he (Lysicles
> or Polemon) suffered], and as for him, in some place the headlands and the grey
>   wave [?of the sea confine him
> (translated by Richard Thomas).[10]

In my opinion, it is impossible to arrive at this meaning without inexplica-
bly relating line 3 to something outside the text: in my view Thomas's gloss
'(Polemon)' cannot be correct. Thomas reached his solution, I presume,
by giving weight to the fact that Lysicles was not the 'first voice of the
Academy', whereas Polemon was just that.

   The facts of the case are these. Lysicles' name is known from Diogenes
Laertius, as (for example) Austin and Bastianini observe in their *apparatus
criticus*.[11] Polemon, head of the Academy from 314 to 269, and his student
Crates were lovers, and, according to Arcesilaus in Diogenes Laertius' *Life
of Crates*, they lived 'as though they were gods, or some kind of relics from
the golden age'. Diogenes continues:[12]

Antigonus reports that he [i.e. Arcesilaus] took his meals in company at Crantor's,
while the two of them [i.e. Polemon and Crates] shared their lives and interests
with Arcesilaus. And Arcesilaus (he writes) shared accommodation with Crantor,
but Polemon with Crates shared the home of Lysicles, one of the citizens. For as
already mentioned, Crates was the beloved [*erômenos*] of Polemon, and Arcesilaus
of Crantor.

The Antigonus whom Diogenes cites is Antigonus of Carystus, author
of the *Successions of the Philosophers*, one of Diogenes' main sources. The
difficulty with his account, as Thomas must have perceived it in order to

---

[8] In Di Nino 2006: 100.   [9] In C. Austin and Bastianini 2002: 115.
[10] In 'Posidippus *Epigrams*, Pap. Mil. Vogl. VIII 309, Translations' (Angiò et al. 2008).
[11] C. Austin and Bastianini 2002: 114. Cf. also Di Nino 2006: 103 n. 6.
[12] Diog. Laert. 4.22. I wish to thank my colleague Trevor Evans for discussing this passage with me.

arrive at his translation of Posidippus, is that Diogenes describes Lysicles as 'one of the citizens' – that is, implicitly not actually a philosopher but just a reasonably close friend of Polemon and Crates, and the man with whom these two philosophers lodged. We need not, however, conclude from Diogenes' description of Lysicles as 'one of the citizens' that he was not also himself a philosopher.

Antigonus wrote that 'he [i.e. Arcesilaus] took his meals in company' (*syssition*) at Crantor's, and that Polemon and Crates 'shared their lives and interests' (*homonoôs symbiountôn*), with two of them living in Crantor's house and two in that of Lysicles, who himself could well have formed part of the group. These indeed were the leading lights of the Academy. Crantor, Diogenes reports elsewhere, had long been fascinated by Polemon.[13] After Polemon departed this life at a great age, Crates succeeded him as head of the Academy (269–266 BC). The next head was Arcesilaus (266–241 BC), the philosopher who steered the Academy into the scepticism which remained the principal feature of its teaching until the time of Antiochus of Ascalon. These five (Polemon and Crates, together perhaps with Lysicles, Crantor and Arcesilaus) were the leading lights of the Academy and, when in Athens, they formed the circle which gave Plato's Academy its present and future direction. Three of the five were heads of the Academy, who between them directed it for a total of seventy-three years. In view of this record, it is, I suggest, unlikely that Lysicles was a citizen of Athens who lacked any special interest in philosophy.

The shipwreck poem, therefore, the first in the 'Shipwrecks' section (*Nauagika*) in the Milan Posidippus papyrus, is on this argument a lament for a leading Academic philosopher, Lysicles, who perished at sea. Inferences can be drawn from this. First, there is an implied destination: the way the epigram is situated in Posidippus' collection suggests that Lysicles died on his way to Alexandria.[14] Posidippus was an Alexandrian courtier. He continued to be known as Posidippus of Pella, but courtiers might retain their original ethnics without compromise in their commitment to Alexandria and the Ptolemaic kingdom, as for example did Menyllus of

[13] Diog. Laert. 4.17: Diogenes writes of how Polemon always dressed the same, looked the same, and his voice was always the same, διὸ καὶ θηραθῆναι Κράντορα ὑπ' αὐτοῦ: 'on which account Crantor was charmed by him' (in C. D. Yonge's translation), but θηραθῆναι is stronger than 'charmed'. R. D. Hicks translates, 'This in fact accounts for the fascination which he exercised over Crantor'; cf. Diog. Laert. 4.24.

[14] I am not convinced by the objections raised to Posidippus' authorship by, for example, Lloyd-Jones 2003a: 613–16, cf. Lloyd-Jones 2003b; Schröder 2004; Ferrari 2007. Thomas 2004: 260 n. 4, while not rejecting Posidippus' authorship, records an open verdict; he would, he writes, be prepared to be persuaded by some argument which he has not yet heard enunciated.

Alabanda,[15] and many others besides. Writing long before the discovery of
the Milan papyrus, Fraser speculated that Posidippus might have moved
home to Pella, and even to the court of Antigonus Gonatas,[16] in the last
years of his life. Since, however, Posidippus' verse celebrates achievements
of the Ptolemaic royal family as late as the 250s or 240s,[17] there is minimal
ambiguity as to what is implied by the epigram: Lysicles died (the reader is
invited to think) on a voyage to visit Alexandria.

    This fits well with Susan Stephens' observations on what she calls the
'geopoetics' of the Milan Posidippus.[18] She identifies geographical movement as a theme across the collection. In the first poem of the 'Dedications'
section (*Anathematika*), Hegeso, a Macedonian girl living in Egypt, ded-
icates an Egyptian linen scarf to Arsinoe;[19] in the 'Gemstones' section
(*Lithika*), gemstones 'seem to migrate from their original locations on
the periphery of empire . . . moving ever closer to Ptolemaic Egypt';[20] in
the 'Bird Portents' section (*Oionoskopika*), cranes migrate from Thrace to
Egypt.[21] More recently, in a chapter of Kathryn Gutzwiller's *New Posidippus*, Stephens has argued that Posidippus 'belonged to the wave of Macedonians who travelled to Egypt to the court of the early Ptolemies': his 'normative geography' extends between Egypt and northern Greece/Macedon.[22]

    Within the programme of the Milan Posidippus, Lysicles should then
be understood as suffering shipwreck on his way to Egypt. A court poet
addresses a cenotaph. Lysicles, at first glance improbably, is called 'the
first voice of the Academy'. Hopes of bringing a top-class philosopher
to Alexandria have been dashed, and not for the first time. Ptolemy I
had unsuccessfully invited Theophrastus to his court, Diogenes Laertius
reports,[23] and when Ptolemy took Megara over (in 308 BC) he invited
Stilpo to his court. Stilpo declined the offer of a new life as an Alexandrian
courtier,[24] though he did at some point (even if briefly) accept Ptolemy's
hospitality, as is implied by Diogenes Laertius in an earlier chapter where
he relates an interchange with Diodorus of Iasus, which is set at Ptolemy's
court:[25]

---

[15] Menyllus of Alabanda (*Pros. Ptol.* VI 14773) spoke in the Roman senate on behalf of Ptolemy VI
Philometor in 163 and 162 (Polyb. 31.10.4 and 20.1).
[16] Fraser 1972: I, 557–8.
[17] Five epigrams in the *Hippika* (Posidippus 78–82) celebrate chariot-racing victories by Berenice II
Euergetis or Berenice Phernophorus (also known as Berenice the Syrian; daughter of Ptolemy II
Philadelphus and Arsinoe I), cf. Fantuzzi 2004: 220–1. C. Austin and Bastianini 2002: note to
Posidippus 78.
[18] Stephens 2004: 170.   [19] Posidippus 36.1–2 and 8.   [20] Stephens 2004: 170.
[21] Posidippus 22.3–4.   [22] Stephens 2005: 231–2; cf. Thompson 2005a: 283.
[23] Diog. Laert. 5.37.   [24] Diog. Laert. 2.115.   [25] Diog. Laert. 2.111–12.

This person [Diodorus], while staying at the court of Ptolemy Soter, was asked certain dialectical questions, which came from Stilpo. Unable to give an immediate solution, he was reproached by the king, among other things by being called 'Cronus', by way of mockery. He left the symposium, wrote an essay on the problem set, and then ended his life in despondency.

The stakes were high, then, at Ptolemy's table. Stilpo was equal to its demands, but would not commit himself to the role of court philosopher. Diodorus Cronus lacked the necessary quick wit, and was subjected to mockery – not only from the king, but (worse) from Callimachus, who wrote derisively in an epigram:[26]

> . . . αὐτὸς ὁ Μῶμος
> ἔγραφεν ἐν τοίχοις, ὁ Κρόνος ἐστὶ σοφός.

> Momus himself kept on writing on the walls: Cronus is wise.

No wonder Diodorus died in a state of despondency.

The analogy with Posidippus' *Lithika* can perhaps be taken a step further than Stephens' observation that the stones come from all corners to the centre of the Ptolemaic world in Alexandria. Ann Kuttner in 'A cabinet fit for a queen' writes about how the gem poems relate to collecting and elite display. These epigrams 'are mostly about pure pleasure, blank stones which are "only" colours and light, not passed off as usefully durable signet hardstones'.[27] She continues by expounding how 'the cult of collecting – "collectionism" – endorsed acquisition, as long as it had a worthy cultural agenda'.[28] This had pay-offs for the status of gem-carvers, as Kuttner observes, and a similar dynamic is in evidence in Ptolemy I's persistent efforts to collect philosophers. The only difference one might note was that Plato, Aristotle and other philosophical luminaries of the past had scored much higher in social esteem than any gem-carver. Philosophy might claim to have the worthiest cultural agenda on the market, though such a claim would not go uncontested.

Invitations to Theophrastus, Stilpo, Diodorus Cronus and (as appears from Posidippus) to Lysicles to visit Ptolemy's court in Egypt show transmarine collectionism in full swing. It is helpful to bear this in mind in interpreting two other poems by Posidippus. First, one known before the Milan papyrus was found:[29]

---

[26] Diog. Laert. 2.111 (= Callim. Frag. 393 (Pfeiffer)).   [27] Kuttner 2005: 141–2.
[28] Kuttner 2005: 144.
[29] Posidippus 123 (*Anth. Pal.* 5.134), with translation in C. Austin and Bastianini 2002.

Κεκροπί, ῥαῖνε, λάγυνε, πολύδροσον ἰκμάδα Βάκχου,
   ῥαῖνε· δροσιζέσθω συμβολικὴ πρόποσις.
σιγάσθω Ζήνων ὁ σοφὸς κύκνος, ἅ τε Κλεάνθους
   μοῦσα, μέλοι δ' ἡμῖν ὁ γλυκύπικρος Ἔρως.

Cecropian jug, pour out the dewy moisture of Bacchus,
   Pour it out: let the toast we all share be refreshed.
Let Zeno the wise swan be silent, and the Muse of Cleanthes.
   Let our concern be with Love the bitter-sweet.

Marco Fantuzzi and Richard Hunter suggest interpreting this as 'simply
one of the various statements of the "suspension" of rationality in favour
of drunkenness and *therefore* of love (and love poetry)'.[30] They prefer this
view of the text over Gutzwiller's argument for placing it as an introductory
epigram for a collection, cast in the form of a *recusatio*.[31] It is not Posidippus'
only reference to the philosophical schools (even if it appeared to be so, until
the discovery of the Milan papyrus), and it certainly does not imply that
Posidippus himself studied in the Stoic school – although the symposium
takes place in Athens, as the 'Cecropian jug' tells the reader.

   Stoicism, merely banished from a symposium, has done better than other
philosophies in Posidippus' work since Lysicles the Academic perished in
a shipwreck; and in the other poem to which I want to draw attention, the
fortuitously anonymous philosopher is already dead and buried:[32]

στῆθι τεταρπ[όμενος – γέρας ε]ὔμετρον, οὐ μέγα σ' αἰτ[ῶ –]
   ὡς γνῶις [±15   ] Ἐρετριέα·
εἰ δὲ βάδην ὑπάγεις, μ[άθ]ε καί, φίλε, τὸν Μενεδήμωι
   συσχολάσαντ' ἐς ὅ[λον, Ζεῦ] πάτερ, ἀνδρὶ σοφῶι.

Be kind [enough] to stop – I ask you a reasonable [favour], nothing great –
   so that you may know [. . . . .] from Eretria.
If you move a step further, learn too, my friend, that I was a fellow-student
   of Menedemus, a [very] wise man, O father Zeus.

In this epigram, in the 'Modes' (*Tropoi*) section of the Milan collection,
the epitaph claims it as the deceased's distinction that he was one of the
(many)[33] pupils of Menedemus, last of the Socratics.[34] As Stefano Pozzi
notes, Posidippus could have known Menedemus, who lived until the

---

[30] Fantuzzi and Hunter 2004: 345.
[31] Gutzwiller 1998: 157–60. Gutzwiller (157, n. 83) cites earlier interpretations of the poem, which run
   in the direction of an understanding similar to that of Fantuzzi and Hunter.
[32] Posidippus 104, with translation in C. Austin and Bastianini 2002.
[33] Plut. *De tranq. anim.* 472e.
[34] At least at Diog. Laert. 2.144, where Diogenes completes his account of the Socratics before moving
   on to Plato. Diogenes' Socratics, in order, are: Socrates, Xenophon, Aeschines, Aristippus, Phaedo,

second half of the 260s.[35] Whether he did ever encounter him is another matter. Menedemus' royal connections ran in another direction, towards the court of Antigonus Gonatas, where he took refuge near the end of his life, when he had to go into exile;[36] earlier he had been the ruler of democratic Eretria.[37] It is, however, just possible that Posidippus came across him in the course of his diplomatic duties.

In sum, Posidippus in his extant work names two Stoics (Zeno and Cleanthes) and a Socratic (Menedemus), as well as Lysicles, an Academic. Collectionism is not avowedly on the agenda in the Zeno–Cleanthes epigram, although Athens is. But the epitaph of Menedemus' pupil and the lament over the shipwreck of Lysicles both seem to combine with Diogenes Laertius' stories to attest to a programme of bringing well-regarded philosophers to Egypt to adorn the king's table and lend *gravitas* to the Ptolemies' empire-building project. In the language of the New Zealand Department of Labour, this might well be described as 'attracting smart capital to Alexandria'.

It may, therefore, be worthwhile questioning Fraser's view of Alexandria as a place of philosophical underachievement. If a broader view is taken, it might be claimed that Alexandria was early on a Peripatetic city. Demetrius of Phalerum, educated by Theophrastus[38] and 'a man of great learning and experience on every subject' with a long list of books to his name on philosophical and other matters,[39] relocated to Alexandria in 307 BC. Aristotle himself was, according to Strabo,[40] the 'first man . . . to have collected books and to have taught the kings in Egypt how to arrange a library'. This, of course, can only have been the case figuratively.[41] Equally importantly, Ptolemy Philadelphus is reported to have bought a set of Aristotle's and Theophrastus' works from Neleus.[42] Although Fraser argued against the view that Theophrastus' pupil Erasistratus studied in Alexandria,[43] G. E. R. Lloyd's re-examination of the question in 1975 seems to show it to be more probable than not that Erasistratus, like Herophilus, received convicts from the prison for vivisection from King Ptolemy,[44] rather than in

---

Euclides, Stilpo, Crito, Simon, Glaucon, Simmias, Cebes, Menedemus. On Menedemus, see also Knoepfler 1991.

[35] Pozzi 2006: 201.   [36] Diog. Laert. 2.142.   [37] Diog. Laert. 2.137.   [38] Strabo 9.1.20.

[39] Diog. Laert. 5.80–1.   [40] Strabo 13.1.54 (= 608).

[41] Andrew Erskine (1995: 39–40) comments that 'this cannot be literally true; Aristotle was dead by the time Ptolemy gained control of Egypt. It is most likely that Strabo means that the organization of material in the Library was modelled on Aristotle's own private library.'

[42] Ath. 1.3b.   [43] Fraser 1972: I, 347–50.

[44] Celsus, *Med.* Proem 23–4: 'They hold that Herophilus and Erasistratus did this in the best way by far, when they laid open men whilst alive – criminals received out of prison from the kings – (24) and, while these were still breathing, observed parts which beforehand nature had concealed'.

another Hellenistic capital such as Antioch.[45] Indeed, it appears at present to be agreed among medical researchers that Alexandria was where Erasistratus worked.[46] And when, in the person of Eratosthenes, Alexandria finally did import a philosopher it could be proud of, his broad range of scientific interests made him in some respects more reminiscent of a sort of Peripatetic than a Stoic or Academic.[47]

Eratosthenes, so the Suda says, was sometimes called 'the new Plato',[48] a more likeable nickname, surely, than 'Beta', as he was also known. The third nickname which the Suda records, 'Pentathlon', was perhaps one whose justice Eratosthenes would have had to acknowledge.

The implication of a passage in Strabo[49] is that Eratosthenes 'frequented the Porch and the Academy';[50] he also commented on teachers who failed to set up a school which lasted beyond their own lifetimes, meaning Arcesilaus as well as Ariston. Something of a Stoic himself, Strabo would have agreed with Diogenes Laertius, who wrote that, among the ghostly presences of mid third-century philosophy in Athens, Chrysippus 'alone had understanding, but the rest flitted about like shadows'.[51] To an impartial observer, however, Chrysippus' contemporary Eratosthenes would seem the more substantial figure. The arrival in Alexandria of this 'new Plato' came near the start of the reign of Ptolemy III Euergetes – at, or after, the end of Posidippus' life. Earlier kings, who invited the great philosophical voices to their court, had achieved a brief visit from Stilpo, and a lengthy tenure from Demetrius of Phalerum once his star was no longer in the ascendant in Athens. And now, from the Milan papyrus, it seems probable both that a pupil of Menedemus died in Alexandria and that Lysicles, the 'first voice of the Academy', perished trying to cross the sea to that city. But under Ptolemy III Euergetes, Eratosthenes, the great thinker of the day, and third Librarian, came to Alexandria via Athens from the Ptolemies' own land of Cyrene.

In summary, Fraser's judgement on Alexandrian philosophy is in need of amplification, or possibly something more radical. The things which were

---

[45] Lloyd 1975: 174–5.

[46] Note, for example, Francisco López-Muñoz and Cecilio Alamo (2009: 516), who write, 'Later, in Ptolemy's Egypt, the two most prominent representatives of the Alexandrian School, Herophilus of Chalcedon (325–280 B.C.) and Erasistratus of Keos (310–250 B.C.), basing themselves on the Stoical legacy of pneumatism, proposed that air, once inhaled by living beings, became transformed into *pneuma* (*spiritus*, in Latin).' Cf. Wills 1999: 1720.

[47] Eratosthenes' philosophy teacher was Ariston of Chios according to the Suda *s.v.* Eratosthenes, *FGrH* 241 T1. Ariston had been taught by Zeno of Citium and by Polemon (Diog. Laert. 7.162), but set up his own school.

[48] Suda *s.v.* Eratosthenes, *FGrH* 241 T1.   [49] Strabo 1.2.2.

[50] So Fraser 1970: 178.   [51] Diog. Laert. 7.183, quoting Hom. *Od.* 10.495 (on Teiresias).

done in the Alexandrian Museum and Library, which we might sum up as 'Homeric and Callimachean scholarship', took Greek culture in a new direction, and it is understandable that Fraser felt inclined to write that 'Alexandrian philosophy in the Ptolemaic period cuts a poor figure'. Fraser's *Ptolemaic Alexandria* is full of value-judgements, some more controversial than this one, and they make his book still 'good to think with', forty years on; and yet, if Fraser did hit on an important issue with his negative comment on philosophy in Alexandria, still the shape of the issue was not exactly as he supposed it to be. Fraser's view seems to have been that philosophy was an exotic plant which did not grow well in Egyptian soil – whereas philology and natural science did.

The way matters developed was more circumstantial. In the case of philosophy, events took a different turn from that they took in other areas of endeavour. As Alexandria developed, all Greek culture came as an investment of imported 'smart capital'; it was a matter of sea transport from all over the world defined by the 'normative geography' (in Susan Stephens' words), and beyond. So although Lysicles was drowned trying to get to Alexandria, there were important philosophers who demonstrated a reluctance to associate themselves with the Successors' courts. Troels Engberg-Pedersen links that reluctance to philosophers' wish to maintain their independence.[52] To some degree, the same reluctance hung on in the second generation and after. Stilpo would not migrate to Egypt, although he would visit and show up the deficiencies there of lesser lights. Theophrastus would not live in Alexandria, although from a certain perspective one might infer that Alexander's links to Aristotle made Alexandria, at one remove, the city the Lyceum built.[53] Zeno, similarly, would not throw his lot in with Antigonus Gonatas, even though the latter went to his lectures every time he was in Athens.

There must have been a reason for such reluctance, even if there is a danger of inference giving way to speculation in the search for it. 'Smart capital' in many cases was mobile, and yet the big philosophical names stayed where they were well established, a fact which was not necessarily a matter of citizenship. Neither Theophrastus of Eresus nor Zeno of Citium was an Athenian citizen, yet they palmed royal invitations off on less celebrated associates. Aethiops, not a big name, did migrate to Egypt; but,

[52] Engberg-Pedersen 1993: 292, after discussing how important it may have been that institutions (Academy, Lyceum) existed already at Athens for philosophy, but not (289) for 'literary theory and "grammar" in the wide sense'.

[53] Engberg-Pedersen (1993: 288) makes the link more direct: Ptolemy I set up the Museum and the Library 'by inviting people from the Lyceum to bring their know-how down to Alexandria'.

as a pupil of Aristippus (who died before the middle of the fourth century), he must have been an old man by the time he reached Ptolemais in Upper Egypt.[54] And there is no evidence that philosophy prospered there beyond Aethiops' days.

As Diogenes the Cynic saw it, royal courts were not fit for a philosopher, while (so the anecdote goes) Aethiops' teacher Aristippus took the opposite view. Diogenes Laertius relates:[55]

Diogenes, washing the dirt from his vegetables, saw [Aristippus] passing and jeered at him, saying, 'If you had learnt to make these your diet, you would not have paid court to kings', to which his response was, 'And if you knew how to associate with men, you would not be washing vegetables.'

It is hard to bring these two outlooks together. The evidence points to Diogenes' stance having been the more influential. The philosophical agenda itself was resistant to royal collectionism. This is the reason behind the 'poor figure' which, over time, philosophy cut in Alexandria.

---

[54] Diog. Laert. 2.86.
[55] Ibid. 2.68: translation adapted from that of R. D. Hicks, Loeb Classical Library 1925.

CHAPTER 9

Aspects of the diffusion of Ptolemaic
portraiture overseas

Olga Palagia

The distribution of imperial portraits around the regions of the Roman empire was anticipated by the Ptolemies, who were in the habit of shipping their portraits to Greek cities and sanctuaries in order to enhance their political influence. Even though we have no artists' signatures, the evidence of sculptural techniques suggests that at least portraits in stone (often mixed with other materials) were manufactured in Alexandria and sent out ready-made. Ptolemaic portraits were set up in sanctuaries that received royal benefactions, especially the healing cults of Asclepius and Amphiaraus, in Ptolemaic outposts in the Aegean and in cities that received financial support from the Ptolemies in order to combat a mutual enemy, usually the kings of Macedon. This chapter deals with a selection of Ptolemaic royal portraits found within the borders of modern Greece and discusses the implications of their distribution.

According to literary and epigraphical sources, Ptolemaic royal portraits were erected in Athens, Olympia, Delphi, Oropus and Thermus, as well as on the islands of Delos, Crete, Poros (at Calaureia), Rhodes and Cos. Ptolemaic portraits have also come to light on Thera and Aegina and in Sparta, offering additional evidence of Ptolemaic involvement in these regions. Here we shall discuss portraits dating from the third century down to 145 BC, when the death of Ptolemy VI Philometor marked the lower limit of Ptolemaic influence in the Aegean.[1]

The identification of royal portraits mainly depends on comparison with coin portraits or with other, securely identified, images. Ptolemaic portraits outside Egypt are easy to distinguish on account of their material. Because

I am grateful to Kostas Buraselis for inviting me to participate in the original conference (see Preface, above) and this volume; to Christian Habicht for help and advice; and to Reinhard Senff for information on the dedication of Callicrates of Samos at Olympia, and for the photo in Figure 9.2. Jari Pakkanen kindly placed at my disposal his article (n. 57 below) on the statue base from Calaureia prior to publication.
[1] Hölbl 2001: 43; Buraselis 2011.

Egypt lacked marble, the artists of Alexandria adopted the acrolithic technique, creating images in wood and plaster, where either the faces were
added like marble masks or the marble heads and necks, made separately,
carried tell-tale cuttings for the attachment of plaster elements.[2] The sculp-
tors of Alexandria almost invariably used marble from Paros, an island that
fell within the Ptolemaic sphere of influence. Because the majority of royal
portraits found outside Egypt are in the acrolithic technique, it follows
that they were made in Alexandria and exported. Ptolemaic portraits in
marble often served as cult statues in dynastic cults which were founded
at Ptolemaic outposts like Thera or allied cities like Athens and Rhodes
either by individual cities or by officials from Alexandria.

There are also isolated examples of exported Ptolemaic portraits made
in local Egyptian stone like granite, and therefore most certainly produced
in Egypt.[3] This is the case of the head of Ptolemy VI now in the Athens
National Museum (Figure 9.10).[4] Bronze honorary statues of Ptolemaic
rulers outside Egypt are amply documented by inscriptions but their place
of manufacture is not stated.

Portraits of Ptolemy I were seen by Pausanias (1.8.6; 6.16.3) in the Athenian Agora and at Olympia, where he was displayed alongside Demetrius
Poliorcetes, both rulers being crowned by a personification of Elis. The
occasion for the erection of this group in Olympia may be the short-lived
treaty of friendship between Ptolemy I and Demetrius in 298 BC.[5] The
area before the entrance of the Odeion in the Athenian Agora was reserved
as a Ptolemaic corner (Paus. 1.8.6–9.3).[6] It included portraits of Ptolemy
II Philadelphus and his sister-wife Arsinoe II, Ptolemy VI Philometor,
Ptolemy IX and his daughter Berenice III. A bronze portrait of Ptolemy III
Euergetes was seen by Pausanias (1.17.2) in the gymnasium, known as the
Ptolemaion, founded by this king in Athens.[7] His portrait was also set up
in the Eponymous Heroes monument in the Agora in 224/223 (Paus. 1.5.5).
A portrait of Cleopatra VII represented as a goddess was set up alongside a
statue of Mark Antony on the Athenian Acropolis.[8] None of these images
has survived.

---

[2] For Ptolemaic royal portraits created in the acrolithic technique, see Palagia 2007: 240–2, with further
references. Marble heads were also touched up in colour, as attested by the head of Berenice II in
Kassel, Antikensammlung Sk 115: *La Gloire d'Alexandrie* 1998: 83, no. 45. See also n. 34 below.
[3] For the production of Ptolemaic portraits in Egyptian granite and other local stones, see Stanwick
2002: 11.
[4] See n. 53 below.
[5] Plut. *Pyrrh.* 4.3; Hölbl 2001: 23. Kotsidu 2000: 125–6, K. 69[L] dates this group to 311–309.
[6] On the relations between Athens and the Ptolemies, see Habicht 1992.   [7] Cf. n. 30 below.
[8] Dio Cass. 50.15.2. The statues must have stood near the south wall of the Acropolis because they
were hurled by thunderbolts into the theatre of Dionysus.

Figure 9.1 Marble head of Ptolemy I Soter from Thera

In the third century the Ptolemaic fleet dominated the Aegean, and we have ample evidence of Ptolemaic presence on the islands and in harbour towns. Delos in particular was the recipient of Ptolemaic portraits up to the reign of Ptolemy VI; some were connected to the dynastic cult. These are documented by inscriptions, but none of the statues has come down to us.[9] A colossal head of Ptolemy I (Figure 9.1) in Parian marble, wearing a royal diadem, was discovered on the island of Thera.[10] The king is readily identified thanks to his coin portraits. The size and material of the head suggest a cult statue. The question here, however, is whether we have a lifetime or a posthumous portrait. Ptolemy I Soter was the first of the Ptolemies to be worshipped as a god. With approval from the oracle of Siwa, the Rhodians established a sanctuary to Ptolemy in 304 with the cult epithet Soter, in gratitude for his help against Demetrius Poliorcetes (Diod. Sic. 20.100.3;

[9] The evidence is collected in Kotsidu 2000: 209–15, K. 134–9.
[10] Thera Archaeological Museum. Kyrieleis 1975: 165, A2, plate 3; Kreikenbom 1992: 22, 122, I12; Kotsidu 2000: 239, K. 157 [E2].

Paus. 1.8.6; Ath. 15.696). The shrine was known as the Ptolemaion.[11] The
Rhodians later erected an honorary statue of Ptolemy IV Philopator (or
Ptolemy IX Philopator II); a bronze group of Ptolemy V Epiphanes and his
mother, Arsinoe III, was also dedicated by Leonidas son of Archinas in the
sanctuary of Athena at Lindos.[12] The League of Islanders voted Ptolemy I
Soter divine honours and an altar on Delos at some unspecified date before
280 BC.[13] Ptolemy I's cult continued after his death not only within Egypt
but also at various spots in the Aegean, usually in association with the
Ptolemaic dynastic cult that tended to accompany military garrisons sent
out from Alexandria. Thera was a Ptolemaic stronghold, and this is attested
from the time of the Chremonidean War (268–262), and again in the reign
of Ptolemy VI Philometor in the first half of the second century.[14] Evidence
for Ptolemaic ruler cult on the island is provided by a shrine dedicated to
Ptolemy III by Artemidorus of Perge.[15] Altars to Ptolemy VI Philometor,
his sister-wife Cleopatra II and their children were dedicated by the demos
of the Theraeans and by Irenaeus, *grammateus* of the troops on Thera,
Crete and at Arsinoe in the Peloponnese (Methana).[16] The temple of Isis
and Sarapis on Thera, erected under Ptolemaic influence in the third century, is the earliest of its kind in the Cyclades and served as a focus for the
dynastic cult.[17]

Kyrieleis identified Ptolemy's head from Thera as a lifetime portrait,
whereas Kreikenbom associated it with the dynastic cult that flourished
in the time of Ptolemy VI. If this was a lifetime portrait, there is no
other evidence of Ptolemaic involvement on Thera in the reign of Soter.
A tentative solution to the chronological problem may depend on stylistic
analysis. The king's agitated features and twisted neck are reminiscent of
second-century Ptolemaic portraits like those of Ptolemy VI in Alexandria
and the putative Cleopatra II in the Louvre.[18] It is therefore possible that

---

[11] Kotsidu 2000: 228, K. 152 [L]. For a cult of Ptolemy III and Berenice II on Rhodes, see Kotsidu
2000: 229, K. 153 [E].

[12] Portrait of Philopator: *IG* XII.1 37. Portraits of Ptolemy V and Arsinoe III: Blinkenberg 1941: 417,
no. 161.

[13] *SIG*[3] 390 ll. 26–7 and 48–9. On divine honours awarded to Ptolemy I by the Rhodians and the
League of Islanders, see Habicht 1970: 111; Hölbl 2001: 93. On the League of Islanders, see Meadows,
Chapter 2 in this volume.

[14] Bagnall 1976: 123–34; Hölbl 2001: 43, 305. On the Chremonidean War, see Habicht 2006: 161–7.

[15] Hiller von Gaertringen 1904: 87, 100–1; *IG* XII.3 464; Hölbl 2001: 96. See also Meadows,
Chapter 2 in this volume.

[16] *IG* XII.3 468 and 466/1390; *SEG* 31.741; Bagnall 1976: 135–6; Gill and Bowden 1997: 273, C12;
Kotsidu 2000: 239, K. 157 [E2].

[17] Bommas 2005: 43–4.

[18] Ptolemy VI, Alexandria, Graeco-Roman Museum 24092: Kyrieleis 1975: 174, F 3, plate 50.
Cleopatra II (?), Paris Louvre Ma 3546: Kyrieleis 1975: 185, M 12, plate 104, 1–2.

Figure 9.2 Fragment of inscribed pedestal of portraits of Ptolemy II Philadelphus and
Arsinoe II dedicated by Callicrates of Samos at Olympia

his colossal cult statue formed part of a dynastic group on Thera, testifying
to the last concentrated efforts of the dynasty to bolster their influence
outside Egypt on the eve of the final collapse of the Ptolemaic empire in
the Aegean.

In the 270s and 260s Ptolemy II and his sister-wife Arsinoe II had a
strong presence in Greece, culminating in their involvement in the Chremonidean War, which began just before Arsinoe's death. Between 278 and
270 their naval commander, Callicrates of Samos, dedicated portraits of the
royal couple at Olympia.[19] The portraits were probably of gilded bronze
and stood on a pair of Ionic columns of Parian marble that reached a
height of about 10 m. The dedicatory inscriptions were written on the
pedestals of the columns (Figure 9.2).[20] The columns were supported by
a platform that was about 20 m long and rested on a base of (probably)
Egyptian limestone imported from Alexandria. According to Pausanias
(6.17.3), another portrait of Ptolemy II was dedicated at Olympia by the
Macedonian Aristolaus. This Aristolaus has been identified by Christian

[19] Hoepfner 1971: 11–54; Mallwitz 1972: 63, 103–4, fig. 66. For Callicrates of Samos, see Hauben,
Chapter 3 in this volume.
[20] Hoepfner 1971: 51, plate 7, Beil. 7.

Habicht as Ptolemy's homonymous general in Caria, son of Ameinias.[21] A group of Ptolemy II and Arsinoe II was dedicated at Delphi probably by Sostratus of Cnidos, responsible for the Lighthouse of Alexandria.[22]

Itanus on Crete was one of the Ptolemaic strongholds established by Ptolemy III's general, Patroclus, in the course of the Chremonidean War, and it lasted until the death of Ptolemy VI Philometor in 145.[23] A *temenos* was erected to Ptolemy III and his wife, Berenice II. Their cult was celebrated with annual games.[24] The Cretan allies of Ptolemy VI dedicated portraits of the king on both Crete and Delos.[25] A much-battered, less-than-life-size head of Ptolemy III (Figure 9.3) in Parian marble in Copenhagen is said to have come from Crete and may well be associated with Itanus.[26] It is flat at the back, and the neck has a tenon for insertion. His bull's horns are a divine attribute, assimilating Ptolemy to Dionysus, a god that associated the Ptolemies with Alexander the Great by alluding to his conquest of India like a new Dionysus. The assimilation of Ptolemaic rulers to various divinities such as Dionysus, Hermes or Hercules was common practice and may be associated with the dynastic cult.[27]

A small head in Parian marble, probably of Ptolemy V Epiphanes as a child, in the Herakleion Museum is also of unknown provenance, but Itanus is a possibility.[28] It is only 10 cm high and shows him wearing a diadem with perhaps a uraeus on the top of his head. Comparison with coin portraits of Ptolemy V supports the identification.

We now move to Athens, Sparta and Aetolia. The 220s marked a turning-point in Ptolemy III's intervention in Greek affairs. As a result of Antigonus Doson's aggressive policy towards Greece and his joining forces with Aratus of the Achaean League, Ptolemy responded to pleas for financial help from Athens, Sparta and Aetolia against their common enemy. The Athenians promptly created a new tribe, the Ptolemais, naming Ptolemy an eponymous hero of Athens in 224/223.[29] A new deme was established, named *Berenikidai* after his wife, Berenice II, and a quadrennial festival,

---

[21] Aristolaus received honours from the Samians: *IG* XII.6 120. Habicht 1957: 218–23.

[22] Amandry 1940–1: 63–5, no. 3, plate VI, 2; Jacquemin 1999: no. 120. Because there is a *rasura* on the base, Amandry suggested that it originally carried a statue of Ptolemy II's first wife, Arsinoe I, which was replaced by a portrait of Arsinoe II after her marriage to her brother.

[23] Bagnall 1976: 120–3; Hölbl 2001: 42, 305.

[24] Bagnall 1976: 121; Kotsidu 2000: 284–5, K. 195 [E]; Hölbl 2001: 96.

[25] Kotsidu 2000: 214–15, K. 139 [E].

[26] Ny Carlsberg Glyptotek 573. Kyrieleis 1975: 168, C3, plate 20; Johansen 1992: no. 48; Hölbl 2001: fig. 3.4.

[27] Cf. Hölbl 2001: 96.   [28] Herakleion Museum 303. Lagogianni-Georgarakou 2001.

[29] On the cult of Ptolemy III in Athens, see Habicht 1992: 74–5; Hölbl 2001: 52; Habicht 2006: 202; Palagia 2007: 237–8.

Figure 9.3 Marble head of Ptolemy III Euergetes probably from Crete

the **Ptolemaea**, was founded in his honour. The gymnasium of Ptolemy (Paus. 1.17.2), endowed by this king rather than by Ptolemy VI, as has also been suggested, may be associated with this festival.[30] As an eponymous hero, Ptolemy III received divine honours, and his cult and priest were shared by Berenice II. The priesthood of Ptolemy and Berenice was probably held within the family of Mikion and Eurykleides that also served the cult of Demos and the Graces, as is attested by adjacent inscribed seats of the priests of these cults in the *prohedria* of the theatre of Dionysus.[31] Statues of Ptolemy III as an eponymous hero were placed in the Eponymous Heroes monuments in the Athenian Agora and at Delphi (Paus. 1.5.5; 10.10.2), and an honorary bronze portrait was set up in the gymnasium

[30] Gymnasium of Ptolemy founded by Euergetes: Habicht 2006: 204, with n. 37; Palagia 2007: 244, with further references. The existence of this gymnasium in the late third century is now attested epigraphically, cf. Palagia 2007: 244.
[31] *IG* II² 5029a; Maass 1972: 110–13, plate 8; Palagia 2007: 237–8 and 243, with further references.

Figure 9.4 Marble head of Berenice II from the Athenian Agora

of Ptolemy (Paus. 1.17.2). None of these has come down to us, but we do
have a possible remnant of the cult statues of the royal couple in a colossal
female head in Parian marble (Figures 9.4–5) that has come to light in the
Athenian Agora.[32]

This head is in fact a marble mask that was once inserted into an
acrolithic statue. The jagged edge of its rear indicates that it was completed
in plaster and can be compared to the stepped outline of a head of Ptolemy I
now in Copenhagen.[33] The rough band modelled around her skull served as
the bedding for a headdress which was additionally supported by two holes
drilled at the top and the left side of this band. The colossal size of the head
and the use of marble rather than bronze suggest that we are dealing with
a cult statue. She need not be a goddess, however. Her corpulent features,
heavy jaw and high forehead indicate an idealised portrait, perhaps of

---

[32] Athens, Agora S 551. Palagia 2007.
[33] Ny Carlsberg Glyptotek 2300, from Egypt. Kyrieleis 1975: 165–6, A3, plates 4–5; Johansen 1992: no.
      36; Palagia 2007: 240, fig. 153.

Figure 9.5 Marble head of Berenice II from the Athenian Agora

an individual assimilated to a goddess. She is close to coin portraits of Berenice II and especially to her large marble portrait head now in Kassel that once belonged to an acrolithic statue.[34] We do not know where in Athens Berenice's cult was located, but an acrolith needed a sheltered space. The gymnasium of Ptolemy, the location of which now eludes us, may have offered her a home.

Ptolemy III's involvement in Cleomenes III's war against the Achaean League and eventually against Macedon amounted to subsidies for Cleomenes' mercenary army from 226/225 to 223/222. Cleomenes had to send his mother and children as hostages to Alexandria, eventually with tragic results for his dynasty.[35] A slightly under-life-size head of Ptolemy III

[34] Antikensammlung Sk 115, from Alexandria. Kyrieleis 1975: 180, K1, plates 83–4.1–3; Gercke and Zimmermann-Elseify 2007: 212–14, no. 66; Palagia 2007: 243, figs. 155–6. See also n. 2 above.

[35] On Ptolemy III's support for Cleomenes III, see Hölbl 2001: 52–3. On the execution of Cleomenes' family following his abortive revolution in Alexandria: Plut. *Cleom.* 22.3–7; 38.1–6.

Figure 9.6 Marble head of Ptolemy III Euergetes from Sparta

(Figure 9.6) in Parian marble from Sparta must date from that three-year period.[36] It happens to be the first artefact in Parian marble found in Sparta after the Archaic period. The king wears a royal diadem; wings grow from his hair, indicating assimilation to Hermes. The symbolism of Hermes as a patron of merchants and communications was obvious and well-suited to Ptolemaic foreign policy. On the Egyptian side, Hermes/Thoth is the dispenser of justice who triumphs over his enemies.[37] The divine attributes of the Spartan head suggest a cult statue, perhaps set up by a Ptolemaic envoy to Cleomenes' court.

As a result of Ptolemy III's financial aid to the Aetolians against Antigonus Doson, a statue group of the king, his wife Berenice II and their children was set up by the Aetolians either in 239/238 or between 224

[36] Sparta, Archaeological Museum 5366. Kyrieleis 1975: 169, C8, plate 24.1; Palagia 2006: 210–12, fig. 6.
[37] For assimilation of Ptolemaic rulers to Hermes and Hermes/Thoth, see Palagia 2006: 211–12.

and 221 in the sanctuary of Apollo at Thermus, meeting place of the Aeto-
lian League.[38] The inscribed statue base once carried eight or nine statues,
including portraits of the future Ptolemy IV and his sister-wife Arsinoe
III. In addition, the Aetolians dedicated a comparable family group of
Ptolemy III and Berenice II in front of the temple of Apollo at Delphi.[39]
The statue base is very fragmentary, and it is now impossible to assess how
many of their children were represented. In addition, a single portrait of
Ptolemy III was dedicated by the Aetolian Sosippus in front of the
opisthodomos of the temple of Apollo.[40]

Although not a Ptolemaic military base, Cos was important to the
Ptolemaic empire as the birthplace of Ptolemy II.[41] He sponsored temple
B at the Asclepieum and encouraged a posthumous cult of Arsinoe II,
organised by the Coan state after 267. Arsinoe was worshipped on the
island as Thea Arsinoe Philadelphos, and had a *temenos* and priestess.[42] The
next royal couple that was heavily involved in Coan affairs was Ptolemy
IV and Arsinoe III. We do not know what the nature of their benefactions
was, but each received a statue in the city of Cos and a bronze statue in the
Asklepieum. Ptolemy's image in the city was in fact a cult statue (ἄγαλμα),
while the bronze in the Asklepieum portrayed him on horseback. We learn
this from an honorary inscription of about 200, which suggests that both
statues may have been posthumous.[43] Arsinoe III's portraits, on the other
hand, were lifetime affairs. Their bases are preserved. A statue of the deified
Arsinoe III was set up in the city of Cos by Callimachus son of Antiphilus,
of Alexandria, who had served as *agônothetês* at some unknown contest,
possibly during the *Arsinoeia* festival.[44] The base is made of granite, but its
colour indicates that it was probably not imported from Egypt but from
some Greek island. Delos, for example, has a granite quarry.[45] The stone
of the base set up by Callimachus is at any rate suitably Egyptianising.
A bronze statue of Arsinoe III was erected by the demos of Cos in the
Asklepieum as a thank-offering for some unknown benefaction bestowed
by the queen.[46] A fragment of the inscribed orthostate base survives. Its

---

[38] *IG* IX I² I 56; Hintzen-Bohlen 1990: 144–5; Kotsidu 2000: 168–9, K. 104 [E] and [A]; Hölbl 2001:
    52; Habicht 2006: 197. Bennett 2002 argues that the group was set up in 239/238 by calculating the
    dates of birth and death for the children of Ptolemy III.
[39] Colin 1930: nos. 232–3.   [40] *IG* IX I² 203; Colin 1930: no. 234; Jacquemin 1999: no. 302.
[41] Sherwin-White 1978: 84.
[42] Sherwin-White 1978: 100–1; Kotsidu 2000: 241, K. 159 [E]; Hölbl 2001: 98.
[43] Höghammar 1993: 204, n. 94a–b.
[44] Stampolides 1982; Höghammar 1993: 112, no. 2. Arsinoe is called θεά on the base.
[45] Hadjidakis, Matarangas and Varti-Matarangas 2009: 276–9.
[46] Höghammar 1993: 173, no. 63, fig. 28.

Figure 9.7 Bronze statue, here identified with Arsinoe III

preserved height is 56 cm and its length is 1 m, indicating that the statue
was over-life-size.

It is tempting also to associate with Cos an over-life-size bronze female
portrait (Figures 9.7–8) that was retrieved in 1995 from the sea near Calymnos by a fisherman.[47] This presumably came from a shipwreck carrying a
cargo of bronze statues, since more were eventually fished out of the sea.
Neither the shipwreck nor the statues have been properly investigated. The
route and date of the ship as well as the nature of its shipment elude us, and
publication of the bronzes, now housed in the new Calymnos Museum, is
pending. Because of the importance of the find, however, I would like to

[47] Calymnos Museum. Tzalas 2007: 362, fig. 38.

Figure 9.8 Bronze head of statue in Figure 9.7, here identified with Arsinoe III

raise a few questions regarding the date and identity of the female statue, which has come to be known as the Lady of Calymnos.

She is a heavily built woman with a youthful face. She stands swathed in a crinkly *chitôn* and voluminous *himation* with a fringed border hanging from her left side. The fringed mantle is transparent, allowing her *chitôn* to show through, and must be a representation of the famous Coan shawl. The garments cloak the entire figure, exposing only her face, right hand and feet, which are shod in sandals. Her waved hair is parted in the middle, forming a bun at the back, outlined by the cloak, which is wrapped up over her head. Spit curls are formed on her cheeks. The body type is well known from, among others, a headless marble statue from Cos dated to around 200 or shortly thereafter.[48] A bronze statuette from the same period and probably from Alexandria, now in New York and known as the Baker Dancer, reproduces a similarly cloaked figure sporting a similar hairstyle.[49]

The face of the Lady of Calymnos (Figure 9.8), albeit idealised, appears to be a portrait. The bun hairstyle and *himation* over the head recall coin

[48] Cos Museum 24. Kabus-Preisshofen 1989: 239–42, no. 53, plate 55.
[49] Metropolitan Museum of Art 1972.118.95. *La Gloire d'Alexandrie* 1998: 265, no. 206; Picón et al. 2007: fig. 237.

Figure 9.9 Bronze head of Arsinoe III

portraits of Ptolemaic queens, for example Arsinoe II and Berenice II.[50] Is the Calymnos Lady one of the lost bronze Ptolemaic portraits documented by inscriptions all over the Aegean? Her bun hairstyle and oval face come closer to the portraiture of Berenice's daughter, Arsinoe III, and especially her bronze portrait now in Mantua (Figure 9.9).[51] Since the Calymnos statue is unpublished, all I can do here is raise the question by suggesting a Ptolemaic identity, also bearing in mind that Arsinoe III was honoured with two bronze portraits on the nearby island of Cos.

Bronze portraits of Ptolemy IV and Arsinoe III were also set up at Oropus in gratitude for their financial support towards the healing sanctuary of Amphiaraus. Only the fragmentary statue base survives *in situ*.[52]

A colossal head of Ptolemy VI Philometor at a young age, made in Egyptian granite, was fished out of the sea in the harbour of Aegina in

---

[50] Cf. *La Gloire d'Alexandrie* 1998: 217, nos. 163–4.
[51] Palazzo Ducale, probably from Alexandria. Kyrieleis 1975: 182, L3, plates 92–4.1.
[52] Statue base: *IG* VII 297; Petrakos 1997b: no. 424. For Ptolemy IV's support of the sanctuary of Amphiaraus, see Petrakos 1997b: nos. 175 (*IG* VII 298) and 325 (*IG* VII 3498).

Figure 9.10 Granite head of Ptolemy VI Philometor probably from a shipwreck near
Aegina

1842 (Figure 9.10).[53] This is in Egyptian format, wearing the double crown
of Upper and Lower Egypt, the *nemes* and the uraeus, but with Greek-
style face, hair and sideburns. The back pillar carries a cartouche with
Philometor's Horus name.

Images of the Ptolemies as pharaohs were set up in temples of the
Egyptian gods in Egypt in order to please their native subjects.[54] The

---

[53] Athens, National Museum ANE 108. First identified by Six 1887. See also Kyrieleis 1975: 174, F1,
plate 47; Ashton 2001: 90, no. 16; Stanwick 2002: 107, B6, figs. 52–3, with further references.
[54] Stanwick 2002: 6–14.

presence of such a portrait in Greece seems odd, and its appearance on Aegina is even more intriguing, for Aegina was under Attalid influence at that time. It has indeed been suggested that the head had been removed in modern times from its original location.[55] Aegina was the first capital of Greece after its liberation from the Ottoman empire. In 1829 the Aegina Museum was founded as the first National Museum of Greece and thus became the recipient of antiquities from other areas, particularly the islands. On this scenario, a modern ship carrying the head of Ptolemy VI to its new home on Aegina sank in the harbour before reaching its destination.

It is usually thought that this granite statue of Philometor originally stood in the sanctuary of Isis at Methana mentioned by Pausanias (2.34.1), where it would be aimed at Egyptian members of the Ptolemaic garrison on the peninsula.[56] Methana not only had a Ptolemaic military presence attested from the Chremonidean War until the death of Ptolemy VI in 145, it was also renamed Arsinoe in the Peloponnese in honour of Arsinoe II.[57] A newly found statue base of Ptolemy II and Arsinoe II from the sanctuary of Poseidon at Calaureia was dedicated to Poseidon by the new city of Arsinoe in the Peloponnese, thus establishing its creation already in the reign of Philadelphus.[58] A dynastic cult of the Ptolemies at Methana is documented by the dedication of an altar to the Great Gods in the name of Ptolemy VI and his family by the Ptolemaic courtier Irenaeus and his men, who were sent out from Alexandria, as a thank-offering for escaping the perils of their crossing.[59]

The alternative view that the granite head was sent to Aegina as a royal gift to the Attalid agents[60] has little to recommend it on account of its Egyptianising style, which would have had no particular significance for the Attalid court.

What we have learned from all this is that Ptolemaic royal portraits in stone were manufactured in Alexandria and shipped on demand to Ptolemaic territories or allied cities. Their diffusion reflects the power and influence of the Ptolemaic empire in the third century and first half of the second century. The central distribution of royal portraits effectively helped

---

[55] Smith 1988: 170, no. 71; Habicht 1992: 90; Gill, Foxhall and Bowden 1997: 73, 75.

[56] Six 1887: 221; Habicht 1992: 90. Egyptians in the military garrison of the Ptolemies on Thera are attested in the reign of Ptolemy VI: Hölbl 2001: 43.

[57] Bagnall 1976: 135–6; Habicht 1992: 90; Gill, Foxhall and Bowden 1997: 73–5; Hölbl 2001: 43, 305; Wallensten and Pakkanen 2009.

[58] Wallensten and Pakkanen 2009, tentatively dated during the Chremonidean War.

[59] *IG* IV 854; *SEG* 37.321; Gill, Foxhall and Bowden 1997: 270, C8. Irenaeus also dedicated an altar on Thera in honour of Ptolemy VI and his wife and children: see above, n. 16.

[60] Felten 2006.

control the royal image. We do not know if this practice was confined to stone or whether it also applied to bronze portraits. It is hardly surprising that, with the exception of Sparta, extant Ptolemaic portraits in Greece were found in harbour towns, accessible to the Ptolemaic fleet. Ptolemaic portraits thus formed part of Ptolemaic trade, albeit at a political rather than a commercial level.

CHAPTER 10

Ptolemies and piracy

Lucia Criscuolo

The aim of this chapter is not ambitious: I shall not try to solve all the mysterious connections that shaped Ptolemaic policy in the eastern Mediterranean, nor do I present new evidence on a subject that has a very poor body of literary and epigraphic witnesses, not to speak of documentary papyri, which are completely absent. Moreover, and just to mention the more recent ones, in the last ten years a number of books and articles have put forward new interpretations of piracy. So, for instance, according to the definition given by Horden and Purcell in their *Corrupting Sea*,[1] piracy is to be treated as a 'normal manifestation of Mediterranean production and redistribution' or a 'systemic epiphenomenon of connectivity suppressed by powerful states only for brief intervals in Mediterranean history'. Another, similar perspective is provided by Bresson, who describes piracy as a violent expression of economic rationalism ('on doit s'interroger sur les formes de rationalité économique que la guerre ou la piraterie peuvent revetir').[2] That is why, in the light of the most recent studies on this key issue, I shall simply summarise what we know, indicating what interpretations should perhaps be modified and what assumptions we may reasonably make about Ptolemaic policies on the subject of Mediterranean piracy and pirates.

It may be useful to start by rehearsing some important observations on, first of all, the terminology currently in use to describe different forms of piracy. The distinction between pirate and privateer (in Italian, *pirata* and *corsaro*, in French *pirate* and *corsaire*, and in German *Seeräuber* and *Kaper*) was one made long ago, but no such distinction existed in antiquity.[3] The two words found for pirates in the ancient sources, *lêstai* (λησταί) and

---

[1] Horden and Purcell 2000: 387.   [2] Bresson 2008: 214.

[3] On privateers, see Jackson 1973: 241–53, though the author is not over-concerned to provide a precise definition of the word, nor with the problems arising from the lack of a specific terminology in Greek; still valid is the brief statement of Tarn 1913: 87 that 'the distinguishing line [between privateersmen and pirates] was often remarkably thin'. Brulé 1978: 132–3 and de Souza 1999: 2–12 give prudent definitions of ancient piracy and examine the terminology used. See also Pritchett 1991: 312–63, on raids and pirates, with a chronological list of all examples from Alexander on (338 ff.). For the trouble

peiratai (πειραταί) (the latter used only from the Hellenistic period on), carried no sense of any distinction between either land banditry and sea piracy or between straightforward outlaws and those types of mercenaries who went raiding on behalf of Hellenistic states. So we cannot expect to find in the ancient authors or inscriptions any lexical key that would allow us to know whether those termed pirates were acting in the context of a war or simply according to some logic of robbery, nor, unless this is described in detail, whether they were attacking communities on the coast or ships sailing on the open sea. This ambiguity, stressed thirty years ago by Garlan and more recently again by de Souza and Gabrielsen,[4] makes more difficult the reconstruction and evaluation of the political and economic context of certain episodes mentioned in classical authors and inscriptions.

On the other hand, it is quite common in the ancient sources, as indeed today, to find *peiratês* or its adjective *peiratikos* used in a pejorative sense when adversaries were involved.[5] Moreover, since most of the epigraphical evidence for piracy lacks any secure date, it is sometimes risky to claim that a piratical attack was made in the context of a war. Further, and this has bearing on the subject of this chapter, it becomes extremely risky to consider Ptolemaic attitudes towards 'piracy' as an adhesion to, or detachment from, some code of moral behaviour on the basis alone of the terms and judgements employed by ancient authors. An approach like this would involve treating the first three Ptolemies as good kings because they took good care of the security of their subjects, while the later Ptolemies, as we shall see, being myopic and corrupt, would even collaborate with pirates. Such a reconstruction also results from the usual historical interpretation of relations between the Ptolemaic kingdom and the League of Islanders as based both on the need for protection against the pirates of the Islanders and on the hegemonic interests of the Ptolemies.[6] When, in the second half of the third century BC, these hegemonic interests could no longer be supported by naval supremacy the level of Ptolemaic protection decreased,

that terminology can give to the anglophone (and indeed other) modern historians, see Little 2005: chap. 2, 10–22, under the title 'Sea rovers: freebooters, filibusters, cruisers, corsaires, buccaneers, privateers, and pirates'.

[4] Garlan 1978: 2; de Souza 1999: 9–12; Gabrielsen 2003: 390–1 and 398 ff.; see also, among others, Ducrey 1999: 171–93, on pirates and privateers, esp. 171–4; so too Eckstein 2006: 79–117, esp. 84. Apart from the obvious observation that pirates were considered enemies, the problem is not treated in Giovannini 2007: esp. 159–60.

[5] See also the cautious and wise considerations of Rigsby 1996: 16–17.

[6] See, e.g., the recent work of L. Gallo 2009: 335 and Hauben 2010: 108–9, who, as most earlier scholars, assign the foundation of the League to Antigonus and Demetrius at the end of the fourth century, soon to be replaced by the Ptolemies. In Chapter 2 of this volume, A. Meadows' different reconstruction and chronology challenges this view and convincingly provides a new, broader interpretation.

and many cities were compelled to find other solutions, and other protectors.[7]

Actually there is one suspicious episode that may show Ptolemy II as a cynical accomplice of bandits, though it is dubious whether pirates were in fact involved.[8] On the other hand, as is clear from inscriptions, the good relations between the Ptolemies and the cities of the Aegean islands continued in the second century when the League no longer existed. Ptolemy VI should not perhaps be compared to his ancestors, but the presence of his 'friend' (*philos*) Aglaus in Aegean waters was quite marked.[9] Is this still nothing to do with pirates?

Secondly, the social and political milieu which produced and hosted piracy has often been analysed in recent years. In such an enquiry three main groups of 'pirate communities' come into question: the Aetolians, the Cretans and the Cilicians.[10] These three major players shared the maritime plunders of the central and eastern Mediterranean during the Hellenistic period. And in part they shared other characteristics too, such as a long tradition in raiding neighbours, few economic resources, and territories difficult to attack and to control from without. In the light of a closer economic analysis, there is now general agreement as to the structural integration of piracy and trade. Thus, precisely when pursuing their piratical activities, these three main pirate peoples were, to a degree, also taking part in an economic process of collecting and distributing specific products such

[7] One solution could be *asylia*, often recognised by Aetolians and Cretans in this period; for a more cautious approach, see Rigsby 1996, introduction. A more political interpretation is given by Buraselis 2003. For a more social and political interpretation, see also Kvist 2003: 214–17, with a list of the Cretan grants of *asylia*, noting the absence from this list of Cretan cities under Ptolemaic influence or control (216). This observation is potentially interesting, but two problems arise: of the sixty-one grants listed, twenty-three are from unknown Cretan cities, and the chronological distribution shows most instances to be overly concentrated in time to be connected to the problem of piracy alone.

[8] According to Paus. 1.7.3, Ptolemy II used *lêstai* to raid Antiochus I's territories and compel him to give up his attack on Egypt. I doubt that they were sea pirates, contra Gabbert 1986: 158; cf. Petropoulou 1985: 39, who notes, moreover, that the Ptolemies did not fight piracy as they should have done.

[9] Cf. now Casa 2010: 219. For continuing strong relations between Cos and the Ptolemies in the second century BC, thanks to Aglaus' family, see Habicht 2007: 146–7; Buraselis 2011: 153–4. The importance and nature of the political role of Ptolemaic *philoi*, especially those from the islands, like Aglaus, or, for instance, Callicrates, still need more careful consideration.

[10] On Aetolians, see Scholten 2000: esp. 114–16, on the ambiguous distinction between 'private' Aetolian piracy and its political use or tolerance, especially by the Ptolemies. On Cretans, see Brulé 1978: esp. 138–42; for the bad reputation of the Cretans and onomastics derived from raid and violence, Perlman 1999: 137–9; Chaniotis 2006: 134–7, noting the many treaties between Cretan *poleis* on the division of booty, slaves or cash acquired 'either by land or by sea'. On Cilicians, see de Souza 1999: 97ff.

as slaves, cash, corn, and so on.[11] But on the main aspect of the economic dimension of the phenomenon, that is, the profits that piracy could earn, I should perhaps also mention the scepticism expressed by de Souza:[12]

profits of piracy are unlikely to have accounted for any dramatic changes in local prosperity over an extended period of time, such as might make some impression on the archaeological record of a particular city. Whatever our literary sources might claim, the contribution of piracy to the economy of any place in Antiquity is unknowable, because it cannot be detected.

So, generally for the first half of the third century BC the Ptolemies, as leaders of the League of Islanders in the period before the destruction and resurrection of Rhodes, are considered one of the protectors (*prostatai*) against piracy, a strong naval power which, besides pursuing political and military targets mainly in Greece, tried to ward off the raids of pirates who assaulted the coasts and ships in the Aegean and eastern Mediterranean.[13] Evidence for such a role is to be found in the well-known Athenian decree of 286 BC in honour of Zenon, a Ptolemaic naval commander who escorted the corn supply for the city.[14]

The Ptolemies had a fleet and military bases in mainland Greece,[15] Crete (Itanus, perhaps the small island of Leuca as well),[16] Thera[17] and Samos,[18] at least until the mid second century. Indeed, from Thera we have a second well-known inscription, *IG* XII.3 1291, which mentions an attack made by pirates (8–10) that was repulsed thanks to the intervention of Ptolemaic troops sent from the main town by another Ptolemaic high officer, whose name is only partly legible (–philos), but whose ethnic was *Rhaukios*,

[11] Horden and Purcell 2000: 157–8; Gabrielsen 2001: 219–40; at 220 he points out, for example, that, despite difficult conditions in the Cyclades, often attacked by pirates, according to the analysis by Reger 1994b their prosperity rose significantly in the second half of the third century, when Ptolemaic protection was no longer effective, and when the Rhodians had not yet completed the development of their power.

[12] de Souza 1999: 60.

[13] See, e.g., Hauben 1983: 112; Hauben 1996: 222, noting that even voyages of exploration and commercial expeditions had a military function against piracy; cf. Gabrielsen 2003: 395 ff., rightly challenging this too-simple recontruction. For the great importance given by the Ptolemies to their Aegean fleet, Van 't Dack 1988: 25–9 remains a key discussion.

[14] *IG* II² 650; on this text, frequently cited as a proof of Ptolemaic concern for Athenian welfare before the Chremonidean War, see Habicht 2000: 146, with n. 14; Buraselis, Chapter 6 in this volume.

[15] For the base at Methana, see Bagnall 1976: 135–6; Meadows above, Chapter 2 in this volume, n. 50.

[16] Bagnall 1976: 117–23; for Itanus, see particularly Spyridakis 1970: 77, and, for the withdrawal of the Egyptians from this base, 86 and 98; for Leuca, the small island for a long time controlled by Itanus, see also Viviers 1999: 225.

[17] See Bagnall 1976: 123–34.

[18] For Ptolemaic control, the naval base and the special position of Samos in the so-called Ptolemaic empire, see Shipley 1987: 185–94 and 298–301.

which means he was a Cretan (3–6).[19] The Therans honoured him and the leader of the soldiers, Hephaestion, who had saved more than 400 people in the raid. This inscription has no date, so it is impossible to know whether these pirates were enemies in a time of war or simply desperate raiders who did not realise that, even when attacking a northern village on the island, they would face the reaction of the Ptolemaic military garrison.[20]

Another episode that could be of a similar nature is attested by the inscription *IG* XII.3 328, perhaps of the mid third century, also found in Thera, which in the last section of an official letter probably sent by a Ptolemaic officer (perhaps the commander of the garrison) to a superior mentions an agreement made with the Allariotes – Cretans and probably pirates – who had taken some captives from Thera;[21] the official had found a solution to the problem this posed in exchanging prisoners with the Allariotes (16–20), thereby recovering the Therans, who in the meantime had spent three years with the Cretans, 'becoming partners in their struggles'.[22]

Thera was not the only Ptolemaic garrison of importance to the Ptolemies. Involving no formal dependence on Egypt,[23] the presence of such garrisons created a special link between the Ptolemaic monarchy and the islands or cities where they were stationed. In Crete, too, a Ptolemaic presence was still active under Ptolemy VI. This king is mentioned, probably a traditional ally of Gortyn, in the treaty between Gortyn and Cnossus dated *c.* 168 BC.[24] The reason for the withdrawal from Crete under Ptolemy VIII is unknown. Roman 'encouragement' has been suggested.[25] The economic difficulties suffered by Ptolemy VIII at the start of his reign may also have played some part in the decision; these were only partially overcome with the help of Ptolemy's general, Hierax.[26]

---

[19] Undated but probably from the second half of the third century BC, cf. Van 't Dack 1988: 126, 146–7. Alongside the traditional presence of Cretans as mercenary troops and particularly in the Ptolemaic army, we must consider the traces left by the first Ptolemies in a fair number of Cretan towns: first Gortyn, but also Olous, Phalasarna, Eleutherna and Lappa; see Bagnall 1976: 117–18; Kreuter 1992: 35–45. For Rhaukos as an ally of Ptolemy, see Brulé 1978: 5, n. 5, on the basis only of this inscription. Given the regular claims of friendship between Rhaukos and Gortyn (see Chaniotis 1996: n. 29), it is highly probable, however, that this commander was recruited by a Ptolemy, but no formal connection is required to explain a professional soldier entering the service of a good master.

[20] For the supplement of the title of the Cretan commander as *phrourarchos*, not *nauarchos*, see Van 't Dack 1988: 127–31 and, definitively, Van 't Dack 1988: 147–50: the *Rhaukios* concerned was also *stratâgos tâs polios* in Thera (l. 6).

[21] For this interesting text, see Bielman 1994: n. 54, with bibliography and detailed commentary; on this inscription as evidence for the transfer and settlement of people, see also Chaniotis 2006: 100–1.

[22] These words are restored in a large lacuna in ll. 5–6: σ[υνδιαπράξαντας αὐτοῖς πλείστους ἀγῶ]νας.

[23] Chaniotis 2002: 106–8.   [24] Chaniotis 1996: 46 and n. 43.   [25] Habicht 1992: 85.

[26] Diod. Sic. 33.20 and 22. For a short survey of relations between Egypt and Crete, see Bagnall 1976: 117–23; Kreuter 1992: 35–45; on economic aspects (e.g. the Cretan production of Hadra vases), Perlman 1999: 151–3; Stefanakis 2000, perhaps over-emphasising the relevance of Ptolemaic coinage on Crete.

Egyptian maritime supremacy was acknowledged, among others, by the Rhodians, who first profited for their trading activities from the security kept by the Egyptian fleet, and who then in turn, from the second half of the third century, replaced Egyptian naval power. From that moment on until the end of the second century, the task of defending commerce between Asia and Europe from piracy was performed by Rhodes.[27]

Such is the reconstruction presented in more or less the same form throughout modern discussions of the Hellenistic period.[28] Nevertheless, we must also agree with de Souza, who writes: 'With no explicit literary testimony and only a couple of apparently fortuitous epigraphic instances of Ptolemaic officers tackling pirates, I do not think that it is reasonable to conclude that the Egyptian kings pursued a major anti-piracy policy in the Aegean in the manner of the Rhodians.'[29] This statement is certainly correct, yet it does not free us from asking some further questions: is it reasonable to exclude the possibility that the kings of Egypt helped or used pirates, as did the Antigonids? Was there ever such a thing as a Ptolemaic policy towards piracy? And if there was, was it a constant one? If not, what weight should be given to political reasons in what we find?

The suspicion that the first six Ptolemies and their generals had dealings and often directly or indirectly collaborated with people who could be considered pirates is very strong. There are documents which easily fit such a picture, such as the inscription from Thera discussed above, reporting the so-called exchange of prisoners.[30] The precise meaning of the text is not so clear, since the restitutions in it are extensive, but the impression in fact given is that the concern of the Ptolemaic officer involved was to ensure the return of a certain number of people taken from Thera, through the convenient exchange of prisoners or slaves in addition to the payment of a sum of money.[31] This is surely not a regular method of policing . . .

In other episodes, there was no direct involvement of Egyptian ships, but it is highly probable that such practices were not unfamiliar to

---

[27] In recent years this picture has been to some degree revised, especially in the evaluation of the forces involved and the political care taken by the Rhodians, also in the identification of Cretans as pirates, see, e.g., Wiemer 2002: 137–44; Gabrielsen, Chapter 4 in this volume.

[28] I simply recall here the statement of Ed. Will 1979: 326: 'on admet qu'à l'époque où les premiers Ptolémées avaient réussi à imposer leur autorité à la Mediterranée orientale et à une partie au moins de l'Egée, la flotte lagide y avait exercé une police efficace'. An implicit distinction between Ptolemaic and Rhodian *prostasia* is made by Pohl 1993: 127–8, who considers the Rhodian one to be based on economic needs, not on claims of hegemony. This is also the implication of Meadows' reconstruction in this volume, at least for the Ptolemies. Of course, the two aspects played equally in Ptolemaic policy, and not only in the third century BC.

[29] de Souza 1999: 54.   [30] *IG* XII.3 328.

[31] Lines 16–18: σ[υ]νχωρηθέντων δὲ [ὧν ἠξίωσαν, ἐν οἷς καὶ ἡ]μεῖς συνεμείν[α]μεν, ἐκομι[σά]μεσθ[α τὰ παρ' ἐκείνοις σώματα ἀντὶ τοῦ] περὶ αὐτῶν συνχωρηθέντος ἀνη[λώματος; for the interpretation of these lines, cf. Bielman 1994: 198.

commanders of the Ptolemaic base in Methana, and perhaps also to Egyptian naval forces in Thera and Itanus. When Athens was under Macedonian control (*c.* 260–230 BC), the Athenians honored Eumaridas from Cydonia (*IG* II² 844.1–32, 228 BC) for the payment (to be refunded) of the prisoners taken to Crete by the Aetolian commander Boucris – an Aetolian usually considered a pirate – perhaps to be sold as slaves, probably during the war with Demetrius, 239–229 BC. Eumaridas had also helped an Athenian embassy in Cnossus and Polyrrhenia, both cities allied or favourable to both the Aetolians and to the Ptolemies at that time.[32] Some years before, in the decree in honour of Heracleitus (*IG* II² 1225, 250–244 BC?),[33] we read that during the war against Alexander, son of Craterus, the Salaminians had been attacked by naval forces coming from Epilimnium and 'behaving like pirates [*peiratikoi*]'.[34] Their identity is unknown,[35] but, whoever they were, Ptolemaic forces certainly would not stop them from attacking their former ally, now under Antigonid control.

Also of note is the naval alliance between Ptolemy III and the Aetolians attested by the Hauniensis papyrus 6.18.[36] Moreover, the 'direct line' of recruitment of mercenaries that connected the Ptolemies, Cretans and Aetolians may also explain some other cases of apparent involvement of the Egyptian king with pirates.

The first case is that of Dicaearchus. According to Diodorus,[37] Dicaearchus was a 'brave' Aetolian enrolled by Philip V, who persuaded him to raid the islands as a way of getting cash; for Polybius, he was the man appointed by Philip V as commander-in-chief of the fleet when the

---

[32] As Bielman 1994 suggests in her commentary to nos. 31, 124.

[33] See Bielman 1994: no. 25. The inscription is also reprinted, with commentary and English translation, by Taylor 1997: 250–6, but with no relevant changes in its interpretation.

[34] Lines 12–13: . . . καὶ πολέμου γενομένου τοῦ περὶ Ἀλέξανδρον καὶ πειρατικῶν ἐκπλεόντων ἐκ τοῦ Ἐπιλιμνίου. This phrase always refers to pirates sailing out of an unknown port. There have been different proposals: e.g. Gabbert 1986: 161–2 suggested that this could be Epidaurus Limera, near Cape Taenarus ('an excellent base for piracy' (sic)), but the most reasonable identification remains Corinthian Epilimnium, the name given to the sanctuary of Poseidon at Schoenus (see Monceaux in Hammond and Walbank 1988: 302, n. 4 and Bielman 1994: 103).

[35] Brulé 1978: 3–6, who excludes Aetolians, argues, not very convincingly, that they were Cretans. All scholars have translated the expression πειρατικῶν ἐκπλεόντων as 'pirates sailing out', but in that case the text would simply have read *peiratôn* (πειρατῶν), as elsewhere. Here I would suggest that the charge made is that the troops of Alexander had made a raid like pirates. However, one might suggest that πειρατικῶν here is an abbreviation for πειρατικῶν νεῶν (pirate ships).

[36] On this fragment of a biographical work on the Ptolemies, see (for the text) I. Gallo 1975: n. 2; Bülow-Jacobsen 1979; for the historical implications, see Habicht 1980; and, in general, on good relations between the Aetolians and Egypt particularly in the second half of the third century BC, see Scholten 2000: 137–8.

[37] Diod. Sic. 28.1.

king attacked the islands and towns of the Hellespont.[38] This episode is
generally dated to 204 BC, while Philip was also aiding the Cretans in their
war against Rhodes and just before his eastern expedition.[39] Later he turned
up in Alexandria, where he was executed by Aristomenes in 197/196 BC,
together with Scopas.[40] It is not known when he had arrived in the city.
According to Walbank, he could have been enlisted directly by Scopas,
another famous Aetolian general, in 204/203 BC,[41] or, according to Westermann, in 200 BC, when Scopas again recruited mercenaries after his defeat
in Palestine.[42] In either case the responsibility for having called upon such
an embarrassing individual would fall on Scopas, another Aetolian, and for
Dicaearchus the real reason for accepting, though not one openly declared,
would exclusively be the cash – as Polybius wrote, a typical example of an
impious man. But besides this literary portrait we also learn more about
him from papyri: he is the well-known owner of a royal gift of income
(a *dôrea*) attested by *P.Col.* inv. 480 (*P.Col.* 1 = *C.Ptol.Sklav.* 5); the text
mentions a 1 per cent tax as a grant for Dicaearchus, to be collected on
the price of slaves sold, and a 1 drachma per slave sold to the crown as a
result of debt. Gabrielsen has stressed the fact that this grant applied to
the slave trade,[43] which, for a former pirate now mercenary commander,
would represent a form of additional income – a familiar one – to the main
payment for his activities. Alhough the sums involved were only potentially
high – we lack information on the approximate number of slave sales in the
Ptolemaic kingdom (not just within Egypt itself) – nevertheless the reputation of Aetolian generals in Egypt, according to Polybius, was that of an
avaricious group.[44] On the other hand, most scholars have missed another
series of documents which serve to illustrate the role of Dicaearchus at
Alexandria. Four demotic papyri exist which record an eponymous priest
of Ptolemais for year 7 of Ptolemy V (199/198 BC) named Clitomachus
son of Dicaearchus.[45] Along with other owners of royal gifts or *dôreai*,
normally 'friends' (*philoi*) or generals in the service of the Ptolemies (such

[38] Polyb. 18.54.6–11; cf. Walbank 1967: 625–6. These events are dated to 197/196 BC.
[39] Cf. Walbank 1967: 416.
[40] Cf. n. 38 above. See also Huß 2001: 493–503, on events in Alexandria and the international background.
[41] Cf. Walbank 1967: 625. [42] Westermann 1929: commentary 23–5, esp. 24.
[43] Gabrielsen 2003: 395. It is surely no coincidence that in the same year the king made a royal order
concerning Egyptians enslaved after the revolt, cf. *SB* 20.14659 = *C.Ptol.Sklav.* 9.6–9, now re-edited
as *P.Sijp.* 45.
[44] See the portrait of Scopas in Polyb. 13.2.
[45] Cf. Clarysse and Van der Veken 1983: no. 92 bis, listing *P.dem.Berl.* 13593 = Lüddeckens, *Ehev-
erträge* no. 28; *P.dem.Dublin* 1639 = Pestman, *Recueil* I, no. 8; *P.dem.Louvre* 2435 = Zauzich,
Schreibertradition, no. 26; *P.BM Andrews* no. 3 is now to be added (see *Pros. Ptol.* online).

as Sosibius, Comanus or Aglaus), Dicaearchus was also granted the honour of having his son appointed eponymous priest in the dynastic cult, and that too in the southern capital of the kingdom, a region that in those years is known to have been in serious trouble.[46] It is possible that the *dôrea* and this further honour were conferred as an incentive to keep the mercenary general loyal to his new Egyptian master, Ptolemy V, represented by his guardians, either Tlepolemus or Aristomenes. For there is no doubt that the two men named Dicaearchus, the Aetolian 'pirate' and the father of the eponymous priest, are one and the same person, so showing a perfect and quite rapid acceptance into the heart of the Alexandrian court.

I wonder, however, if we may change perspective or, better, the starting-point: perhaps Dicaearchus had already been in Egypt since the reign of Philopator. It has indeed been observed that 'most of the key commanders in the Fourth Syrian War were Aetolians'.[47] The events in Alexandria and the bad atmosphere that, according to Polybius, Agathocles had created for all the most important individuals (*epiphanestatoi andres*) could well then have persuaded Dicaearchus to leave Egypt for a while, perhaps accompanying Ptolemy, the son of Sosibius, in his embassy to Pella to arrange a marriage alliance between Ptolemy V (later Ptolemy V Epiphanes) and Phila, the daughter of Philip V of Macedon, in 204 or 203 BC.[48] On that occasion Philip, who was preparing the naval expeditions that followed in the Aegean against the Cyclades and Rhodes, might have offered him the chief command of the fleet when negotiations over the marriage broke down.[49] In either case (whether the Aetolian arrived back in Alexandria after serving Philip or had for some time earlier exercised the role of pirate under this monarch), Egypt became seriously compromised by men who, in the words of Polybius, demonstrated a questionable morality. The political implications are also baffling: the decision to host a general after his service to the king of Macedon, to close their eyes in the face of Philip's initiatives against the Aegean islands and Rhodes, went in the opposite direction to the traditional setting of the maritime policy of the Ptolemies, if indeed such ever existed. Friendly relations with Rhodes, now under attack from Cretans and Macedonians, could apparently be abandoned by Egypt.

---

[46] On the great revolt in the Thebaid during those years, see Veïsse 2004: 11–25.

[47] Scholten 2000: 182–3.

[48] Polyb. 15.25. Cf. Hammond and Walbank 1988: 411–16, for the date and reconstruction of events of the following three years, until 200 BC. In this period, according to sources that are not always reliable, Egypt had to cope with an internal crisis, the more or less secret alliance between Macedonia and Syria, and the attack that followed from Antiochus IV.

[49] The date would in this case be 203/202 BC. Dicaearchus seems to be the only Aetolian among the friends of the Antigonids listed by O'Neil 2003: 516 and 521–2.

At a lower level, but again in the milieu of prominent mercenaries, we find a Cretan woman, married to a governor of the city of Citium on Cyprus, who honours his father-in-law, one Melancomas. He too had served as governor of the city. Melancomas was an Aetolian, described as general and cavalry commander (*hegemôn, hipparchês*), priest of the Gods Euergetai and in charge of the city (*epi tês poleôs*).[50] Crete and Aetolia were thus associated under the Egyptian flag in the name of military professionalism. In Aptera, recognised as a pirate base, some Aspendians, probably from the Ptolemaic garrison of Thera, were honoured in the second century,[51] not to mention the well-known Delian inscription of Cretan mercenaries for Aglaus, the celebrated Coan commander.[52] Were these all pirates? Probably not. Could they have something to do with pirates sometimes? Probably so.

And the suspicion that the use of such mercenaries could indeed take place probably lies at the base of the later allegation reported by Strabo concerning the Ptolemies, as also Rhodes, in his well-known discussion of the birth and development of Cilician piracy first headed by Diodotus Tryphon in the mid second century BC, a phenomenon which he ascribes to the economic boom that followed the Roman victories over Carthage and Corinth. He writes that:

> the Romans, becoming wealthy following the destruction of Carthage and Corinth, employed a large number of slaves [*oiketeia*]. The pirates as a group, recognising this favourable situation, flourished as a result; they themselves both went out in search of captives and trafficked in slaves. The kings of both Cyprus and Egypt worked together with them, as joint enemies of Syria; nor did the Rhodians enjoy friendly relations with the Syrians, to whom they gave no help.[53]

There is a slight difference between the behaviour of the two groups: both Ptolemies concerned, apparently Ptolemy VI Philometor and Ptolemy VIII Euergetes II, were active in favour of the pirates (*sunergoun*), that is, they collaborated with the pirates, while the Rhodians had a more passive

---

[50] *I.Kition* 2024 = *OGIS* 134; the date 145–116 BC, i.e. under Ptolemy VIII Euergetes II, is given by Launey 1987: 194, who considers Melancomas to be a descendant of the Melancomas in Polyb. 8.15.9 ff. Perhaps, however, the date should be changed; if the father / *epi tês poleôs* was priest of Euergetes II, the son / *epi tes poleôs* was in charge probably after 120 BC, but I doubt that the writing of the inscription can be so late (see *I.Kition* plate 27). I would suggest that the priesthood was in the cult of Euergetes I and his wife; in that case, Melancomas would be another Aetolian in the service of Ptolemy III or IV, perhaps even, but not necessarily, the same Melancomas as in Polybius. The inscription would in this case date from the early second century BC.

[51] Cf. Robert 1963: esp. 416 ff., who comments on the honours, noting that they had been decided because those involved were Ptolemaic officers, rather than because of their origin.

[52] For an updated bibliography on Aglaus, see now also Casa 2010: 216–19; as mentioned above, some of the inscriptions come from the Cyclades.

[53] Strabo 14.5.2.

attitude: they 'did not help' the Seleucids. In this way they would weaken their rivals, the Seleucids. Or, to quote Gabrielsen, on Rhodes: 'The naval *prostates* looked the other way because it suited his own political interest'[54] and, implicitly, the economic interests of Rome. Cilician pirates would sail the eastern Mediterranean routes until the end of the Mithridatic Wars and the final intervention by Pompey, but, as Appian states (probably taking his information straight from Strabo), these pirates were not only Cilicians but also Syrians, Cypriots, Pamphylians and, naturally, from Pontus.[55] Here we find Cyprus mentioned for a second time in connection with piracy in the period around the turn of the second to first century BC. The statement of Strabo, probably influenced by a certain contempt for the Ptolemaic dynasty, should probably be understood as referring to the final decade of the second century and the beginning of the first, when there were different Ptolemies on the thrones of Cyprus and Egypt. The allegation Strabo (or his sources) makes sounds reasonably reliable. The cross war between the Ptolemaic and Seleucid kings (Ptolemy IX and Antiochus IX vs Ptolemy X and Antiochus VIII) and the need for funds to pay the mercenaries might, as Josephus suggests, plausibly induce a certain unscrupulousness in fund-raising.[56] Ptolemy IX Soter II, for example, though in exile on Cyprus, could employ an army of 30,000 soldiers for his expedition from Cyprus to Ptolemais-Akkô in 103 BC. Where did Ptolemy get the cash to pay these soldiers from? And what ships did he use? It comes, therefore, as no surprise to find Ptolemaic kings, despite their long-time friendship with Rome, detailed along with other more traditional adversaries in the *lex de provinciis praetoriis*. This law, incidentally, gives us a description of how complicity with the pirates worked:[57]

And likewise] to the king ruling in the island of Cyprus, to the king [ruling in Alex]andria and Egyp[t, and to the king ruling in Cyr]ene and to the kings ruling

---

[54] Gabrielsen 2001: 233.   [55] App. *Mith.* 92.
[56] *AJ* 13.12.3, 30,000 infantry and cavalry combined.
[57] M. H. Crawford 1996: no. 12, Delphi Copy, Block B, 8:

ὁμοίως τ]ε καὶ πρὸς τὸν βασιλέα τὸν ἐν τ[ῇ ν]ήσῳ Κύπρωι βασιλεύοντα καὶ πρὸς τὸν βασιλ[έα τὸν ἐν Ἀλε]ξανδρείαι καὶ Αἰγύπ[τωι βασιλεύοντα καὶ πρὸς τὸν βασιλέα τὸν ἐπὶ Κυ]ρήνη βασιλεύοντα καὶ πρὸς τοὺς βασιλεῖς τοὺς ἐν Συρίαι βασιλεύον[τας, πρὸς οὓς] φιλία καὶ συμμαχία ἐ[στὶ τῶι δήμωι τῶι Ῥωμαίων, γράμματα ἀποστελλέ]τω καὶ ὅτι δίκαιόν ἐστ[ιν αὐ]τοὺς φροντίσαι, μὴ ἐκ τῆς βασιλείας αὐτ[ῶν μήτε] τῆ[ς] χώρας ἢ ὁρίων πειρατὴ[ς μηδεὶς ὁρμήσῃ, μηδὲ οἱ ἄρχοντες ἢ φρούραρχοι οὓς κ]αταστήσουσιν τού[ς] πειρατὰς ὑποδέξωνται, καὶ φροντίσαι, ὅσον [ἐν αὐ]τοῖς ἐσ[τι] τοῦτο, ὁ δῆμος ὁ Ῥωμαίω[ν ἵν' εἰς τὴν ἁπάντων σωτηρίαν συνεργοὺς ἔχῃ].

For a vivid description of the way pirates might behave in the vicinity of a great port, see also the episode (no matter if untrue) in Philostr. *VA* 3.24.

in Syria who have [relationship of friendship and alliance with the Roman people, he (i.e. the senior consul) is to send letters] to the effect that it is right for them both to see that [no] pirates [use] their kingdom or land or territories [as a base for operations and that no officials or garrison commanders whom] they shall appoint harbour the pirates and to see that, insofar as it shall be possible, the Roman people [have them as contributors to the safety of all].

A generation later, Pompey's victories over the Cilician pirates in the well-known campaign of 67 BC rendered no less credible the fears of Gabinius, who, charged with treason and extortion, declared that between 56 and 55 BC he had left Syria – his province together with Cilicia – to go to Egypt and restore Ptolemy XII in order to save his province from the danger posed to it by an Egypt serving as a base for piracy while under the control of Archelaus and Berenice.[58] Egypt, no longer *prostatês*, not even an honest friend to be trusted, after Rome's annexation of Cyprus had become the last possible new base for piracy: ripe for a purge with the good Roman medicine.

A few words to conclude. From such scanty sources it is obviously difficult to answer with certainty all the questions asked at the start of this enquiry, but I would venture to claim that the Ptolemies, like other Hellenistic naval powers, did not have any one policy towards pirates, even in the third century BC, the period of their so-called protectorate (*prostasia*) of the Aegean. First, as is often claimed, this was because the definition of piracy, especially in time of war, might depend on one's point of view, and, more substantially, because the political and economic behaviour of the Ptolemies was always characterised by an extreme and flexible pragmatism, though one that was not always successful. They defended and offered help to friends, be they small Greek towns in the islands or free traders and merchants, as a political and economic expression of their supremacy, but above all they took care of their own interests, showing indeed few scruples in their dealings with somewhat shady individuals. 'Prevention is better than cure', and, as far as we can tell, whether in war or in peace, to keep their kingdom safe from the pirates, whatever territories might be involved, their naval strength or their cash worked equally well.

[58] Cic. *Rab. Post.* 20: Gabinius se id fecisse dicebat rei publicae causa, quod classem Archelai timeret, quod mare refertum fore praedonum putaret. But cf. Dio Cass. 39.56.1, 'Gabinius greatly harmed Syria, so that he caused them more damage than they suffered from piratical attacks', then at their peak; and at 59, the allegations against Gabinius, who had not defended them from the pirates, came from the Syrians.

CHAPTER 11

The Nile police in the Ptolemaic period

Thomas Kruse

Travelling on the Nile was a dangerous matter, since one might, for example, quite easily become a victim of piracy, as the following report on such an incident well indicates. In a letter from the Arsinoite nome dating from 224 BC a certain Amadocus addresses a man named Cleon, telling him that the person who will deliver his letter to Cleon told him the following story:

Amadocus to Cleon, greetings. The man who will hand you over the letter says that the ship of Asonides, on board of which were also Dorion and the helmsman Erobastis, while sailing along the area of Tmoienetis, intercepted a barge in which were found some women, and they [i.e. the robbers] departed carrying with them a large footbath made of bronze and a small one, three drinking vessels made of bronze, a big ladle . . . a sifter, a wine strainer, a lampstand made of bronze, a bowl made of bronze, a woollen pillow, a casket for perfumes containing perfumes worth 10 drachmas, 66 drachmas in cash, an unguent-box made of ivory, a plate made of ebony and ivory, a woollen cloak and two linen tunics, two jars of wine . . . [1]

and here the text breaks off.

Although this does not concern us here, . . . does it still not strike one as just a little odd that, while our Amadocus knows practically everything about the value of the loot and the value and condition of the precious goods that the robbers (whom he obviously also knows!) took from the women, he does not say a single word about the women themselves? Who, and how many, were they? Where were they from? Why, and to where, were they travelling, all alone? What happened to them? Were they harmed by the pirates? Well, . . . Amadocus is clearly not interested in their fate, so we too have to leave these poor women alone.

---

[1] *P.Coll.Youtie* I 7.1–17, Ἀμάδοκος Κλέωνι χαίρειν. Ὁ τὰ γ[ράμμα]|τά σοι ἀποδιδούς φησιν τ[ὸ πλοῖον] | τὸ Ἀσωνίδου τοῦ . . . δ . . . ἐφ᾿ οὗ ἐπέπλει | ˙ Δωρίων καὶ κυβερνήτης Ἐροβάστις, ἀνα|⁵πλέον κατὰ Τμοιενέτιν περικόψαι | βᾶριν ἐν ἧι ἐπέπλεον γυναῖκες, ὤι|χοντο δ᾿ ἔχοντες ποδανιπτῆρα χαλ|κοῦν μέγαν καὶ ἄλλον μικρόν, κόν|δυα χαλκᾶ γ, κύαθον μέγ[αν] κ.τ.λ.; for the date of the letter, cf. *BL* IX 59.

However, it was not just private citizens like these women travelling the Nile in small boats who could fall prey to brigandage. This could happen even to government officials and the state vessels they were allowed to use while on duty, vessels which were protected by special guardsmen, as we learn from the following document, a *prosangelma*, that is to say, a complaint, which was submitted to a police officer in the thirty-sixth year of Ptolemy VIII (135 BC):

In the 36th year, Hathyr 11[?]. To Demetrius, one of the diadochi, hipparch over men and *epistatês*, from Paalas son of Harmais, ship's guard of the cabin cruiser [*thalamêgos*] of Apollonius, one of the first friends and *stratêgos* and superintendent of revenues. On the [...] of Phaophi of the 36th year, the said cabin cruiser being at anchor, certain persons approaching in their own boat came to anchor outside it[?] and broke off some of our gear, and when I rebuked them, telling them to keep clear, they leapt on board with unseemly shouts and gave me many blows, with the result that in the tussle I lost a cloak worth 3,000 copper drachmas as well as the broken gear, which was likewise worth 3,000 copper drachmas.[2]

These two examples of piracy and robbery on the Nile make clear, though in a negative light, that the oft-cited description of the Nile as the 'lifeline of Egypt', trivial as it may be, nevertheless remains fully true, for they very well illustrate how vulnerable this lifeline was. The river was the country's lifeline not only because it fed the population by flooding the arable land and bringing the fertile mud onto the fields, but also because it was by far Egypt's most important and fastest transport route, on which was shipped state grain and other important goods destined for Alexandria and for export overseas. Further, it was the vital line of communication along which, day after day, government and adminstrative officials, soldiers, traders and other people, official records, files, messages and so on were transported. In what follows I shall concentrate on this second aspect of the Nile's role as regards Egypt and its population. In particular, the focus of this chapter is on the institutions and various measures by means of which the government and administration of Ptolemaic Egypt tried to secure the safety of shipping on the Nile.

---

[2] *P. Tebt.* III.1 802.1–20, (ἔτους) λς Ἀθὺ[ρ .]α. | [Δημ]ητρίωι τ[ῶ]ν διαδόχων καὶ ἱππάρχηι | ἐπ᾽ ἀνδρῶν καὶ ἐπιστάτει [ ]. | Παρὰ Πααλ[ᾶ]τος τοῦ Ἁρμάιος τοῦ [ ] |⁵ ναυφυλακοῦντος τὴ[ν] Ἀπολλων[ίου] | τῶν (πρώτων) φίλων καὶ στρα(τηγοῦ) καὶ ἐ[πὶ τῶν] | προσόδων θαλαμηγόν. τῆι [το]ῦ | Φαῶφι τοῦ λς (ἔτους) τῆς δ[εδη]λωμένης | θαλαμηγοῦ οὔσης ἐφόρμ[ου] ἐπελθόντες |¹⁰ τινὲς ἐν ἑαυτῶν πλοίω[ι] | ἐκτὸς ᾳ [....]ς προσόρμισαν καὶ τινα | τῶν ἡμετέρων ὅπλω[ν] ἐξέκλασαν, | οἷς καὶ ἐπιτιμήσαντός μου ὅπως | διαχωρισθῶσι, οἱ δ᾽ ἐμπηδήσαντες |¹⁵ φωινὰς ἀπρεπεῖς προείεντο κἀμοὶ | πληγὰς καὶ πλείους ἔδωκαν, | ὥστ᾽ ἄν ἐν τῆι ἀψιμαχίαι ἀπολέσαι με | ἱμάτιον ἄξιον χα(λκοῦ) (δραχμῶν) ᾽Γ[ ] χω[ρ]ὶς τῶν |²⁰ ἐκκλασθέν-των ὅπ[λων] ἃ ἦ]ν | ἄξια ὁμοίως χα(λκοῦ) (δραχμῶν) ᾽Γ. [ἀξιῶ οὖν] | συ[ντάξ]αι κ.τ.λ.

The importance such measures had from the point of view of the government is illustrated by the fact that a decree on the safety of Nile shipping is found among the compilation of royal ordinances (*prostagmata*) in
P.Hib. II 198, which is most probably to be dated to the reign of Ptolemy III
Euergetes I shortly after 242 BC. In this royal ordinance, the text of which
is unfortunately rather mutilated, we find, introduced by the clause 'Let
the judges to whom it is appointed to judge also brigands judge [them]',[3]
the following regulations:

Persons sailing on the river are to moor... [here there is a lacuna in the
text] ... in the appointed places [during the day?]. But [they are not to sail?][4]
at night... [another lacuna in the text] ... Any persons who are driven by storm
and [forced] to anchor on the bank are to go before the competent [authorities]
and inform the police of the reason and the place in which they have anchored. To
those who have reported, the chief of police shall send a guard adequate to protect
them while they are moored, so that no violence may be done. And if any persons
sent from [the king? here there is another lacuna] ... are sailing in haste and wish
to sail at night, they are to be given an escort.[5]

For the most part in the restoration and interpretation of this text I
follow the *editio princeps*, whose editors, in my view, rightly considered
these regulations to be concerned with the safety of ship traffic *on the
Nile*.[6] Roger Bagnall, on the contrary, in an article dating from 1969 took
the passage to refer to ships coming *from the open sea to the mouth of the
Nile* (i.e. for example the Canopic branch of the river).[7] But this is in my
view very doubtful, since shipping usually reached Egypt via the seaport of
Alexandria. Moreover, the interpretation of the editors was confirmed by
Lionel Casson, who, in his study on the *Periplus Maris Erythraei*,[8] pointed
out that the expression *apodedeigmenos hormos* ('designated port') is found
in the *Periplus* for the seaports of Myos Hormos and Berenice, the two

---

[3] *P.Hib.* II 198 V 109–10, διακρινέτ[ω]σ[α]ν δὲ περ[ὶ αὐτῶν οἱ κρι] | ταὶ οἵ[σπερ καὶ το]ὺς λῃστὰς
κρίνειν συντέ[τακται (cf. ll. 85–6).

[4] A probable supplement of the lacuna because of the superscript *mu* in l. 112, which possibly hints at
an abbreviation for μή (see also further below).

[5] *P.Hib.* II 198 V 110–22, τοὺς δὲ] | πλείον[τας κατὰ π]οταμὸν ὁρμίζεσθαι πρὸ τ[± 11] | ἐν τοῖς
ἀ[ποδεδει]γμένοις τ[ό]ποις, νυκτὸς δὲ \μ/ μ[± 11] | οὖνται [c. 9] [...ἀπ]ολέσωσιν ευ [c. 11] | ἐὰν
δέ τι[νες ὑπὸ] χειμῶνος [ἐπι]κληθέντες [± 11] |¹¹⁵ ἐπ' ἀκτῆς ὁ[ρμισ]θῆναι παρελθόντ[ε]ς ἐπὶ τ[ὰ
± 11] | συγκύρον[τα] προσαγγελλέτωσαν τοῖς φυ[λακίταις τήν] | τε αἰτίαν κ[α]ὶ τὸν τόπον
ἐν ὧι ὡρμίσθησαν [καὶ τοῖς προσ]|αγγείλασιν συναποστελλέτω ὁ ἀρχιφυλακ[ίτης φυλακὴν]
| ἱκανὴν οἵτινες φυλάξουσιν τοὺς ὁρμοῦντα[ς ὅπως μηθὲν] |¹²⁰ βίαιον γένηται· καὶ ἐάν τινες
παρὰ τοῦ [βασιλέως? ἀπεσ]|ταλμένοι κατὰ σπουδὴν πλείωσιν καὶ βούλ[ωνται πλεῖν] | νυκτός,
συμπρ[ο]πεμπέτωσαν τούτους καὶ [.

[6] See the commentary of the editors to *P.Hib.* II 198.110–22 (p. 102).

[7] Bagnall 1969: 93–6.   [8] Casson 1989: 271–4.

major ports of Egypt on the Red Sea,[9] as well as for Moscha, which was a minor port on the coast of southern Arabia.[10] Casson convincingly argued that the designation of these ports as *apodedeigmenoi hormoi* must have the same meaning as the *apodedeigmenoi topoi* in *P.Hib.* II 198, that is to say 'designated places' or 'designated harbours' in their function as suitable and as the safest places to moor, which skippers were obliged to head for when they sailed the Nile.[11] But if, as we have seen, they were unable to do this because of bad weather and were forced to drop anchor elsewhere, they were to hurry to the nearest police station and report their position so that a guard could be sent out to protect the ship and its cargo. Obviously these places were 'designated' (*apodedeigmenoi*) because the government maintained police posts there to provide safety against pirates and other bandits. On the other hand, if a ship was not able to moor in such places it ran the risk of attack and became easy prey for brigands. This was even more the case if a ship sailed the river at night. Therefore the regulations which are laid out in *P.Hib.* II 198 presumably either prohibited navigation at night in principle or made special arrangements in cases such as may have been detailed in the fragmentary passage in ll. 112–14.[12] Indeed, as we learn from the last preserved lines of the text, these special provisions were made specifically in the case of persons who were sent on a special mission (presumably by the government) and were, therefore, in a hurry

[9] *Peripl. M. Rubr.* 1, Τῶν ἀποδεδειγμένων ὅρμων τῆς Ἐρυθρᾶς θαλάσσης καὶ τῶν περὶ αὐτὴν ἐμπορίων πρῶτός ἐστιν λιμὴν τῆς Αἰγύπτου Μυὸς ὅρμος, μετὰ δὲ αὐτὸν εἰσπλεόντων ἀπὸ χιλίων ὀκτακοσίων σταδίων ἐν δεξιᾷ ἡ Βερενίκη. – 'Of the designated ports on the Erythraean Sea, and the market-towns around it, the first is the Egyptian port of Mussel Harbor [= Myos Hormos]. To those sailing down from that place, on the right hand, after eighteen hundred stadia, there is Berenice.'

[10] *Peripl. M. Rubr.* 32, καὶ μετ᾽ αὐτοὺς ὅρμος ἀποδεδειγμένος τοῦ Σαχαλίτου λιβάνου πρὸς ἐμβολήν, Μόσχα λιμὴν λεγόμενος. – 'And beyond this is a port designated for receiving the Sachalitic frankincense; the harbour is called Moscha.'

[11] See also the contract for shipping freight on the Nile *P.Oxy.Hels.* 37 (AD 176), in which is included a clause prohibiting skippers from sailing at night or during storms and prescribing that they are to moor 'each day at the designated and safest harbours at the proper hours': οὐ νυκ[τοπλοῶν οὐδὲ χιμ]ῶνος ὄντος, προσορμίζων δὲ καθ᾽ ἑκάστην ἡμέραν ἐπὶ τῶν ἀποδεδιγμέ|νων καὶ ἀσφαλεστάτων ὅρμων ταῖς καθηκούσαις ὥραις (ll. 6–7). This, or a very similarly styled, clause was also inserted in the freight contract *P.Oxy.* XLIII 3111 (Antinoopolis, AD 257), but the passage in l. 12 is too mutilated to be restored with certainty (see also the editors' note). The term ἀποδεδειγμένοι ὅρμοι also occurs in *P.Laur.* I 6.5–6 (freight contract of unknown provenance, AD 98–103; for the date, see *BL* VIII 161); *P.Lond.* II 295 (p. 99) (AD 118): receipt of a camel driver to deliver barley εἰς τοὺς ἀποδεδειγμένους ὅρμους (ll. 7–8); *P.Aberd.* 20.9 (presumably also a freight contract, second century AD). For ἀποδεδειγμένοι τόποι (by which harbours are also meant), see also *P.Ross.Georg.* II 18.33 (notary's register of contracts AD 139–40).

[12] I am inclined to accept the editors' (and also Bagnall's) opinion that the νυκτὸς δέ in l. 112 indicates that the preceding passage deals with ship traffic by day, while at night other rules must have been applied, i.e. to the effect that one should not sail by night, except for urgent needs (the latter is stated explicitly in l. 121).

and wished to sail, or had to do so, at night. For these skippers and their ships an escort was provided which accompanied them – one might think of guards on the escorted ship itself or smaller escort-vessels, like the boats of the river patrol which were called *phylakides*, or *potamophylakides*, with which I shall also deal in a moment.

We have seen that already in the third century BC there existed a river guard or river patrol in Egypt. By the middle of the second century a considerable part of this guard was clearly garrisoned in the capital Alexandria itself. We get some information about this from a passage in *UPZ* I 110, surely one of the most spectacular highlights of papyrology and one of the central pieces in Wilcken's monumental edition of the *Urkunden der Ptolemäerzeit*. This papyrus, which is 1.80 m long and is housed in Paris, contains the famous decrees of the *dioikêtês* Herodes, who was in office around 164 BC and had to cope with the consequences of the revolt of Dionysius in that year; his main task was the restructuring of the economy and the restoration of social peace among the population after this rebellion. His decrees are concerned with the incorrect interpretation and handling by certain local officials in the Egyptian *chôra* of the regulations of a royal order (*prostagma*) issued shortly before, which regulated the imposition of a land lease at a reduced rent (presumably to cover the losses caused by *basilikoi georgoi* who participated in the revolt of Dionysius) and the number and status of the groups of people who were to be compulsorily enrolled to lease the plots pertaining to this measure. From l. 20 onwards we read that the guards and the Egyptian *machimoi* with *klêroi* of 7 and 5 arouras and 'the marine *machimoi* stationed on the police boats' who were garrisoned in Alexandria addressed the *dioikêtês*, complaining that their kinsmen and family members at home were being harrassed by the local administration, whose officials apparently tried to force them into the aforementioned compulsory leases of land.[13]

---

[13] *UPZ* I 110.i.20–8:

οἱ παρε[φ]εδ[ρε]ύοντες ἐν Ἀλεξανδ[ρ]είαι τῶν | τ᾿ ἐπιλέκτων καὶ τῶν (ἑπταρούρων) καὶ (πενταρούρων) μαχίμων καὶ | τῶν ἐπὶ τῶν φυλακίδων [τ]εταγμένων ναυκλη|ρομαχίμων ἐντετεύχασιν ἡμῖν προφερόμενοι | τοὺ<ς> παρ᾿ αὐτῶν ἀπολελειμμένους ἐπὶ τῶν τόπων | σκύλλεσθαι μὴ μετρ[ί]ως, τῶν πρὸς ταῖς πραγματεί|αις οὐ κατὰ τὸ βέλτιστον ἐγδεχομένων τὸν τοῦ πε|ρὶ τῆς γεωργίας προστάγματος νοῦν, ἀλλ᾿ οἰομένων | <δεῖν> ἕκαστον αὐτῶν γεω[ργ]ήσειν ἐπὶ τὸ ἔλασσον κε(φάλαιον) κ.τ.λ.

The picked forces and *machimoi* with a *klêros* of 7 or 5 arouras, as well as the marine *machimoi* stationed on the police boats who are garrisoned in Alexandria, have petitioned us, bringing forward that the people they left at home are being immoderately harrassed, as the local officials don't interpret the royal decree on the cultivation of the land in its best sense but believe that every one of them has to take over the cultivation of the land at a reduced rent.'

Clearly by this time there existed among the *nauklêromachimoi* a special troop of soldiers who in times of peace were on duty on the police boats patrolling the Nile. Like other *machimoi* these were recruited from among the native Egyptian population and were provided by the government with a *klêros* of land to secure their livelihood. These *nauklêromachimoi* are also mentioned in a fragmentary passage of a decree of Ptolemy VIII Euergetes II and the two Cleopatras ('sister' and 'wife') (*P. Tebt.* I 5.44 ff.) issued shortly after 118 BC. This forms part of a collection of decrees compiled by the *kômogrammateus* of the Arsinoite village of Kerkeosiris, Menches. These decrees, bestowing several *philanthrôpa* on various groups of the population after the reconciliation between Ptolemy VIII and Cleopatra II, were also aimed at the restoration of peace after the internal strife between the Ptolemaic siblings which had resulted in outright civil war in the preceding years. In this text the *nauklêromachimoi* are, as in *UPZ* I 110, again mentioned together with other *machimoi* and *klêros*-holders of 7 and 10 arouras. The decree guaranteed them the legal possession of land which had been granted them at the time of the recent civil war. Together with these *nauklêromachimoi*, troops of the 'river fleet' (*potamou stolos*) are possibly also mentioned, if the respective reading and restoration of the damaged passage of the papyrus are correct, as indeed is most probably the case.[14]

The police boats (*phylakides*) on which such *nauklêromachimoi* were stationed could very well have been part of the Ptolemaic 'royal river fleet' (*potamios basilikos stolos*) just mentioned. For this river fleet, apart from its restoration in the text just mentioned, until recently we had only a single certain reference in a very mutilated collection of royal *prostagmata* probably dating from 95/94 BC. The relevant passage seems to deal with problems concerning the equipment of soldiers, among which are mentioned persons 'of the river fleet' (*ek tou potamou stolou*).[15] Fortunately, however, we now have another testimony provided by a papyrus of the collection of the University Library of Trier in Germany and recently edited by Bärbel

---

[14] *P. Tebt.* I 5.44–8 (= *C.Ord.Ptol.*² 53), [τοὺς δὲ ἐπιλέ]κ̣[τους] κ̣α̣ὶ μαχ(ίμους) [καὶ] (δεκαρούρους) καὶ (ἑπταρούρους) κ̣[αὶ τοὺς το]ύ̣|⁴⁵[τ]ων ἡ[γου]μέν[ο]υς καὶ τοὺς ἄλλους τοὺς φερομ[ένους ἐν τῆι συντ]ά̣(ξει) | [καὶ τοὺς] να̣[υκ]ληρομαχ(ίμους) καὶ τοὺς ἐκ τοῦ πολ[± 10] | [κρατεῖν] ὧν κατεσχήκασι κλή(ρων) ἕως τοῦ [νβ (ἔτους) ἀκατηγο]|[ρήτου]ς καὶ ἀνεπιλήπτους ὄντας. – 'And that the picked forces, and the *machimoi* who own 10 or 7 arourae, and their leaders, and all others placed in that class, and the *nauklêromachimoi*, and those who . . . shall have the legal ownership of the lands which they have possessed up to the . . . year, and shall not be subject to accusation or interference.' For l. 46 Daris 1990: 6 proposed restoring ἐκ τοῦ ποτ[αμοῦ στόλου].

[15] *SB* XX 14106.6 (*editio princeps*: Daris 1990); see also B. Kramer in the commentary to *P.Poethke* 18.5 (with n. 15).

Kramer.[16] This text, coming from the Heracleopolite nome and dating from 137 BC, is an instruction from the royal scribe (*basilikos grammateus*) of this nome to his representative (the *antigrapheus*) concerning provisions for the *thalamêgos* of the *epistratêgos* Boethus. The supply designated for this ship amounted to 160 artabas of wheat, which was to be handed over to 'Leon, representative of Damon, superintendent of the royal river fleet'.[17] We further learn from this text that the Ptolemaic river fleet clearly had an important base in the Heracleopolite nome – a point to which we shall have occasion to return later on.

This fleet, however, about which we are unfortunately only poorly informed, and also the police boats were only part of the system built up by the government to provide for the safety of shipping on the Nile. We have already learned from the royal ordinances in *P.Hib.* II 198, dating from shortly after 242 BC, that there must have existed guard posts along the banks of the Nile and (one may presume) of its branches as well as the larger canals whose duty it was to watch over water traffic and to react to unusual incidents. This was the case should they receive information on ships which were forced to moor outside the prescribed places and which they then had to protect, or on those for which they had to provide an escort when they needed to sail at night. This is to assume that these guard posts were manned by the so-called *potamophylakes*, who occur in a couple of documents of the Ptolemaic period.

We get some information about their duties and competence from a text which was edited in 2006 by Charikleia Armoni in her fine edition of the delicate, complicated and badly mutilated documents belonging to the archive of the royal scribe Dionysius, who was in office in the Heracleopolite nome between 159 and 157 BC. Among the papers of this nome official is found a fragmentary draft of an official letter dating from 12 June 158 BC which he addressed to the *potamophylax* Haspheus (*P.Heid.* IX 428). In this letter Dionysius reports that Leonides, the *nauklêros* of the *kerkouros* – a type of transport vessel – belonging to Castor, the captain of that ship, called Maron, and another person who was the official ship's-attendant (*epiploos*) had together submitted a memorandum to Dionysius in which they reported that, while their ship was at anchor in the harbour of Ankyron Polis in the Heracleopolite nome, it was attacked and plundered by certain individuals. These took off with them goods or part of the cargo – the text of the passage is too mutilated to get more details – worth altogether 3,000

---

[16] *P.Poethke* 18.
[17] *P.Poethke* 18.4–6: Λέοντι τῶι παρὰ Δάμωνος τῶι πρὸς τῶι ποταμίωι βασιλικῶι στόλωι.

talents of copper, and they burned (and probably also stole) parts of the ship's equipment with the effect that it was now impossible to navigate the ship any more.[18] After this the crew of the *kerkouros* had obviously notified the *potamophylax* about the assault, but because nothing had been done by him on their behalf since then they now addressed his superior, the royal scribe Dionysius, who for his part now admonishes the *potamophylax* to do what he is supposed to do. We are not told what exactly Haspheus should do now or what he already should have done before, because at this point the text breaks off, but it is clear from this document that it was the responsibility of a *potamophylax* to receive notification of such attacks made on shipping and to take all necessary action in such cases, which (as I understand from the Heidelberg papyrus) included arrangements for the repair of the ship if it was damaged in the course of the assault.

Further information about the duties of the *potamophylakes* is provided by a document in the Berlin collection (*BGU* VIII 1784). This text is also an official letter from the Heracleopolite nome, but of a much later date than the document just discussed. It dates from the period between 64 and 44 BC, that is to say either the reign of Ptolemy XII Neos Dionysus or of his daughter, the famous Cleopatra VII. The letter is addressed to a certain Mandrobes, presumably an army officer. The sender of the letter, who does not tell us his name, reports to him that a subordinate of Mandrobes, a man named Hierax, delivered to him a written instruction from Mandrobes concerning the *potamophylakes* and others. In compliance, he had ordered the *potamophylakes* to escort (*propempsai*) the *ouragia* – probably the rearguard or rear detachment of a larger military unit together, maybe, with its equipment and baggage – to Hiera Nesos (a village in the Heracleopolite nome). When they got there, they were to hand the assignment over to the river police of the Troites (presumably a toparchy also in the Heracleopolite nome),[19] who for their part should accompany the *ouragia*

---

[18] *P.Heid.* IX 428.2–11, Ἀσφεῖ ποταμοφύ(λακι)· Λεωνίδου ναυκλήρου τοῦ Κάστορος | κερκούρου καὶ Μάρωνος ..[± 6] .... | ἐπ' αὐτῶι ἐπίπλου δόντων ἡμῖν ὑπ[όμνημα] |⁵ ὑπὲρ τοῦ τῆι [number τοῦ] Φαρ]μοῦθι περὶ ὥρα[ν ± 4] | ὁρμοῦντος τοῦ πλοίου ἐπ[ὶ τοῦ κατ' Ἀγκυρῶν πόλιν] | ὅρμου ἐπιθεμένους τινὰ[ς ± 17] | [ἐπὶ τὸ προωνομ]ασμένον πλ[οῖον ± 15] | [2]τ.[± 40] |¹⁰ ὠιχῆσθαι ἔχον[τ]ας λα....ε.[± 15] | ὧν εἶναι τὴν διατίμησιν εἰς χα(λκοῦ) (τάλαντα) κ.τ.λ.

[19] The Troites mentioned here cannot very well be identified with the homonymous area in the Memphite nome, way further north of the Heracleopolite, since later in the text we hear that the river police of the Troites should escort the *ouragia* to the Cynopolite, the nome on the south-eastern border of the Heracleopolite. The journey of the *ouragia* is obviously directed to the south. The toponym Troites is also mentionend in two other documents from the Heracleopolite nome (*BGU* VIII 1807.3; XVI 2630.13), and in both cases this certainly designates an area *within* this administrative district. It is therefore somewhat puzzling that Falivene 1998 makes no mention of this.

to its final destination, the village of Chie in the Cynopolite nome, which bordered the Heracleopolite on the south-east. Before the text breaks off, Mandrobes, who is clearly to take part in the journey, is urged by the sender of the letter 'to summon the *potamophylakes* to perform their difficult task courageously'.[20] It looks as if the sender of the letter is here anticipating that the trip could become a dangerous one. This may be due to the times of unrest in Egypt during the later years of the reign of Ptolemy XII, who was, first, forced by the Alexandrians to go into exile, then had to raise a lot of money to win the support of the Romans and, after having been finally reinstalled by Rome with military force in 56 or 55 BC, had to permit a gangster like Rabirius Postumus to squeeze as much cash and tribute out of the country's population as was possible. But this, of course, is simply hypothesis. The text could also very well belong to the reign of Cleopatra VII and/or the time of Caesar's stay in Egypt. But these times were in no way any calmer for the country than those of her father had been.

Be that as it may, what is important for us here is that we learn from the text just discussed some details of the organisation of the river police. It is clear that single guard posts consisting of *potamophylakes* were responsible for certain sections of the river and its channels, and for the canals as well. The latter is also confirmed by the fact that in line 3 of *BGU* VIII 1784 the writer clearly at first intended to write: 'to the river guards of the channel [or branch] called *Ptolemaikos*' (*tou Ptolemaikou potamophylaxi*)[21] and then corrected the passage (at least in part, since while he put the *potamophylaxi* in brackets he forgot to delete *Ptolemaikou*, which now reads somewhat strangely). In any case, the original intention of the writer implies that river guards also existed for the *Ptolemaikos potamos*, which may be identified either with the Bahr Yussuf, on the bank of which was situated the harbour of Heracleopolis, or with the Memphis canal.[22]

The *potamophylakes* had to watch over the crossings of the particular waterway assigned to them, or, as two written payment orders for *potamophylakes* from 63 BC put it, they were 'river guards assigned to watch

---

20 *BGU* VIII 1784.1–10, Μανδρόβηι | Ἱέραξ ὁ παρὰ σ[ο]ῦ συμμείξας ἀπέδωκέ μοι | ἃ ἐγεγράφει<ς> ὑπέρ τε τῶν ποταμοφυλάκων | καὶ ἄλλων. \τού/τοις μὲν οὖν [ποταμοφύλαξι] \τοῦ Πτολε- μαικοῦ/ |⁵ γέγραφα προπέμψαι [ὑμᾶς] \τὴν οὐραγίαν/ μέχρι Ἱερᾶς καὶ | \παραδοῦναι/ τοῖς ἀπ[ὸ] τοῦ Τρω[ί̈τ[ου], καὶ ἐκείνοις δὲ ὅπως | σὺν ὑμῖν γένωντ[αι πρ]ὸς τὸ Χιὴ τοῦ Κυνο|πολίτου· ὀρθῶ[ς οὖν ποιήσ]εις τοὺς δηλου|μένους ποτα[μοφύλακα]ς συντάξας |¹⁰ εὐθαρσεῖς ποι[εῖσθαι καμ]άτους, κ.τ.λ.
21 τοῖς μὲν οὖν τοῦ Πτολεμαικοῦ ποταμοφύλαξι.
22 The Πτολεμαϊκὸς ποταμός is also attested in *P.Strasb.* V 356, a very mutilated fragment of a land survey dating from the second century AD.

over the crossings of the river'.[23] Consequently these guards, if necessary, had to escort official transports from one police post to the next. How exactly such an escort was organised we do not know. It could be that several *potamophylakes* travelled on board the ship or ships they had to accompany, but I consider this rather unlikely and would think rather that they escorted them in their police boats, the so-called *(potamo)phylakides*, and in this way they built up a convoy.

Michael Rostovtzeff, in an article entitled 'Πλοῖα θαλάσσια on the Nile' published more than seventy years ago, thought such escorts were also used for sea-going ships of the Ptolemaic warfleet,[24] since in a number of Heracleopolite documents dating from 64/63 BC there are mentioned deliveries of state grain to the 'serving crews assigned to the *dioikêtês* from the sea fleet'.[25] I consider this highly doubtful, because not only do we not know the purpose of the mission for which these crews were sent into the Egyptian *chôra*, we are also not explicitly told whether these men even had their sea-going ships (*ploia thalassia*) with them at the time. But even if this were the case, it could very well be, as the editor Wolfgang Kunkel thought, that crews from the sea-going fleet were put at the disposal of the *dioikêtês* (the highest-ranking official of the civil administration) for the needs of the civil service, such as building activities or the like.[26]

One certainly has to admit, however, that sea-going ships and at least smaller warships were able to navigate the Nile and the Bahr Yussuf as well.[27] We do, for example, know for certain that already by the middle of the second century BC a *trihêmiolia*,[28] manned by Egyptian *machimoi* who obviously functioned as marines, was stationed in the harbour of Heracleopolis.[29] The mission of this ship could have been of a military

---

[23] οἱ πρὸς τῇ τηρήσει τῶν κατὰ ποταμὸν πόρων ποταμοφύλακες; *BGU* VIII 1743 (*editio princeps*: Kunkel 1927: 188–90, no. 3) + *BGU* XIV 2368 cols. II and III (Heracleopolite nome, 23 August 63 BC). For πόρος meaning 'crossing place' or 'ferry' in this context, cf. LSJ *s.v.*

[24] Rostovtzeff 1940: 374–6.

[25] λειτουργοὶ τεταγμένοι τῷ διοικητῇ ἐκ τοῦ θαλασσίου στόλου. See *BGU* VIII 1744–6.1755.

[26] See the introduction to the *editio princeps* of these texts by Kunkel 1927: 191–3. We learn also from *P.Berl.Salm.* 1.16–17 (Heracleopolis, 86 BC), where a certain Ptolemaeus is mentioned with the title ὁ πρὸς τῶι διοικητικῶι στόλωι ('the one responsible for the fleet of the *dioikêtês*'), that the *dioikêtês* might indeed have had a fleet at his disposal. The purpose of this fleet is described as συμπλεούσης Ἀλεξάνδρωι τῶι ἐπὶ τῆς ὑπηρεσίας προκεχειρισμένωι εἰς τὴν χώραν (ll. 18–19) – 'sailing in the company of Alexandros, who has been appointed to take care of the [expedition?] to the countryside'. This sounds not like a military but rather like a civil mission.

[27] In *BGU* VIII 1755.4 (Heracleopolite nome, 52 BC), e.g., θαλάσσια σκάφη on the Nile are attested, which I consider to be sea-going transport vessels.

[28] For this type of ship invented by the Rhodians, see Casson 1971: 127–32.

[29] See *P.Hamb.* I 57 (160 BC); *P.Phrur.Diosk.* 4 (153 BC?); *SB* XXVI 16698, cf. also the *editio princeps* by Kramer 2001.

character, since about this time the Heracleopolite was developed into some form of military stronghold with a fortress (*phrourion*) both in the metropolis itself and in its harbour, and with several minor *phrouria* across the countryside of the nome.[30] But of course this *trihêmiolia* could also have been part of the royal river fleet mentioned above and could therefore have provided regular escorts for official transports; as we saw earlier, at least one unit of the Ptolemaic river fleet was stationed in the Heracleopolite.[31] It may thus not necessarily be by mere accident that most of the papyrus documents attesting activity of ships, a fleet or its crews come from this nome.

But let us return to the *potamophylakes*. They show up also in a group of land registers from the Heracleopolite nome dating from the second or first century BC;[32] these provide us with information on the social status of these river guards. The registers are arranged by toparchies and/or villages and by the occupational categories of the landholders. From these texts we learn that the *potamophylakes*, like soldiers and other state officials, were *klêrouchoi*, holders of a *klêros*, a plot of land granted to them by the king. So they were part of the cleruchic system by means of which the Ptolemaic state aimed at securing the living of its army and its administrative officials.

Let us now take a closer look at the *klêroi* of the *potamophylakes*. In *BGU* XIV 2441.225–8 we have an entry concerning an unknown Heracleopolite village which, under the heading 'From the *potamophylakes*', mentions two *potamophylakes*: Heracleides, son of Aratomenes, and Heracleides, son of Theocharis, each holding a *klêros* of ten arouras, one part of which was planted with wheat, the other with grass and farmed by a tenant (*geôrgos*).[33] Ten arouras seems to have been the normal size of the *klêros* of a *potamophylax*, as is confirmed by the other land registers of this series containing entries on such *klêroi*. These were, admittedly, not very large parcels of land, but the *potamophylakes*, of course, were not very high-ranking officials, and the *klêroi* of Egyptian *machimoi* were even smaller, consisting of 7 or 5 arouras, as we saw in the passage from *UPZ* I 110 from 164 BC concerning the Egyptian *machimoi* and *nauklêromachimoi*, and as discussed in an earlier

---

[30] See also Kruse 2011.   [31] See above on *P.Poethke* 18.

[32] *BGU* XIV 2437.46–7; 2440.50–61; 2441.225–8; 2444.1–3; see also *P.Amh.* II 32.13–14 (unknown provenance, second century BC).

[33] ἐκ πο(ταμο)φυ(λάκων)· Ἡρακλείδου τοῦ Ἀρατομένου ἐκ (τοῦ) Κορράγου | ⟦ . ⟧ ι γεω(ργὸς) Φίλων (πυρῷ) ς χό(ρτῳ) δ (γίνονται) ι | Ἡρακλείδου τοῦ Θεοχάριδος ἐκ (τοῦ) Νικαίου ι γεω(ργὸς) Ἑρμίας (πυρῷ) ε χό(ρτῳ) ε (γίνονται) ι | γίνονται ἐκ πο(ταμο)φυ(λάκων) ἐσπαρ(μένης) σ(πορίμου) ἧς μέ(ρος) κ; the phrase ἐκ (τοῦ) Κορράγου as well as ἐκ (τοῦ) Νικαίου designate former holders of the land allotments of which the respective *klêroi* (now held by the two *potamophylakes*) once formed part.

section of this chapter. The normal policemen, the *phylakitai*, who are also mentioned in the land registers received a *klêros* of 10 arouras as well.

The Heracleopolite land registers from the second or first century BC attest *klêroi* of *potamophylakes* in quite a number of villages of this nome. Of course this only means that their plot was situated there; the relevant village was not necessarily also the place where these *potamophylakes* performed their duties. To sum up: the Ptolemaic river police consisted of a special troop of river guards, the *potamophylakes*, who had cleruchic status and occupied guard posts alongside the banks of the Nile and its channels, and the larger canals as well. These guardposts were called *phylakai*, like the 'lower *phylakê*' (*katô phylakê*) which in the later third century BC is attested for Schedia at the entrance of the *Alexandreôn chôra*[34] or the *Hermopolitikê phylakê* in the Hermopolite nome mentioned by the geographer Strabo.[35] These posts were where customs dues from merchant vessels were collected too. It may well be that collecting such customs dues also formed part of the role of the *potamophylakes*, though up to now we lack any hard proof for this. Certainly part of their duties was to watch over the section of the Nile or waterway assigned to them, to receive notifications from skippers about unusual incidents, such as attacks on their ships or about their possible mooring-place outside the prescribed harbours, and to provide not only protection for such vessels but also, in certain cases, escorts for ships and transports alike. For this purpose they used their guard or patrol boats, the *potamophylakides*. Where stronger protection was needed, it was also possible to station marines, the *nauklêromachimoi*, on such vessels, which perhaps formed part of the 'river fleet' (*potamou stolos*).

It is by no means surprising that the institution of the *potamophylakia* survived the Ptolemies. The problem of piracy and brigandage on the Nile of course remained the same also after the Romans took over control of Egypt, as is illustrated by an inscription on a gravestone now in the Musée du Louvre dating from the Roman imperial period, which tells us that three sailors from Ptolemais in Upper Egypt – two brothers and their uncle – were killed by raiders in the harbour of Pouchis in the Antaeopolite nome, and their ship was also burned.[36]

---

[34] See *P.Hib.* I 110,25 (postal register, 225 BC), ἐπὶ τῆς κάτω φυ[λα]κ(ῆς) [ἐν] Σχεδίαι.

[35] Strabo 17.1.41 (C 813), Ἑξῆς δ' ἐστὶν Ἑρμοπολιτικὴ φυλακή, τελώνιόν τι τῶν ἐκ τῆς Θηβαΐδος καταφερομένων – 'Then follows the Hermopolite guard post, a place where the toll is collected from merchandise brought down from the Thebais.'

[36] *IEgLouvre* 90 = *OGIS* II 697, Ἀντιλαβοῦ, κύριε Σάραπι. Βῆσις | πρεσβύτερος καὶ Βῆσις νεώτε|ρος, ἀμφότεροι Σεντώσυτος | κυβερνήτου ἀπὸ Πτολεμαίδος |⁵ καὶ Βῆσις κάρβας ἀδελφὸς τῆς | μητρὸς αὐτῶν, ἐσφαγμένοι ἐν ὅρ|μῳ Πούχεως τοῦ Ἀνταιοπολεί|του νομοῦ, καὶ τὸ πλῦ(ο)ν

The Romans, however, seem to have undertaken some institutional changes regarding the river police. First of all, at some time during the first or early second century AD, the *potamophylakia* was placed under the control of the *praefectus classis Alexandrinae*; guarding the river and the larger waterways, from then on, was presumably at least in part the duty of the Alexandrian fleet. This is attested by an inscription from Málaga in Spain. The *patronus* of this town in the years around AD 130 was L. Valerius Proculus, who at some time during his career was ... *praef(ectus) classis Alexandrin(ae) et potamophylaciae.*[37] The Romans obviously also introduced a new tax called 'apportionment (*merismos*) for the police boats on the river' which was a poll-tax to cover the expenses for the maintenance and supply of the guard ships and their crews.[38] The *potamophylakes* themselves are only poorly attested from this period, but this may well be due also to the chance preservation of our source material. But it seems that by now the *potamophylakes* had become liturgists, whom the towns and villages of the *chôra* had to nominate for their territory. But, as we have indicated, the testimonies are *very* few. We have only four documents dating from the Roman period which mention *potamophylakes*,[39] compared to around a hundred receipts on *ostraca* and papyrus attesting the '*merismos* for the police boats on the river'.

But the Romans do not concern us further here, and the texts just mentioned merely serve to outline some aspects of the later development of the institution of the *potamophylakia* after the Ptolemies.

αὐτῶν ἐνπέ|πρηκαν. – 'Be our aid, lord Sarapis! Bêsis the elder, and Bêsis the younger, both sons of the skipper Sentôous from Ptolemais, and Bêsis a builder of small boats, the brother of their mother, were killed in the harbour of Pouchis in the Antaeopolite nome, and [the raiders] burned their ship.'

[37] *CIL* II 1970 = *ILS* 1341.

[38] μερισμὸς ὑπὲρ ποταμοφυλακίδος (or ποταμοφυλακίδων). For this tax see F. Reiter in the introduction to *P.Köln* IX 377.

[39] *P.Aberd.* 94 (Upper Egypt, second century AD); *P.Brem.* 11 col. III (AD 117–18); *P.Oxy.* XLIV 3184a (AD 296); *CPL* 106 (= *P.Gen.lat.* 1) recto col. I D (AD 81–90).

CHAPTER 12

Hellenistic royal barges

Dorothy J. Thompson

Enobarbus The barge she sat in, like a burnish'd throne,
     Burnt on the water. The poop was beaten gold,
     Purple the sails, and so perfumed that
     The winds were love-sick with them; the oars were silver,
     Which to the tune of flutes kept stroke, and made
     The water which they beat to follow faster,
     As amorous of their strokes. For her own person,
     It beggar'd all description: she did lie
     In her pavilion – cloth of gold, of tissue –
     O'er-picturing that Venus where we see
     The fancy outwork nature; on each side her
     Stood pretty-dimpled boys, like smiling Cupids,
     With divers-colour'd fans, whose wind did seem
     To glow the delicate cheeks which they did cool,
     And what they undid did.
       Shakespeare, *Antony and Cleopatra*, Act 2, scene 2, ll. 223–37

In autumn 41 BC, Cleopatra VII, queen of Egypt, answered the summons of the Roman general Antony by taking control of the occasion. Her arrival in Tarsus up the river Cydnus is best known from the wonderful evocation of Shakespeare, quoted above. Here, however, I start with Plutarch's account on which this was based:[1]

Though she received many letters of summons from him and his friends, Cleopatra so despised and laughed openly at the man that she sailed up the river Cydnus in a barge with gilded poop and purple sails outspread; the sailors pulled back their silver oars to the music of flutes accompanied by pipes and lyres. The queen reclined beneath a canopy embroidered with gold, adorned like Aphrodite in a scene, and young boys, like Cupids in a picture, took their stand on either side and fanned her. Likewise, the fairest of her serving maids, wearing the dress of

 I wish to thank participants at the Ptolemaic Waterways and Power conference together with S. M. Burstein. Their input is acknowledged with gratitude.
[1] Plut. *Ant.* 26.1–3. Shakespeare used Thomas North's translation (from French) of Plutarch's *Lives.*

Nereids and Graces, stood some at the helm, others at the sheets. Wondrous scents from the many incense burners suffused the banks. Of the people there, some escorted her on both sides directly from the river, while others went down from the city to see the sight. The crowd poured out from the market-place and finally Antony himself was left alone, sitting on his platform. Word went round among them all how Aphrodite would come in revelry to Dionysus, for the good of Asia.

My interest in this chapter is in the role of Hellenistic royal barges, like that of Cleopatra, both as essential accoutrements of royalty and in their development over time.[2] As symbols of regal wealth and power, I shall suggest, barges formed part of the competition for primacy played out among the successors of Alexander. No less than horses, ceremonial craft were prized possessions of kings and queens, important to their image both at home and abroad. For the Hellenistic rulers of Egypt, with the Nile running the length of their kingdom and, in the third century BC, an Aegean thalassocracy (the League of Islanders), travel by water was the norm, but Egypt was not the only kingdom where a special ship or ceremonial barge might exemplify a monarch's standing. As we shall find, the royal ship of Macedon also played a role in the process of the Roman conquest of the Hellenistic world.

Nevertheless, Ptolemaic Egypt stands out as the centre of development for royal ships. For here the main artery of the Nile provided a navigable waterway within the country, along which pharaohs would regularly travel in a symbolic act of the unification of Upper and Lower Egypt,[3] while the new capital of Alexandria gave access to the Aegean world from which the new rulers came. Further, as well illustrated in earlier chapters, the Ptolemaic empire of the third century BC consisted in the main of islands and depended on naval power.

Cleopatra's arrival in Tarsus makes a vivid scene. She came as Aphrodite, Plutarch tells us, to revel with Dionysus, who for Egyptians was also Osiris.[4] The tableau of the queen on board her royal barge is a striking one, in which the visual impact of Plutarch's account depends on the detail he gives.[5] There is nothing here as to the size or construction of Cleopatra's barge. We are not even told if this was the same as the ship in which she had

---

[2] As in Shakespeare, the term barge is used here also for royal craft with sails.
[3] For Ptolemaic royal progresses, see Clarysse 2000.
[4] Cf. Plut. *Ant.* 24.3, Antony as Dionysus in Ephesus earlier the same year; Dio Cass. 48.39.2, as the new Dionysus in Athens (with Octavia) in 39 BC; Plut. *Ant.* 60.3, and later in Alexandria. In 34 BC, Cleopatra dressed as the new Isis, Plut. *Ant.* 54.6.
[5] See Pelling 1988: 186–9.

sailed across to Cilicia.[6] Nor do we know whether its hold contained all that the queen required for the lavish series of entertainment she provided in the following days or whether this came along in separate carriers.[7] Such ceremonial barges had become a standard means of transport for Hellenistic monarchs, and in Egypt the need for ceremonial craft was recognised early in the Ptolemaic dynasty. If Appian may be trusted, already at the start of the period, in the third century BC, Ptolemy II counted 800 ships, with cabins, gilded poops and prows, as part of his naval strength – ships more specifically designated for the ceremonial aspect of war.[8]

In the first half of the third century, however, the record is primarily of fighting ships, reflecting the troubled international scene of the early Hellenistic period. Increasingly large, yet still efficient ships were constructed for dynasts and kings in which to fight and, at the same time, parade the splendour of their power. From Plutarch's parallel life to that of Antony, we learn of the Fifteen and Sixteen of Demetrius Poliorcetes, which had been added to his fast-growing naval force by 288 BC.[9] What precisely these numbers refer to is debated,[10] but such a designation underlines the importance of size as a defining feature of these ships. Such ships were not just beautiful but also good for fighting, combining magnificence of equipment with practical use; their speed and manoeuvrability were, Plutarch reports, even more remarkable than their great size. Demetrius was important for naval developments in the period, and a prime player in the competition for the construction of great ships among the early generations of Alexander's successors.[11] Plutarch describes how his enemies, standing on the shore, would stare in amazement as his ships sailed by.[12] These large ships of the early third century BC were built not just for display: they also served as flagships for the king in major battles.

Others followed suit. Though they were regularly rivals, when involved in the siege of Cilician Soli Lysimachus requested Demetrius to

---

[6] The description of this boat as a πορθμεῖον, Plut. *Ant.* 26.1, the term used for ferries on the Nile, suggests that it was another craft.

[7] Plut. *Ant.* 26.3–27.1, purple tapestries with threads of gold, drinking cups of gold inlaid with gems, cup stands, silver trappings for the horses, cooks, Ethiopian slaves to carry torches, etc.; cf. Ath. 5.147e–148c (Socrates of Rhodes). The roses for weaving into a net (and covering the floor to a cubit's depth), together with other supplies, could well have been purchased locally. For supply vessels, see Max.Tyr. 30.82, ὁλκάδες δημοτικαί.

[8] App. *Praef.* 10, ἐς πολέμου πομπήν.

[9] Plut. *Demetr.* 43.4–5, with at least one Fifteen (πεντεκαιδεκήρης) and Sixteen (ἑκκαιδεκήρης), cf. 20.4, in the plural.

[10] Morrison and Coates 1996: xiv and 90, number of files of oarsmen each side of the ship in a banked system of oars; Casson 1995: 106, the number of oarsmen to one bank of oars.

[11] Casson 1995: 137–40, a naval arms race; cf. Tarn 1930: 129–41; Murray 2012: 3–12.

[12] Plut. *Demetr.* 20.4; his 'city-takers', ἑλεπόλεις, also provided a θέαμα for those under siege.

demonstrate his siege engines and to show him his ships under sail. Demetrius complied, and, so Plutarch reports, Lysimachus wondered and left.[13] Sometime later, however, Lysimachus' own Eight appeared on the scene – a Super-Eight equivalent to a Sixteen, which Casson suggests was a double-hulled catamaran.[14] This large ship served as the flagship of Ptolemy Ceraunus in 280 BC and played a notable part in the sea battle when he defeated Antigonus Gonatas.[15] It was known as the *Leontophoros*, most probably from a lion as its crest, and it is this which connects the ship to Lysimachus.

The changing fortunes of the rival dynasts of the period may be charted through the fate of their flagships, which, when captured, were put by the other side to a similar use. The fate of the Sixteen of Demetrius remains a puzzle. Casson follows Tarn in suggesting that it entered the navy of Ptolemy I around the time that Demetrius surrendered to Seleucus in 285 BC.[16] In that case, it could not have served as flagship for Demetrius' son Antigonus in the naval battle of 280 just mentioned, when Ceraunus was victorious in the *Leontophoros*. On the other hand, that particular battle would seem a more likely occasion for its transfer to the Egyptian fleet. It perhaps came back into Antigonus' hands some three decades later when he defeated Ptolemy II at the battle of Cos. For that battle Antigonus had his own flagship, a 'sacred trireme'.[17]

Eights, Fifteens and Sixteens were certainly impressive but, as so often, Ptolemy II Philadelphus went one better. Two records survive of the navy of this king, whose control of the League of Islanders played a key part in confirming Ptolemaic power in the Aegean. The details of these accounts are hard to reconcile, but that is not really relevant here.[18] They agree, however, in recording the naval supremacy of the king and his success in surpassing his contemporaries in the construction of large ships. Appian's account is the more general, recording the make-up of Ptolemy II's navy in round figures, while Athenaeus provides the greater detail. According to Athenaeus, Philadelphus' navy contained, as the largest of many large ships, two Thirties and one Twenty. So, whereas for naval parades Ptolemies probably used those smaller craft with gilded poops and prows,[19] when he

---

[13] Plut. *Demetr.* 20.4.   [14] Casson 1995: 112–15 ; cf. Murray 2012: 171–8.
[15] Memnon, *FGrH* 434 F1.8.5–6.   [16] Casson 1995: 139, n. 12.
[17] Ath. 5.209e. Tarn, followed by Casson 1995: 139, n. 14, suggests that this was the ship dedicated on Delos; cf. Buraselis 1982: 148.
[18] App. *Praef.* 10; Ath. 5.203c–d, cf. *OGIS* 39, a royal dedication from Paphos for Pyrgoteles, designer of the Thirty and Twenty.
[19] App. *Praef.* 10, οἷς αὐτοὶ διαπλέοντες ἐπέβαινον οἱ βασιλεῖς.

went into battle in his later years Philadelphus had a choice between two large and impressive Thirties for his flagship.

Overall, however, for some hundred years following the death of Alexander, the competition among Hellenistic dynasts was played out with ships that were suited to the dual purpose of ceremony and naval conflict. The royal craft of this period mainly doubled up as flagships; their impressive size was matched by their suitability for this task. This remained the case until in Egypt, in the last decades of the third century, Ptolemy IV Philopator went beyond any previous excess, and we enter a new phase in the construction of royal barges.

In his *Table Talk*, Athenaeus reports the description from Callixeinus of Rhodes of the innovatory ship construction sponsored by Ptolemy IV. Earlier in the same book, Callixeinus was the source for the pavilion and the great procession of Ptolemy II. His account of Philopator's ships presents similar paradoxographical characteristics – the detail, concern for size, number, material, all forms of excess, and the unexpected.[20] Philopator was responsible for the building of two great ships, a huge Forty, which required the construction of a special dock to launch it, and a monster river barge.[21] The Forty was perhaps originally conceived as a flagship to outdo all flagships, but, according to Plutarch, it barely differed from buildings fixed to the ground; it moved unsteadily and with difficulty, and was constructed not for use but for show.[22] The same could certainly be said of the second great vessel, his houseboat, which may have spent most of its life moored at Schedia, close by Alexandria.[23]

This royal river boat of catamaran design, with a double hull supporting structures between, is reported to have had a length of half a stade (i.e. 200 cubits), a breadth of 30 cubits and a height, including its superstructure, of a little under 40 cubits. In metres, this is approximately 105 m in length, 15.75 m in breadth and 21 m in height.[24] Its mast (of 70 cubits) was 36.75 m high, and the sail of byssos had a purple topsail. For comparison, the last Bucintoro of the Doge of Venice, that of 1729 depicted with its crimson

[20] Ath. 5.196a–197c, σκηνή, 197d–203b, πομπή. On Callixeinus, probably a courtier and recipient of a *dôrea* under Ptolemy VI, see Thompson 2000: 368, n. 8.
[21] Ath. 5.203e–204d, the Forty (τεσσαρακοντήρης) with 400 sailors and 4,000 rowers; 204d–206c, the river boat (ποτάμιον πλοῖον) described as ἡ θαλαμηγός.
[22] Plut. *Demetr.* 43.4–5. Hauben 1981 draws attention to the devastating effect of the use of huge quantities of imported timber for building these ships; cf. Erskine, Chapter 5 in this volume at n. 50.
[23] Cf. Strabo 17.1.16, τὸ ναύσταθμον τῶν θαλαμηγῶν πλοίων, later used by (Roman) prefects at Schedia, which also served as a customs post.
[24] In contrast, the royal rowbarge *Gloriana*, built for the diamond jubilee of Queen Elizabeth II in 2012, is just 94 ft (under 28.6 m) in length; the luxurious fittings of this barge carry a range of symbolic resonances for this latter-day monarchy.

canopy by Canaletto and Francesco Guardi, measured just one-third that length. Exaggeration was certainly a feature of the form of account of which Callixeinus was master.

Athenaeus' account of Philopator's barge is overwhelming, both in its length and in its detail. Here I simply take the reader on a whistle-stop tour of the craft, guided by the plans I have provided (see Figure 12.1); these in turn are based on those to be found in Caspari's 1916 art-historical study of this pleasure-boat, modified in part by my own understanding of Athenaeus' text.[25] These plans serve well to guide us round the covered walkways and rooms of the ship, with its numerous columns, costly decoration and luxurious fitments. We enter the main deck at the stern through a series of entrance halls before reaching the central lounge. Public rooms were measured by the number of couches they held, and the main reception room (the *oikos megistos*) was a twenty-couch room with columns all around it. Most of the room was walled with split cedar and cypress wood from Miletus. The twenty doors of the portico were made of planks of citron wood and decorated with ivory. Their column shafts were of cypress wood with Corinthian capitals ornamented in ivory and gold. And so the description continues . . . This was a pleasure-ship, a place of entertainment and delight, and after the narrow passage (the *syrinx*) lay the women's quarters. After a dining-room with nine couches we reach a further bedroom and the stairway to the upper deck.

Here space was put to a different use, and royalty moves into the religious sphere. There was a *tholos*-shaped temple with a marble statue of Aphrodite, the goddess, that is, of the queen, and towards the bows a thirteen-couch room dedicated to Dionysus with a cave.[26] The outside of this cave was inlaid with precious jewels and gold; inside stood translucent statues of the royal family, most probably the object here of cult. The large central area of the upper deck went uncovered except for wooden slats, but when the ship was underway a purple awning protected those who reclined beneath it. Costly Tyrian purple was the colour for kings and queens, as found in the sails of Cleopatra's barge with which we started; the sails of her flagship at Actium were also coloured purple.[27] The Bucintoro of the Doge of Venice sailed, in contrast, with a crimson ensign and canopy.[28]

---

[25] Caspari 1916: opp. 22 (outward appearance) and 25 (deck plans); plans followed quite closely by M. Pfrommer in Grimm 1998: 54–5, fig. 54c, cf. 54a–b and 54d, for visual reconstructions. I modify Caspari's plan of the upper deck, positioning the Dionysiac room with its cave further towards the bow (Ath. 5.205e). I am grateful to Lacey Wallace for drawing these plans.

[26] Cf. Ath. 4.148b, ritual of (more simple) Bacchic caves in Athens copied by Mark Antony.

[27] Plin. *HN* 19.5.22, as also for imperial flagships in Rome; coloured sails are here traced back to Alexander on the Indus.

[28] As illustrated by Canaletto in *Il ritorno del Bucintoro nel Molo il giorno dell'Ascensione* (1730).

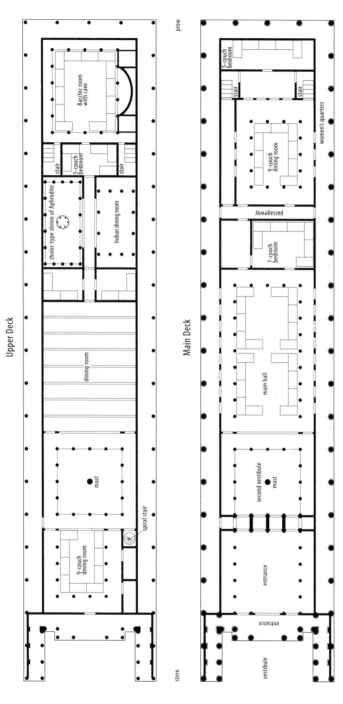

Upper Deck

prow

Bacchic room
with cave

stair

5-couch
bedroom

stair

tholos-type shrine of Aphrodite

Indian dining room

dining room

mast

9-couch
dining room

spiral stair

stern

Main Deck

5-couch
bedroom

stair

stair

9-couch
dining room

women's quarters

passageway

7-couch
bedroom

main hall

second vestibule

mast

entrance

entrance

vestibule

Figure 12.1 The royal barge of Ptolemy IV Philopator

Moving aft along the upper deck, we pass the mast and spiral stairway to reach the final room in our brief tour – a further nine-couch dining-room, where the decoration seems strikingly different. This was an Egyptian room, at odds with the rest of the ship. The columns grew wider towards their top, with alternate drums of black and white, 'for this was the Egyptian way'.[29] Buds, barely opened, formed their capitals, encased by lotus and fruiting palms. Other floral motifs made up the decoration of this room, with alabaster set into its coloured walls. Egypt, it is clear, was different. Yet here Egyptian materials and motifs were adopted into the decoration of a royal ship, as though required but at the same time something rather exotic, not really part of the overall decor.

The rest lay within the bowels of the ship.[30] For further detail here, we may turn to the description given in Athenaeus' account of the great Sicilian ship of Hieron II, the *Syrakosia*.[31] There, in the hold, lay the ship's tackle, the water tanks and kitchens, the bath houses, the wine jars and the stores, the cooks and the sailors in their quarters, and all that lies behind the proper functioning of a floating palace like that of Philopator. Hieron's ship, in contrast, was a sea-going vessel, clad in lead, with defences and engines of war, as well as vast storage areas for grain and well-appointed passenger quarters. On the *Syrakosia*, mosaic floors carried tales from the *Iliad*, and a library was located in a study.[32] There was no such sign of culture to be found on the ship of Philopator.

With Philopator's monstrous barge (as indeed with his elaborately decorated Forty) utility has given way to appearance.[33] No longer was this a ship to double up for war; this was a barge built rather for pleasure and display.[34] The same is the case with the next royal ship to be considered, a vessel which, despite its author's claim to veracity, is probably little more than a literary construct employed to a moral end.

In a disquisition on the old adage that 'it is hard to be good', the second-century AD author Maximus of Tyre recounts the voyage from Egypt to Troy of a royal boat built by a king who lacked any understanding of the sea.[35] Here the tale is summarised. This was another monster ship built to serve as its owner's palace, with beautiful porticoes and walkways, lounges, dining rooms and all that anyone could need. An orchard grew on board,

---

[29] Ath. 5.206c.   [30] Ath. 5.206c, 'many other rooms'.

[31] Ath. 5.206d–209b; for a detailed discussion of this ship, see Lehmler 2005: 210–32.

[32] Ath. 5.207d, *Iliad*; 207e, library.

[33] Cf. Plut. *Demetr.* 43.5, on Philopator's Forty: θέαν μόνην ἐκείνη παρέσχε.

[34] On the Hellenistic vogue for pleasure-boating, see Horden 2005: 187, quoting Purcell.

[35] Max.Tyr. 30.57–104.

with pomegranates, pear-trees, apples and vines. There were baths and a gymnasium, cooks' quarters and bedchambers for the courtesans. All was brightly coloured, and gleamed with silver and gold.[36] The Egyptians who saw it wondered at the sight and envied those who sailed it. When this huge and extravagant ship set sail accompanied by normal merchant ships,[37] it drew away from port like a floating island to the happy sound of music; smells of roasting meat filled the air. Once out at sea, however, a storm blew up and the ship was soon in peril. The accompanying merchant ships could reef in their sails, but the floating palace lurched around like a drunkard on the water. Speedily it all broke up in wreckage, and that was the end of a hapless mariner, a no-good ship and an untimely display of wealth.

This barge resembles an amalgam of Hieron's great grain transport, which had gardens on board with a concealed watering system, and Philopator's monster palace on the Nile, with its women's quarters and decorated halls. As from Cleopatra's barge, the sound of music combined with odours to entrance those who wondered at the giant craft, for ships like this were built to impress, not for practical ends. In the words of Seneca, these were 'the playthings of kings in their revels on the sea'.[38] At the same time they reflected royal wealth and power.

To what other uses were they put? Their prime purpose, of course, was for the transport of their owners in suitable style and comfort. We have already noted the ceremonial use of barges and the larger craft of third-century BC dynasts, which served as flagships in battle as well as visible measures of status. When the British queen still had her yacht *Britannia*, this was the scene of countless diplomatic encounters as she played host to foreign dignitaries. And so it has always been with royal ships that can also be used for diplomatic ends. When Cleopatra answered Antony's summons to Tarsus, the barge she sailed in played its part in the outcome. So too, much earlier in the period, when Demetrius in 300/299 BC sailed to Rhosus in northern Syria in response to Seleucus' request to marry his daughter, it was on board his *Thirteen* – his then flagship – that he returned the initial hospitality offered by that king. 'There was relaxation', reports Plutarch, 'joint discussions, and days spent in each other's company without

---

[36] Similarly, the 3,500-guest luxury liner *Phoenicia* being prepared for Hannibal Gaddafi, son of the former Libyan leader, was to have marble columns, statues and gold-framed mirrors (plus an enormous tank full of sharks), *Independent*, 17 March 2012: 21.

[37] On the economic significance of smaller vessels accompanying larger ships, see Braudel 1972: 1, 292, 298.

[38] Sen. *Ben.* 20.3, *ludibria regum in mari lascivientium*; cf. Purcell's observation on the Hellenistic vogue for pleasure-boating, Horden 2005: 187.

the presence of guards or weapons until the moment when Seleucus left, taking Stratonice off in splendour to Antioch.'[39]

The ultimate use of a royal ship is one familiar to all from seafaring nations – its use as a funeral barge.[40] Again Demetrius Poliorcetes may serve as an example. On his death in the Syrian Chersonese, his remains were dispatched home for burial. Immediately he heard the news, Antigonus sailed out with his whole fleet to meet his father's remains already encased in a golden casket. He placed them on the stern of the largest of his leading ships and set out on tour. Garlands and escorts met the ship as it visited various cities. As the boat put in to Corinth en route to its final resting place, the funerary urn shone out on the vessel's poop, adorned with royal purple and a diadem; young men with spears and in armour stood all around. And the best flute-player of the day accompanied the rowers with a most solemn dirge.[41] Once again the visual effect was enhanced by accompanying music.

In conclusion, a consideration of royal ships in the process of conquest by Rome of the Hellenistic kingdom of Macedon will illuminate further the symbolic role of these craft. There can be no better illustration of the importance to Hellenistic kings of their ships than the meeting at Locris in November 198 BC, during the Second Macedonian War, of Philip V with the Aetolians and Titus Quinctius Flamininus.[42] On that occasion the king refused to disembark from his war galley (described as a *pristis*), and he parleyed with the Romans on shore from the safety of his ship. The importance of the king's naval strength was well recognised by the Romans. So, following the Macedonian defeat at Cynoscephalae, when it came to the final peace the terms imposed by Rome on Philip V in 196 BC involved the surrender of all of his ships, with the exception of light craft and his royal Sixteen.[43]

Whether the Sixteen which Philip retained was the s   Demetrius' earlier flagship from 288 BC has been a subject much deb   MS *Victory*, Nelson's flagship at the battle of Trafalgar in 1805, may   an instructive parallel. Launched in 1765, this ship was commissi   1778. Aged just 36 years old, it was rebuilt in 1801, so Nelson's flags   rafalgar was a comparatively recent rebuild. *Victory* then remained   ntline duty

[39] Plut. *Demetr.* 31.1, 3–4; 32.2–3.
[40] A picture, for instance, in the Hellenic Maritime Museum in the Peira   the naval vessel *Amphitrite* used in the funeral of King George I of Greece in 1913.
[41] Plut. *Demetr.* 52.3–53.3.
[42] Polyb. 18.1.5–9, with Walbank 1967: 548–9, for the date; Livy 32.32.
[43] Polyb. 18.44.6, with Walbank 1967: 611–12, and Walbank 1979a: 790–1; cf. Livy 33.30.5, *regia una*; App. *Mac.* 3.9.3, calling it a Six (ἑξήρους).

until (just eleven years old in its rebuilt form) it was brought to moorings in Portsmouth harbour in 1812. There it remained in use for a further 110 years in both practical and ceremonial roles and was only moved to dry dock in 1922, when restoration work returned the ship to its earlier state.[44] Had Philip's Sixteen in 196 BC been the same ship as that of Demetrius earlier it would already have been over 90 years old when the king of Macedon was allowed by Rome to keep it, and some 120 years old when it later made the journey across the sea to Rome. Even with lead cladding, this seems an unrealistic age for any such ship, though less incredible perhaps than the case of Theseus' ship still claimed as that employed at the *Oschophoria* in Athens at the time when Plutarch was writing.[45] Unless, like HMS *Victory*, Demetrius' ship survived in seriously rebuilt form, the balance of probability is against the identification of the two Macedonian flagships.

Be that as it may, the more interesting question to ask is why in 196 BC the Romans left the Macedonian king in possession of his Sixteen. Various explanations have been given. Livy describes the ship as 'of almost unmanageable size',[46] whereas Casson, accepting its identification as Demetrius' earlier flagship, believes it was 'so old and antiquated that Rome . . . had no hesitation in letting him keep it'.[47] Another explanation should be considered. For a vanquished king left in post, however much his power was diminished, a minimum of status was still required. A royal ship was, I suggest, a bare necessity if Philip was to retain any standing at all in the Hellenistic world. Rome recognised this situation, and Philip kept his Sixteen.[48]

As is well known, from the Roman point of view Macedon did not fully understand its new role. The Third Macedonian War ensued, and the settlement that followed Rome's victory at Pydna was very different. This time the terms were pronounced in Latin, not Greek,[49] and the victor, Lucius Aemilius Paullus, confiscated the royal Sixteen. He himself sailed up the Tiber in this ship decorated with Macedonian spoils, with hangings from the palace and shining armour, as crowds lined the banks to gape.[50]

---

[44] www.hms-victory.com
[45] Plut. *Thes.* 22.3. *Thes.* 23.1 provides further detail: this triaconter was preserved complete until the fourth century BC; later the planks were so constantly renewed that whether or not it remained the same became a subject for philosophical debate.
[46] Livy 33.30.5, *inhabilis prope magnitudinis.*   [47] Casson 1995, 139, n. 12.
[48] A similar form of reasoning may have applied later when, in the Treaty of Apamea in 188 BC, Rome required Antiochus III to surrender all his longships but allowed him to keep ten undecked ships (perhaps used for ceremonial use), Polyb. 21.43.13, reading *aphrakta*, cf. Walbank 1979a: 159. Rhodian *aphrakta*, however, were used ten years later to escort Perseus' bride Laodice when the journey exceeded the limits allowed to Seleucid sailing, Polyb. 25.4.8–10.
[49] Livy 45.29.3.   [50] Livy 45.35.3, *regia nave ingentis magnitudinis.*

And as a sort of coda, this iconic ship appears again in Polybius' account of the build-up to the Third Carthaginian War, preserved in an especially constructed dry dock in Rome, where in 149 BC it was used to incarcerate Carthaginian hostages.[51] Such was the fate of this Macedonian Sixteen, matched, as it were, by that of the kingdom itself at the hands of the new power of Rome. And the later royal barges that we hear of are those of Roman emperors.[52]

---

[51] Polyb. 36.5.9.
[52] Suet. *Calig.* 37.2, Liburnian galleys with gem-encrusted sterns, baths, colonnades, banquet-halls, vines and fruit trees. The two large early imperial pleasure-ships brought up from Lake Nemi in Italy were, unfortunately, destroyed in 1944.

CHAPTER 13

Eudoxus of Cyzicus and Ptolemaic exploration of the sea route to India

Christian Habicht

Let me begin with a few words about Cyzicus, the city of Eudoxus, who is the hero of this chapter. The place is far to the north of Ptolemaic Egypt, on the southern shore of the Propontis, the Sea of Marmara. It was founded by the Ionian city of Miletus early in the seventh century BC. The land was fertile, the waters rich in tuna fish, the harbours excellent.[1] Cyzicus was 'a city of merchants and sailors'. Its silver staters, the Κυζικηνοί, were for more than 200 years, down to the days of Alexander the Great, one of the three dominant currencies of the Mediterranean, rivalled only by the golden Δαρεικοί of the Great King and the silver tetradrachms of Athens. They have been called 'the most interesting coin series of all times and countries'.[2] They are found in particularly large numbers in the area of the Black Sea and the Crimea, where some coin hoards contained close to 200 *Cyzicenes*. This reflects the importance of the city as a major place for the grain trade. Another, less well-known feature is its role as a centre of science, especially in mathematics and astronomy, during the later fourth and early third centuries. It was Eudoxus of Cnidus, a namesake of our man from Cyzicus, whose students were active there and in lively competition with Epicurus and his followers based in Lampsacus. The details have been worked out from some Herculaneum papyri by David Sedley, who suggests that the work of the astronomers at Cyzicus may even have influenced the great Archimedes of Syracuse about a century later.[3]

Cyzicus was a strong fortress, withstanding over the course of time several assaults by potent figures. Only once did it come close to being taken, by King Mithridates Eupator of Pontus in 73 BC. It barely escaped, due to its stubborn resistance and the superior strategy of the Roman general

---

[1] Hasluck 1910; Ruge 1924; Ehrhardt 1988; Avram 2004.

[2] Regling 1931: 3 ('die interessanteste Münzreihe aller Zeiten und Länder'), quoted with approval by Mildenberg 1993: 1.

[3] Sedley 1976. A recent quotation, 'Eudoxe de Cyzique, F 277 Lasserre', should read 'Eudoxe de Cnide...' (Counillon 2007: 42, n. 31).

Lucullus. The citizens themselves, however, were convinced that their main goddess, Kore (or Persephone), the daughter of Demeter, had in person come to their rescue.[4] Somewhat earlier, they followed a model set in 241 by the citizens of Cos for their festival in honour of Asclepius, the *Asclepieia*, and then repeated by other cities such as Magnesia on the Maeander and Teos. They transformed Kore's festival in the early second century from an annual local event into a much more splendid quadrennial festival, the *Koreia*. The entire Greek world was invited to participate.[5] As had happened in these earlier cases, the change was approved and sanctioned by an oracle of Apollo. It was this festival that set Eudoxus on his path to become the discoverer of the sea route to India 'and the one and only precursor of Vasco da Gama' (Thiel 1966: 10). The events were recorded by his slightly younger contemporary Posidonius of Apamea, the eminent philosopher, historian and universal scholar. He heard in Gades in Spain about Eudoxus and his adventures. His report, from his work *On the Ocean*, is preserved for us by Strabo in the second book of his *Geography*.[6] Strabo faithfully copied Posidonius' account and then severely criticised it as a web of lies and fantasies. Modern scholars, however, agree that what Posidonius narrates is basically true, and that Strabo's polemics are mean and of little value.[7] The story, in Ian Kidd's translation, reads as follows:

In the reign of Ptolemy Euergetes II, Eudoxus came to Egypt as ambassador and herald for the games at the festival of Kore. He joined up with the king and his court, most particularly in his voyages up the Nile, for he was a man most naturally curious of strange places, and not untutored in them. It so happened that an Indian was brought to the king by the garrison of the Red Sea, who reported that they had found him half-dead, shipwrecked and alone; but who he was or where he had come from they had no idea, as they couldn't understand his language. He was handed over to people to teach him Greek. Once he had learned it, his story was that he was sailing from India when he happened to lose his way and ended up safely here after his fellow sailors had died of starvation. He was taken at his word and promised to act as guide for the route to India to a crew selected by the king. Eudoxus was one of them. So he sailed off with presents and returned with a cargo of perfumes and precious stones . . . But Eudoxus was deceived in his hopes; King Euergetes appropriated the whole cargo.

---

[4] Plut. *Luc.* 10.1; App. *Mith.* 75.323–5.   [5] More in my paper, Habicht 2010: 311–22.
[6] Posidonius, *FGrH* 87 F28.4–5 (F49C Edelstein-Kidd). Strabo 2.3.4–5 (C 98–102). Recent studies: Otto and Bengtson 1938: 194–218, 'Die Aufnahme des direkten Seeverkehrs mit Indien seit der Zeit des 2. Euergetes'; Delbrueck 1955–6: esp. 44–7; Laffranque 1963; Thiel 1966; Fraser 1972: I, 181–4; II, 314–17; Dihle 1974; Desanges 1978: 151–73: 'Les navigations d'Eudoxe de Cyzique'; Dihle 1978: esp. 546–50; Raschke 1978: esp. 659–61; Casson 1984: 473–9; R. Grzybek 2002; Tomber 2008.
[7] F. Jacoby comments on *FGrH* 87 F28, p. 176: 'besonders kleinlich und wertlos'; Laffranque 1963: 205–6; Desanges 1978: 151: 'particulièrement féroce'; Kidd 1988: 252–7.

And the account continues with a record of his further voyages.

Eudoxus had come as ambassador and herald (θεωρὸς καὶ σπονδ-οφόρος) to Alexandria, to announce the upcoming *Koreia* in his home town.[8] For such an important mission people were elected by their fellow citizens, which means that Eudoxus must have been of mature age and a member of a highly respected and wealthy family of his town. He was, in the words of Richard Delbrueck, 'an independent gentleman, a man of the world, polyglot, with the audacity of a pirate and the knowledge of a highly educated man'.[9] In his official capacity he was introduced at court, and this event changed not only the direction of his life but also the maritime policy of the Ptolemies, because it so happened that at this time the shipwrecked Indian captain had been found and the king had received intelligence that it might be possible to sail to India and back across the sea, thereby avoiding the usual route along the coast of Arabia, where vessels were plagued by people exacting tolls and by pirates (see Map 13.1). Furthermore, Egyptian merchants did not sail all the way to India, but were met somewhere along the coast by ships of their Indian partners and their cargo.

The circumstances that led to Eudoxus' first voyage to India certainly sound somewhat fanciful, but the main event, the direct crossing to India, is well attested. The king who had sent him on his way seized the luxury goods that he brought back; he may have exercised a right of monopoly. Furthermore, it had been a royal mission, not a private enterprise. That happened no later than 116, the year during which the king died. The king's widow, Cleopatra III, then prepared another expedition on a larger scale and sent Eudoxus out again. On the way back he was carried round Cape Guardafui (the northern tip of Somalia) and stranded on the coast, somewhere between the Cape and Zanzibar. When the ship got free, he made it back to Alexandria, where now Cleopatra's son was reigning, probably Ptolemy Soter II. If so, Eudoxus' return happened in 107 at the latest.[10] Once again, the king, a different one this time, confiscated all the goods brought back from the expedition; Eudoxus may have violated the deal he had struck before leaving. During the following years he briefly returned to his native city and sold all his possessions before undertaking

[8] Strabo 2.3.4 (C 98); the same designation again in 2.3.5 (C 101).
[9] Delbrueck 1955–6: 46: 'ein unabhängiger Herr, welt- und sprachkundig, mit dem Wagemut eines Piraten und dem Wissen eines hochgebildeten Mannes'.
[10] Eudoxus' return before 107 is favoured by Fraser 1972: 1, 183 and Desanges 1978: 152–3. For a later date, see Laffranque 1963: 207. It is difficult to see what led Dihle to say that Eudoxus returned from his second voyage to India precisely in 102 (Dihle 1965: 45).

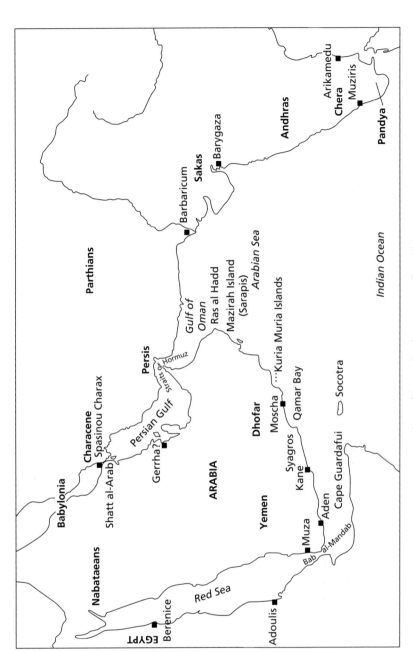

Map 13.1 The Red Sea and Indian Ocean, after Salles 1993: 497

a third and a fourth voyage, both times on his own account. He sailed out of Gades in Spain and tried to find India by circumnavigating Africa from the west. He did not come very far, but again extricated himself from a mild crash. Somehow he made his way to the court of King Bocchus I of Mauretania, well known from Sallust's *Bellum Iugurthinum* as Jugurtha's father-in-law and ally, who turned traitor and delivered him into the hands of Sulla and his commander, Marius, in 106. Eudoxus was unsuccessful in his efforts to persuade the king to send him out to India. He barely escaped before being deported to a desert island. Nothing is known about Eudoxus' fourth attempt. When Posidonius left Gades in about 100 BC, people still thought Eudoxus might return one day.

The prevailing view of the large majority of scholars is that what the Indian captain revealed to the authorities in Egypt was the use of the monsoon winds, and that Eudoxus was the first Greek to make use of this knowledge. W. W. Tarn, however, was sceptical.[11] He said that while it is not stated which way the Indian led Eudoxus to India, it could only have been the way he had come himself, that is, along the coast. But this is arbitrary and seems to me (and to most scholars as well) very unlikely, since the whole story makes sense only if what the Indian revealed was something new to the Ptolemaic side, that is to say, a direct route across the open ocean. It then follows that he guided Eudoxus that same route, only in the opposite direction. This must have happened during the summer months, when the south-west monsoon constantly blows from March to September and brings rain to India.[12] For the return voyage, the north-east monsoon blowing (less heavily) from October to February was used.

So far, so good. Eudoxus, however, is not the only one credited with having been the first to travel to India directly across the ocean. There is also Hippalus. The *Periplus Maris Erythraei*,[13] written in the middle of the first century AD, says in section 57 that the pilot (κυβερνήτης), Hippalus, guided by his knowledge of the *emporia* and of the formation of the sea (σχῆμα τῆς θαλάσσης), was the first who, supported by the monsoon winds, found the direct route to India, τὸν διὰ πελάγους ἐξεῦρε πλοῦν. The author of the *Periplus* adds that the south-west monsoon was for this reason given the name *Hippalus*. At about the same time as the *Periplus*, the elder Pliny to a degree confirms that statement.[14] He gives the itinerary for

---

[11] Tarn 1939: 323–4, reviewing Otto and Bengtson 1938.   [12] Böker 1962: 403–11.
[13] Casson 1989. A date of *c.* AD 45 is favoured by Groom 1995.
[14] Plin. *HN* 6.101–6, speaking of sailing to India in the time after Alexander the Great: *postea ab Syagro Arabiae promunturio* [Ras Fartak] *Patalen favonio, quem hippalum [hipalum] ibi vocant, peti certissimum videbatur*: the south-west monsoon is called *Hippalus* by the locals.

the monsoon routes and notes the various stages of such a voyage and their duration. From Iuliopolis, the harbour of Alexandria, to Okelis took fifty days. Okelis, known as the 'monsoon harbour', is Bab el Mandeb, where the Red Sea opens into the Gulf of Arabia. He continues: from Okelis to Muziris in south-western India the ships sail *vento Hippalo*, 'with the wind called Hippalus', and reach their destination in forty days.[15] The whole voyage amounted to ninety days.

Nothing is known about the person and the date of Hippalus. The name is not uncommon in Ptolemaic Egypt and is found, for instance, for some high-ranking officials in the first half of the second century BC.[16] The author of the *Periplus* adds that this route was used 'from that time on until now' (ἀφ' οὗ μέχρι καὶ νῦν), a remark that suggests a very long time, which would bring Hippalus way back from Pliny's own time, perhaps close in time to Eudoxus. Both could well be called 'first', if they travelled different routes, if, for instance, Hippalus found soon after Eudoxus a new and even shorter way across the sea. There were various routes; those discovered first led to places close to the mouth of the Indus river, but after a while shorter ways were found to places further south. The possibility, however, that Hippalus antedates Eudoxus cannot entirely be ruled out.[17] Some scholars have even tried to harmonise the seemingly contradictory statements: they make Hippalus the pilot of Eudoxus, putting both men in one and the same boat. Others disagree, with good reason in my opinion, since such a conciliatory approach seems methodologically unsound.[18]

The result so far is that shortly before 116 BC Eudoxus returned from the first direct passage to India and some years later from the second. Since that time major Egyptian merchants or state fleets could make use of the direct route for the trade with India, whereas trade on a smaller scale continued the old way along the coast, described in precious detail by the *Periplus*. For about a century trade remained limited: Strabo says that under the Ptolemaic kings only very few dared to cross over the ocean to India, and in another context that annually barely twenty ships made the trip, a statement which may have minimised the actual volume.[19] Trade in any

---

Böker 1968: 2299, lines 22–40.

[16] Delbrueck 1955–6: 45 suggests that he might have been a high-ranking Ptolemaic commander. For persons of that name in Ptolemaic Egypt, see *Prosopographia Ptolemaica*.

[17] Raschke 1978: 661.

[18] Otto and Bengtson 1938: 202. In favour: Thiel 1966: 50; Mooren 1972: 132–3 ('possibly'); Desanges 1978: 158–9; Huß 2001: 618. Against: Güngerich 1950: 29–30, n. 48; Fraser 1972: I, 83; Raschke 1978: 661. Undecided: Dihle 1974: 7.

[19] The two statements by Strabo are, respectively, 2.5.12 (C 118) and 17.1.13 (C 798). On these, see Raschke 1978: 662; Young 2001: 19.

case exploded in the period of Augustus and flourished in the time of Pliny and the *Periplus*. The Roman annexation of Egypt in 30 BC contributed to this. Already in the time of Aelius Gallus, the Roman prefect of the country in 25 BC, 120 ships were sailing annually from Myos Hormos in the Red Sea en route to India.[20] In this respect, the well-known fact must be mentioned that during the reign of Augustus several embassies from Indian kings came to see the Roman Princeps, as Augustus himself states in his *Res Gestae*.[21] The imports to Egypt were always of much higher value than the exports to India. Perfumes and precious stones made up much of what was brought from India, and also cinnamon and pepper.[22] Apart from genuine and so-called 'luxury goods', there were also some for medical purposes, such as Indian spices against infections, and other expensive items used for religious ceremonies, such as frankincense and myrrh. Luxury goods included silk, which came from China by land to India, and besides the gemstones and perfumes came ivory and tortoise shell.[23] A good deal of the profit went to the coffers of the Ptolemies and, later, to the emperor's *fiscus*.

The development of such an important trade route (see Map 13.2) has been connected with an innovative element in the Ptolemaic administration: the appearance of a new high-level office, that of the commander in charge of the Red Sea and the Indian Ocean, ἐπὶ (or στρατηγὸς) τῆς Ἐρυθρᾶς καὶ Ἰνδικῆς θαλάσσης. The position was open to courtiers of the highest ranks, since the incumbent always carried the title of 'kinsman (of the king)', συγγενής. Otto and Bengtson identified the year 110/109 as the first in which the new post is attested.[24] This is in an inscription from Coptus, one of the places on the way from Egypt to India and back. The text is published as *SB* V 8036 = *IPortes du désert* 49. A person, whose name is lost, appears as 'kinsman and *stratêgos*, and in charge of the [Red Sea and Indian] Ocean' (ὁ συγγενὴς καὶ στρατηγὸς καὶ ἐπὶ τῆς [Ἐρυθρᾶς καὶ Ἰνδικῆς] θαλάσσης), and the date is given as 'year eight'. That seems clear enough, but, alas, it is not, in fact. Otto and Bengtson take it as year eight of the joint rule of Cleopatra III and Ptolemy Soter II, that is, 110/109.

[20] Strabo 2.5.12 (C 118).
[21] Embassies arrived in 25 BC at Tarragona, in 20 on Samos and another from King Porus at Antioch in Syria. The numerous literary testimonies are conveniently listed in the editions of the *Res Gestae* by Volkmann 1969 and Scheid 2007 in their notes to chapter 31.
[22] See Sidebotham 1986: 20–4 for Roman imports from India and 24–32 for goods exported from Rome to India. See also Casson 1989: 39–43.
[23] Young 2001: 14–18.
[24] Otto and Bengtson 1938: 1–22 and 197, followed by Tarn 1939: 324: 'more probable'; Volkmann 1939: 1009 and Fraser 1972: I, 182.

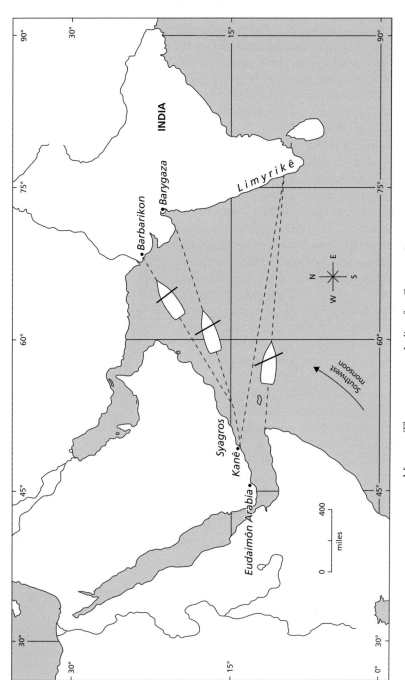

Map 13.2 The sea routes to India, after Casson 1989: 225

Leon Mooren, however, the specialist in Ptolemaic court titles, disagrees and finds that the titles of this man and of his brother Apollodorus mentioned before him point to a later date. The possibilities are 74/73, year eight of Ptolemy XII Auletes, or 45/44, year eight of the famous Cleopatra VII.[25]

Another holder of that office, Callimachus, held the position for almost thirty years and is attested as the incumbent in five inscriptions from various places in Egypt, namely for the years 79, 75, 62 (twice) and 51. The post may have existed as early as 110/109, but it existed in any event in 79 BC. Either way, these dates are compatible with those for the two voyages of Eudoxus in *c.* 118 to 110. It is another question whether the designation of the office means what is generally believed: control over the trade with India. Does the expression Ἰνδικὴ θάλασσα really mean the ocean between Arabia and India? Etienne Bernand, in his edition of the inscriptions from Philae in Egypt, points out in his comments on one of the Callimachus texts that Indian elephants (ἐλέφαντες Ἰνδικοί) in the Adoulis inscription of Ptolemy III are Ethiopian beasts, not Indian, and are also called in that same inscription Τρωγλοδυτικοὶ καὶ Αἰθιοπικοί, that is, Nubian and Ethiopian elephants. It may therefore be that Indian Ocean (Ἰνδικὴ θάλασσα) here means in fact the sea off the coast of Somalia and Ethiopia.[26] Even so, the connection with the Indian trade would still exist, since Cape Guardafui on the coast (this is the spice post called Ἀρώματα) was an important station in this trade.

I must once again return to Hippalus. We have seen that he and Eudoxus were most certainly not partners on one and the same boat and cannot share the credit of being the first to have reached India across the open ocean. One or the other has to be our choice – unless those scholars are right who claim that the pilot Hippalus is nothing but a myth. This view was expressed by Santo Mazzarino in a paper of 1987.[27] Mazzarino observes that the manuscript reading in Pliny (*HN* 6.100) was rather *hypalus* and that this does not designate a person, but the wind that carried the sailors from the coast of Arabia to India. He identified that wind as blowing from the sea (rather than from under the sea), ἄνεμος ὕφαλος. He concludes that the pilot Hippalus is the result of a wrong etymology which used the well-known personal name Hippalus. If there was no person Hippalus, that would explain why Posidonius does not mention him when he speaks of Eudoxus. This view has recently gained some momentum: it was supported

[25] Mooren 1972: 127–33. He and Raschke 1978: 661 are both inclined to accept the date of 74/73.
[26] E. Bernand 1969: 310–11.   [27] Mazzarino 1982–7: VII–XIV.

in the 1990s with new arguments by A. Tchernia[28] and by Mazzarino's pupil
Federico de Romanis,[29] although it was rejected by Jehan Desanges.[30] None
of these authors, strangely enough, mentions the fact that in 1913 Emil
Kiessling had already categorically stated that the famous pilot Hippalus
was just a fiction.[31] He noted that the geographer Ptolemy attests a *mare
Hippalum*, πέλαγος Ἱππάλου,[32] in the area of the Somali coast, and Pliny
a promontory *Hispalum* or *Hippalum*.[33] Kiessling concluded that the wind
got its name from the promontory (Hippalus is the wind that blows from
the promontory Hippalum) and that the author of the *Periplus* invented
the person Hippalus as the eponym of that wind. From another angle
Kiessling came to the same conclusion as Mazzarino much later: that the
pilot Hippalus is a myth, a fiction.[34] If this is correct (and it has at least
a chance to be), then Eudoxus remains the only one who is credited as
having been the first to have crossed the ocean to reach India. He had the
right idea (as against the view of Eratosthenes), that India could be reached
by circumnavigating Africa from the west (as Vasco da Gama eventually
did in 1497). But, unfortunately, he was stranded twice in his attempts to
prove it. In all probability, the second attempt cost him his life.

---

[28] Tchernia 1995: 991–1009.   [29] De Romanis 1997: 671–92.

[30] Desanges 1999: 339–43, and in his Budé edition of Pliny, *HN* 6.75–6, n. 172.

[31] Kiessling 1913.

[32] Ptol. *Geog.* 4.7.41: Τὸ δὲ ἀπ' ἀνατολῶν τῶν νήσων τούτων πέλαγος Ἱππάλου (Ἱππάδος ω,
Ἵππαλος Χ) καλεῖται, ᾧ συνάπτει ἀπ' ἀνατολῶν τὸ Ἰνδικὸν πέλαγος μέχρις ἀνατολῶν.

[33] *HN* 6.172: *hinc Azanium mare, promunturium quod aliqui Hippalum* (Detlefsen; Mayhoff: *Hispalum*
codd.) *scripsere*.

[34] Schmitthenner 1979: 103 came very close to this conclusion when he called Hippalus, referring to
Tarn 1951: 369, a 'semi-mythical figure'.

CHAPTER 14

Timosthenes and Eratosthenes: sea routes and Hellenistic geography

Francesco Prontera

The relationship between knowledge and power runs right through world history. In classical antiquity this relationship can most easily be charted in Egypt under the first Ptolemies, not only because the expansion of the kingdom gave a new impetus to the development of geographical knowledge, both in theory and practice, but mainly because we know a fair amount about the activities and work of the protagonists. In fact, the ancient literary sources offer a great deal of information on the relationship between Ptolemaic politics and geography, while such information is missing for imperial Rome in the second century BC, for the era of Pompey the Great, or even for that of Augustus. We know very little about the world map of Agrippa, but we can reconstruct the geometric structure of the world map of Eratosthenes; and, what is more important, we can see the close bonds between the cartographic pattern and the network of the land and sea routes. The historical and cultural context in which Timosthenes, Eratosthenes, Ptolemy II and Ptolemy III operated might even remind us of some more recent experiences (such as France in the seventeenth century). The comparison is obviously anachronistic; however, it can give us an idea of how peculiar the relationship was between monarchic power and geographical science in Hellenistic Egypt, a relationship which has no parallel in the ancient world.

The activity of Timosthenes[1] as an admiral of Ptolemy II precedes the appointment of Eratosthenes (c. 245 BC) as the head of the Library in Alexandria. We have no information about the career of Timosthenes before he was appointed admiral. His city of origin, Rhodes, offered the environment most suited to naval activities in the ancient Mediterranean. His experiences – among which some diplomatic missions for the

---

[1] Still fundamental is Gisinger 1937; see further Fraser 1972: I, chap. 10; II, 521–2, esp. 751, n. 13; Prontera 1992; Hauben 1996; Meyer 1998.

monarch may perhaps be included[2] – provided Timosthenes with first-hand information. He used this to write a work of ten books *On Harbours*, which has survived only in some forty fragments. Basically, this work is the first such monograph for which we can get some sense of its character.

Probably the title *periplous* had already appeared in Greek literature as a report of personal experience of naval exploration, while the systematic description of peoples and countries of the world was named *periodos gês* (tour of the earth).[3] Clearly, thanks to the special knowledge that the writer had acquired in the field, the work *On Harbours* presented itself as something new, as shown already by its title. Here the title has indeed its own significance, given the huge task of classification and criticism of Greek literature carried out in the Library of Alexandria. However, the ten books of the *On Harbours* of Timosthenes are not a portolan, in the medieval and modern sense of the term, but rather a work of descriptive geography.

In fact, Timosthenes proceeds to a review of the three continents in the form of a circumnavigation of the Mediterranean, beginning from Egypt and following an anti-clockwise course until reaching Libya. Together with the information acquired from his naval experience, in this work we can detect some interest in certain mythistorical details and note the literary elaboration of the writer, who plainly refers to his famous predecessors, such as Aristotle, Eudoxus (of Cnidus) and Ephorus, and who himself is later referred to by well-known geographers such as Eratosthenes, Hipparchus, Posidonius, Strabo, Marinus of Tyre and Ptolemy. The fact that neither Timosthenes himself nor those who used his geographical work ever thought to name it a *periodos gês* means that this work was something original in the geographical literature. In the climate of Augustan classicism, Strabo criticised the Hellenistic authors of treatises entitled *Harbours* and *Periploi*: '[they] leave their investigation incomplete, if they have failed to add all the mathematical and astronomical information which properly belonged in their books'.[4] Quite different was the judgement on Timosthenes expressed by Eratosthenes (Strabo 1.1.40); in all probability, Eratosthenes was the first to use the word *geôgraphia* in the scientific sense that this neologism retained up to the time of Claudius Ptolemy.

---

[2] His diplomatic activities should also include his performance at Delphi of the *nomos pythikos* (Strabo 9.3.10), a musical piece intoned with the flute without any vocal accompaniment; cf. Aujac 1986: 16–18 and Baladié 1996: 213.

[3] Arist. *Pol.* 2.1262a.19; *Rh.* 1.1360a.

[4] Strabo 1.1.21, trans. H. L. Jones, Loeb Classical Library 1917. On works of descriptive geography known as *Limenes* (*On Harbours*), cf. Strabo 8.1.1.

Some comments contained in the fragments of Timosthenes certainly derive from autopsy of the writer himself. However, he must have consulted literary sources widely, and probably other sources as well (e.g. archives of the Ptolemaic navy perhaps), in order to compose his description of the inhabited earth in ten books. Inevitably, the information on the western half of the Mediterranean is far briefer, compared with that on the eastern Mediterranean. The records of distances, along the coast or in ocean crossings, are combined with a careful attention devoted to topographical description. Timosthenes has good knowledge of the sailing route along the African coast, mainly from Cyrene to Carthage, and he provides an estimate of the length of the sides that create the scalene triangle of Sicily (frag. 22 W.). The position of the Cyanean rocks in relation to the sanctuary of the Twelve Gods on the Thracian Bosporus (frag. 26 W.), as well as that of Artace in the land of Cyzicus, constitute good examples of his power of description of particular places (frag. 31 W.): 'there is a deep harbour for eight boats in the elbow shaped by the mountain where the sandy beach ends' (this indeed is one of the few verbatim references to his work). The same can be said of some of the details he gives on the morphology of the coast of Salamis (frag. 40 W.) and the Malian Gulf, where – for someone coming from Thermopylae – a sandy headland is described as suitable as a station for a warship.[5]

Certain fragments of the work *On Harbours* on sailing on the open sea require separate discussion, since Timosthenes does not confine himself simply to an estimate of distances: he also indicates the relative position of places. On the coast west of Carthage, the Metagonion (Cape Tres Forcas, near modern Melilla, in Morocco) lies 'opposite' Marseilles. Naturally, the possibility of a straightforward route is to be excluded here, although this is attested later between Metagonion and New Carthage in Spain (Strabo 17.3.6). In order to place Metagonion in relation to the European coast opposite it, Timosthenes refers to the site of Marseilles, which from the end of the fourth century BC (Pytheas) had become the main reference point for the delineation of the western Mediterranean.

As in the representation of historical time, where certain memorable events stand out as key points in the framework of collective memory, so also in the representation and ordering of geographical space, too vast to be taken in by the human eye, certain places play a special role. On modern maps, a north–south alignment of Marseilles and Metagonion would be

---

[5] Didym., Dem. *Phil.* 11, col. II, 30–8: see Fraser 1972: 11, 781, n. 13 (this quotation from Timosthenes was unknown to E. A. Wagner (see Wagner 1888).

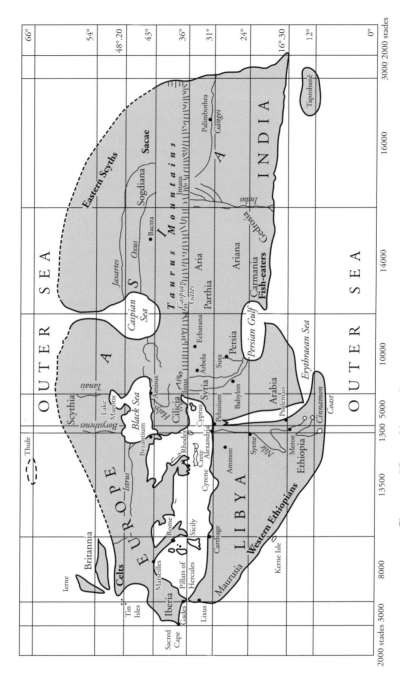

Figure 14.1 The world map of Eratosthenes: a reconstruction, after Aujac 2001: 81

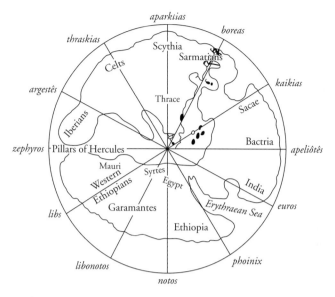

Figure 14.2 The 'windrose' of Timosthenes: a reconstruction, after Miller 1898: 49, fig. 16

met with a smile. No one would ever claim that Melilla is opposite Provence rather than the Sierra Nevada. But at the time of Timosthenes the shape of the western side of the Mediterranean was still largely a matter of conjecture, especially in comparison with what was known of the eastern side. So Timosthenes tried to establish in the western sector, as in the eastern sector, of the 'internal sea' an alignment between the European and African coasts. The favoured candidate for alignment with the Metagonion promontory was Marseilles, on the assumption that the extension of the African coastline to the west of Carthage was roughly the same as the extension of the European coastline to the west of southern Italy.

It is significant that the same 'error' should characterise Eratosthenes' map of the Mediterranean (Figure 14.1). The idea that Marseilles lies 'opposite to' Metagonion does not seem so aberrant here as it would on modern maps, since Carthage, the strait of Messina and Rome are all located on the same meridian.[6] The mental map underlying the nautical geography of Timosthenes is thus materialised in the geometric construction of Eratosthenes. The importance of Marseilles as a fundamental reference point for

---

[6] Prontera 2009: 143.

the delineation of the western Mediterranean is also based on the astronomical calculation of its latitude. As effected by Pytheas by means of the
gnomon,[7] this calculation yielded a result very close to reality (c. 43°N).
Pytheas used this finding to estimate the distance travelled northward
during his famous Atlantic *periplous*. On Eratosthenes' map, the position
of Marseilles, on whose latitude Byzantium is also mistakenly located,[8]
marked the maximum amplitude of the maritime space between Europe
and Africa to the west of the strait of Messina.

Other alignments in the eastern Mediterranean lead us to the sphere of
the geopolitical interests of the Ptolemies: these are the sea routes between
Cyprus, the southern coast of Asia Minor (the Chelidonian Islands) and
the Delta of the Nile (with the Canopic and Sebennytic mouths). Almost
four centuries later, the cartographer Marinus of Tyre still relied on the
information of Timosthenes in order to draw certain meridians in the
region of the Levant.[9]

The relationship between the tradition of Mediterranean navigation,
with its own relative systems for the orientation and localisation of places,
and the world map clearly emerges from the so-called windrose of Timosthenes (Figure 14.2). The circular form of the old Ionian world maps is
divided into twelve sectors, which correspond to the sectors of the horizon
whence the twelve winds blew. This pattern, which was already known
to Aristotle (*Met.* 2.6), was used by Timosthenes in order to place certain
peoples on the periphery of the inhabited world.[10]

See Agathem. 2.6–7 Diller = frag. 6b W.:

6. The winds blow: from equinoctial sunrise *apeliôtês*, from equinoctial sunset
zephyros, from midday *notos*, from the Bear *aparctias*, from summer solstice (sunrise) *kaikias*, and next from equinoctial sunrise *apeliôtês*, and from winter sunrise
euros, and in the west, from winter sunset *libs*, and next again from equinoctial
sunset *zephyros*, from summer sunset *argestês* or *Olympias* also called *Iapyx*, then
notos and *aparctias* blowing opposite each other; so there are eight. 7. But Timosthenes, who wrote the circumnavigations, says there are twelve [winds], adding
boreas between *aparctias* and *kaikias*, *phoinix* also called *euronotos* between *euros*
and *notos*, *leukonotos* or *libonotos* between *notos* and *libs*, *thraskias* or *kirkios* (as
called by the local people) between *aparctias* and *argestês*. He says nations dwell on
the borders of the earth, towards *apeliôtês* Bactrians, towards *euros* Indians, towards
phoinix the Red Sea and Ethiopia, towards *notos* Ethiopia beyond Egypt, toward
leukonotos Garamantes beyond the Syrtes, towards *libs* western Ethiopians beyond

---

[7] Strabo 1.4.4; 2.5.41. Cf. Aujac 1966: 43–5; Bianchetti 1998: 160–1.   [8] Prontera 2007/8a: 47–8.
[9] Ptol. *Geog.* 1.15.5 = frag. 16 W. (cf. frag. 36 a–b W.). Cf. Geus, Chapter 15 in this volume.
[10] Aujac 1966: 260–1; Masselink 1956: 75–84 ; Prontera 2007/8b: 179–80.

Moors, towards *argestê* Iberia, now Hispania, towards *thraskias* Celts and their neighbours, towards *aparktias* Scythians beyond Thrace, towards *borras* Pontus, Maeotis and Sarmatians, towards *kaikias* the Caspian Sea and Sacae.[11]

The centre of the map (Figure 14.2) doubtless lies in the Aegean Sea, in all probability in Rhodes. The central position of the Aegean Sea – the first 'Mediterranean' in Greek history – is indicated by the position of the wind that blows from Olympus, in the west-north-western sector, the position of the wind *phoinix* (south-south-eastern), or even the wind *kaikias* also called by some the 'wind from Hellespont' (*hellespontias*), the direction of which is opposite the south-west wind (*libs*).

Timosthenes summarised his work *On Harbours* in one book; he also reworked in a further book the estimates of distances in stades (*stadiasmos*). Indeed, the *stadiasmos* of Timosthenes, in the sense of a 'handbook of sea distances', seems to begin a line that continues down to the *Stadiasmus Maris Magni*, an anonymous work dating to the imperial period. The systematic quantification of data is a characteristic of the Hellenistic kingdoms; this involves a form of 'rationality' which finds its expression in the administration, in international relations and in military practice as well. In any case, Timosthenes was certainly the one from whom Eratosthenes borrowed most of the maritime distances he used in drawing the Mediterranean in his map of the world.

The name of Eratosthenes of Cyrene is connected with the measurement – well known even today – of the circumference of the earth and, consequently, with the foundation of 'scientific' geography on an astronomical and mathematical basis.[12] In fact, the sphericity of the earth demanded – at least theoretically – new approaches to cartography; one of the most significant contributions to be attributed to Eratosthenes is surely his effort to apply new principles in outlining the inhabited earth. The number of astronomical data concerning the position of significant places was nevertheless very small (only four measurements, and these of geographical latitude: Syene–Aswan, Alexandria, Rhodes and Marseilles). Under these circumstances, the geometric pattern of the map of the earth was based on the network of land routes as far as Asia was concerned and on the network of sea routes for the Mediterranean. If we take into account the fact that the bases of this lay-out are empirical, it becomes clear that the map of Eratosthenes not only signals 'progress' in the development of geography and ancient science, it is also the result of political and military history, and, from this point of view, it can be considered a particular form of

---

[11] Trans. Diller 1975: 67–8.   [12] Aujac 2001; Geus 2007.

evidence for the representation of the maritime sphere of influence of the Ptolemaic kingdom.

The geographical coordinates of Eratosthenes can be compared only outwardly with the network of meridians and parallels of modern geography. The first step in the map of the world was the drawing of the two rectangular axes that crossed at Rhodes. At irregular intervals – according to the available information and to the historical and geographical significance of the places involved – Eratosthenes drew a number of parallel lines on either side of the two main axes. However, the main parallel and the main meridian were not a discovery made by Eratosthenes. In fact, the parallel corresponds to the extent of the Mediterranean from the Pillars of Hercules as far as the Gulf of Issus. The main meridian, which to the south follows the stream of the Nile from Alexandria to Meroe, connects the two climatic poles of the furthest north (Scythia) and the furthest south (Ethiopia), while Greece, the Aegean Sea and Asiatic Ionia hold the central position. This north–south axis forms the basis of orientation already to be found in the Herodotean 'map' of Anatolia and the Levant: according to Herodotus (2.34; 1.72.3), the Nile Delta lies opposite that of the Danube, and this alignment draws a line through Cyprus, Cilicia and Sinope. Together with the foundation of Alexandria and the development of the maritime interests of the Ptolemies, the course of this axis partially changed, as the main meridian of Eratosthenes shows; and in the alignment of Alexandria–Rhodes–Byzantium we can observe at close quarters the interaction between naval experience and cartography.

The sea-passage from Rhodes to Alexandria is, with the north wind [*boreas*], approximately 4,000 stadia, while the coasting-voyage [*periplous*] is double that distance. Eratosthenes says that this is merely the assumption made by navigators in regard to the length of the sea-passage, some saying it is 4,000, others not hesitating to say it is even 5,000 stadia, but that he himself, Eratosthenes, by means of the shadow-catching sun-dial, has discovered it to be 3,750 stadia (Strabo 2.5.24: transl. H. L. Jones, Loeb Classical Library 1917).[13]

The alignments of the relevant places, selected through naval experience, *precede* their placement on geographical coordinates. In other words, the use of the *gnomon* in the astronomical calculation of geographical latitude is not applied to an undifferentiated and 'neutral' area. On the contrary, it is the specific historical conditions that determine the network of the relations in a certain area, and it is on the basis of this selective geography that the ancient cartographer works. The expression 'with the north wind' cannot refer here

---

[13] Eratosth. IIB.28 Berger.

to the direction of navigation: in fact, there was no need to refer to the southern location of Alexandria in relation to Rhodes. The time required for the crossing (before this calculation was translated into stadia) clearly depended on the wind: this explains the peculiar assertion that the distance would be '4,000 stadia before the wind', as if the distance was one of the variables of the crossing. Since the voyage along the coast requires twice the time, it is likely that this sentence refers not to the circumnavigation of the entire Levant, but to a route that included Cyprus.[14]

In the context of Strabo (2.5.24), where the reference to Eratosthenes occurs, the 'Egyptian Sea' extends from the Syrian–Palestinian coast to the Delta of the Nile.[15] While the waters that wash the southern coast of Asia Minor are named after the adjacent region (the Gulf of Pamphylia and the Gulf of Issus), the maritime area of influence of Egypt covers the entire region south-east of Cyprus: in fact, the waters of Phoenicia do not have a name of their own to compete with this denomination. When later, in the *Geography* of Ptolemy, along the coast of Phoenicia we encounter the 'Syrian Sea', this name dates from after the establishment of the Roman province (by Pompey in 64/63 BC). As Strabo describes the eastern Mediterranean, largely relying on Timosthenes[16] and Eratosthenes, the extension of the 'Egyptian Sea' up to the waters of Cyprus and Issus seems likely to reflect the historical reality of the third century BC.[17]

As Pascal Arnaud stressed in a monograph on this subject, travel on the open sea in this region during the summer months to a large extent depends on the – clearly predominant – northern and north-western winds.[18] On the contrary, along the coasts of the Levant the south-western winds regularly blow, which allows navigation northwards. This means that in maritime communications between Rhodes and Alexandria the direct route was normally possible from north to south but not in the opposite direction. Therefore, in the system of sea routes (Map 14.1) which ensured communications between Ptolemaic Egypt and its overseas possessions, Cyprus

---

[14] On the sea trade between Alexandria and Rhodes, see Gabrielsen, Chapter 4, and Buraselis, Chapter 6 in this volume.

[15] Cf. Strabo 14.6.1, with the comments of Arnaud 2005: 207: 'Le découpage sectoriel de la Méditerranée orientale tel qu'il se dégage des géographes anciens fait en effet nettement apparaître l'existence d'un espace maritime réputé égyptien, l'Égypte en constituant à la fois le centre de gravité économique et le point d'ancrage terrestre le plus révélateur des conditions qui régissent la haute mer.'

[16] See Strabo 17.3.21, which in all probability also derives from Timosthenes: 'The naval base of the Cyrenaeans lies opposite the western promontory of Crete, Kriometopon, the distance between being one thousand stades. The voyage is made by Leukonotos' (trans. H. L. Jones, Loeb Classical Library 1932).

[17] Burr 1932: 48–50.   [18] Arnaud 2005: 207–23.

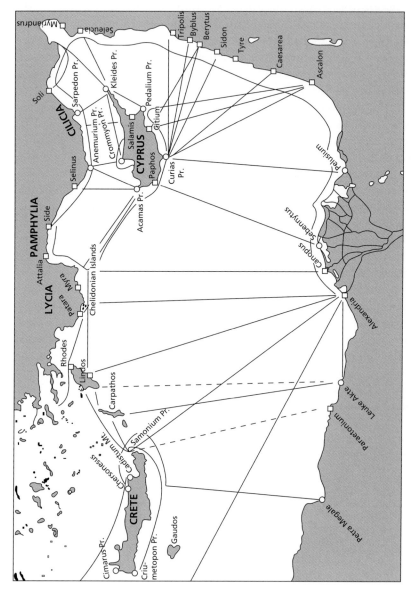

Map 14.1 Seaways in the eastern Mediterranean according to ancient geographers, after Arnaud 2005: 212

certainly played a key role.[19] According to Eratosthenes, 'in ancient times' (*to palaion*) Cyprus was literally covered with forests, which were exploited for metal smelting and later for shipbuilding. However, the size of the forests remained so vast that individuals were allowed to cut down the trees and then become holders of the arable land created in this way, land which was free of tax (Strabo 14.6.4–5 = Eratosth. IIIB.91 Berger). The historical background to this important provision is not known,[20] but the problem was certainly on the agenda in the period of Eratosthenes.

As a final reflection, I would like once again to draw attention to the geography of the Mediterranean, comparing the windrose of Timosthenes (Figure 14.2) with the map of Eratosthenes (Figure 14.1). The geometric pattern of the Mediterranean in the map of Eratosthenes is based on the equivalence between the estimated distances along the axis of the Mediterranean (from Issus to the Pillars of Hercules) and the estimated distances along the coast of North Africa to the west of Alexandria, about which Timosthenes was well informed. The circular frame in the windrose of Timosthenes presupposes, of course, organisational principles very different from the rectangular projection of the meridians and parallels. However, what the two frames do have in common is the new central position of Rhodes and of the Egyptian Sea, a position which was now added to the older centrality of the Aegean. In the pattern of Timosthenes, it is a geometric centre in relation to the circle of the world. In the parallelogram map of Eratosthenes, it is a functional centre because the geographer draws the plan of the inhabited earth starting from the maritime area of influence of the Ptolemaic kingdom. In the same way, therefore, as an interest in geography was promoted by this kingdom so too cartography reflected the considerations of Ptolemaic power.

---

[19] Strabo 16.6.2–3; Arnaud 2005: 216–17.
[20] Meiggs 1982: 397: 'There is no certain mark of time in this statement.' Cf. Berger 1880: 338–9; Biffi 2009: 333–4; Roller 2010: 211.

CHAPTER 15

Claudius Ptolemy on Egypt and East Africa

Klaus Geus

Ptolemy, arguably the most important geographer of all time, provides a detailed description of the *oikoumenê* in his *Handbook of Geography* (*geographikê hyphêgêsis*), written around AD 150. As a native citizen of Alexandria, Ptolemy is likely to have drawn upon Ptolemaic sources for his description of Africa, Asia Minor and Arabia. This chapter aims to evaluate why and to what extent Ptolemy used sources from Ptolemaic times.

It is a well-known fact that the ancient geographical handbooks transmitted much outdated information, or, to put it mildly, that the ancient geographers were not always able to get hold of new or reliable information about all parts of the *oikoumenê*. For example, Eratosthenes drew upon Alexander's bematists ('step-counters') for the description of most parts of Asia or upon Pytheas for the north-western parts of Europe, thus upon sources which were more than a century old at the time of the publication of his *Geography*. On the other hand, Eratosthenes and especially his map of the *oikoumenê* were not only in use at Strabo's times but were also considered one of the standard works of geography, even in Roman times.

This should remind us that we have to reckon with a long persistency of information in the field of ancient geography. But this persistency also enables the historical geographer, at least theoretically, to find worthwhile information about Hellenistic times in much later texts. I limit myself here to the following question: what sources did Ptolemy use in his description of North Africa, and especially for Egypt and its adjacent countries?

As already noted, as a native citizen of Alexandria Ptolemy is likely to have drawn upon personal and/or Ptolemaic sources for his description of Africa, Asia Minor and Arabia. Some scholars even think that Egypt, or at least parts of Egypt, were measured by himself. According to the preface of his work, this is most unlikely. To a large extent, Ptolemy's data rest on

I should like to thank Dorothy Thompson, Irina Tupikova, Nicola Zwingmann, Hartmut Blum and Peter Nadig for their valuable suggestions, and Przemyslaw Jaworek for drafting the charts.

older works, most probably on Hipparchus of Nicaea (second century BC) and Marinus of Tyre (*c.* AD 100). Marinus in particular is criticised throughout the introduction, thus suggesting he was the most important source for Ptolemy.[1] Modern scholars such as Albert Herrmann tend to think that nearly all of Ptolemy's data go back to Marinus.[2] But Ptolemy also made use of certain travellers' logs and merchants' reports, as is clear from his introduction. Since some of these sources concern East Africa, I shall come to them later. But before that I shall discuss an example of Ptolemy's criticism of Marinus in order to show where the problems of interpretation lie.

As I have already mentioned, Ptolemy repeatedly criticised Marinus in his introduction. Normally Ptolemy gives ample reason for his criticism, sometimes drawing upon sources which Marinus either overlooked or ignored. One of these sources was the work *On Harbours* by Timosthenes of Rhodes, an admiral of Ptolemy II in the first half of the third century BC.[3] Ptolemy writes in 1.15.4:

Similarly he [Marinus] says that the Chelidoniai lie opposite Kanopos, and Akamas opposite Paphos, and Paphos opposite Sebennytos, where again he sets the stades from Chelidoniai to Akamas as 1,000, and Timosthenes sets those from Kanopos to Sebennytos as 290; but this distance [between Kanopos and Sebennytos] should actually have been larger if it lay between the same meridians [as the interval between the Chelidoniai and Akamas] because it subtends a [similar] arc of a larger parallel (translated by Berggren and Jones 2000).

The Chelidonian islands (here Chelidoniai) or cliffs of modern Beş Adaları lie off the south-western coast of Turkey. Canopus or modern Abukir is near the most western branch of the Nile Delta; Acamas, modern Cape Arnauti or Hagios Epiphanios, is at the north-western corner of Cyprus. By Paphos[4] Ptolemy probably means Paphos Nea (modern Paphos), not Paphos Palaia (modern Kuklia), but this would make no great difference here. Paphos lies at the south-western corner of Cyprus, a little more to the east than Acamas; the city of Sebennytus (modern Samannud) in the middle of the Nile Delta lies at some distance off the branch of the river with

[1] Apart from the Arab author al-Masudi (died AD 956/957), Ptolemy is our sole source for Marinus. According to this author, Marinus lived 'in our time' (1.6.1, καθ' ἡμᾶς). Since Ptolemy knew of certain editions and works based on Marinus, and since Marinus seems to have mentioned certain cities in the context of Trajan's Dacian wars, Marinus' last work was probably published *c.* AD 110.
[2] Herrmann 1930: 45–54.
[3] The new edition of his fragments in *FGrH* is eagerly anticipated. Wagner 1888 is still useful. Cf. also Prontera, Chapter 14 in this volume.
[4] Paphos is mentioned by Ptolemy only here. In his catalogue he has both Paphos Palaia (Kuklia; 5.14.1) and Paphos Nea (Paphos; 5.14.1; 8.20.3).

the same name. Like most scholars,[5] I think that by Sebennytus Ptolemy meant not the city, but the Sebennytic mouth, since Sebennytus was an island town. What is more, both Canopus and the Sebennytic mouth lie at the same parallel of 31° 05′ north, a fact which enables Ptolemy to measure the arc distance between the meridians of the two localities.[6]

On Ptolemy's reckoning (Figure 15.1), Acamas is about 1,080 stades east and slightly south of the Chelidonian islands, while the distance between the Canopic and the Sebennytic mouths of the Nile is given by Ptolemy in his catalogue as 35′.[7] On a parallel of 31° 05′ north, this equals about 250 stades, very close to the figure of 290 stades transmitted by Timosthenes.[8]

Ptolemy's point of criticism is that Marinus 'placed the Chelidonian islands opposite Canopus, and Acamas opposite Paphos, and Paphos opposite Sebennytus' (Figure 15.2). Ptolemy clearly refers to two meridians with an arc distance of nearly 1,000 stades. So what is involved is one distance, not two 'distances', as for example Berggren and Jones imply.[9] The second distance between the Canopic and the Sebennytic mouths, which is credited to Timosthenes, was not used by Marinus in the first place, but was

---

[5] Cf. Mžik 1938: 50–1, n. 9; Berggren and Jones 2000: 159; Müller 1883 suggested a conjecture here. Ambiguous are Stückelberger and Graßhoff 2006: 99, who identify Sebennytus with Samannud in the text, but write in n. 105: 'Sebennytos wird der mittlere Mündungsarm des Nil nach der gleichnamigen Stadt Sebennytos/Samanud in der Mitte des Deltas genannt.' In fact, Sebennytus lies near the Damietta branch.

[6] The coordinates of these localities in Ptolemy´s catalogue are as follows:

Chelidonian islands (5.3.9)	61° 30′	36°
Canopus (4.5.9)	60° 45′	31° 05′
[Heracleotic or Canopic mouth (4.5.10)	60° 55′ (50′)	31° 05′]
(Cape) Acamas (5.14.1)	64° 10′	35° 30′
Paphos [Nea] (5.14.1)	64° 20′	35° 10′
(Paphos [Palaia] 5.14.1	64° 30′	′35°)
Sebennytus (4.5.51)	62° 20′	30° 20′
[Sebennytic mouth (4.5.10)	61° 30′	31° 05′]

[7] According to the so-called ⲱ recension, 40′ according to the so-called Ξ recension.

[8] Berggren and Jones 2000: 159 have 320 stades between Canopus and the Sebennytic mouths.

[9] Berggren and Jones 2000: 159 interpret this passage thus:

'Ptolemy thus preserved Marinos' distances; but the localities in Cyprus are shifted quite far west of the meridian through the Sebennytic mouth. As it happens, Marinos was approximately correct in stating that Chelidoniai is 'opposite' Canopus, and Paphos opposite to the Sebennytic mouth; and the distance from Chelidoniai to Akamas is indeed about 1,100 stades, though in a southeast direction. The error of assuming that Akamas was close to due east of Chelidoniai (which might be Ptolemy's rather than Marinus') together with the fact that Timosthenes' figure for the distance from Canopus to the Sebennytic mouth is less than half the correct distance, account for the inconsistency.

So Berggren and Jones put the blame on Ptolemy, not Marinus. I think that they fail here to understand Ptolemy's point.

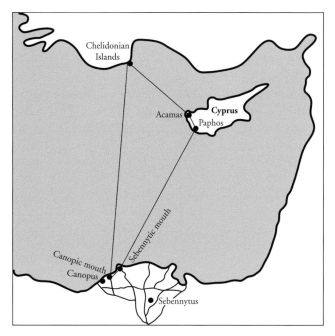

Figure 15.1 Some eastern Mediterranean coordinates according to Ptolemy

introduced by Ptolemy against Marinus, as is evident from the contrast implied in ὑπ᾽ αὐτοῦ and ὑπὸ Τιμοσθένους.

I have attempted a sketch of how Marinus' original map might have looked (Figure 15.2). Probably, on his map, the Delta of the Nile was much bigger, extending over 1,000 stades between the Canopic and the Sebennytic mouths. This gross error is in line with another geographical misconception on Marinus' part. Marinus considered the length of the *oikoumenê* – the distance between the Island of the Blessed in the West and the Chinese metropolis Sera in the East – to be 225°, thus making it nearly double what it should be. He usually stretched all distances in a west–eastern direction.

In support of my interpretation, I would like to point out that only on this interpretation does the next sentence make sense.[10] Ptolemy says that the arc distance of 1,000 stades between the Canopic and the Sebennytic mouths should actually – at least on a map – be greater than the 1,000 stades between the Chelidonian islands and Acamas, because the latter

---

[10] This sentence is, regrettably, ignored by Berggren and Jones in their commentary.

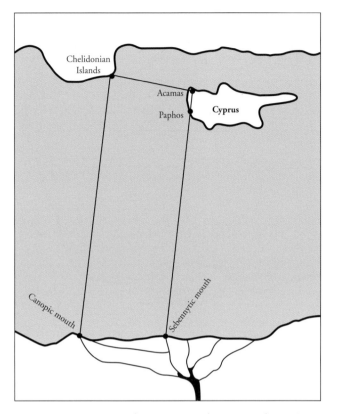

Figure 15.2 Some eastern Mediterranean coordinates according to Marinus

localities lie further to the north than do the former. As we all know, all
meridians converge at the North Pole, thus shortening the meridian arc
distance at the equator from 500 stades to a zero degree at the pole. It is
clear then that Ptolemy here accused Marinus of ignoring this important
principle of map projection.

As a result, I would like to put two points on the record. First, even
in Marinus' time, despite a lot of accumulated data, ancient geographers
had some difficulty in drawing accurate maps. The main reason for errors
such as we have seen is probably the geographical preconception of the
breadth and length of the *oikoumenê*. This preconception compelled the
geographers to distort the real conditions to some extent. It is interesting
to see that this distortion concerns not only the lesser-known parts of the
world but also very familiar regions like the Nile Delta. Secondly, we find

the puzzling case that Ptolemy corrected Marinus, an author who may still have been alive in Ptolemy's own time, from a much older source dating back to the Ptolemaic period.[11] Since Timosthenes is also cited a second time in Ptolemy's introduction on another matter against Marinus, the wrong distance given between the Canopic mouth and the Sebennytic mouth was not simply an oversight or blunder by Marinus. It is reasonably certain that Marinus was unaware of Timosthenes' *On Harbours*, a fact which is not really surprising since Timosthenes wrote at least 350 years before Marinus.[12]

Our second example concerns two of the most important waterways in Africa, namely the Nile and the stretch along the east coast of Africa called Aromata (1.15.10–11):[13]

He [Marinos] even says that the river Nile, from where it is first seen [πρῶτον ὁρᾶται] up to Meroē, will be drawn correctly [going] from south to north. Likewise, he [Marinos] says, that the sail from Arōmata to the lakes from which the Nile flows is effected by the Aparktias [north] wind. But Arōmata is quite far east of the Nile; for Ptolemais Thērōn is east of Meroē and the Nile by a march of ten or twelve days, and <the Bay of Adoulis is . . . stades> from Ptolemais, and the straits between the peninsula of Okēlis and Dērē are 3,500 stades from Ptolemais, and the cape of Great Arōmata is 5,000 stades to the east of these (translated by Berggren and Jones 2000).

This passage contains two points where Marinus is again criticised.[14] From its first appearance down to Meroe the Nile flows straight from south to north. The voyage along the east coast of Africa from the Aromata as far as the Nile lakes is effected only by the north wind. Firstly, we have to clarify

---

[11] Compare also 1.15.2, where Ptolemy argues against Marinus, again following Timosthenes (Pachynus/Leptis Magna and Himera/Thena).

[12] It is worth noting here that Timosthenes' work is the only source out of nearly a dozen in Ptolemy's *Geography* which we also know of from external evidence.

[13] Cooley 1854 has been completely superseded.

[14] What is meant by πρῶτον ὁρᾶται? According to Ptolemy in the fourth book of his *Geography* (4.8.3), the upper Nile gets its water from the snow melt in the so-called Moon mountains (ἀφ' οὗ ὑποδέχονται τὰς χιόνας αἱ τοῦ Νείλου λίμναι) and flows down to the two Nile lakes in a northern direction. The lakes may be identified with Lake Victoria and Lake Albert, although this is far from sure, since Ptolemy placed these too far to the south. From each of these lakes there flow branches of the Nile, which meet at a northern point. Therefore, the Nile was 'seen' or, better, 'known' to Ptolemy from the Moon mountains, presumably the Ruwenzori range. I here ignore the question whether Ptolemy's information was based on autopsy or simply conjecture. It is unknown whether Marinus had ever heard of the Moon mountains and the headstreams of the Nile. Even if he had, Ptolemy could not have accused Marinus of mapping the Nile in a northerly direction, because Ptolemy himself speaks of a river only from its outlet from the lakes. Therefore, πρῶτον ὁρᾶται meant the point where the Nile flows out of the lakes. This coincides with what Ptolemy tells us in the next sentence, when he criticised Marinus for putting the Nile lakes directly south of the Aromata.

what exactly Ptolemy had in mind when he criticized Marinus as drawing the Nile in a straight line from south to north.[15]

According to Ptolemy, following the conjunction of its two branches the Nile flows at 60° East mostly in a northerly direction, but bends off slightly to the east before Meroe. At the confluence of the Nile and the Astapus the deviation is a full degree, at Meroe one and a half degrees.[16]

We have no reason to doubt Ptolemy's assertion that Marinus really thought of the Nile as running in a straight line from south to north. Quite to the contrary! It seems that Marinus' opinion was not particularly unusual. I quote a much-discussed passage of the geographer Strabo (17.4.8):[17]

Into the Nile fall two rivers flowing from some lakes in the east, and embracing the great island of Meroe. That which runs on the eastern side of the island is the Astaboras; the other, on the western side, the Astapus; but some call this the Astaboras, for they suppose the Astapus to be another river, which, flowing from some lakes in the south nearly in a straight line, constitutes the main body of the Nile.

What we have here basically is a fragment of the Hellenistic geographer Eratosthenes. He is mentioned both shortly before and after this passage. Strabo cites Eratosthenes and 'others' on the upper part of the Nile.

According to Eratosthenes, whose knowledge of Ethiopia was rather limited,[18] two rivers flow from 'some lakes' to the east. Together with

---

[15] On Ptolemaic maps Meroe is placed on a parallel of 16° 25′ N, which is nearly correct (it is in fact 16° 56′ N). Apart from three cities (Sakolche, Eser and Daron) lying on the banks of the Nile, Ptolemy only mentions the confluence of Nile and Astapus (at 12° N), the confluence of Astaboras and Astapus (at 11° 30′) and the conjunction of the two arms of the Nile (at 2° N), which pour out of the lakes. Pomponius Mela, Pliny, Diodorus and Agatharchides call the river to the west of Meroe Astapus. Ptolemy instead considers the west arm the 'real' Nile and places the Astapus with its tributary Astaboras in the east. He places the Astapus, which flows from Lake Coloe (Lake Tana), to the west, but knows about another tributary to the east, the Astaboras (where this comes from is unclear from either the text or the maps), which joins the river Astapus to the south-east of Meroe. According, therefore, to Ptolemy, the western branch of the Nile is the 'real' Nile.

[16] A full degree on a latitude of 12° N equals nearly 460 stades or 90 km, one and half degrees nearly 700 stades or 135 km in the eastern direction. One cannot easily see this on Ptolemy's map. We have again to look up the coordinates of the respective localities in Book 4:

Meroe	61° 30′
Nile/Astapus	61°
Conjunction of frontal flows	60° (62°)
Lake to the west	57°
Lake to the east	65°

[17] See, e.g., Postl 1970: 30, 68, 98–100; Huß 1990: 334–42; Radt 2009: 398.
[18] See, e.g., Roller 2010: 224.

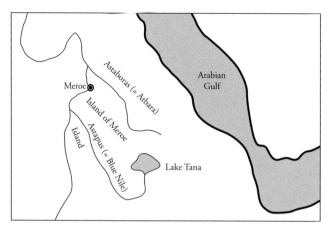

Figure 15.3 The upper reaches of the Nile according to Eratosthenes

the Nile they embrace Meroe (Figure 15.3). It is fairly certain that by the two rivers Eratosthenes meant the Atbara (normally called Astaboras in antiquity) and the Blue Nile (normally called Astapus in antiquity). Despite the plural 'some lakes' he clearly meant Lake Tana (normally called Coloe in antiquity).[19]

But Strabo also knows of another view, which he attributes to anonymous 'others'. According to these 'others', the Astaboras and the Astapus do not flow from the east, but from some lakes to the south nearly in a straight line (Figure 15.4).

It seems clear that on this interpretation the Astapus is not to be identified with the Blue Nile but with the Bahr el-Djebel. By 'some lakes', Lake Albert and Lake Victoria are meant here. It is surprising that the Sobat river is not mentioned by 'others', but Strabo or his source may have shortened the original text.

Unfortunately, we cannot say who looms behind these 'others', but since they are mentioned by Strabo and probably wrote after Eratosthenes, they belong to the Hellenistic age.

How then does their theory relate to Marinus and Ptolemy?[20] It is important to understand that both Marinus and the 'others' think of one arm of the Nile as flowing 'nearly in a straight line'. True, the 'others' refer

---

[19] The maps are borrowed (with slight modifications) from Huß 1990.

[20] Ptolemy does know of three arms of the Nile: the 'real' Nile in the west, the Astaboras, and the Astapus. It would be interesting to know what rivers Ptolemy means by Nile, Astapus and Astaboras, but I must ignore this question here.

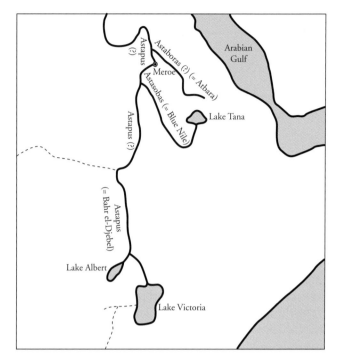

Figure 15.4 The upper reaches of the Nile according to 'others'

to the Astapus, while according to Ptolemy it is the Nile which Marinus drew in such a way. But, as can be seen from the map and the catalogue, Ptolemy's description of the Nile is in some regards confused. And the 'others' seem to have spoken of the 'main body' of the Nile, which is, at least according to Ptolemy, the western branch of the Nile.

This all makes it very likely that Marinus drew on the 'others', i.e. a Hellenistic source, for his description of the Upper Nile.

Now let us return to Ptolemy's second point in his criticism of Marinus. It will be useful to repeat the passage here:

> Likewise, he [Marinus] says, that the sail from Arōmata to the lakes from which the Nile flows is effected by the Aparktias [north] wind. But Arōmata is quite far east of the Nile; for Ptolemais Thērōn is east of Meroē and the Nile by a march of ten or twelve days, and <the Bay of Adoulis is . . . stades> from Ptolemais, and the straits between the peninsula of Okēlis and Dērē are 3,500 stades from Ptolemais, and the cape of Great Arōmata is 5,000 stades to the east of these (translated by Berggren and Jones 2000).[21]

---

[21] Translated by Stückelberger and Graßhoff 2006: 101 thus:

The text poses some difficulties. Berggren and Jones think that there is a lacuna in the text. Their reasoning is that Adoulis is not on the same meridian as Ptolemais Theron but rather a full degree more to the east (see Figure 15.5).

But since Okelis is also half a degree further east than Dere, it seems more probable that Ptolemy is not aiming to be as accurate as possible but rather to make his whole argument as simple as possible. So the result is just loose speech on the part of Ptolemy. The editors of the new Bern edition are right to ignore Berggren and Jones' conjecture.

Again, Ptolemy based his point of criticism of Marinus on an addition of meridian arc distances between these cities:[22] Ptolemais Theron is said to be ten or twelve days east of Meroe and the Nile. These ten or twelve days are translated by Ptolemy in the catalogue of his fourth book as $4°\ 30'$.

The distance from Ptolemais Theron and/or the Bay of Adoulis (*Adoulikos kolpos*) to the straits between Dere and Okelis is said to be 3,500 stades, and the distance from the straits between Dere and Okelis to the Aromata is said to be another 5,000 stades.

The most interesting fact here is probably Marinus' notion that one can reach the Nile lakes from the Aromata via a voyage along the coast of East Africa. Even if we allow for a certain room for interpreting ἐπὶ τὰς λίμνας, ἐξ ὧν ὁ Νεῖλος ῥεῖ, there is no denying the fact that Marinus placed the Nile lakes to the south of the Aromata.[23]

In this case, fortunately, we do know how Marinus reached this view. Ptolemy wrote in 1.9.1:

Denn Ptolemaïs Theron/Marsa Aqiq ist etwa 10 bis 12 Tagesreisen östlicher als Meroë und der Nil, und die Meerenge/Bab al-Mandeb bei der Halbinsel Okelis und bei Dere/am Ras Siyan ist weitere 3500 Stadien von Ptolemaïs und dem Adulischen Gold/der Annesley Bay entfernt; von dort sind es nochmals 5000 Stadien nach Osten bis zum Kap der Grossen Aromata.

Translated by Mžik 1938: 52 thus:

Denn 'Ptolemaïs im Jagdgebiet' liegt 10 oder 12 Tagereisen östlich von Meroë und vom Nil; die Meerenge bei der Halbinsel Okelis und Deire aber liegt weitere 3500 Stadien östlich von Ptolemaïs und vom Adulitischen Meerbusen; von dort sind noch 5000 Stadien weiter nach Osten bis zum Vorgebirge Groß-Aromata.

[22]		
Meroe	$61°\ 30'$	$16°\ 25'$
Ptolemaios Theron/Marsa Aquiq	$66°$	$16°\ 25'\ (30')$
Okelis (6.7.7)	$75°$	$12°$
Dere/at Ras Siran	$74°\ 30'$	$11°$
[Adoulis/Massawa	$67°$	$11°\ 20'\ (40')]$
Aromata	$83°$	$6°$

[23] If we are to identify the Nile lakes with Lake Albert and Lake Victoria, this would mean that Marinus ignored a vast distance of nearly $20°$ to Cape Guardafui!

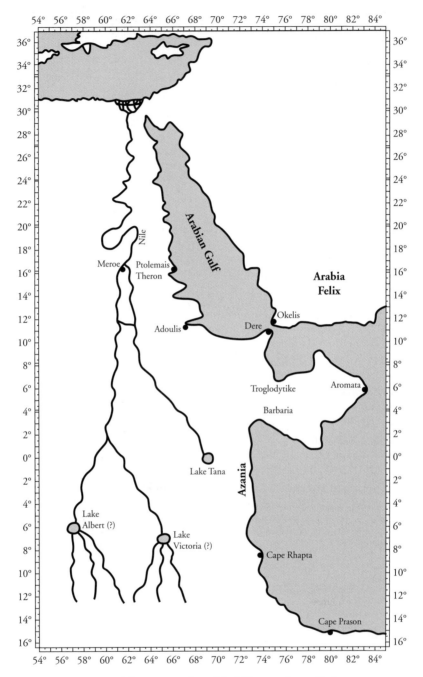

Figure 15.5 The upper reaches of the Nile according to Ptolemy

Next, concerning the sail between Aromata and Rhapta, he says that a certain Diogenes, who was one of those who sailed to India, returning the second time, was driven back when he got to Arōmata by the Aparktias [north] wind and had Trōglodytikē on his right for twenty-five days, and [he then] reached the lakes from which the Nile flows, slightly to the south of which is Cape Rhapta (translated by Berggren and Jones 2000).

Ptolemy knows of Diogenes' voyage only through Marinus.[24] Since we have no further information, the date of Diogenes is difficult to ascertain. I shall argue below for the late Ptolemaic period. First, we need to consider the geographical conception of the east coast in Ptolemy's work.

As we have seen before, Ptolemy used his own sources for his description of the east coast of Africa. In 1.17.6–7 he wrote:

As we learn [μανθάνομεν] from the merchants who have crossed from Arabia Felix to Arōmata and Azania and Rhapta (they give all these [places] the special name Barbaria) that the sail is not exactly to the south; but rather this part is to the west and south, while they make the sail across from Rhapta to Prason toward the east and south. And the lakes from which the Nile flows are not right by the sea but quite far inland. [We learn] also that the sequence of beaches and bluffs to Cape Prason from the Cape of Arōmata is different from what it is according to Marinos (translated by Berggren and Jones 2000).

Ptolemy corrected Marinus' notion that the lakes from which the Nile flows are right by the sea from the reports of merchants, whom, as the present tense 'we learn' (μανθάνομεν) implies,[25] he probably questioned himself. If this is true, then Marinus' (wrong) opinion that the lakes lie to the south of the Aromata must have been the traditional one. This makes it probable that Marinus' original source, Diogenes, was a merchant not of the time of Marinus and Ptolemy, but of a much older age, probably of the Ptolemaic period.

As a second argument for a Ptolemaic date for Diogenes, I would like to advance the observation that Diogenes probably had in mind Eratosthenes' geographical conception that the Nile flows from lakes to the east, not to the south as the 'others' cited by Strabo have it.[26] So the most probable

---

[24] Diogenes, who is otherwise unknown, must have taken the southern trade route by the southwest monsoon from Arōmata to southern India. The return voyage was begun in December or January, using the northeast monsoon to cross the open ocean and seasonal east winds to pass through the Gulf of Aden. Presumably Diogenes hit the African coast too far south to enter the Gulf and was driven further south (transl. by Berggren and Jones 2000: 68, n. 33).

[25] In 1.17.5 Ptolemy has ἐμάθομεν.

[26] This theory was probably superseded by later authors such as Artemidorus and Posidonius.

date for Diogenes would be the end of the second century or the beginning of the first century BC.[27]

Again we find that both Marinus and Ptolemy used sources from Ptolemaic times for their respective descriptions of East Africa. We know at least of Timosthenes, Eratosthenes, Hipparchus, probably of Diogenes and some 'others'.

We need to tackle one last question: to what extent did Ptolemy draw on sources from Hellenistic times? There is no clear-cut answer to this question, as the author himself does not provide much information. Nevertheless, we may try to give some clues.

The most important source was surely the above-mentioned Marinus, who studied 'with great care' (μετὰ πάσης σπουδῆς) and 'meticulously' (μετ' ἐπιμελείας) 'nearly all reports of his fore-runners' (τὰς πάντων σχεδὸν τῶν πρὸ αὐτοῦ [sc. ἱστορίας]) (1.6.1), which surely included Hellenistic works like that of Eratosthenes. If we take this statement at face value, and we have no reason to think otherwise, nearly every geographical author of this period was used by Ptolemy, at least indirectly. Given the large quantity of data on Egypt and its neighbouring areas, Ptolemaic sources featured prominently in the work of Marinus.

We know that Ptolemy also processed additional material. Apart from Marinus, ten authors (or rather voyagers) are cited by name in his introduction (and not a single one is mentioned in later books, since Ptolemy is reluctant to give more than names and coordinates in his meagre catalogue).[28] Six of these undertook maritime expeditions; only four of them travelled over land. This ratio is not surprising. *Periploi* play a greater role than itineraries in Ptolemy's work. His account is drafted primarily along the coastlines; the sequences of localities are structured according to the shores, not the coordinates. Streets, even the biggest Roman *viae publicae*, are nowhere mentioned.

Other kinds of source are even harder to grasp. Maps are very rarely mentioned (*Geogr.* 1.19.1; cf. 8.1.2) and surely had little effect on Ptolemy's own ones, which were plotted either in his peculiar cone projection or drawn according to his own mathematical principles.

---

[27] Hartmut Blum informs me that this date is in accord with Albrecht Dihle's view that regular travel between East Africa and India started only in the late Ptolemaic period, cf. Dihle 1984: 109–52. Diogenes' second return trip bears some resemblance to the second Indian voyage of Eudoxus of Cyzicus, who, also on his way back to Egypt, was driven off course by winds to the south and stranded 'beyond Ethiopia' (Strabo 2.3.4). Habicht (see Chapter 13 in this volume) takes this as 'somewhere between the Cape and Zanzibar'. Either Diogenes suffered a similar fate or Ptolemy (or Marinus?) confused the two.

[28] Stückelberger 2009: 123–4.

Ptolemy may have had access to the documents of the Roman central administration in Alexandria, as Stückelberger contended,[29] but these were surely not his main source. In the case of Egypt, we can even notice that when mentioning nomes Ptolemy does not use the Roman units but rather has the Pharaonic situation in mind (mediated again presumably through Ptolemaic sources).

These considerations strengthen our contention that even in works of the most accomplished geographers of the Roman Principate such as Ptolemy and Marinus, Hellenistic sources and, especially, sources from Ptolemaic Egypt play a major role. And this was surely a desirable thing.

It is a well-known fact that the Ptolemaic kings were trying to get hold of all kinds of geographical data. They may even have tried to revise what they acquired, as Geminus tells us casually in regard to the region between the summer tropic and the equator (*Elem. Astr.* 16.24), with this comment: 'The account about these places has been recorded and investigated through the kings in Alexandria.'

Strabo confirms Geminus' statement and underlines the distinction between the Ptolemaic and the 'older kings' in this respect (17.1.5):[30]

These kings were concerned with things of this kind; and especially the Ptolemy surnamed Philadelphus, since he was of an inquiring disposition [*philhistorôn*], and on account of the infirmity of his body was always searching for novel pastimes and enjoyments. But the kings of old were not at all concerned with such things, although they proved themselves congenial to learning, both they and the priests, with whom they spent the greater part of their lives.

It was, however, another Ptolemy who harvested the geographical fruits of the Ptolemaic past some centuries later. His name, therefore, and his knowledge went back to an earlier royal tradition of important research and expertise.

---

[29] Stückelberger 2009: 129.
[30] Cf. also 2.1.5: ταῦτα γάρ ὁ Ἐρατοσθένης λαμβάνει πάντα ὡς ἐκμαρτυρούμενα ὑπὸ τῶν ἐν τοῖς τόποις γενομένων ἐντετυχηκὼς ὑπομνήμασι πολλοῖς, ὧν εὐπόρει βιβλιοθήκην [i.e. of Alexandria] ἔχων τηλικαύτην ἡλίκην αὐτὸς Ἵππαρχός φησι.

Bibliography

Abulafia, D. (2005) 'Mediterraneans', in Harris 2005: 64–93.

Acosta-Hughes, B., Kosmetatou, E. and Baumbach, M. (eds.) (2004) *Labored in Papyrus Leaves: Perspectives on an Epigram Collection Attributed to Posidippus (P.Mil.Vogl. VIII 309)*. Hellenic Studies 2. Washington D.C.

Ager, S. L. (2003) 'An uneasy balance: From the death of Seleukos to the battle of Raphia', in Erskine 2003: 35–50.

(2005) 'Familiarity breeds: Incest and the Ptolemaic dynasty', *JHS* 125: 1–34.

Ahrweiler, H. (1966) *Byzance et la mer. La marine de guerre, la politique et les institutions maritimes de Byzance aux VIIe–XVe siècles*. Paris.

Amandry, P. (1940–1) 'Dédicaces delphiques', *BCH* 64–5: 60–75.

Ameling, W. (2000) 'Patroklos 2', in *Der Neue Pauly*, vol. IX. Stuttgart: 419–20.

Ameling, W., Bringmann, K. and Schmidt-Dounas, B. (1995) *Schenkungen hellenistischer Herrscher an griechische Städte und Heiligtümer*, vol. I: *Zeugnisse und Kommentare*. Berlin.

Anastassiades, A. (1998) 'Ἀρσινόης Φιλαδέλφου: Aspects of a specific cult in Cyprus', *RDAC*: 129–40.

Andronikos, M. (1950) *Archaiai epigraphai Beroias*. Thessalonica.

Angiò, F., Cuypers, M., Acosta-Hughes, B. and Kosmetatou, E. (eds.) (2008) 'New poems attributed to Posidippus: An electronic text in progress, version 10.0 (November 2008)', in The Center for Hellenic Studies: Harvard University/Classics@ Issue 1: Posidippus/Epigrams (February 2011) (http://chs.harvard.edu/wb)

Archibald, Z. H., Davies, J. K. and Gabrielsen, V. (eds.) (2011) *The Economies of Hellenistic Societies, Third to First Centuries BC*. Oxford.

Arnaud, P. (2005) *Les routes de la navigation antique. Itinéraires en Méditerranée*. Paris.

Ashton, S.-A. (2001) *Ptolemaic Royal Sculpture from Egypt*. Oxford.

Aujac, G. (1966) *Strabon et la science de son temps*. Paris.

(1986) 'Strabon et la musique', in *Strabone. Contributi allo studio della personalità e dell'opera*, vol. II, ed. G. Maddoli. Perugia: 9–25.

(2001) *Eratosthène de Cyrene, le pionnier de la géographie*. Paris.

Austin, C. and Bastianini, G. (eds.) (2002) *Posidippi Pellaei quae supersunt omnia*. Milan.

Austin, M. M. (2006) *The Hellenistic World from Alexander to the Roman Conquest: A Selection of Ancient Sources in Translation.* 2nd edn. Cambridge.

Avram, A. (2004) 'Cyzicus', in *An Inventory of Archaic and Classical Greek Poleis*, ed. M. H. Hansen. Oxford: 983–6.

Badian, E. (1961) 'Harpalus', *JHS* 81: 16–43.

Bagnall, R. S. (1969) 'Some notes on *P.Hib.* II 198', *BASP* 6: 73–101.

(1975) 'Ptolemaic foreign correspondence in *P. Tebt.* 8', *Journal of Egyptian Archaeology* 61: 168–80.

(1976) *The Administration of the Ptolemaic Possessions outside Egypt.* Columbia Studies in the Classical Tradition 4. Leiden.

(1979) 'The date of the foundation of Alexandria', *American Journal of Ancient History* 4: 46–9, reprinted in Bagnall 2006: chapter 4.

(1980) Review of T. Leslie Shear, Jr, *Kallias of Sphettos and the Revolt of Athens in 286 B.C.*, Princeton 1978, *AJP* 101: 244–7.

(1984) 'The origin of Ptolemaic cleruchs', *BASP* 21: 7–20, reprinted in Bagnall 2006: chapter 8.

(2005) 'Egypt and the concept of the Mediterranean', in Harris 2005: 339–47.

(2006) *Hellenistic and Roman Egypt: Sources and Approaches.* Variorum Collected Studies. Aldershot.

Bagnall, R. S. and Drew Bear, Th. (1973) 'Documents from Kourion: A review article', *Phoenix* 27: 99–117 and 213–44.

Baines, J. and Málek, J. (1980) *Atlas of Ancient Egypt.* Oxford.

Baladié, R. (1996) *Strabon, Géographie livre* IX. Paris.

Barbantani, S. (2005) 'Goddess of love and mistress of the sea: Notes on a Hellenistic hymn to Arsinoe–Aphrodite (*P. Lit. Goodsp. 2, I–IV*)', *AncSoc* 35: 135–65.

Baslez, M.-F. (2008) *Saint Paul, artisan d'un monde chrétien.* 2nd edn. Paris.

Bass, F. (ed.) (2005) *Beneath the Seven Seas.* London.

Bekker-Nielsen, T. (2004) *The Roads of Ancient Cyprus.* Copenhagen.

Bengtson, H. (1967) *Die Strategie in der hellenistischen Zeit. Ein Beitrag zum antiken Staatsrecht*, vol. III. 2nd edn. MünchBeitr 36. Munich.

Bennett, C. J. (2002) 'The children of Ptolemy III and the date of the exedra of Thermos', *ZPE* 138: 141–5.

(2011) 'Berenice Phernophoros' (28 February 2011), www.tyndalehouse.com/egypt/ptolemies/berenice_a_fr.htm

Berger, H. (1880) *Die geographischen Fragmente des Eratosthenes.* Leipzig.

Berggren, J. L. and Jones, A. (2000) *Ptolemy's Geography: An Annotated Translation of the Theoretical Chapters.* Princeton and Oxford.

Bernand, A. (1992) *La prose sur pierre dans l'Égypte hellénistique et romaine*, vols. I–II. Paris.

(1995) *Alexandrie des Ptolémées.* Paris.

Bernand, E. (1969) *Les inscriptions grecques de Philae.* Paris.

Berthold, R. M. (1984) *Rhodes in the Hellenistic Age.* Ithaca and London.

Berve, H. (1926) *Das Alexanderreich auf prosopographischer Grundlage.* Munich.

Beyer-Rotthoff, B. (1993) *Untersuchungen zur Aussenpolitik Ptolemaios' III.* Bonn.

Bianchetti, S. (1998) *Pitea di Marsiglia, L'Oceano.* Pisa and Rome.

Bielman, A. (1994) *Retour à la liberté.* Études épigraphiques 1. Athens and Lausanne.

Biffi, N. (2009) *L'Anatolia meridionale in Strabone. Libro XIV della Geografia.* Bari.

Bilde, P., Engberg-Pedersen, T., Hannestad, L., Zahle, J. and Randsborg, K. (eds.) (1993) *Centre and Periphery in the Hellenistic World.* Studies in Hellenistic Civilization 4. Aarhus.

Billows, R. A. (1990) *Antigonos the One-eyed and the Creation of the Hellenistic State.* Hellenistic Culture and Society 4. Berkeley.

Bing, P. (2003) 'Posidippus and the admiral: Kallikrates of Samos in the Milan epigrams', *GRBS* 43: 243–66.

Bingen, J. (2002) 'La victoire pythique de Callicratès de Samos', *CE* 77: 185–90.

(2007) *Hellenistic Egypt: Monarchy, Society, Economy, Culture.* Edinburgh.

Blinkenberg, C. (1941) *Lindos*, vol. ii: *Inscriptions.* Berlin and Copenhagen.

Blümel, W. (1992) 'Brief des ptolemäischen Ministers Tlepolemus an die Stadt Kildara in Karien', *Epigraphica Anatolica* 20: 127–33.

Boiy, T. (2007) *Between High and Low: A Chronology of the Early Hellenistic Period.* Frankfurt am Main.

Böker, R. (1962) 'Monsunschiffahrt', *RE* Suppl. IX: 403–11.

(1968) 'Winde', *RE* VIII A2: 2211–2387.

Bommas, M. (2005) *Heiligtum und Mysterium. Griechenland und seine ägyptischen Gottheiten.* Mainz am Rhein.

Bonneau, D. (1971) *Le fisc et le Nil. Incidences des irrégularités de la crue du Nil sur la fiscalité foncière dans l'Égypte grecque et romaine.* Paris.

Bousquet, J. (1988) 'La stèle des Kyténiens au Létôon de Xanthos', *REG* 101: 12–53.

Braudel, F. (1972) *The Mediterranean and the Mediterranean World in the Age of Philip II*, transl. Siân Reynolds. 2 vols. London.

(2001) *The Mediterranean in the Ancient World.* London.

Breccia, E. (1926) *Le rovine e i monumenti di Canopo.* Monuments de l'Égypte gréco-romaine I.1. Bergamo.

Bresson, A. (2000) *La cité marchande.* Scripta Antiqua 2. Paris and Bordeaux.

(2002) 'Wine, oil and delicacies at the Pelusion customs', in *Widerstand, Anpassung, Integration. Die griechische Staatenwelt und Rom. Festschrift für Jürgen Deininger zum 65. Geburtstag*, ed. N. Ehrhardt and L.-M. Günther. Stuttgart: 69–88.

(2005) 'Ecology and beyond: The Mediterranean paradigm', in Harris 2005: 94–114.

(2007) *L'économie de la Grèce des cités (fin vi^e–i^er siècle a.C.)*, vol. i: *Les structures et la production.* Paris.

(2008) *L'économie de la Grèce des cités (fin vi^e–i^er siècle a.C.)*, vol. ii: *Les espaces de l'échange.* Paris.

Briant, P. (2002) *From Cyrus to Alexander: A History of the Persian Empire*, transl. P. T. Daniels. Winona Lake, Ind.

Brulé, P. (1978) *La piraterie crétoise hellénistique.* Centre de recherches d'histoire ancienne 27. Annales littéraires de l'Université de Besançon 223. Paris.

Brun, P. (1991) 'Les Lagides à Lesbos. Essai de chronologie', *ZPE* 85: 99–113.

Bruneau, P. (1970) *Recherches sur les cultes de Délos à l'époque hellénistique et à l'époque impériale.* Bibliothèque des écoles françaises d'Athènes et de Rome 217. Paris.

Bülow-Jacobsen, A. (1979) '*P. Haun.* 6. An inspection of the original', *ZPE* 36: 91–100.

Buraselis, K. (1982) *Das hellenistische Makedonien und die Ägäis. Forschungen zur Politik des Kassandros und der drei ersten Antigoniden im Ägäischen Meer und in Westkleinasien.* MünchBeitr 73. Munich.

(1993) 'Ambivalent roles of centre and periphery: Remarks on the relations of the cities of Greece with the Ptolemies until the end of Philometor's age', in Bilde et al. 1993: 251–70.

(2003) 'Zur Asylie als außenpolitischem Instrument in der hellenistischen Welt', in *Das antike Asyl*, ed. M. Dreher. Cologne, Weimar and Vienna: 143–58.

(2005) 'Kronprinzentum und Realpolitik. Bemerkungen zur Thronanwartschaft, Mitregentschaft und Thronfolge unter den ersten vier Ptolemäern', in *ΔΙΑΔΟΧΟΣ ΤΗΣ ΒΑΣΙΛΕΙΑΣ. La figura del sucesor en la realeza helenística*, ed. V. Alonso Troncoso. Gerión Anejos 9. Madrid: 91–102.

(2008) 'The problem of the Ptolemaic sibling marriage: A case of dynastic acculturation?', in McKechnie and Guillaume 2008: 291–302.

(2010) 'God and king as synoikists: Divine disposition and monarchic wishes combined in the traditions of city foundations for Alexander's and Hellenistic times', in *Intentional History: Spinning Time in Ancient Greece*, ed. L. Foxhall, H.-J. Gehrke and N. Luraghi. Stuttgart: 265–74.

(2011) 'A lively "Indian summer": Remarks on the Ptolemaic role in the Aegean under Philometor', in Jördens and Quack 2011: 151–60.

Burr, V. (1932) *Nostrum mare. Ursprung und Geschichte der Namen des Mittelmeeres und seiner Teilmeere im Altertum.* Stuttgart.

Burstein, S. M. (1982) 'Arsinoe II Philadelphos: A revisionist view', in *Philip II, Alexander the Great and the Macedonian Heritage*, ed. W. L. Adams and E. N. Borza. Washington D.C.: 197–212.

(1985) *The Hellenistic Age from the Battle of Ipsos to the Death of Kleopatra VII.* Cambridge.

(1996) 'Ivory and Ptolemaic exploration of the Red Sea: The missing factor', *Topoi* 6: 799–807.

(2008) 'Elephants for Ptolemy II: Ptolemaic policy in Nubia in the third century BC', in McKechnie and Guillaume 2008: 135–47.

Carney, E. D. (1987) 'The reappearance of royal sibling marriage in Ptolemaic Egypt', *Parola del Passato* 237: 420–39.

Caroli, C. A. (2007) *Ptolemaios I. Soter. Herrscher zweier Kulturen.* Historia Orientis & Africae. Constance.

Cartledge, P. and Spawforth, A. (2002) *Hellenistic and Roman Sparta: A Tale of Two Cities.* 2nd edn. London.

Casa, G. (2010) 'A new honorific inscription from Naxos', *Studi Ellenistici* 24: 211–21.

Caspari, F. (1916) 'Das Nilschiff Ptolemaios' IV.', *JDAI* 31: 1–74.

Casson, L. (1954) 'The grain trade of the Hellenistic world', *TAPhA* 85: 168–67.

(1971) *Ships and Seamanship in the Ancient World*. Princeton.

(1984) 'The sea-route to India: *Periplus Maris Erythraei* 57', *CQ* 34: 473–9.

(1989) *The Periplus Maris Erythraei: Text with Introduction, Translation and Commentary*. Princeton.

(1991) *The Ancient Mariners: Seafarers and Sea Fighters of the Mediterranean in Ancient Times*. 2nd edn. Princeton.

(1995) *Ships and Seamanship in the Ancient World*. 2nd edn. Baltimore and London.

Chaffin, C. E. (1991–3) 'The tessarakonteres reconsidered', *BICS* 38: 211–28.

Chaniotis, A. (1991) 'Vier kretische Staatsverträge. Verträge zwischen Aptera und Kydonia, einer ostkretischen Stadt und Melos, Olus und Lyttos, Chersonesos und Rhodos', *Chiron* 21: 241–64.

(1993) 'Ein diplomatischer Statthalter nimmt Rücksicht auf den verletzten Stolz zweier hellenistischer Kleinpoleis (Nagidos und Arsinoe)', *Epigraphica Anatolica* 21: 33–42.

(1996) *Die Verträge zwischen kretischen Poleis in der hellenistischen Zeit*. Stuttgart.

(2002) 'Foreign soldiers – native girls? Constructing and crossing boundaries in Hellenistic cities with foreign garrisons', in *Army and Power in the Ancient World*, ed. A. Chaniotis and P. Ducrey. Stuttgart: 99–113.

(2005) *War in the Hellenistic World: A Social and Cultural History*. Oxford.

(2006) 'Die hellenistischen Kriege als Ursache von Migration', in *'Troianer sind wir gewesen.' Migrationen in der antiken Welt*, ed. E. Olshausen and H. Sonnabend. Stuttgarter Kolloquium zur Historischen Geographie des Altertums 8, 2002. Stuttgart: 98–103.

Chankowski, V. (2007) 'Les catégories du vocabulaire de la fiscalité dans les cités grecques', in *Vocabulaire et expression de l'économie dans le monde antique*, ed. J. Andreau and V. Chankowski. Ausonius editions. Études 19. Paris and Bordeaux: 299–331.

Cherry, J. F. and Davis, J. L. (1991) 'The Ptolemaic base at Koressos on Keos', *ABSA* 86: 9–28.

Chilton, L. et al. (2004) *The Rough Guide to the Greek Islands*. 5th edn. New York, London and Delhi.

Chryssanthaki, K. (2005) 'Les monnaies lagides en Égée', in *L'exception égyptienne. Production et échanges monétaires en Égypte hellénistique et romaine*, ed. F. Duyrat and O. Picard. Cairo: 159–75.

Clarysse, W. (1985) 'Greeks and Egyptians in the Ptolemaic army and administration', *Aegyptus* 65: 57–66.

(2000) 'The Ptolemies visiting the Egyptian chora', in Mooren 2000: 29–53.

(2009) 'The Zenon Papyri thirty years on', in *100 Anni di istituzioni fiorentine per la papirologia. Atti del Convegno internazionale di Studi. Firenze, 12–13 giugno 2008*, ed. G. Bastianini and A. Casanova. Studi e Testi di Papirologia, N.S. 11. Florence: 31–43.

Clarysse, W. and Thompson, D. J. (2009) 'An early Ptolemaic bank register from the Arsinoite nome', *APF* 55: 230–60.

(2011) 'An early Ptolemaic bank register from the Arsinoite nome revised', *APF* 57: 33–54.

Clarysse, W. and Van der Veken, G. (1983) *The Eponymous Priests of Ptolemaic Egypt: Chronological Lists of the Priests of Alexandria and Ptolemais with a Study of the Demotic Transcriptions of their Names*. Pap. Lugd.-Bat. 24. Leiden.

Clarysse, W. and Vandorpe, K. (1995) *Zénon, un homme d'affaires grec à l'ombre des pyramides*. Leuven.

Cohen, G. M. (1995) *The Hellenistic Settlements in Europe, the Islands, and Asia Minor*. Berkeley, Los Angeles and Oxford.

(2006) *The Hellenistic Settlements in Syria, the Red Sea Basin, and North Africa*. Berkeley and London.

Cole, S. G. (1984) *Theoi Megaloi: The Cult of the Great Gods at Samothrace*. Études préliminaires aux religions orientales dans l'empire romain 96. Leiden.

Colin, G. (1930) *Fouilles de Delphes*, vol. III. 4: *Inscriptions de la terrace du temple et de la région nord du sanctuaire*. Paris.

Collombert, Ph. (2008) 'La "stèle de Saïs" et l'instauration du culte d'Arsinoé II dans la chôra', *AncSoc* 38: 83–101.

Constantakopoulou, C. (2007) *The Dance of the Islands: Insularity, Networks, the Athenian Empire, and the Aegean World*. Oxford.

Cooley, W. D. (1854) *Claudius Ptolemy and the Nile; or An Inquiry into that Geographer's Real Merits and Speculative Errors, his Knowledge of Eastern Africa and the Authenticity of the Mountains of the Moon*. London.

Counillon, P. (2007) 'L'ethnographie dans le "Périple" du Ps.-Skylax entre Tanaïs et Colchide', in *Une koinè pontique. Cités grecques, sociétés indigènes et empires mondiaux sur le littoral nord de la mer noire (VIIe s. a.C.–IIIe s. p.C.)*, ed. A. Bresson, A. Ivantchik and J.-L. Ferrary. Mémoires (Ausonius) 18. Bordeaux: 37–45.

Crawford, D. J. (1971) *Kerkeosiris: An Egyptian Village in the Ptolemaic Period*. Cambridge.

Crawford, M. H. (ed.) (1996) *Roman Statutes. BICS* Suppl. 64. London.

Criscuolo, L. and Geraci, G. (eds.) (1989) *Egitto e storia antica dall'Ellenismo all'età araba. Bilancio di un confronto. Atti del Colloquio Internazionale, Bologna, 31 agosto–2 settembre 1987*. Bologna.

Crowl, P. A. (1986) 'Alfred Thayer Mahan, the naval historian', in *Makers of Modern Strategy from Machiavelli to the Nuclear Age*, ed. P. Paret. Princeton.

Daris, S. (1990) 'Papiri inediti della Collezione dell'Università Cattolica di Milano – Frammento di ordinanze reali', *Aegyptus* 70: 3–8.

De Romanis, F. (1997) 'Hypalos: Distanze e venti tra Arabia e India nella scienza ellenistica', *Topoi* 7: 671–92.

de Souza, P. (1999) *Piracy in the Graeco-Roman World*. Cambridge.

(2007) 'Naval Forces', in *A Cambridge History of Greek and Roman Warfare*, vol. I: *Greece, the Hellenistic World and the Rise of Rome*, ed. P. Sabin, H. van Wees and M. Whitby. Cambridge: 357–67.

Debord, P. (1994) 'Essai sur la géographie historique de la région de Stratonicée', in *Mélanges Pierre Lévèque 8*, ed. M. M. Mactoux and E. Geny. Paris: 107–21.

Delbrueck, R. (1955–6) 'Südasiatische Seefahrt im Altertum', *BJb* 155–6: 8–58 and 229–308.

Derow, P. S. (1994) 'Historical explanation: Polybius and his predecessors', in *Greek Historiography*, ed. S. Hornblower. Oxford: 73–90.

Desanges, J. (1978) *Recherches sur l'activité des Méditerranéens aux confins de l'Afrique*. Rome.

(1996) 'Sur la mer hippale au souffle du vent Hippale', *Topoi* 6.2: 665–70, reprinted in Desanges 1999: 339–43.

(1999) *Toujours Afrique apporte fait nouveau. Scripta minora*. Paris.

Di Nino, M. M. (2006) 'Posidippus' shipwrecks', *Mediterranean Historical Review* 21.1: 99–104.

Dihle, A. (1965) *Umstrittene Daten. Untersuchungen zum Auftreten der Griechen am Roten Meer*. Cologne.

(1974) *Der Seeweg nach Indien*. Innsbruck.

(1978) 'Die entstehungsgeschichtlichen Voraussetzungen des Indienhandels in der römischen Kaiserzeit', in *Aufstieg und Niedergang der römischen Welt*, vol. II 9.2. Berlin: 546–60.

(1984) *Antike und Orient. Gesammelte Aufsätze*, ed. Viktor Pöschl and Hubert Petersmann. Heidelberg.

Diller, A. (1975) 'Agathemerus, *Sketch of Geography*', *GRBS* 16: 59–76.

Domingo Gygax, M. (2000) 'Ptolemaios, Bruder des Königs Ptolemaios III. Euergetes, und Mylasa. Bemerkungen zu I. Labraunda Nr. 3', *Chiron* 30: 353–66.

(2001) *Untersuchungen zu den lykischen Gemeinwesen in klassischer und hellenistischer Zeit*. Bonn.

(2002) 'Zum Mitregenten des Ptolemaios II. Philadelphos', *Historia* 51: 49–56.

Dorandi, T. (1991) *Ricerche sulla cronologia dei filosofi ellenistici*. Beiträge zur Altertumskunde 19. Stuttgart.

Dreyer, B. (1999) *Untersuchungen zur Geschichte des spätklassischen Athen (322-ca. 230 v.Chr.)*. Historia Einzelschr. 137. Stuttgart.

Ducrey, P. (1999) *Le traitement des prisonniers de guerre dans la Grèce antique des origines à la conquête romaine*. 2nd edn. Paris.

Duncan-Jones, R. P. (1977) 'Giant cargo-ships in antiquity', *CQ* 71: 331–2.

Durrbach, F. (1904) 'Fouilles de Délos (1902). Inscriptions', *BCH* 28: 93–190.

(1905) 'Fouilles de Délos exécutées aux frais de M. le Duc de Loubat (1903). Inscriptions (suite)', *BCH* 29: 417–573.

(1907) 'ΑΝΤΙΓΟΝΕΙΑ ΔΗΜΗΤΡΙΕΙΑ. Les origines de la Confédération des Insulaires', *BCH* 31: 208–27.

(1921–3) *Choix d'inscriptions de Délos*. Paris.

Eckstein, A. M. (2006) *Mediterranean Anarchy, Interstate War, and the Rise of Rome*. Berkeley.

(2008) *Rome Enters the Greek East: From Anarchy to Hierarchy in the Hellenistic Mediterranean, 230–170 BC*. Oxford.

Ehrhardt, N. (1988) *Milet und seine Kolonien*. Frankfurt am Main.

Empercur, J.-Y. (1982) 'Les anses d'amphores timbrées et les amphores, aspects quantitatifs', *BCH* 106: 219–33.

(1995) *A Short Guide to the Graeco-Roman Museum, Alexandria.* Alexandria.

(1998) *Alexandria Rediscovered*, transl. M. Maehler. London.

Engberg-Pedersen, T. (1993) 'The relationship between intellectual and political centres in the Hellenistic world', in Bilde et al. 1993: 285–315.

Errington, R. M. (1977) 'An inscription from Beroea and the alleged co-rule of Demetrius II', *in Ancient Macedonia II, Papers Read at the Second International Symposium Held in Thessaloniki, 19–24 August, 1973.* Thessaloniki: 115–22.

(2008) *A History of the Hellenistic World 323–30 BC.* Oxford.

Erskine, A. (1990) *The Hellenistic Stoa: Political Thought and Action.* London.

(1995) 'Culture and power in Ptolemaic Egypt: The Museum and Library of Alexandria', *G&R* 42.1: 38–48.

(2003) *A Companion to the Hellenistic World.* Oxford.

Etienne, R. (1985) 'Le Koinon des Hellènes à Platées et Glaucon, fils d'Etéoclès', in *La Béotie antique. Lyon–Saint-Étienne, 16–20 mai 1983*, ed. P. Roesch and G. Argoud. Paris: 259–63.

(1990) *Ténos II. Ténos et les Cyclades: Du milieu du IVe siècle av. J.-C. au milieu du IIIe siècle ap. J.-C.* Bibliothèque des écoles françaises d'Athènes et de Rome 263 bis. Athens.

Falivene, M. R. (1998) *The Herakleopolite Nome: A Catalogue of the Toponyms with Introduction and Commentary.* American Studies in Papyrology 37. Atlanta.

Fantuzzi, M. (2004) 'The structure of the *Hippika* in *P.Mil.Vogl.* VIII 309', in Acosta-Hughes, Kosmetatou and Baumbach 2004: 212–24.

Fantuzzi, M. and Hunter, R. (2004) *Tradition and Innovation in Hellenistic Poetry.* Cambridge.

Felten, F. (2006) 'Ägypter im Saronischen Golf', in *Timelines: Studies in Honour of Manfred Bietak*, vol. III, ed. E. Czerny et al. Leuven, Paris and Dudley: 1926.

Ferrari, F. (2007) 'Posidippo, il papiro di Milano e l'enigma del *soros*', in *Proceedings of the 24th International Congress of Papyrology, Helsinki, 1–7 August, 2004*, vol. I, ed. J. Frösén, T. Purola and E. Salmenkivi. Commentationes Humanarum Litterarum 122.1. Helsinki: 331–9.

Filimonos, M. (1989) 'Ένα νέο γυμνάσιο στη Ρόδο και η μαρτυρία του Διοδώρου, ΧΧ, 100, 3–4. Μέρος πρώτο: Το γυμνάσιο', *AC* 58: 128–56.

Fisher, J. and Garvey, G. (2001) *The Rough Guide to Crete.* 5th edn. London.

Fraser, P. M. (1958) Review of first edition of Habicht 1970, *Classical Review* 8: 153–6.

(1960) *Samothrace: Excavations Conducted by the Institute of Fine Arts of New York University*, vol. II.1: *The Inscriptions on Stone.* Bollingen Series 60, 2. New York.

(1961) 'The foundation date of the Alexandrian *Ptolemaieia*', *Harvard Theological Review* 54: 141–5.

(1970) 'Eratosthenes of Cyrene', *Proceedings of the British Academy* 56: 175–207.

(1972) *Ptolemaic Alexandria*, 3 vols. Oxford.

(1981) 'Alexandria from Mohammed Ali to Gamal Abdal Nasser', in *Alexandrien. Kulturbegegnungen dreier Jahrtausende im Schmelztiegel einer mediterranen Großstadt*, ed. N. Hinske et al. Aegyptiaca Treverensia 1. Mainz am Rhein: 63–74.

(2009) *Greek Ethnic Terminology*. Oxford.

Fraser, P. M. and Bean, G. E. (1954) *The Rhodian Peraea and Islands*. Oxford.

Fraser, P. M. and Matthews, E. (eds.) (1997) *A Lexicon of Greek Personal Names*, vol. III. A: *Peloponnese, Western Greece, Sicily and Magna Graecia*. Oxford.

Frazer, A. (1990) *Samothrace: Excavations Conducted by the Institute of Fine Arts of New York University*, vol. X: *The Propylon of Ptolemy II*. Bollingen Series 60, 10. Princeton.

Frier, B. W. and Kehoe, D. P. (2009) 'Law and economic institutions', in *The Cambridge Economic History of the Greco-Roman World*, ed. W. Scheidel, I. Morris and R. Saller. Cambridge: 113–43.

Furley, W. D. (2001) 'Sotades 2', in *Der Neue Pauly*, vol. XI. Stuttgart: 750–1.

Gabba, E. (ed.) (1974) *Polybe*. Entretiens sur l'antiquité classique 20. Geneva.

Gabbert, J. J. (1986) 'Piracy in the Hellenistic period: A career open to talents', *G&R* 33: 156–63.

Gabrielsen, V. (1997) *The Naval Aristocracy of Hellenistic Rhodes*. Studies in Hellenistic Civilization 6. Aarhus.

(2000) 'The synoikized *polis* of Rhodes', in *Polis and Politics: Studies in Ancient Greek History Presented to Mogens Herman Hansen on his Sixtieth Birthday, August 20, 2000*, ed. P. Flensted-Jensen, T. Heine Nielsen and L. Rubinstein. Copenhagen: 177–205.

(2001) 'Economic activity, maritime trade and piracy in the Hellenistic Aegean', *REA* 103: 219–40.

(2003) 'Piracy and the slave-trade', in Erskine 2003: 389–404.

(2007) 'Trade and tribute: Byzantion and the Black Sea straits', in *The Black Sea in Antiquity: Regional and Interregional Economic Exchanges*, ed. V. Gabrielsen and J. Lund. Black Sea Studies 6. Aarhus: 287–324.

(2011) 'Profitable partnerships: Monopolies, traders, kings, and cities', in Archibald, Davies and Gabrielsen 2011: 216–50.

Gallo, I. (1975) *Frammenti biografici da papiri*, vol. I. Rome.

Gallo, L. (2009) 'La lega dei Nesioti. Le vicende storiche', in *Immagine e immagini della Sicilia e di altre isole del Mediterraneo antico*, vol. I, ed. C. Ampolo. Pisa: 335–9.

Gallotta, S. (2009) 'L'organizzazione istituzionale dei Nesioti', in *Immagine e immagini della Sicilia e di altre isole del Mediterraneo antico*, vol. I, ed. C. Ampolo. Pisa: 341–5.

Garlan, Y. (1978) 'Signification de la piraterie grecque', *Dialogues d'histoire ancienne* 4: 1–16.

Garnsey, P. (1988) *Famine and Food Supply in the Graeco-Roman World*. Cambridge.

Gauthier, P. (1979) '"Ἐξαγωγὴ σίτου": Samothrace, Hippomédon et les Lagides', *Historia* 28: 76–89.

(1985) *Les cités grecques et leurs bienfaiteurs (IVe–Ier siècle avant J.-C.). Contribution à l'histoire des institutions*. BCH Suppl. 12. Athens and Paris.

(2003) 'Deux décrets hellénistiques de Colophon-sur-mer', *REG* 116: 470–93.

Geagan, D. J. (1968) 'Inscriptions from Nemea', *Hesperia* 37: 381–5.

Geertz, C. (1979) 'Suq: The bazaar economy of Sefrou', in *Meaning and Order in Moroccan Society: Three Essays in Cultural Analysis*, ed. C. Geertz, H. Geertz and L. Rosen. Cambridge and London: 123–313.

Gera, D. (1998) *Judaea and Mediterranean Politics 219–161 BCE*. Leiden.

Gercke, P. and Zimmermann-Elseify, N. (2007) *Antike Steinskulpturen und neuzeitliche Nachbildungen in Kassel*. Mainz am Rhein.

Geus, K. (2002) *Eratosthenes von Kyrene. Studien zur hellenistischen Kultur- und Wissenschaftsgeschichte*. MünchBeitr 92. Munich, reprinted Oberhaid 2011.

(2007) 'Die Geographika des Eratosthenes von Kyrene. Altes und Neues in Terminologie und Methode', in *Wahrnehmung und Erfassung geographischer Räume in der Antike*, ed. M. Rathmann. Mainz am Rhein: 111–22.

Gill, D. W. J. (2007) 'Arsinoe in the Peloponnese: The Ptolemaic base on the Methana peninsula', in *Egyptian Stories: A British Egyptological Tribute to Alan B. Lloyd*, ed. T. Schneider and K. Szpakowska. Alter Orient und Altes Testament 347. Münster: 87–110.

Gill, D., Foxhall, L. and Bowden, H. (1997) 'Classical and Hellenistic Methana', in *A Rough and Rocky Place: The Landscape and Settlement History of the Methana Peninsula, Greece*, ed. C. Mee and H. Forbes. Liverpool: 62–76.

Giovannini, A. (2007) *Les relations entre états dans la Grèce antique*. Historia Einzelschr. 19. Stuttgart.

Gisinger, F. (1937) 'Timosthenes', in *RE* VI A2: 1310–22.

Goddio, F. (2011) 'Heracleion-Thonis and Alexandria, two ancient Egyptian emporia', in *Maritime Archaeology and Ancient Trade in the Mediterranean*, ed. D. Robinson and A. Wilson. Oxford Centre for Maritime Archaeology Monograph 6. Oxford: 121–37.

Gorre, G. (2010) 'Une première mention d'Hippalos, stratège de la Thébaïde?', *CE* 85: 230–9.

Gounaropoulou, L. and Hatzopoulos, M. B. (1998) *Inscriptiones Macedoniae Inferioris (inter Bermium montem et Axium flumen repertae)*, vol. 1: *Inscriptiones Beroeae*. Athens.

Gow, A. S. F. (1965) *Theocritus, Edited with a Translation and Commentary*. 2nd edn. Reprint. 2 vols. Cambridge.

Grač, N. L. (1984) 'Discovery of a new historical source at Nymphea', *Vestnik Drevnej Istorii* 167: 81–2. (In Russian with English summary and illustrations.)

Graindor, P. (1906) 'Fouilles de Karthaia', *BCH* 30: 92–102.

Griffith, G. T. (1935) *The Mercenaries of the Hellenistic World*. Cambridge.

Griffiths, F. T. (1979) *Theocritus at Court*. Leiden.

Griffiths, J. Gwyn (1970) *Plutarch's De Iside et Osiride*. Cardiff.

Grimal, N. (1988) *Histoire de l'Égypte ancienne*. Paris.

Grimm, G. (1998) *Alexandria. Die erste Königsstadt der hellenistischen Welt*. Mainz am Rhein.

Groom, N. (1995) 'The *Periplus*, Pliny and Arabia', *ArabA Epigr* 6: 180–95.

Grzybek, E. (1990) *Du calendrier macédonien au calendrier ptolémaïque. Problèmes de chronologie hellénistique.* Basle.

(1993) 'Eine Inschrift aus Beroea und die Jahreszählweisen der Diadochen', in *Ancient Macedonia V: Papers Read at the Fifth International Symposium Held in Thessaloniki, October, 10–15, 1989.* Thessaloniki: 521–7.

Grzybek, R. (2002) 'Coptos et la route maritime des Indes', *Topoi* Suppl. 3: 337–47.

Guimiers-Sorbet, A.-M. (2004) 'Mosaics of Alexandria', in Hirst and Silk 2004: 67–73.

Güngerich, R. (1950) *Die Küstenbeschreibung in der griechischen Literatur.* Münster.

Gutzwiller, K. J. (1998) *Poetic Garlands: Hellenistic Epigrams in Context.* Berkeley and Los Angeles.

(ed.) (2005) *The New Posidippus: A Hellenistic Poetry Book.* Oxford. (Paperback 2008.)

Habicht, C. (1957) 'Samische Volksbeschlüsse der hellenistischen Zeit', *MDAI(A)* 72: 152–270.

(1970) *Gottmenschentum und griechische Städte.* Zetemata; Monographien zur klassischen Altertumswissenschaft 14. 2nd edn. Munich.

(1980) 'Bemerkungen zu *P. Haun. 6*', *ZPE* 39: 1–5, reprinted in Habicht 1994: 47–51.

(1992) 'Athens and the Ptolemies', *Classical Antiquity* 11: 68–90, reprinted in Habicht 1994: 140–63.

(1994) *Athen in hellenistischer Zeit. Gesammelte Aufsätze.* Munich.

(1995) *Athen. Die Geschichte der Stadt in hellenistischer Zeit.* Munich.

(1997) *Athens from Alexander to Antony.* Cambridge and Harvard.

(2006) *Athènes hellénistique. Histoire de la cité d'Alexandre le Grand à Marc Antoine.* Paris.

(2007) 'Neues zur hellenistischen Geschichte von Kos', *Chiron* 37: 123–52.

(2010) 'The city of Kyzikos client of oracles', in *Studies in Greek Epigraphy and History in Honor of Stephen V. Tracy*, ed. G. Reger, F. X. Ryan and T. F. Winters. Bordeaux: 311–22.

Hadjidakis, P., Matarangas, D. and Varti-Matarangas, M. (2009) 'Ancient quarries in Delos, Greece', in *ASMOSIA* VII, ed. Y. Maniatis. *BCH* Suppl. 51: 273–88.

Hammond, N. G. L. (1984) 'Alexander's veterans after his death', *GRBS* 25: 51–61.

(1996) 'Alexander's non–European troops and Ptolemy I's use of such troops', *BASP* 33: 99–109.

Hammond, N. G. L. and Walbank, F. W. (1988) *A History of Macedonia*, vol. III: *336–167 BC.* Oxford.

Hardie, P. (2006) 'Virgil's Ptolemaic relations', *JRS* 96: 25–41.

Harris, W. V. (ed.) (2005) *Rethinking the Mediterranean.* Oxford.

Harris, W. V. and Ruffini, G. (eds.) (2004) *Ancient Alexandria between Egypt and Greece.* Columbia Studies in the Classical Tradition 26. Leiden and Boston, Mass.

Hasluck, F. W. (1910) *Cyzicus.* Cambridge.

Hatzopoulos, M. B. (1990) 'Un nouveau document du règne d'Antigone Gonatas', in *Poikila*. Meletemata 10. Athens: 135–48.

(1996) *Macedonian Institutions under the Kings*. Meletemata 22. Athens.

Hauben, H. (1970) *Callicrates of Samos: A Contribution to the Study of the Ptolemaic Admiralty*. Studia Hellenistica 18. Leuven.

(1974) 'A royal toast in 302 BC', *AncSoc* 5: 105–17.

(1975) *Het Vlootbevelhebberschap in de Vroege Diadochentijd (323–301 vóór Christus). Een Prosopografisch en Institutioneel Onderzoek*. Verhandelingen van de Koninklijke Academie voor Wetenschappen, Letteren en Schone Kunsten van België, Klasse der Letteren 77. Brussels.

(1976) 'Fleet strength at the battle of Salamis (306 BC)', *Chiron* 6: 1–5.

(1977) 'Rhodes, Alexander, and the Diadochi from 333/332 to 304 BC', *Historia* 26: 307–39.

(1981) 'A neglected detail of Philopator's policy', *AC* 50: 398–403.

(1983) 'Arsinoé II et la politique extérieure de l'Égypte', in *Egypt and the Hellenistic World. Proceedings of the International Colloquium, Leuven, 24–26 May 1982*, ed. E. Van 't Dack, P. Van Dessel and W. Van Gucht. Studia Hellenistica 27. Leuven: 99–127.

(1985a) 'Les vacances d'Agréophon (253 av. J.-C.)', *CE* 60: 102–8.

(1985b) '"Ceux qui naviguent sur la mer extérieure" (*SB* III 7169)', *ZPE* 59: 135–6.

(1987a) 'Cyprus and the Ptolemaic navy', *RDAC*: 213–26.

(1987b) 'Philocles, king of the Sidonians and general of the Ptolemies', in *Phoenicia and the East Mediterranean in the First Millennium BC. Proceedings of the Conference Held in Leuven from the 14th to the 16th of November 1985*, ed. E. Lipiński. Studia Phoenicia 5 = Orientalia Lovaniensia Analecta 22. Leuven: 413–27.

(1989) 'Aspects du culte des souverains à l'époque des Lagides', in Criscuolo and Geraci 1989: 441–67.

(1990a) 'L'expédition de Ptolémée III en Orient et la sédition domestique de 245 av. J.-C. Quelques mises au point', *APF* 36: 29–37.

(1990b) 'Triérarques et triérarchie dans la marine des Ptolémées', *AncSoc* 21: 119–39.

(1992) 'La chronologie macédonienne et ptolémaïque mise à l'épreuve. À propos d'un livre d'Erhard Grzybek', *CE* 67: 143–71.

(1996) 'Timosthène et les autres amiraux de nationalité rhodienne au service des Ptolémées', in *Proceedings of the International Scientific Symposium Rhodes: 24 Centuries, October 1–5, 1992*, ed. G. Gizelis. Athens: 220–42.

(2004) 'A Phoenician king in the service of the Ptolemies: Philocles of Sidon revisited', *AncSoc* 34: 27–44.

(2006) 'Kriton, stolarque au service d'Apollonios le diœcète', *AncSoc* 36: 175–219.

(2010) 'Rhodes, the League of the Islanders, and the Cult of Ptolemy I Soter', in *Philathenaios: Studies in Honour of Michael J. Osborne*, ed. A. M. Tamis, C. J. Mackie and S. G. Byrne. Athens: 103–21.

Hazzard, R. A. (1987) 'The regnal years of Ptolemy II Philadelphos', *Phoenix* 41: 140–58.

(1992) 'Did Ptolemy I get his surname from the Rhodians?', *ZPE* 93: 52–56.

Heinen, H. (1972) *Untersuchungen zur hellenistischen Geschichte des 3. Jahrhunderts v. Chr. Zur Geschichte der Zeit des Ptolemaios Keraunos und zum Chremonideischen Krieg.* Historia Einzelschr. 20. Wiesbaden.

(1984) 'The Syrian-Egyptian Wars and the new kingdoms of Asia Minor', in *The Cambridge Ancient History*, vol. VII.1: *The Hellenistic World*, ed. F. W. Walbank et al. 2nd edn. Cambridge: 412–45.

Hennig, D. (1989) 'Böoter im ptolemäischen Ägypten', in *BOIOTIKA. Vorträge vom 5. Internationalen Böotien-Kolloquium zu Ehren von Prof. Dr. Siegfried Lauffer*, ed. H. Beister and J. Buckler. Munich: 169–82.

Herrmann, A. (1930) 'Marinus von Tyrus, Geograph und Kartograph', in H. Wagner, *Gedächtnisschrift: Ergebnisse und Aufgaben geographischer Forschung. Dargestellt von Schülern, Freunden und Verehrern des Altmeisters der Deutschen Geographen.* Petermanns Mitteilungen Ergänzungsheft 209. Gotha: 45–54.

Hicks, R. D. (transl.) (1925) *Diogenes Laertius: Lives of the Eminent Philosophers*. Cambridge, Mass. and London.

Hiller von Gaertringen, F. (ed.) (1899) *Thera. Untersuchungen, Vermessungen und Ausgrabungen in den Jahren 1895–1902*, vol. I. Berlin.

(1904) *Thera*, vol. III: *Stadtgeschichte von Thera*. Berlin.

(1931) 'Rhodos', *RE* Suppl. V: 731–840.

Hintzen-Bohlen, B. (1990) 'Die Familiengruppe – ein Mittel zur Selbstdarstellung hellenistischer Herrscher', *JDAI* 105: 129–54.

Hirst, A. and Silk, M. (eds.) (2004) *Alexandria, Real and Imagined*. Centre for Hellenic Studies, King's College London, Publications 5. Aldershot.

Hoepfner, W. (1971) *Zwei Ptolemaierbauten: Das Ptolemaierweihgeschenk in Olympia und ein Bauvorhaben in Alexandrien*. MDAI(A) Beiheft 1. Berlin.

(2003) *Der Koloss von Rhodos. Neue Forschungen zu einem der sieben Weltwunder.* Mainz am Rhein.

Höghammar, K. (1993) *Sculpture and Society: A Study of the Connection between the Free-standing Sculpture and Society on Kos in the Hellenistic and Augustan Periods*. Uppsala.

Hölbl, G. (2001) *A History of the Ptolemaic Empire*, transl. T. Saavedra. London and New York.

Holleaux, M. (1938–68) *Études d'épigraphie et d'histoire grecques*, vols. I–VI. Paris.

Horden, P. (2005) 'Travel sickness: Medicine and mobility in the Mediterranean from Antiquity to the Renaissance', in Harris 2005: 179–99.

Horden, P. and Purcell, N. (2000) *The Corrupting Sea: A Study of Mediterranean History*. Oxford and Malden, Mass.

(2005) 'Four years of corruption: A response to critics', in Harris 2005: 348–75.

Hunt, P. (2007) 'Military forces', in *A Cambridge History of Greek and Roman Warfare*, vol. I: *Greece, the Hellenistic World and the Rise of Rome*, ed. P. Sabin, H. van Wees and M. Whitby. Cambridge: 108–46.

Hunter, R. (2003) *Theocritus: Encomium of Ptolemy Philadelphus*. Berkeley and London.

Huß, W. (1976) *Untersuchungen zur Außenpolitik Ptolemaios' IV*. MünchBeitr 69. Munich.

(1990) 'Die Quellen des Nils', *CE* 65: 334–43.

(1998) 'Ptolemaios der Sohn', *ZPE* 121: 229–50.

(2001) *Ägypten in hellenistischer Zeit: 332–30 v. Chr*. Munich.

(2008) 'Die Tochter Berenike oder die Schwiegertochter Berenike? Bemerkungen zu einigen Epigrammen des Poseidippos von Pella', *ZPE* 165: 55–7.

Ijsewijn, J. (1961) *De sacerdotibus sacerdotiisque Alexandri Magni et Lagidarum eponymis*. Verhandelingen van de Koninklijke Vlaamse Academie voor Wetenschappen, Letteren en Schone Kunsten van België, Klasse der Letteren 42. Brussels.

Jackson, A. H. (1973) 'Privateers in the ancient Greek world', in *War and Society: Historical Studies in Honour and Memory of J. R. Western*, ed. M. R. D. Foot. New York: 241–53.

Jacobsen, T. W. and Smith, P. M. (1968) 'Two Kimolian dikast decrees from Gairestos in Euboia', *Hesperia* 38: 184–99.

Jacobson, D. M. (2004) 'Marisa tomb paintings recently discovered', *Biblical Archaeology Review* 30.2: 24–39.

(2007) *The Hellenistic Paintings of Marisa*. The Palestine Exploration Fund Annual 7. Leeds, including reprint of Peters and Thiersch 1905.

Jacoby, F. (2004) 'Bilistiche', *Simblos* 4: 193–212.

Jacquemin, A. (1999) *Offrandes monumentales à Delphes*. Paris.

Jeffreys, D. G. (2008) 'Archaeological implications of the moving Nile', *EA* 32: 6–7.

Jördens, A. and Quack, J. F. (eds.) (2011) *Ägypten zwischen innerem Zwist und äußerem Druck. Die Zeit Ptolemaios' VI. bis VIII*. Philippika. Marburger altertumskundliche Abhandlungen 45. Wiesbaden.

Johansen, F. (1992) *Greek Portraits, Ny Carlsberg Glyptotek*. Copenhagen.

Jones, C. P. and Habicht, C. (1989) 'A Hellenistic inscription from Arsinoe in Cilicia', *Phoenix* 43: 317–46.

Kabus-Preisshofen, R. (1989) *Die hellenistische Plastik der Insel Kos*. MDAI(A) Beiheft 14. Berlin.

Kidd, I. G. (1988) *Posidonius*, vol. II: *Commentary*. Cambridge.

Kiessling, E. (1913) '*Hippalon pelagos*', *RE* VIII 2: 1656–7.

Knoepfler, D. (1991) *La vie de Ménédème d'Érétrie de Diogène Laërce. Contribution à l'histoire et à la critique du texte des 'Vies des philosophes'*. Basle.

(1993) 'Les *kryptoi* du stratège Épicharès à Rhamnonte et le début de la guerre de Chrémonidès', *BCH* 117: 327–41.

(1995) 'Note additionnelle: Arrhéneidès à Athènes et Pleiston à Delphes', *BCH* 119: 159.

Konstantinopoulos, G. (1972) *Ο Ροδιακός κόσμος*, vol. I: *Λίνδος*. Athens.

Kotsidu, H. (2000) *Timē kai doxa. Ehrungen für hellenistische Herrscher im griechischen Mutterland und in Kleinasien unter besonderer Berücksichtigung der archäologischen Denkmäler*. Berlin.

Kramer, B (2001) 'Königseid eines Offiziers aus dem Jahr 152 v.Chr.', in *Punica – Libyca – Ptolemaica. Festschrift für Werner Huß, zum 65. Geburtstag dargebracht von Schülern, Freunden und Kollegen*, ed. K. Geus and K. Zimmermann. Studia Phoenicia 16. Leuven, Paris and Sterling, Va.: 323–44.

Krasilnikoff, J. A. (2009) 'Alexandria as *place*: Tempo-spatial traits of royal ideology in early Ptolemaic Egypt', in *Alexandria: A Cultural and Religious Melting Pot*, ed. G. Hinge and J. A. Krasilnikoff. Aarhus: 21–41.

Kreikenbom, D. (1992) *Griechische und römische Kolossalporträts bis zum späten ersten Jahrhundert nach Christus*. Berlin and New York.

Kreuter, S. (1992) *Aussenbeziehungen kretischer Gemeinden zu den hellenistischen Staaten im 3. und 2. Jh. v. Chr.* Munich.

Kroll, J. H. (1993) *The Greek Coins*. Athenian Agora 26. Princeton.

Kruse, Th. (2011) 'Die Festung in Herakleopolis und der Zwist im Ptolemäerhaus', in Jördens and Quack 2011: 255–67.

Kunkel, W. (1927) 'Verwaltungsakten aus spätptolemäischer Zeit', *APF* 8: 169–215.

Kuttner, A. (2005) 'A cabinet fit for a queen: The Λιθικά as Posidippus' gem museum', in Gutzwiller 2005: 141–63.

Kvist, K. (2003) 'Cretan grants of asylia – violence and protection as interstate relations', *Classica et Mediaevalia* 54: 185–222.

Kyrieleis, H. (1975) *Bildnisse der Ptolemäer*. Berlin.

La'da, C. A. (1994) 'Ethnicity, occupation and tax-status in Ptolemaic Egypt', in *Acta Demotica: Acts of the Fifth International Conference for Demotists, Pisa 4–8 September 1993*, ed. E. Bresciani. Pisa: 183–9.

  (1996) 'Ethnic Designations in Hellenistic Egypt'. PhD, University of Cambridge (unpubl.).

  (2002) *Foreign Ethnics in Hellenistic Egypt. Pros. Ptol. x.* Leuven.

Labarre, G. (1996) *Les cités de Lesbos, aux époques hellénistique et impériale.* Collection de l'Institut d'archéologie et d'histoire de l'antiquité 1. Paris.

Laffranque, M. (1963) 'Eudoxe de Cyzique et la circumnavigation de l'Afrique', *Revue philosophique de la France et de l'étranger* 153: 199–222.

  La gloire d'Alexandrie (exhibition, Paris, Musée du Petit Palais, 7 May–26 July 1998). Paris.

Lagogianni-Georgakarakou, M. (2001) 'Εικονιστική κεφαλή του Πτολεμαίου Ἐ Επιφανούς', in Ἄγαλμα. Μελέτες για την αρχαία πλαστική προς τιμήν του Γιώργου Δεσπίνη, ed. D. Tsiafaki. Thessaloniki: 317–23.

Launey, M. (1945) 'Études d'histoire hellénistique II. L'exécution de Sotadès et l'expédition de Patroklos dans la mer Égée (266 av. J.-C.)', *REA* 47: 33–45.

  (1987) *Recherches sur les armées hellénistiques (addenda et mise à jour en postface par Garlan Y. – Gauthier Ph. – Orrieux Cl.).* 2nd edn. Paris.

Le Rider, G. (1997) 'Cléomène de Naucratis', *BCH* 121: 71–93.

Lee, J. W. I. (2006) 'Warfare in the Classical Age', in *A Companion to the Classical Greek World*, ed. K. Kinzl. Oxford: 480–508.

Lehmler, C. (2005) *Syrakus unter Agathokles und Hieron II. Die Verbindung von Kultur und Macht in einer hellenistischen Metropole*. Frankfurt am Main.

Leonard, J. R. and Hohlfelder, R. L. (1993) 'Paphos harbour, past and present: The 1991–1992 underwater survey', *RDAC*: 365–79.

Lesquier, J. (1911) *Les institutions militaires de l'Égypte sous les Lagides.* Paris.

Levi, A. (1931) *Sculture greche e romane del Palazzo Ducale di Mantova.* Rome.

Lewis, N. (1986) *Greeks in Ptolemaic Egypt: Case Studies in the Social History of the Hellenistic World.* Oxford.

Little, B. (2005) *The Sea Rover's Practice: Pirate Tactics and Techniques, 1630–1730.* Washington D.C.

Lloyd, G. E. R. (1975) 'A note on Erasistratus of Ceos', *JHS* 95: 172–5.

Lloyd-Jones, H. (1963) 'The seal of Posidippus', *JHS* 83: 75–99.

(2003a) Review of G. Bastianini and C. Gallazzi (eds.), *Posidippo di Pella, Epigrammi (P.Mil. Vogl. VIII 309)*, Milan 2001, *International Journal of the Classical Tradition* 9.4: 612–16.

(2003b) 'All by Posidippus?', in *Des Géants à Dionysos. Mélanges offerts à F. Vian*, ed. D. Accorinti and P. Chuvin. Alexandria: 277–80.

Longega, G. (1968) *Arsinoe II.* Università degli Studi di Padova. Pubblicazioni dell'Istituto di Storia Antica 6. Rome.

Lonis, R. (2000) *La cité dans le monde grec. Structures, fonctionnement, contradictions.* 2nd edn. Paris.

López-Muñoz, F. and Alamo, C. (2009) 'Historical evolution of the neurotransmission concept', *Journal of Neural Transmission* 116: 515–33.

Loukopoulou, L. et al. (2005) *Επιγραφές της Θράκης του Αιγαίου.* Athens.

Lucas, A. (1932) 'The occurrence of natron in ancient Egypt', *Journal of Egyptian Archaeology* 18: 62–6.

Lund, J. (1999) 'Rhodian amphorae in Rhodes and Alexandria as evidence of trade', in *Hellenistic Rhodes: Politics, Culture, and Society*, ed. V. Gabrielsen et al. Studies in Hellenistic Civilization 9. Aarhus: 187–204.

(2011) 'Rhodian transport amphorae as a source for economic (ebbs and) flows in the eastern Mediterranean in the 2nd century BC', in Archibald, Davies and Gabrielsen 2011: 280–95.

Lutley, K. and Bunbury, J. (2008) 'The Nile on the move', *EA* 32: 3–7.

Ma, J. (1999) *Antiochos III and the Cities of Western Asia Minor.* Oxford.

Ma, J. T., Derow, P. S. and Meadows, A. R. (1995) '*RC* 38 (Amyzon) reconsidered', *ZPE* 109: 71–80.

Maass, M. (1972) *Die Prohedrie des Dionysostheaters in Athen.* Munich.

Mahan, A. T. (1890) *The Influence of Sea Power upon History 1660–1783.* Boston, Mass.

Mallwitz, A. (1972) *Olympia und seine Bauten.* Munich.

Marek, C. (1984) *Die Proxenie.* Europäische Hochschulschriften III. 213. Frankfurt am Main, Bern and New York.

(2006) *Die Inschriften von Kaunos.* Vestigia 55. Munich.

Marquaille, C. (2008) 'The foreign policy of Ptolemy II', in McKechnie and Guillaume 2008: 39–64.

Masselink, J. F. (1956) *De Grieks-Romeinse Windroos.* Utrecht and Nijmegen.

Matthaiou, A. P. (2005) 'A new honorary decree from Antissa (Lesbos)', in *Epigraphic Research in Greece and Turkey, First Greek–Turkish Epigraphic Colloquium. Epigraphical Museum, Athens 27–30 January 2005* (unpubl.).

Mazzarino, S. (1982–7) 'Sul nome del vento hipalus ("ippalo") in Plinio', *Helikon* 22/27: VII–XIV.

McCredie, J. R., Roux, G. and Shaw, S. M. (1992) *The Rotunda of Arsinoe.* Samothrace 7. Princeton.

McGing, B. (1997) 'Revolt Egyptian-style: Internal opposition to Ptolemaic rule', *APF* 43: 273–314.

(2010) *Polybius' Histories.* Oxford.

McKechnie, P. and Guillaume, P. (eds.) (2008) *Ptolemy II Philadelphus and his World.* Mnemosyne Supplements. History and Archaeology of Classical Antiquity 300. Leiden and Boston, Mass.

McKenzie, J. (2007) *The Architecture of Alexandria and Egypt 300 BC–AD 700.* New Haven, Conn. and London. (Paperback 2010.)

Meadows, A. (2006) 'The Ptolemaic annexation of Lycia: *SEG* 27.929', in *Proceedings of the Third International Lycia Congress. Symposion Proceedings* 2, ed. K. Dörtlük et al. Antalya: 459–70.

(2008) 'Fouilles d' Amyzon 6 reconsidered: The Ptolemies at Amyzon', *ZPE* 166: 115–20.

(2012) 'Deditio in fidem: The Ptolemaic conquest of Asia Minor', in *Imperialism, Cultural Politics, and Polybius*, ed. C. Smith and L. M. Yarrow. Oxford: 113–33.

Mee, C. and Forbes, H. (eds.) (1997) *A Rough and Rocky Place: The Landscape and Settlement History of the Methana Peninsula, Greece: Results of the Methana Survey Project, Sponsored by the British School at Athens and the University of Liverpool.* Liverpool.

Meiggs, R. (1982) *Trees and Timber in the Ancient Mediterranean World.* Oxford.

Meijer, F. (2000) *Paulus' Zeereis naar Rome. Een Reconstructie.* Amsterdam.

Mélèze Modrzejewski, J. (1983) 'Le statut des Hellènes dans l'Égypte lagide. Bilan et perspectives de recherches', *REG* 96: 241–68.

(1998) '"Paroles néfastes" et "vers obscènes". À propos de l'injure verbale en droit grec et hellénistique', *Dike* 1: 151–69, reprinted in *Anthropologies juridiques. Mélanges Pierre Braun*, ed. J. Hoareau-Dodinau and P. Texier. Limoges 1998: 569–85.

(2008) 'Le troisième livre des Maccabées. Un drame judiciaire judéo-alexandrin', *JJP* 38: 157–70.

Merker, I. L. (1970) 'The Ptolemaic officials and the League of Islanders', *Historia* 19: 159–60.

Meyer, D. (1998) 'Hellenistische Geographie zwischen Wissenschaft und Literatur: Timosthenes von Rhodos und der griechische Periplus', in *Gattungen wissenschaftlicher Literatur in der Antike*, ed. W. Kullmann, J. Althoff and M. Asper. Tübingen: 193–215.

Mildenberg, L. (1993) 'The Cyzicenes: A reappraisal', *AJN* 5/6: 1–12.

Miller, K. (1898) *Mappae Mundi. Die ältesten Weltkarten*, vol. VI: *Rekonstruierte Karten.* Stuttgart.

Mitford, T. B. (1939) 'Contributions to the epigraphy of Cyprus: Some Hellenistic inscriptions', *APF* 13: 13–38.

(1959) 'Helenos, governor of Cyprus', *JHS* 79: 94–131.

(1961) 'The Hellenistic inscriptions of Old Paphos', *ABSA* 56: 1–41.

(1971) *The Inscriptions of Kourion*. Philadelphia.

Moore, J. M. (1965) *The Manuscript Tradition of Polybius*. Cambridge.

Mooren, L. (1972) 'The date of *SB* V 8036 and the development of the Ptolemaic maritime trade with India', *AncSoc* 3: 127–33.

(1975) *The Aulic Titulature in Ptolemaic Egypt: Introduction and Prosopography*. Verhandelingen van de Koninklijke Academie voor Wetenschappen, Letteren en Schone Kunsten van België, Klasse der Letteren 78. Brussels.

(2000) (ed.) *Politics, Administration and Society in the Hellenistic and Roman World. Proceedings of the International Colloquium, Bertinoro 19–24 July 1997*. Studia Hellenistica 36. Leuven.

Moreno, A. (2007) *Feeding the Democracy: The Athenian Grain Supply in the Fifth and Fourth Centuries* BC. Oxford.

(2008) 'Hieron: The ancient sanctuary at the mouth of the Black Sea', *Hesperia* 77: 655–709.

Mørkholm, O. (1991) *Early Hellenistic Coinage from the Accession of Alexander to the Peace of Apamea (336–186 BC)*, ed. P. Grierson and U. Westermark. Cambridge.

Morrison, J. S. and Coates, J. F. (1996) *Greek and Roman Oared Warships, 399–31 BC*. Oxford.

Moyer, I. S. (2011) *Egypt and the Limits of Hellenism*. Cambridge.

Mueller, K. (2005) 'Geographical Information Systems (GIS) in papyrology: Mapping fragmentation and migration flow to Hellenistic Egypt', *BASP* 42: 63–92.

(2006) *Settlements of the Ptolemies: City Foundations and New Settlement in the Hellenistic World*. Studia Hellenistica 43. Leuven, Paris and Dudley, Mass.

Müller, C. (1883–1901) *Claudii Ptolemaei geographia e codicibus recognovit, prolegomonis, annotatione, indicibus, tabulis instruxit*, vol. 1. Paris.

Murray, W. M. (2012). *The Age of Titans: The Rise and Fall of the Great Hellenistic Navies*. Onassis Series in Hellenic Culture. Oxford.

Mžik, H. von (1938) *Des Klaudios Ptolemaios Einführung in die darstellende Erdkunde. 1. Teil: Theorie und Grundlage der darstellenden Erdkunde (ΓΕΩ-ΓΡΑΦΙΚΗ ΥΦΗΓΗΣΙΣ I und II Vorwort), ins Deutsche übertragen und mit Erläuterungen versehen, unter Mitarbeit von Friedrich Hopfner*. Clotho: historische Studien zur feudalen und vorfeudalen Welt 5.1. Vienna.

New Zealand Government Department of Labour (2011) *Labour Market Outcomes for Immigrants and the New Zealand-born 1997–2009*. Wellington. www.immigration.govt.nz

Nisetich, F. (2005) 'The poems of Posidippus', in Gutzwiller 2005: 17–66.

Nye, Joseph H. (1990) *Bound to Lead: The Changing Nature of American Power*. New York.

(2002) *The Paradox of American Power: Why the World's Only Superpower Can't Go It Alone*. Oxford.

O'Neil, J. L. (2003) 'The ethnic origins of the friends of the Antigonid kings of Macedon', *CQ* 53: 510–22.

(2008) 'A re-examination of the Chremonidean War', in McKechnie and Guillaume 2008: 65–89.

Obbink, D. (2004) 'Posidippus on papyri old and new', in Acosta-Hughes, Kosmetatou and Baumbach 2004: 16–28.

(2005) 'New Old Posidippus and old New Posidippus: From occasion to edition in the epigrams', in Gutzwiller 2005: 97–118.

Oliver, G. J. (2001) 'Regions and micro-regions: Grain for Rhamnous', in *Hellenistic Economies*, ed. Z. H. Archibald, J. K. Davies, V. Gabrielsen and G. J. Oliver. London and New York: 137–55.

(2007) *War, Food, and Politics in Early Hellenistic Athens*. Oxford.

Opelt, I. and Kirsten, E. (1989) 'Eine Urkunde der Gründung von Arsinoe in Kilikien', *ZPE* 77: 55–66.

Orrieux, Cl. (1983) *Les Papyrus de Zénon. L'horizon d'un grec en Égypte au IIIᵉ siècle avant J.C.* Préface d'Édouard Will. Paris.

Otto, W. and Bengtson, H. (1938) *Zur Geschichte des Niederganges des Ptolemäerreiches.* ABAW NF 17. Munich.

Palagia, O. (1992) 'Cult and allegory: The life story of Artemidoros of Perge', in *ΦΙΛΟΛΑΚΩΝ: Lakonian Studies in Honour of Hector Catling*, ed. J. M. Sanders. London: 171–7.

(2006) 'Art and royalty in Sparta of the third century BC', *Hesperia* 75: 205–17.

(2007) 'Berenike II in Athens', in *Early Hellenistic Portraiture: Image, Style, Context*, ed. P. Schultz and R. von den Hoff. Cambridge: 237–45.

Panagopoulou, K. (2005–6) 'Cross-reading images: Iconographic "debates" between Antigonids and Ptolemies during the third and second centuries BC', *EYΛIMENH* 6–7: 163–81.

Paschidis, P. (2008) *Between City and King: Prosopographical Studies on the Intermediaries between the Cities of the Greek Mainland and the Aegean and the Royal Courts in the Hellenistic Period (322–190 BC).* Meletemata 59. Athens.

Pédech, P. (1964) *La méthode historique de Polybe.* Paris.

Pelling, C. B. R. (ed.) (1988) *Plutarch, Life of Antony.* Cambridge Greek and Latin Classics. Cambridge.

Peremans, W. (1931–2) 'De Handelsbetrekkingen van Egypte met het Middellandsche-Zeegebied in de 3ᵉ eeuw v.C. De verhandelde Waren', *Philologische Studiën* 3: 3–21 and 81–94.

(1933) 'De zeeslag van Kos en de opstand van Ptolemaios van Ephese. Chronologisch onderzoek', *Revue Belge de Philologie et d'Histoire* 12: 49–58.

(1939) 'La date de la bataille navale de Cos', *AC* 8: 401–8.

Peremans, W. and Van 't Dack, E. (1968) 'Prolégomènes à une étude concernant le commandant de place lagide en dehors de l'Égypte', in *Antidoron Martino David oblatum*, ed. E. Boswinkel, B. A. van Groningen and P. W. Pestman. Pap. Lugd.-Bat. 17. Leiden: 81–99.

Peremans, W. and Van 't Dack, E. et al. (1950–81) *Prosopographia Ptolemaica*, vols. I–IX. Leuven.

Perlman, P. (1999) 'KRĒTES AEI LĒISTAI? The marginalization of Crete in Greek thought and the role of piracy in the outbreak of the First Cretan War', in *Hellenistic Rhodes: Politics, Culture, and Society*, ed. V. Gabrielsen et al. Aarhus: 132–61.

Pestman, P. W. et al. (eds.) (1981) *A Guide to the Zenon Archive*. 2 vols. Pap. Lugd.-Bat. 21. Leiden.

Peters, J. F. and Thiersch, H. (1905) *Painted Tombs of the Necropolis of Marissa (Marêshah)*. London, reprinted in Jacobson 2007.

Petrakos, B. C. (1967) 'Νέαι πηγαὶ περὶ τοῦ Χρεμωνιδείου πολέμου', *AD* 22.1: 38–52.

(1997a) 'La forteresse de Rhamnonte', *CRAI* 605–30.

(1997b) *Οι επιγραφές του Ωρωπού*. Athens.

Petropoulou, A. (1985) *Beiträge zur Wirtschafts- und Gesellschaftsgeschichte Kretas in hellenistischer Zeit*. Frankfurt am Main.

Pfeiffer, R. (1949) *Callimachus*, vol. I. Oxford.

Pfeiffer, S. (2004) *Das Dekret von Kanopos (238 v.Chr.). Kommentar und historische Auswertung*. APF Beiheft 18. Munich.

Picón, C. A. et al. (2007) *Art of the Classical World in the Metropolitan Museum of Art*. New Haven, Conn. and London.

Pirenne-Delforge, V. (1994) *L'Aphrodite grecque. Contribution à l'étude de ses cultes et de sa personnalité dans le panthéon archaïque et classique*. Athens and Liège.

Pohl, H. (1993) *Die römische Politik und die Piraterie im östlichen Mittelmeer vom 3. bis zum 1. Jh. v. Chr.* Berlin and New York.

Pollitt, J. J. (1986) *Art in the Hellenistic Age*. Cambridge.

Porten, B. and Yardeni, A. (1993) *Textbook of Aramaic Documents from Ancient Egypt*, vol. III: *Literature, Accounts, Lists*. Winona Lake, Ind.

Postl, B. (1970) *Die Bedeutung des Nil in der römischen Literatur*. Vienna.

Pozzi, S. (2006) 'Sulle sezioni Iamatikà e Tropoi del nuovo Posidippo (95–105 A.-B.)', *Eikasmos* 17: 181–202.

Préaux, C. (1939) *L'économie royale des Lagides*. Brussels.

(1975–6) 'Sur le naufrage de la littérature historique de l'âge hellénistique', in *Miscellanea in honorem Josephi Vergote*, ed. P. Naster, H. De Meulenaere and J. Quaegebeur. Orientalia Lovaniensia Periodica 6/7. Leuven: 455–62.

Pritchett, W. K. (1991) *The Greek State at War*, vol. V. Berkeley, Los Angeles and London.

Prontera, F. (1992) 'Perìploi: Sulla tradizione della geografia nautica presso i Greci', in *L'uomo e il mare nella civiltà occidentale. Da Ulisse a Cristoforo Colombo*. Atti della Società Ligure di Storia Patria, N.S. 32.2. Genova: 25–44.

(2007–8a) 'Il Mediterraneo. Scoperta e rappresentazione', *Geographia Antiqua* 16–17: 41–60.

(2007–8b) 'Centro e periferia nei mappamondi greci', *Geographia Antiqua* 16–17: 177–86.

(2009) 'La Sicilia nella cartografia antica', in *Immagine e immagini della Sicilia e di altre isole del Mediterraneo antico*, ed. C. Ampolo. Pisa: 141–7.

Pryor, J. H. (1988) *Geography, Technology, and War: Studies in the Maritime History of the Mediterranean, 649–1571.* Cambridge.

Purcell, N. (2005) 'The ancient Mediterranean: The view from the customs house', in *Rethinking the Mediterranean*, ed. W. V. Harris. Oxford: 200–32.

Radt, S. (2009) *Strabons Geographika*, vol. VIII: *Buch XIV–XVII: Kommentar.* Göttingen.

Raschke, M. G. (1978) 'New studies in Roman commerce with the East', in *Aufstieg und Niedergang der römischen Welt*, vol. II 9.2. Berlin: 604–1361.

Rathbone, D. (1983) 'The grain trade and grain shortages in the Hellenistic East', in *Trade and Famine in Classical Antiquity*, ed. P. Garnsey and C. R. Whittaker. Cambridge: 45–55.

Rauh, N. K. (2003) *Merchants, Sailors and Pirates in the Roman World.* Stroud.

Rawlings, L. (2010) 'The Carthaginian navy: Questions and assumptions', in *New Perspectives on Ancient Warfare*, ed. G. Fagan and M. Trundle. Leiden: 253–87.

Reddé. M. (1986) *Mare nostrum. Les infrastructures, le dispositif et l'histoire de la marine militaire sous l'empire romain.* BEFAR 260. Paris.

Reger, G. (1985) 'The date of the Battle of Kos', *American Journal of Ancient History* 10: 155–77.

(1994a) 'The political history of the Kyklades 260–200 BC', *Historia* 43: 32–69.

(1994b) *Regionalism and Change in the Economy of Independent Delos.* Berkeley.

Regling, K. (1931) 'Der griechische Goldschatz von Prinkipo', *Zeitschrift für Numismatik* 41: 1–46.

Rhodes, P. J. and Lewis, D. M. (1997) *The Decrees of the Greek States.* Oxford.

Rhodes, P. J. and Osborne, R. (2003) *Greek Historical Inscriptions (404–323 BC).* Oxford.

Rice, E. E. (1983) *The Grand Procession of Ptolemy Philadelphus.* Oxford.

Ricketts, M. (2002) *The Economics of Business Enterprise: An Introduction to Economic Organization and the Theory of the Firm.* Cheltenham.

Rigsby, K. J. (1980) 'Bacchon the nesiarch on Delos', *AJP* 101: 194–6.

(1996) *Asylia: Territorial Inviolability in the Hellenistic World.* Berkeley, Los Angeles and London.

Robert, L. (1946) 'Contributions à un lexique épigraphique, I, Trihémiolies athéniennes et *PHYLAKIDES*', *Hellenica* 2: 123–6.

(1960) 'Sur un décret des Korésiens au musée de Smyrne', *Hellenica* 11–12: 132–76.

(1963) *Noms indigènes dans l'Asie Mineure gréco-romaine.* Paris.

(1966a) 'Sur un décret d'Ilion et sur un papyrus concernant des cultes royaux', in *Essays in Honor of C. Bradford Welles.* American Studies in Papyrology 1. New Haven, Conn.: 175–211.

(1966b) *Documents de l'Asie Mineure méridionale, inscriptions, monnaies et géographie.* Hautes études du monde gréco-romain 2. Geneva.

Robert, L. and Robert, J. (1983) *Fouilles d'Amyzon en Carie*, vol. I: *Exploration, histoire, monnaies et inscriptions*. Paris.

Rodriguez, P. (2000) 'L'intervention ptolémaïque dans la guerre de Chrémonidès au vu du monnayage lagide', *Revue Numismatique* 155: 17–34.

(2004) 'Les Égyptiens dans l'armée de terre ptolémaïque', *REG* 117: 104–24.

Roller, D. W. (2010) *Eratosthenes' Geography: Fragments Collected and Translated, with Commentary and Additional Material*. Princeton and Oxford.

Rood, T. (2004) 'Polybius', in *Narrators, Narratees and Narratives in Ancient Greek Literature*, ed. I. De Jong, R. Nünlist and A. Bowie. Mnemosyne Supplement 257. Leiden: 147–64.

Rostovtzeff, M. I. (1922) *A Large Estate in Egypt in the Third Century* BC: *A Study in Economic History*. Madison, Wis.

(1937) 'Alexandrien und Rhodos', *Klio* 30: 70–6.

(1940) 'Πλοῖα θαλάσσια on the Nile', in *Études dédiées à la mémoire d'André M. Andréadès*. Athens: 367–76.

(1953) *The Social and Economic History of the Hellenistic World*, ed. P. M. Fraser. 2nd edn. 3 vols. Oxford.

Rougé, J. (1966) *Recherches sur l'organisation du commerce maritime en Méditerranée sous l'empire romain*. Paris.

Ruge, W. (1924) 'Kyzikos', *RE* XII.1: 228–33.

Salles, J.-F. (1993) 'The Periplus of the Erythraean Sea and the Arab–Persian Gulf', *Topoi* 3: 493–523.

Scheid, J. (2007) *Res Gestae Divi Augusti. Hauts faits du divin Auguste*. Paris.

Schmitt, H. H. (1964) *Untersuchungen zur Geschichte Antiochos' des Großen und seiner Zeit*. Wiesbaden.

(1969) *Die Staatsverträge des Altertums*, vol. III: *Die Verträge der griechisch-römischen Welt von 338 bis 200 v. Chr.* Munich.

Schmitthenner, W. (1979) 'Rome and India: Aspects of universal history during the Principate', *JRS* 69: 90–106.

Scholl, R. (1997) 'Ein Trierer Papyrusfragment als Zeugnis für Handel und Wirtschaft im ptolemäischen Ägypten', *APF* 43: 261–72.

Scholten, J. B. (2000) *The Politics of Plunder*. Berkeley and London.

Schorn, S. (2001) 'Eine Prozession zu Ehren Arsinoes II. (*P. Oxy.* XXVII 2465, fr. 2: Satyros, *Über die Demen von Alexandreia*)', in *Punica–Libyca–Ptolemaica. Festschrift für Werner Huß, zum 65. Geburtstag dargebracht von Schülern, Freunden und Kollegen*, ed. K. Geus and K. Zimmermann. Studia Phoenicia 16 = Orientalia Lovaniensia Analecta 104. Leuven: 199–220.

Schröder, S. (2004) 'Skeptische Überlegungen zum Mailänder Epigrammpapyrus (*P.Mil.Vogl.* VIII 309)', *ZPE* 148: 29–73.

Sedley, D. (1976) 'Epicurus and the mathematicians of Cyzicus', *Cronache Ercolanesi* 6: 23–54.

Segrè, M. (1932) 'Due nuovi testi storici', *Rivista di Filologia e di Istruzione Classica* 60, N.S. 10: 446–61.

Shear, T. C. (1978) *Kallias of Sphettos and the Revolt of Athens in 286* BC. Hesperia Suppl. 17. Athens.

Sherwin-White, S. M. (1978) *Ancient Cos: An Historical Study from the Dorian Settlement to the Imperial Period*. Hypomnemata 51. Göttingen.

Shipley, G. (1987) *A History of Samos 800–188 BC*. Oxford.

Sidebotham, S. E. (1986) *Roman Economic Policy in the Erythra Thalassa 30 BC–AD 217*. Leiden.

Six, J. (1887) 'Ein Porträt des Ptolemaios VI. Philometor', *MDAI(A)* 12: 212–22.

Skeat, T. C. (1969) *The Reigns of the Ptolemies*. MünchBeitr 39. Munich.

Smith, R. R. R. (1988) *Hellenistic Royal Portraits*. Oxford.

Spyridakis, S. (1970) *Ptolemaic Itanos and Hellenistic Crete*. Berkeley, Los Angeles and London.

Stampolides, N. (1982) 'Καλλίμαχος Ἀλεξανδρεὺς ἀγωνοθετήσας', *AAA* 15: 297–310.

Stanwick, P. E. (2002) *Portraits of the Ptolemies: Greek Kings as Egyptian Pharaohs*. Austin, Tex.

Stefanakis, M. I. (2000) 'Ptolemaic coinage and Hellenistic Crete', in *Κρήτη και Αίγυπτος. Πολιτισμικοί δεσμοί τριών χιλιετιών*. Herakleion: 195–207.

Stefanou, M. (2008) 'The Ethnic Origin of Ptolemaic Cleruchs until 145 BC'. MA Thesis, University of Athens (unpubl., in Greek).

Steinby, C. (2007) *The Roman Republican Navy: From the Sixth Century to 167 BC*. Helsinki.

Stephens, S. (2004) 'For you, Arsinoe . . .', in Acosta-Hughes, Kosmetatou and Baumbach 2004: 161–76.

(2005) 'Battle of the books', in Gutzwiller 2005: 229–48.

Stewart, A. (1990) *Greek Sculpture: An Exploration*. 2 vols. New Haven, Conn. and London.

Strathern, P. (2007) *Napoleon in Egypt: 'The Greatest Glory'*. London.

Stroud, R. (1998) *The Athenian Grain-Tax Law of 374/3 BC*. Hesperia Suppl. 29. Princeton.

Stückelberger, A. (2009) 'Zu den Quellen der *Geographie*', in *Klaudios Ptolemaios: Handbuch der Geographie. Ergänzungsband*, ed. A. Stückelberger and F. Mittenhuber. Basle: 122–33.

Stückelberger, A. and Graßhoff, G. (eds.) (2006) *Klaudios Ptolemaios: Handbuch der Geographie, Griechisch–Deutsch*. 2 vols. Basle.

Svoronos, J. N. (1904) *Τὰ νομίσματα τοῦ κράτους τῶν Πτολεμαίων*. 3 vols. Athens.

Świderek, A. (1974) Review of Hauben 1970, *JJP* 18: 302–4.

Talbert, R. J. A. (ed. in collaboration with Bagnall, R. S. et al.) (2000) *Barrington Atlas of the Greek and Roman World*. Princeton.

Tarn, W. W. (1911) 'Nauarch and nesiarch', *JHS* 31: 251–9.

(1913) *Antigonos Gonatas*. Oxford.

(1930) *Hellenistic Military and Naval Developments*. Cambridge.

(1933) 'Two notes on Ptolemaic history', *JHS* 53: 57–68.

(1939) Review of Otto and Bengtson 1938, *JHS* 59: 323–4.

(1951) *The Greeks in Bactria and India*. Cambridge.

Tataki, A. B. (1998) *Macedonians Abroad: A Contribution to the Prosopography of Ancient Macedonia*. Meletemata 26. Athens.

Taylor, M. C. (1997) *Salamis and the Salaminioi: The History of an Unofficial Athenian Demos*. Amsterdam.

Tchernia, A. (1995) 'Moussons et monnaies. Les voies du commerce entre le monde gréco-romain et l'Inde', *Annales HSS* 5: 991–1009.

Thiel, J. H. (1954) *A History of Roman Sea-power before the Second Punic War*. Amsterdam.

(1966) *Eudoxos of Cyzicus: A Chapter in the History of the Sea-Route to India and the Route round the Cape in Ancient Times*. Groningen.

Thomas, R. (2004) '"Drownded in the tide": The *Nauagika* and some "problems" in Augustan poetry', in Acosta-Hughes, Kosmetatou and Baumbach 2004: 259–75.

Thompson, D. J. (1983) 'Nile grain transport under the Ptolemies', in *Trade in the Ancient Economy*, ed. Peter Garnsey, Keith Hopkins and C. R. Whittaker. London: 64–75 and 190–2.

(2000) 'Philadelphus' procession: Dynastic power in a Mediterranean context', in Mooren 2000: 365–88.

(2001) 'Hellenistic Hellenes: the case of Ptolemaic Egypt', in *Ancient Perceptions of Greek Ethnicity*, ed. Ir. Malkin. Washington D.C.: 301–22.

(2003) 'The Ptolemies and Egypt', in Erskine 2003: 105–20.

(2005a) 'Posidippus, poet of the Ptolemies', in Gutzwiller 2005: 269–83.

(2005b) 'The exceptionality of the early Ptolemaic Fayum', in *New Archaeological and Papyrological Researches on the Fayum. Proceedings of the International Meeting of Egyptology and Papyrology. Lecce, June 8th–10th 2005*, ed. M. Capasso and P. Davoli. Papyrologica Lupiensia 14. Lecce: 303–10.

(2012) *Memphis under the Ptolemies*. 2nd edn. Princeton.

Tipps, G. (1985) 'The Battle of Ecnomus', *Historia* 34: 432–65.

Tomber, R. (2008) *Indo-Roman Trade: From Pots to Pepper*. London.

Touloumakos, J. (2006) 'Politischer Witz und Karikatur in der hellenistischen Zeit. Ausdrucksformen und Stellenwert', *AncSoc* 36: 111–34.

Tracy, S. V. (1990) 'Hands in Samian inscriptions of the Hellenistic period', *Chiron* 20: 63–96.

Tréheux, J. (1992) *Inscriptions de Délos. Index I. Les étrangers, à l'exclusion des Athéniens de la clérouchie et des Romains*. Paris.

Tunny, J. A. (2000) 'Ptolemy "the Son" reconsidered: Are there too many Ptolemies?', *ZPE* 131: 83–92.

Turner, E. G. (1984) 'Ptolemaic Egypt', in *The Cambridge Ancient History*, vol. VII.1, ed. F. W. Walbank, A. E. Astin, M. W. Frederiksen and R. M. Ogilvie. 2nd edn. Cambridge: 118–74.

Tzalas, C. E. (2007) 'Bronze statues from the depths of the sea', in Valavanis 2007: 342–63.

Uebel, F. (1968) *Die Kleruchen Ägyptens unter den ersten sechs Ptolemäern.* Abhandlungen der Deutschen Akademie der Wissenschaften zu Berlin, Klasse für Sprachen, Literatur und Kunst 3. Berlin.

Valavanis, P. (ed.) (2007) *Great Moments in Greek Archaeology.* Los Angeles.

van Groningen, B. A. (1933) *Aristote. Le second livre de l'Économique.* Leiden.

Vandorpe, K. (2008) 'Persian soldiers and Persians of the Epigone: Social mobility of soldiers-herdsmen in Upper Egypt', *APF* 54: 87–108.

Van 't Dack, E. (1988) *Ptolemaica Selecta, études sur l'évolution des institutions militaires lagides.* Studia Hellenistica 29. Leuven.

Van 't Dack, E. and Hauben, H. (1978) 'L'apport égyptien à l'armée navale lagide', in *Das ptolemäische Ägypten,* ed. H. Maehler and V. M. Strocka. Mainz am Rhein: 59–94.

Veïsse, A.-E. (2004) *Les 'révoltes égyptiennes'. Recherches sur les troubles intérieurs en Égypte du règne de Ptolémée III à la conquête romaine.* Studia Hellenistica 41. Leuven, Paris and Dudley, Mass.

Vélissaropoulos, J. (1980) *Les nauclères grecs. Recherches sur les institutions maritimes en Grèce et dans l'Orient hellénisé.* Hautes Études du Monde Gréco-Romain 9. Geneva and Paris.

Vittmann, G. (2003) *Ägypten und die Fremden im ersten vorchristlichen Jahrtausend.* Mainz am Rhein.

Viviers, D. (1999) 'Economy and territorial dynamics', in *From Minoan Farmers to Roman Traders,* ed. A. Chaniotis. Stuttgart: 221–33.

Völcker-Janssen, W. (1993) *Kunst und Gesellschaft an den Höfen Alexanders des Großen und seiner Nachfolger.* Quellen und Forschungen zur antiken Welt 15. Munich.

Volkmann, H. (1939) Review of Otto and Bengtson 1938, *Philologische Wochenschrift* 1939: 1007–11.

(1969) *Res Gestae Divi Augusti. Das Monumentum Ancyranum.* 3rd edn. Berlin.

Wagner, E. A. (1888) *Die Erdbeschreibung des Timosthenes von Rhodus.* Leipzig.

Walbank, F. W. (1957, 1970) *A Historical Commentary on Polybius,* vol. I. Oxford.

(1967) *A Historical Commentary on Polybius,* vol. II. Oxford.

(1979a) *A Historical Commentary on Polybius,* vol. III. Oxford.

(1979b) 'Egypt in Polybius', in *Glimpses of Ancient Egypt: Studies in Honour of H. W. Fairman,* ed. J. Ruffle, G. A. Gaballa and K. A. Kitchen. Warminster: 280–9, reprinted in Walbank 2002: 53–69.

(1982) 'Sea-power and the Antigonids', in *Philip II, Alexander the Great, and the Macedonian Heritage,* ed. W. Adams and E. Borza. Washington D.C.: 213–36, reprinted in Walbank 2002: 107–2.

(1993) 'Η ΤῶΝ ΟΛῶΝ ΕΛΠΙΣ and the Antigonids', in *Ancient Macedonia V: Papers Read at the Fifth International Symposium Held in Thessaloniki, October 10–15, 1989.* Thessaloniki: 1721–30, reprinted in Walbank 2002: 127–36.

(2002) *Polybius, Rome and the Hellenistic World: Essays and Reflections.* Cambridge.

Wallensten, J. and Pakkanen, J. (2009) 'A new inscribed statue base from the sanctuary of Poseidon at Kalaureia', *Opuscula* 2: 155–65.

Weber, G. (1993) *Dichtung und höfische Gesellschaft. Die Rezeption von Zeitgeschichte am Hof der ersten Ptolemäer.* Hermes Einzelschr. 62. Stuttgart.

(1998–9) 'The Hellenistic rulers and their poets. Silencing dangerous critics?' *AncSoc* 29: 147–74.

Wehrli, C. (1968) *Antigone et Démétrios.* Geneva.

(1970) Review of Hauben 1970, *CE* 45: 403–4.

Welles, C. B. (1934) *Royal Correspondence in the Hellenistic Period.* New Haven Conn.

(1970) *Alexander and the Hellenistic World.* Toronto.

West, W. C. (1977) 'Hellenic homonoia and the new decree from Plataea', *GRBS* 18: 307–19.

Westermann, W. L. (1929) *Upon Slavery in Ptolemaic Egypt.* New York (= *P.Col.* I).

Wheatley, P. V. (1998) 'The chronology of the Third Diadoch War', *Phoenix* 52: 257–81.

Wiemer, H. U. (2002) *Krieg, Handel und Piraterie. Untersuchungen zur Geschichte des hellenistischen Rhodos.* Klio Suppl. 10. Berlin.

Will, Ed. (1979) *Histoire politique du monde hellénistique*, vol. i. 2nd edn. Nancy.

(1982) *Histoire politique du monde hellénistique*, vol. ii. 2nd edn. Nancy.

Will, Er. (1955) *Exploration archéologique de Délos faite par l'École Française d'Athènes. Fascicule xxii: Le Dôdékathéon.* Paris.

Willcocks, W. (1904) *The Nile in 1904.* London.

Wills, A. (1999) 'Herophilus, Erasistratus, and the birth of neuroscience', *Lancet* 354/9191 (13 November 1999): 1719–20.

Wilson, A. (2011) 'The economic influences of developments in maritime technology in antiquity', in *Maritime Technology in the Ancient Economy: Ship-Design and Navigation*, ed. W. V. Harris and K. Iara. Journal of Roman Archaeology Supplementary Series 84. Portsmouth, R.I.: 211–33.

Wilson, P. J. (1997–8) 'The illiterate trader?', *BICS* 42: 29–56.

Winnicki, J. K. (1985) 'Die Ägypter und das Ptolemäerheer', *Aegyptus* 65: 41–55.

(1989) 'Das ptolemäische Heer und das hellenistische Heerwesen', in Criscuolo and Geraci 1989: 213–30.

(1991) 'Der zweite syrische Krieg im Lichte des demotischen Karnak-Ostrakons und der griechischen Papyri des Zenon-Archivs', JJP 21: 87–104.

(2009) *Late Egypt and her neighbours.* JJP Suppl. 12. Warsaw.

Winter, E. (2010) 'Formen ptolemäischer Präsenz in der Ägäis zwischen schriftlicher Überlieferung und archäologischem Befund', in *Militärsiedlungen und Territorialherrschaft in der Antike*, ed. F. Daubner. *Topoi*: Berlin Studies of the Ancient World 3. Berlin and New York: 65–77.

Wörrle, M. (1971) 'Ägyptisches Getreide für Ephesos', *Chiron* 1: 325–40.

(1977) 'Epigraphische Forschungen zur Geschichte Lykiens I', *Chiron* 7: 43–66.

(1978) 'Epigraphische Forschungen zur Geschichte Lykiens II', *Chiron* 8: 201–46.

(1991) 'Epigraphische Forschungen zur Geschichte Lykiens IV', *Chiron* 21: 203–39.

Yonge, C. D. (transl.) (1853) *Diogenes Laertius: The Lives and Opinions of Eminent Philosophers*. London.
Young, G. K. (2001) *Rome's Eastern Trade: International Commerce and Imperial Policy, 31 BC–AD 305*. London and New York.
Zimmermann, M. (1992) 'Die lykischen Häfen und die Handelswege im östlichen Mittelmeer. Bemerkungen zu P.Mich. I 10', *ZPE* 92: 201–17.

Index

Abdemoun (of Sidon), 79, 81
Academy
See philosophy
Acamas (promontory), 219–22
Achaean League, 34, 89, 104, 125, 130, 148, 151
  cleruchs from, 125
administration, 98, 213
  Ptolemaic, 9, 29, 84, 88, 99, 101, 103, 173, 176, 203
  Roman, 231
Adoulis, 223, 226–9
  inscription from, 127, 205
Aegean, 4, 5, 12, 47, 82, 103, 106, 109, 110, 127, 130, 145, 156, 168, 171, 188, 213, 214, 217
  cleruchs from, 115, 127–30
Aegina, 3, 66, 105
  statues from, 143, 156–8
Aelius Gallus (prefect), 203
Aemilius Paullus, Lucius, 195
Aenus, 6, 84, 91, 128
  garrison at, 128
Aeolis, 128
Aethiops (philosopher), 141, 142
Aetolia, 148
Aetolian League, 153
Aetolians, 152, 153, 162, 166, 168, 194
  See Dicaearchus, Melancomas, Scopas, Sosippus, Theodotus, pirates
Africa, 15, 99, 212, 218
  circumnavigation of, 16, 17, 201, 206
  East, 219, 223–30
  North, 217, 218
Agatharchides (of Cnidus), 17
Agathocles, 90, 168
Aglaus (of Cos), 162, 169
agriculture, 2, 102
Agrippa
  world map of, 207
Alexander (son of Craterus), 23, 166
  revolt of, 119

Alexander III of Macedon (the Great), 1, 4, 9, 12, 16, 34, 40, 46, 67, 97, 98, 120, 121, 122, 160, 186, 187, 189, 190, 197, 201, 218, 233, 234, 235, 242, 243, 249, 256, 257
  and Aristotle, 141
  and Dionysus, 148
  army of, 122, 125
  corpse of, 121
  cult of, 39, 46
Alexandria, 1, 2, 3, 4, 29, 38, 90, 155, 167, 168, 176, 213, 214
  and Rhodes, 13, 66–81, 214, 215, 217
  as capital, 4, 18, 102, 176, 186, 231
  as destination, 125, 135, 139, 199
  citizens of, 218
  cults in, 8, 30, 31
  culture in, 139, 140, 141
  depravity in, 92
  food for, 173
  foundation of, 1, 214
  harbours of, 1, 4, 14
  manufacture in, 9, 143, 144
  philosophers in, 133–42
  port of, 1, 12, 15, 81, 174
  portrait of, 6
  Roman, 72
  See also Iuliopolis, Library, Lighthouse
Alexandris
  See ships (*Syrakosia*)
altars, 20, 30, 158
  to Ptolemies, 8, 9, 29, 146
Amasis (pharaoh), 3, 66
ambassadors, 27, 198, 199
  See envoys
Amon (god), 102
Amorgos, 8, 30, 35
  cult of Arsinoe on, 30
  garrison on, 30
Amphiaraus
  cult of, 143, 156

259

amphictyony
  Delian, 35
  Delphic, 31
Amphipolis, 120
amphorae
  Cnidian, 72
  Rhodian, 14, 68
Andros, 35
  battle of, 45, 83
  garrison on, 27
Ankyron Polis, 178
Antaeopolite nome, 183
Antigoneia (festival), 20, 21, 22, 23, 26,
    37–8
Antigonids, 118, 119, 120, 165, 166
Antigonus (of Carystus), 134
Antigonus I Monophthalmus, 4, 20–2, 24, 27,
    37, 40, 44, 67, 104
  and Nesiotic League, 24
  army of, 121
Antigonus II Gonatas, 20–3, 37, 39, 42, 60, 62,
    119, 139, 141, 188, 194
  joint rule with Demetrius II, 22–3
Antigonus III Doson, 23, 24, 88, 95, 148,
    152
Antioch, 140, 194, 203
Antiochus (of Aptera)
  as eponymous priest, 46
Antiochus (of Ascalon), 133, 135
Antiochus I, 42, 162
Antiochus II, 42
Antiochus III, 85, 86, 87, 88, 89, 93, 195
  pact with Macedon, 90
Antiochus IV Epiphanes
  war with Egypt, 82, 125, 168
Antiochus VIII Grypus, 170
Antiochus IX Cyzicenus, 170
Antirrhodos, 13, 14, 69
Antissa, 120
  garrison at, 29–31, 127
Antony (Marcus Antonius), 11, 185, 190
  portraits and statues, 144
Anubis, 9, 50
Apamea, 195
Aphrodite, 3, 49, 185, 190
  Zephyritis, 9, 29, 47
  See also Arsinoe II, Berenice I, Cleopatra VII
Apollo, 3, 36, 49, 153, 198
  Hylates, 49
  Karneios, 9
  Qos as, 11
Apollodorus (nesiarch), 32, 36
Apollodotus (*epistatês*), 56–8
Apollonius (of Aphrodisias), 104
Apollonius (*dioikêtês*), 42, 43, 79, 81

Apollonius (of Rhodes), 17
Apollonius (*stratêgos*), 173
Appian
  on Ptolemaic fleet, 82, 187
Aptera, 46, 54, 169
Arabia, 16, 175, 199, 202, 205, 229
  Ptolemy on, 218
  spices from, 16
Aramaic
  customs record, 3
Aratus (of Sicyon), 11, 125, 148
Arcesilaus (philosopher), 134–5, 140
Archimedes (of Syracuse), 197
Aristippus (philosopher), 142
Aristolaus (son of Ameinias), 147
Aristomenes, 167, 168
Ariston (of Chios), 140
Aristotle, 137, 139, 208, 212
  and Alexander, 141
army, 2
  of Cleomenes III, 151
  Ptolemaic, 9, 15, 99, 108, 120, 126, 127, 128,
    130
  Ptolemaic reformed, 110
Aromata, 16, 205, 223, 226–9
Arsinoe I, 136, 148
Arsinoe II, 35, 39, 48, 105
  as Aphrodite, 29, 30, 36, 39, 47
  cities named after, 10, 52, 58, 158. *See* Coressus,
    Methana
  cult of, 9, 29–31, 36, 52, 136, 153
  death of, 46, 51
  influence of, 41, 46, 47–8, 147
  marries brother, 32
  portraits and statues, 49, 144, 148, 156, 158
  Rotunda of, 29
  See Arsinoeia Philadelpheia
Arsinoe III
  portraits and statues, 146, 153–4, 156
Arsinoeia (festival), 153
Arsinoite nome, 9, 123, 172, 177
  See Fayum
Artemidorus (of Perge), 35, 146
  on Thera, 9, 10, 27, 29, 36
Artemisium
  battle of, 94
artists, 15, 16, 143, 144
Asclepieia (festival), 198
Asclepieum
  on Cos, 153
Asclepius (god), 143, 198
Asia, 86, 213
  geography of, 218
Asia Minor, 3, 14, 104, 109, 130
  cleruchs from, 115, 128

coast of, 129, 212, 215
geography of, 218
settlements in, 120
trade with, 77
Astaboras (river), 224–6
Astapus (river), 224–6
astronomy, 197, 208, 212, 213
Aswan, 2, 213
asylia, 162
Atbara
  See Astaboras
Athenaeus
  on barge of Philopator, 189–92
  on *Kaunos*, 55
  on Ptolemaic fleet, 83, 188
  See Callixeinus (of Rhodes)
Athena
  temple at Lindos, 66, 146
Athens, 33, 138, 140, 141
  Acropolis, 144
  Agora, 144, 149, 150
  and Ptolemies, 143, 148
  as naval power, 74
  coinage of, 12, 197
  cults in, 144, 149
  fall of, 38
  imports to, 76
  loss of possessions, 26
  merchants from, 72
  moneylenders in, 80
  Odeion, 144
  Oschophoria at, 195
  philosophy in, 140
  protects seas, 13, 76
  siege of, 105, 106
Attalids, 158
Attica, 46, 53, 54, 56, 57, 60, 61
  honey from, 72
Augustus, 203, 207

Babylon, 121, 122
Bacchon (nesiarch), 8, 27, 36, 59, 64
  career of, 32
Bactrians, 212
Bahr Yussuf, 180, 181
barges
  royal, 12, 19, 185–96
  See ships (*thalamêgoi*)
Belistiche, 65
benefaction
  royal, 24, 28, 99, 100, 101, 143, 153, 167, 177
Berenice (on Red Sea), 174
Berenice (princess), 136
Berenice I, 35
  and Aphrodite, 47

Berenice II, 6, 100
  cult of, 148, 149
  honoured in Athens, 148
  portraits and statues, 151, 152, 153, 156
Berenice III
  portraits and statues, 144
Berenice IV, 171
Beroea
  decree from, 22, 37
Bithynia, 104
Black Sea, 3, 4, 75, 103, 197
  trade, 80
  See grain, Pontus
boats
  See ships
Bocchus I (of Mauretania), 201
Boethus (*epistratêgos*), 178
Bosporus
  Ptolemies and, 104
  Thracian, 209
brigandage
  See piracy
brigands, 174, 175
  See also pirates
bronze
  objects of, 172
  See coinage, statues
Byzantium, 104, 105, 214

cabotage, 14
Calaureia, 58, 143, 158
Callias (of Sphettus), 8, 33, 105
Callicrates (of Samos), 7, 9, 30, 36, 39–53, 63, 64,
  147, 162
  and religion, 50
  as eponymous priest, 36, 39, 46, 50
  as nauarch, 39, 45, 47, 51–3, 64
Callimachus (*epistratêgos*), 205
Callimachus (governor of Upper Egypt),
  102
Callimachus (poet), 133, 137, 141
Callixeinus (of Rhodes), 11, 28, 189
  on Ptolemaic fleet, 41
Calymnos, 127
  statues from, 154–6
Camirus, 66
canals, 1, 178, 180, 183
  Memphis canal, 180
  See Bahr Yussuf
Canopus, 50, 219–22
  decree, 100–1
  Nile, mouth of, 212, 220–2, 223
Cape Guardafui, 199, 205, 227
Cape Sunium, 61
Cape Zephyrium, 39, 47

capital
  human ('smart'), 132–3. *See* intellectuals
cargoes, 3, 14, 72, 73, 78, 80, 106, 154, 175, 178, 198, 199
Caria, 3, 26, 28, 116
  Chrysaoric League in, 34
Carians, 3
Carpathos, 75
Carthaea, 54, 56, 57
Carthage, 169, 209, 211
  and Rome, 100
Carthaginian Wars
  Third, 196
Carthaginians, 17, 93
  See fleet
cartography, 18, 213–15, 217, 221–3
cartouche, 157
cash, 163, 167, 170, 171, 172, 180
Caspian Sea, 213
Cassandrea, 29
Caunus, 15, 30, 43–4, 53, 65
  cult of Arsinoe at, 30
cavalry, 125
Celts, 213
Ceos, 31, 35, 56, 57, 58
  cult of Arsinoe on, 31
  garrison on, 56
Chalcis, 106
Chares (of Lindos), 13
cheese, 15
Chelidonian Islands, 212, 219–22
Chersonese, Syrian, 194
Chersonesus, 75
China
  silk from, 203
Chios, 3, 127
  wine from, 15, 72
chôra (countryside), 60, 116, 176, 181, 183, 184
Chremonidean War, 10, 31, 37, 38, 39, 46, 48, 51, 53, 59, 60–1, 62, 64, 146, 147, 148, 158, 163
Chrysippus (philosopher), 140
Cilicia, 77, 128, 130, 171, 187, 214
  See pirates
Cimolos, 35, 71
cinnamon, 203
Citium, 141, 169
Clazomenae, 3, 106
Cleanthes (Stoic philosopher), 139
Cleomenes (of Naucratis), 12, 14, 67, 80, 81
  as satrap, 78–9, 98
Cleomenes III, 11, 87, 90, 95
  in Alexandria, 88–9, 116, 151
Cleopatra II, 177
  cult of, 146

dynastic disputes, 177
portraits and statues, 146
Cleopatra III, 177, 199, 203
Cleopatra VII, 12, 102, 179, 180, 205
  as Aphrodite, 186
  barge of, 185–6, 193
  portraits and statues, 144
cleruchs
  from Greece, 124–6
  origin of, 108–31
  royal ruling on, 108
cleruchy
  as institution, 108, 116, 131
Clitomachus (son of Dicaearchus), 167
clothes, 15, 155, 172, 173
Cnidus, 3, 17
Cnossus, 164, 166
Coele Syria, 6, 87, 89, 92, 93, 128
  Ptolemaic control, 84, 85, 90
  struggle over, 85
  Syrian control, 91
coinage
  bronze, 11, 12, 76
  copper, 173, 179
  gold, 10, 197
  of Athens, 197
  of Cyzicus, 197
  Ptolemaic, 10, 105, 164
  silver, 10, 76, 197
  Spartan, 11
coins
  circulation of, 103
  hoards, 197
  See also portraits
collectionism, 139
  Ptolemaic, 137–8, 142
Colossus of Rhodes, 13
commerce, 12, 14, 19, 67, 107, 163
  protection of, 12
  Ptolemaic, 16
  See also networks, trade
competition, 8, 16, 186, 187, 189, 197
contracts
  loan, 16
  shipping, 71, 78, 175
coordinates, 214, 220, 224, 227, 230
copper, 15. *See also* coinage
Coptus, 18, 203
Coresia
  See Coressus
Coressus (Coresia), 60
  as Arsinoe, 31, 57
Corinth, 24, 169, 194
cornucopia, 105

corruption
  Ptolemaic, 92, 161
Corupedion, 28
Cos, 127, 155
  battle of, 38, 43, 62, 83, 188
  birthplace of Ptolemy II, 11, 153
  festival at, 198
  Ptolemaic aid for, 105
  sacred envoys from, 33
  statues from, 143, 153–4, 155, 156
cotton, 15
court, 2, 141, 142
  Alexandrian, 41, 48, 50, 51, 65, 84, 87, 90, 92,
    96, 136–7, 140, 168, 198, 199, 205
  Antigonid, 136, 139
  Attalid, 158
  Byzantine, 90
  ideology of, 47
  Mauretanian, 201
  Spartan, 152
courtesans, 193
courtiers, 39, 51, 61, 135, 136, 158, 203
Crantor (philosopher), 134–5
Craterus, 122
Crates (philosopher), 134–5
Cretan Wars
  Second, 75
Cretans, 162, 164, 167
  as mercenaries, 164
Crete, 46, 54, 59, 65, 146, 163
  and Ptolemies, 127, 164
  and Rhodes, 75
  dedications from, 143, 148
  soldiers from, 127
  See pirates
Crimea, 197
crown
  double Egyptian, 157
cult
  See royal cult
culture, 8, 15, 50, 141, 192, 197
  See Alexandria
Curium, 49, 52
customs dues, 14, 71, 72, 81, 103, 183, 199
  Aramaic record of, 3
  See taxes
Cyclades, 21, 26, 38, 59, 83, 146, 168
Cydnus (river), 185
Cynopolite nome, 179, 180
Cynoscephalae, 194
Cyprus, 3, 4, 6, 30, 49, 72, 91, 92, 128, 169, 170,
    212, 214, 215, 219
  Antigonid victory on, 21
  Callias on, 33
  cleruchs from, 115, 128

cult of Arsinoe on, 30
governors of, 59, 92
grain from, 101
importance of, 84
Ptolemaic control, 84
Roman annexation, 171
shipbuilding on, 42
See pirates
Cyrene, 4, 91, 140, 209
  cleruchs from, 115, 117, 125, 128, 130
  grain from, 99
  rule of Ptolemy VIII, 130
  special status, 129
  See Eratosthenes
Cythnos, 15, 35
Cyzicus, 9, 17, 33, 197–8, 209

Danube, 214
decrees
  Athenian, 27, 106, 163
  honorific, 27, 29, 31, 33, 54, 57, 60, 66, 103,
    128, 153, 166
  official, 8, 20–1, 22–3, 176
  priestly, 100–1, 102
  royal, 102, 174, 177
  See League of Islanders
Delos, 30, 33, 49, 51, 52, 105, 153
  and freedom from Athens, 21
  and Ptolemies, 31, 32, 35
  archon, 21
  central role of, 33
  garrison on, 30
  Ptolemaieia on, 32
  royal cults on, 8, 30
  statues and portraits, 143, 145, 148
  temple accounts, 21, 32, 59
Delphi, 153
  dedications from, 143
  Pythian games, 50, 51
  statues at, 148, 149
Delta (Nile), 2, 3, 6, 43, 122, 212, 214, 215, 219,
    221
Demeter, 198
Demetrieia (festival), 20, 21, 22, 37–8
Demetrius (of Phalerum), 133, 139, 140
Demetrius I Poliorcetes, 6, 13, 20, 21, 37, 40, 43,
    44, 105, 122, 193
  and Athens, 105
  and Nesiotic League, 24
  at Salamis, 21, 94
  fleet of, 187–8
  funeral of, 194
  portraits and statues, 144
  ships of, 194
  See Demetrieia, Rhodes, siege of

Demetrius II, 20, 21, 37, 166
  joint rule with Gonatas, 22–3
Dere, 223, 226–9
desert, 2, 15, 18
diadem, 145, 148, 152
Dicaearchus (Aetolian), 166–8
Diocles (Athenian archon), 27
Diodorus Cronus, 136–7
Diodorus Siculus, 166
  on Antigonid activities, 25
  on Phoenician navy, 25
  on Rhodes, 67
Diodotus Tryphon, 169
Diogenes
  on East Africa, 230
  voyage of, 229–30
Diogenes (the Cynic), 142
Diogenes Laertius
  on philosophers, 134–5, 139, 140, 142
Diognetus (admiral), 94
dioikêtai, 181
  See Apollonios, Herodes
Dionysius (royal scribe), 178, 179
Dionysius Petosarapis, 176
Dionysus (god), 186
  Alexander connection, 148
  as Osiris, 186
  cave of, 190
  theatre of, 144, 149
Dioscurides (nephew of Antigonus), 21,
  25–6
Dorians, 3
dynastic cult
  Ptolemaic, 7, 8, 10, 12, 36, 144, 145, 146–7, 148,
    152, 158, 190
  See royal cult

eagle
  Ptolemaic, 10–12
earthquake
  See Rhodes
ebony, 172
economy, 107, 163, 176
  forms of, 81
  growth in, 69, 132, 169
  local, 60
  problems in, 164
Egypt, 169, 171
  and Rhodes, 13–14
  geography of, 97, 218
  immigration to, 123, 128
  in Polybius, 96
  Lower, 102, 157, 186
  population of, 173
  Roman conquest, 203

  temples in, 157
  unity of, 18, 186
  Upper, 142, 157, 183, 186
Egyptian Sea, 215, 217
Egyptianisation, 153, 192
Elaea, 17
Elateians, 104
elephants, 15, 16
  Indian, 205
Elis, 144
embassies, 31, 104, 203
  Athenian, 166
  from India, 203
  Ptolemaic, 168
  See envoys
empire, 7
  British, 7
  Ottoman, 7, 39, 158
  Ptolemaic, 6, 7–8, 9, 10, 16, 40, 52, 83, 89, 91,
    130, 131, 158, 215
  Venetian, 7
envoys, 8, 10, 32
  sacred (*theôroi*), 8, 9, 12, 17, 31, 33
Ephesus, 89, 91
  battle of, 67, 106
Ephorus (historian), 208
Epichares (*stratêgos*), 60
Epicurus (philosopher), 197
Epinicus (governor), 103, 128
Erasistratus (scientist), 139
Eratosthenes (of Cyrene), 17, 140, 207, 208, 217,
  224, 225
  and circumference of earth, 17, 213
  and Timosthenes, 208, 213
  as Librarian, 207
  geography of, 213–17, 218, 229, 230
  map of, 207, 211, 212, 213, 217, 218
  on East Africa, 230
  on route to India, 206
Eretria, 30, 138, 139
  cult of Arsinoe at, 30
Ethiopia, 15, 205, 212, 214, 224, 230
ethnics, 109–30, 135
  fictitious, 110, 124
Euclid, 133
Eudoxus (of Cnidus), 208
Eudoxus (of Cyzicus), 8, 17, 197–206, 230
Eumaridas (of Cydonia), 166
Eumenes II, 104
Euphrates, 42
Europe, 212
  geography of, 218
exploration, 2, 16, 17, 18, 163
  Red Sea, 16
  route to India, 197–206

exports, 3, 100
  from Egypt, 12, 15, 98, 99, 144, 203
  from Rhodes, 69
  grain, 98, 99
  of portraiture, 144

famine, 97, 98, 99, 101, 102
Fayum
  drainage of, 122
festivals, 8–9, 37, 38, 50, 148
  See games, *Antigoneia, Arsinoeia, Asklepieia,*
    Demetrieia, Koreia, Ptolemaieia
figs, 15, 62
fish, 15, 72, 197
Flamininus, Titus Quinctius, 194
fleet
  Alexandrian, 184
  Athenian, 75, 94
  Carthaginian, 93, 94, 95
  expense of, 42, 95
  of Demetrius Poliorcetes, 44
  of Ptolemy I, 94
  of Ptolemy II, 83
  Phoenician, 25
  Ptolemaic, 4, 6, 7, 25, 30, 40, 52, 53, 74, 83, 89,
    92–6, 99, 105, 145, 159, 163, 181, 188, 202,
    209
  Rhodian, 67, 73–4
  river, 177–8, 182, 183
  Roman, 94, 95
  Seleucid, 94
  See naval power
foodstuffs, 13, 15, 62, 102, 104, 142
  See also fish, grain
foreign policy
  Ptolemaic, 84–92, 102–5, 152, 171, 199
frankincense, 15, 175, 203
freight charges, 81
friends
  royal, 48, 51, 59, 162, 167, 173

Gabinius (Aulus), 171
Gades, 198, 201
games, 8, 31, 50, 148, 198
Garamantes, 212
garrisons
  Ptolemaic, 6, 8, 10, 22, 26, 27, 29, 30, 35, 54,
    57, 58, 60, 93, 120, 127, 128, 129, 146, 158,
    163–4, 181
Gaudos (isle of), 65
Gaza
  battle of, 121, 122
geography, 2, 13, 17, 18, 40, 64, 77, 89, 110, 141,
    218–31
  geographers, 17

geôgraphia as neologism, 208
  Hellenistic, 207–17
  in Posidippus, 136, 137
gnomon, 212, 214
gods
  Egyptian, 7, 9, 50
gold, 11, 185, 190, 193, 194
  Nubian, 15
  See coinage
Gortyn, 164
grain, 2, 15, 76, 101, 163, 181, 192
  Egyptian, 68, 78, 80, 97–107
  from Black Sea, 66
  gifts of, 68, 74, 97, 100, 105
  shortage, 78, 99–102
  supply, 34, 163
  trade, 14, 77, 104, 197
  transport, 105–6, 173
granary
  royal, 105
granite, 144, 153, 156, 158
Greece, 5, 14, 26, 143, 159, 214
  cleruchs from, 115, 124–6, 127,
    130
  mainland, 109
  northern, 136
Greek language, 195, 198
guard posts, 178, 180, 183. *See* garrisons
gymnasium, 99, 193
  of Ptolemy. *See* Ptolemaion (Athens)

hairstyles, 152, 155, 156, 157
Halicarnassus, 3, 42
harbours, 4, 40, 84, 145, 159, 175, 178, 197,
    209
  of Alexandria, 1, 12, 71, 202
  of Coressus, 57
  of Methana, 58
  of Rhodes, 13, 71, 77
  on Nile, 180, 181, 182, 183
  See ports
Haspheus (river guard), 178, 179
Helios
  statue of, 13
Hellespont, 6, 26, 84, 91, 104, 127, 128, 130, 167,
    213
Hera (goddess), 41, 50
Heraclea (Cyclades), 35
Heraclea (Pontus), 105, 114
Heracleides (ship captain), 72, 81
Heracleopolis, 180, 181
Heracleopolite nome, 178, 179, 182,
    183
Hercules
  Ptolemies as, 148

Hermeias, 87
Hermes
    as Thoth, 152
    Ptolemies as, 148, 152
Hermias (nesiarch), 36
Hermopolite nome, 183
Herodes (*dioikêtês*), 176
Herodotus (historian), 66, 214
Herophilus (scientist), 133, 139
Hiera Nesos, 179
Hierapytna, 75
Hierax (general), 164
Hieron (of Syracuse), 56, 57
    garrison commander, 58
Hieron II
    Syrakosia of, 100, 192, 193
Hippalus, 201–2, 205
    See monsoons
Hipparchus (of Nicaea), 208, 219
    on East Africa, 230
Hippomedon (governor), 103, 127
Hispania, 213
Homer, 141, 192
Homonoia (goddess), 36, 37
honey, 15, 72
hostages, 151, 196
Hymettus, 61

Ialysus, 66
Iasus, 136
Iberia. *See* Hispania
Icaros, 35
Idumaea, 11
Imbros, 76
immigrants, 3, 15, 121
    See cleruchs
immigration, 121
    to Egypt, 110, 129, 130, 131
imports, 3, 104
    to Athens, 105
    to Egypt, 15, 68, 72, 81, 99, 101, 102,
        203
India, 148, 229, 230
    sea route to, 198–206
Indian Ocean, 15, 17, 203, 205
Indians, 198, 199, 201, 203, 212
Indus, 190, 202
information
    role in market, 71, 78, 80
intellectuals, 16, 55, 132–42
    See also philosophers
interest
    rates of, 77, 80
Ionia, 3, 130, 214
Ionians, 3

Ios, 27, 30, 34, 35
    decree from, 27
irrigation, 2, 193
Isis, 9, 50, 146, 158, 186
    ship's name, 3
Issus, 217
    Gulf of, 214, 215
Italy, 17, 114, 211
    cleruchs from, 115
Itanus, 46, 48, 54, 59, 60, 75, 148, 166
    garrison at, 127, 163
    statues from, 148
Iuliopolis, 202
Iulis (Ceos), 56, 58
ivory, 15, 172, 190, 203

jewels, 15
    See stones, precious
Jews, 116
judges, 50, 56, 58, 174

Kerkeosiris, 177
kingship
    Antigonid declaration of, 21
    joint, 21, 22–3
klêros, 176, 177, 182
    inheritance of, 123, 124
    See cleruchs, cleruchy
Kore, 198
Koreia (festival), 17, 198, 199
Koroni, 58, 61

Lachares (tyrant), 105
Lake Mareotis, 1
Lake Moeris, 122
land registers, 182, 183
Laodice, 195
Larissa, 125
Latin language, 195
latitude, 212, 213
    calculation of, 214
League of Islanders, 6, 19–38, 127, 186, 188
    and Antigonids, 20–6
    and piracy, 161–2, 163
    as foundation of Ptolemy II, 19–36
    decrees of, 20–1, 29, 49. *See also* Nicuria
        decree
    loss of Ptolemaic control, 37–8, 83
    members of, 35
    nature of, 34
    Nicuria decree, 8, 27–8, 31, 32, 146
    Rhodian revival of, 19
    See Nesiotic League
Lebedos, 104
Lemnos, 26, 76

Leonidas son (of Archinas), 146
Lesbos, 29, 120, 127
Levant, 212, 214, 215
libraries
  of Aristotle, 139
  on *Syrakosia*, 192
Library (at Alexandria), 17, 139, 141, 231
  librarians of, 17, 140, 207
Libya, 208
Lighthouse (Pharos), 1, 13, 148
limestone, 147
Lindos, 66, 146
  temple chronicle, 66
linen, 103, 136, 172
loans, maritime, 77, 78
Locris, 194
lotus, 192
Lucullus, Lucius Licinius, 198
luxury, 12, 190, 199
Lycia, 28, 34, 44
Lycian League, 34
Lysicles (philosopher), 133–6, 137, 138, 139, 140,
  141
Lysimachea, 6, 84, 91, 127, 128
Lysimachus, 48, 65
  death of, 28, 29
  ships of, 187–8

Macedon, 6, 84, 110, 136, 151, 168, 194
  cleruchs from, 115, 116–24, 125, 126, 127, 130
  royal ship of, 186
Macedonian Wars
  Second, 194
  Third, 195
Macedonians
  in Egypt, 136
  See Macedon (cleruchs)
machimoi (Egyptian), 123, 176, 181, 182
Maeotis, 213
Magnesia (on the Maeander), 198
Magnesia (Thessaly), 125
Malian Gulf, 209
manpower
  military, 95, 130
  needs, 129
  recruitment, 120
manumission, 22
maps, 212, 213, 221, 222, 224, 230
  See cartography
marble, 144, 150
  Parian, 144, 145, 147, 148, 150, 152
  See statues
Marinus (of Tyre), 208, 212
  and Ptolemy, 219–30
  map of, 221

Marisa, 11
markets, 12, 14, 73, 80, 97, 98, 103, 132, 137
  taxes in, 71
Maronea, 6, 84, 91, 103, 128
  garrison at, 128
Marseilles, 209–12, 213
Massaliotes, 17
mathematics, 17, 197, 208, 213
Maximus (of Tyre), 192
medicine, 140, 203
Mediterranean, 1, 2, 3, 4, 12, 13, 18, 42, 45,
  213
  circumnavigated, 208
  eastern, 47, 82, 97, 160, 162, 163, 170, 209, 211,
    212, 215
  geography of, 217
  western, 209–12
Megara, 136
Melancomas (Aetolian general), 169
Melanias (of Perge), 18
Melos, 35
Memnon (of Rhodes), 67
Memphis, 3, 102
  canal, 180
Memphite nome, 179
Menches (village scribe), 177
Menecles (of Barca), 16
Menedemus (philosopher), 138–9, 140
Mentor (of Rhodes), 66
Menyllus (of Alabanda), 136
mercenaries, 3, 15, 108, 109, 120, 127, 128, 129,
  167, 169, 170
  as pirates, 161, 166, 169
  See also soldiers
merchants, 2, 14, 67, 71, 72, 75, 76, 81, 98, 152,
  171, 197, 199, 202, 219, 229
  See traders
meridians, 211, 212, 214, 217, 220, 222, 227
Meroe, 214, 223, 224
Messina, 211, 212
Metagonion (Cape Tres Forcas), 209
metals, 3
  See coinage, bronze, gold, silver
metal-work, 15
Methana (Arsinoe), 31, 58, 59, 60, 146, 158, 166
  refoundation of, 31, 58
Methymna, 29
Miletus, 3, 30, 48, 51, 190, 197
Min
  as Pan, 18
Mithridates Eupator (of Pontus), 197
Mithridatic Wars, 170
Molon (satrap), 87
money, 32, 37, 50, 68, 76, 77, 95, 165, 180
  See coinage

moneylenders, 80
monopoly, 199
monsoons, 15, 201–2, 229
  See Hippalus
Moors, 213
Morocco, 209
mosaics, 6, 192
Muhammad Ali (1805–48), 39
Museum (of Alexandria), 141
music, 193, 194
Muziris, 202
Myconos, 35
Myos Hormos, 174, 203
myrrh, 15, 203
Mytilene, 3

Napoleon, 60
natron, 3
nauarch, 36
  See Callicrates (of Samos)
Naucratis, 1, 3
  Hellenion at, 66
  hermeneus at, 66
  See Cleomenes
nauklêroi, 178
nauklêromachimoi, 176, 177, 182, 183
naval power, 2, 4, 6, 12, 40
  Antigonid, 82
  Athenian, 75, 76
  Hellenistic, 187
  Macedonian, 168, 195
  of Rhodes, 67, 74, 76
  Ptolemaic, 4–6, 11, 12, 16, 17, 18, 34, 41, 45, 60, 62, 82–96, 107, 161, 163, 165, 171, 186, 187, 188
  See thalassocracy
navigation, 175, 215
  Mediterranean, 212
navy
  See fleet
Naxos, 35
Nephereus (pharaoh), 97
nesiarchs, 33, 34, 36
  See Apollodorus, Bacchon, Hermias
Nesiotic League, 8
  See League of Islanders
networks
  strategic, 52
  trade, 14, 33, 42, 78, 79, 80, 81
  See Delos
New Carthage, 209
New Zealand, 132, 139
Nicomedes I, 104
Nicuria
  See League of Islanders

Nile, 1–2, 4, 15, 18, 19, 83, 174, 181, 183, 186, 193, 198, 214
  Blue, 225–6. *See* Astapus
  Canopic branch, 174
  course of, 223–6
  flood, 100, 173
  lakes, 223, 224, 225, 226–9
  mouths, 212, 220–2
  piracy on, 13
  police, 172–84
  protection on, 74, 76, 174
  role of, 19, 173, 186
  valley, 122
Nisyros, 35
North Pole, 222
Nymphaeum (Crimea), 3

officials, Ptolemaic, 9, 10, 35, 56, 144, 173, 176, 182, 202
Okelis (Bab el Mandeb), 202, 223, 226–9
olive oil, 3, 72, 81, 99
Olus, 46, 51, 53, 54, 75
Olympia, 36, 49
  statues at, 143, 144, 147
Olympus, 213
oracles, 198
  See Siwa
orchards, 192
Oropus, 143, 156
Osiris
  See Dionysus
ostraca, 184
  from Rhodes, 79, 81

Paerisades II, 104
Palaepaphos, 51, 52
Palestine, 120
palms, 192
Pamphylia, 6, 18, 34, 77, 84, 130
  Gulf of, 215
  See pirates
Pan (as Min), 18
Paphos, 4, 49, 188, 219–22
papyri, 15, 167
  of Herculanaeum, 197
  survival pattern, 118, 119, 122, 160
  See Posidippus, Zenon
paradoxography, 189
parallels (of latitude), 214, 217, 219, 220, 224
Parmeniscus (grain merchant), 78, 80, 81
Paros, 30, 35, 144
  cult of Arsinoe on, 30
  garrison on, 30

partnerships
  trading, 78, 81
Patroclus (of Macedon), 7, 52, 53–64, 148
  and Sotades, 64
  as eponymous priest, 39, 46, 53, 63
  as *stratêgos*, 53, 63, 64
  island of, 61
  son of Patron, 45, 53
Patron (ship captain), 72, 81
patronage
  Ptolemaic, 15–16, 18, 139
Pausanias
  on Patroclus, 53, 60
  on portraits, 144
pedlars, 14, 78, 79, 80, 81. *See* traders
Pella, 120, 135, 168
Peloponnese, 25, 31, 88, 89, 115, 124, 146, 158
Peloponnesian War, 94
Pelops (son of Alexander), 64
  as eponymous priest, 59
  islets of, 60
Pelusium, 71, 72
pepper, 203
Perdiccas, 121
perfumes, 15, 172, 198, 203
Perge
  See Artemidorus, Melanias
Perigenes (admiral), 94
Persephone
  See Kore
Perseus, 106, 195
Persian Wars
  Second, 94
phalanx, 122, 124
Pharos
  See Lighthouse
Phaselis, 3
Phila (daughter of Philip V), 168
Phila (wife of Demetrius I), 23
Philadelpheia (festival), 36
Philadelphia (Arsinoite nome), 9
Philip Arrhidaeus, 23
Philip II, 66
Philip V, 82, 87, 91, 95, 120, 166, 194
  pact with Antiochus, 90
Philocles (of Sidon), 4, 8, 36, 39, 43, 44, 45, 46,
  52, 53, 59, 63, 64
philosophers, 133–42
philosophy, 140
  Academic, 133
  dogmatism, 133
  Peripatetic, 139
  scepticism, 133, 135
  Socratic, 138
  Stoic, 138, 139, 140

Phocaea, 3
Phoenicia, 3, 4, 6, 14, 25, 26, 40, 77, 79, 101, 215
Phoenicians, 3
phoenix, 11
Pillars of Hercules, 214, 217
piracy, 12, 71, 106, 160–71
  collaboration with, 165–8
  control of, 12–13
  cost of, 73
  on Nile, 172–3, 183
  profits of, 163
  See pirates
Piraeus, 75, 77, 80
pirates, 2, 12, 60, 73, 74, 76, 160–4, 165, 168, 171,
  175, 199
  Aetolian, 162, 166, 169
  Cilician, 73, 162, 169–70
  Cretan, 73, 75, 162, 163–4, 166, 169
  Cypriot, 73, 170
  from Pontus, 170
  Pamphylian, 73, 170
plaster, 144
Plataea, 36
Plato, 135, 137, 140
Pliny, 203, 205
  on monsoon, 201
Plutarch, 185, 189, 193, 195
Polemon (philosopher), 134–5, 140
police, 123, 173, 174, 175, 179, 180, 183
  See potamophylakes, protection, ships
    (*phylakides*)
Polybius, 12, 196
  on Achaean League, 125
  on impiety, 167, 168
  on Ptolemaic empire, 6, 82–96
  on Ptolemies VI and VIII, 125
  on Ptolemy IV, 84–5, 90
  on Raphia, 127
Polyrrhenia, 166
Pompey (Gnaeus Pompeius), 170, 171
Pontus, 197, 213
  cleruchs from, 115
  produce from, 72
  See Black Sea
port, 14, 15
portraits, 6
  of Ptolemies, 9, 143–59
  on coins, 105, 143, 145, 148, 151, 156
  Roman imperial, 9, 143
portraiture
  technique, 143–4
ports, 2, 3, 18, 42, 54, 175
  See harbours
Porus (king), 203
Poseidon (god), 58, 158, 166

Posidippus (poet), 9, 13, 29, 30, 47, 140
  on Arsinoe, 30, 42
  on Callicrates, 30, 47, 50, 51
  on gems, 136, 137
  on Lysicles, 133–6
Posidonius (of Apamea), 17, 201, 208, 229
  on Eudoxus, 198–9, 205
potamophylakes (river guards), 176, 178, 182–4
  Roman period, 184
power, 207
  economic, 12
  hard and soft, 8, 9, 12
  maritime, 1, 4
  Ptolemaic, 6, 10, 12, 15, 18, 22, 158, 217
  Roman, 93, 196
  royal, 2, 6, 33, 186, 193, 207
  See also naval power
prejudice
  anti-Egyptian, 61
prices, 73, 80, 98
  grain, 98, 101, 105
priestess
  in dynastic cult, 153
priests
  Egyptian, 100, 102
  in dynastic cult, 29, 39, 46, 50, 53, 60, 63, 149, 167
Proculus, L. Valerius, 184
Propontis, 3, 103, 197
  cleruchs from, 115, 127
prosopography
  of cleruchs, 109, 110, 117
prosperity, 11, 18, 39, 42, 69, 105, 163
protection
  for shipping, 13, 73–6, 106, 161, 165, 173, 175–82, 183
  military, 107
province (Roman), 171, 215
proxenia
  grants of, 34, 46, 54, 66
Psammetichus I, 3
Ptolemaea
  See Ptolemaieia
Ptolemaieia (festival), 8, 10, 31–2, 35
  at Athens, 149
  foundation of, 28
  on Delos, 31, 32, 35
Ptolemaion
  at Athens, 144, 149, 150, 151
  at Rhodes, 67, 146
Ptolemais, 89, 93, 94
Ptolemais (Athenian tribe), 148
Ptolemais Hermeiou, 142, 167, 183
Ptolemais Theron, 223, 226–9
Ptolemais-Akkô, 170

Ptolemy (geographer), 206, 208, 215, 231
  See also Marinus, Timosthenes
Ptolemy (son of Sosibius), 168
Ptolemy Ceraunus, 188
Ptolemy I Soter (son of Lagus), 1, 4, 8, 11, 25, 27, 28, 39–40, 122
  and Cyrene, 129
  and Delos, 8, 35
  and Rhodes, 13, 67, 105, 145
  army of, 109, 116, 118, 121–2, 126
  as Soter, 31
  cult of, 31, 32, 40, 67, 146
  deification of, 8
  in Aegean, 26–7, 28
  patronage of, 136–7
  portraits and statues, 144, 145–6, 150
  settles cleruchs, 122
  takes title of king, 67
Ptolemy II Philadelphus, 6, 7, 8, 13, 17, 28, 34, 35, 36, 38, 40, 41, 45, 48, 62, 100, 104, 108, 118, 123, 136, 148, 162, 188, 189, 207, 219
  Aegean policy, 8, 10, 58, 67, 83, 105, 130, 136, 147, 162
  and Aratus, 125
  and Asia Minor, 128
  and League of Islanders, 20–36
  army of, 121
  born on Cos, 11, 127, 153
  character of, 231
  cult of, 32, 104
  cultural policy, 139
  drainage works, 122, 123
  fleet of, 42, 83, 187, 188
  marries sister, 9, 32, 41, 64
  portraits and statues, 49, 144, 147, 148, 158
  ships of, 188
  wealth of, 108
  See Theoi Adelphoi
Ptolemy III Euergetes, 9, 17, 38, 40, 87, 88, 89, 100, 103, 105, 127, 140, 166, 205, 207
  aids Rhodes, 68, 74, 76, 105
  and Achaean League, 125
  and Sparta, 11, 151
  cult of, 146, 148, 149
  expands control, 130
  honoured in Athens, 148–50
  portraits and statues, 144, 148, 151–3
  See Canopus decree
Ptolemy IV Philopator, 3, 11, 40, 88, 95, 105, 127, 168
  army of, 95, 127
  barge of, 189–92
  in Polybius, 82, 84–5, 90
  portraits and statues, 146, 153, 156

Ptolemy V Epiphanes, 51, 75, 90, 91, 168
  portraits and statues, 146, 148
Ptolemy VI Philometor, 16, 110, 146, 149, 158,
    169, 189
  and Achaea, 125
  and Rome, 136
  cult of, 146
  dynastic disputes of, 91–2
  end of empire under, 12, 59, 143, 145, 148
  portraits and statues, 144, 146, 148, 156
Ptolemy VIII Euergetes II, 16, 17, 164, 169, 177,
    198
  and Achaea, 125
  dynastic disputes of, 91–2, 177
  expels intellectuals, 16
  rules Cyrene, 91, 130
Ptolemy IX Soter II, 146, 170, 199
  portraits and statues, 144
Ptolemy X Alexander, 170
Ptolemy XII Neos Dionysus (Auletes), 179, 180,
    205
  restored, 171
Ptolemy the Son, 48
Punic Wars
  First, 93, 94, 95
purple, 185, 189, 190, 194
Pydna
  battle of, 92, 195
Pyrgoteles (ship designer), 188
Pytheas, 209, 212, 218

Qos (god)
  See Apollo
quarries, 2

Rabirius Postumus, 180
Ramses II, 97
Raphia
  battle of, 82, 90, 95, 127
  stele, 90
recruitment
  military, 60, 118, 120, 125, 130, 166
recruits
  See cleruchs
Red Sea, 16, 18, 83, 175, 198, 202, 203, 212
  coast, 2, 18
  trade, 15, 16
revolts, 87, 119
  Egyptian, 90, 167, 168, 176
Rhamnus
  decree from, 60, 61
Rhapta, 229
Rhenea, 15, 35
Rhithymna, 54
Rhodes, 14, 66, 143, 163, 167, 168, 213, 214

and Alexandria, 13–14, 66–81, 106, 214, 215,
    217
and pirates, 169, 170
as trade centre, 66, 77–81
cult of Soter, 67, 145
Dorians from, 3
dynastic cult at, 144
earthquake, 68, 74, 105
necropolis of, 79
produce from, 15, 72
protects seas, 13, 106, 165
siege of, 13, 67, 68, 105, 145
See Colossus, sanctuaries, ships (*phylakides*)
Rhosus, 193
robbers, 172
  See pirates
Romans, 183, 185, 194
Rome, 87, 169, 195, 211
  and Egypt, 92, 97, 203
  and Macedon, 194, 195–6
  defeats Carthage, 93
  protects seas, 13
  Ptolemies and, 16, 170–1, 180
  senate of, 136
routes
  by land, 18, 213
  by sea, 69, 75, 209, 212, 213, 214, 215, 229
  See India
royal cult
  Ptolemaic, 7
  See Arsinoe II, dynastic cult, Ptolemy I,
      Ptolemy II, Ptolemy III, Ptolemy VI
royal scribes, 178

Sacae, 213
sailors, 61, 183, 189, 192, 197, 198, 205
Salamis, 209
Salamis (Cyprus), 4, 6
  battle of, 6, 43, 44, 94
Sallust, 201
Samos, 3, 30, 49, 51, 52, 89, 91, 95, 163, 203
  cult of Arsinoe on, 30
  garrison on, 60, 163
  Heraeum on, 49, 54, 59
  See Callicrates
Samothrace, 18
  Ptolemies and, 29, 103
  royal cult on, 30
Samothracian gods, 29
sanctuaries, 49, 156, 158, 209
  at Thermus, 153
  for dynastic cult, 9, 49
  in Egypt, 18
  on Cyprus, 49
  on Rhodes, 145, 146

sanctuaries (*cont.*)
  on Samos, 49
  on Samothrace, 29, 30
  See temenos
Sarapis, 9, 146
  statue of, 3, 105
Sarmatians, 213
Schedia, 183, 189
science, 197, 213
scientists, 16
Scopas (Aetolian), 167
Scyros, 76
Scythia, 214
Scythians, 213
Sea of Marmara
  See Propontis
Sebennytus, 219–22
  as Nile mouth, 212, 220–2, 223
Seleuceia (in Pieria), 89, 93, 101, 105
Seleucids, 40, 83, 87, 91, 94, 170
  See fleet
Seleucus I Nicator, 4, 193
Seleucus II, 42
Sera, 221
Seriphos, 35
settlers
  military, 108–31
  See cleruchs
Sextus Empiricus, 133
Shakespeare, William, 185
ship captains, 175, 176, 178, 183, 184
shipbuilding, 6, 42, 217
ships, 3, 170, 181, 202
  Amphitrite, 194
  Britannia, 193
  Bucintoro, 189, 190
  Eight, 188
  elephant-carriers, 16
  Fifteen, 187, 188
  flagships, 187, 188, 189, 190, 193, 194, 195
  Forty, 95, 189, 192
  Gloriana, 189
  HMS *Victory*, 194
  Isis, 3
  lead-clad, 192, 195
  merchant, 71, 75, 76, 77, 183, 193
  of Theseus, 195
  on Nile, 172, 173
  phylakides, 14, 74, 106, 176, 177, 178, 181, 183
  Sixteen, 187, 188, 194–5
  Syrakosia, 100, 192
  thalamêgoi, 173, 178
  Thirteen, 193
  Thirty, 42, 188
  transport, 6, 94, 106, 178, 181, 183, 187, 193

triêreis, 76, 94
trihêmioliai, 74, 181
Twenty, 42, 188
undecked (*aphrakta*), 27, 106, 195
warships, 6, 42, 75, 83, 93, 94, 105, 181, 187–8, 194, 209
  See barges (royal), fleet
shipwrecks, 17, 72, 133, 135, 136, 138, 139, 154, 193, 198, 199
Sicily, 4, 209
  and Egypt, 100, 115
Sicyon, 22, 26
  See Aratus
Sidon, 4, 79
  See Philocles
siege engines, 188, 192
sieges, 13, 25, 67, 68, 93, 105, 106, 187
Sierra Nevada, 211
silk, 203
silver, 15, 33, 185, 193
  See coinage
Sinope, 3, 105, 214
Siphnos, 35
Siwa, 145
slaves, 27, 163, 165, 187
  trade in, 13, 73, 166, 167, 169
soldiers, 60, 61, 89, 108, 116, 164, 170, 173, 177, 182
  cavalry, 110, 122, 125
  infantry, 110, 122, 125
  See cleruchs
Soli, 4, 106, 187
Somalia, 199, 205
  coast of, 16, 206
Sosibius, 87, 88, 89, 91, 95
Sosippus (Aetolian), 153
Sostratus (of Cnidos), 148
Sotades (of Maronea), 53, 54, 55–6, 62, 64–5
Spain, 184, 198, 201, 209
  See Hispania
Sparta, 11, 159
  dedications from, 143, 152
  Ptolemies and, 97, 148
Spartans, 16, 61
spices, 15, 16, 203
  See Aromata
statues, 49
  acrolithic, 144, 150, 151
  bronze, 13, 50, 144, 146, 147, 149, 153, 154, 155, 156, 159
  colossal, 145, 147, 150, 156
    See Colossus of Rhodes
  Egyptian, 157–8
  Egyptianising, 153
  marble, 144, 155
    See marble, Parian

royal, 9, 190
   See portraits
stone, 143, 144, 159
Stilpo (philosopher), 136–7, 140, 141
stones
   precious, 15, 136, 190, 198, 203
   See granite, limestone, marble, statues
Strabo, 15, 183, 198, 202, 208, 218
   on Cilician piracy, 169–70
   on libraries, 139
   on Mediterranean, 215
   on Nile, 224, 225, 229
   on Ptolemy II, 231
   on Rhodes, 74
   on Timosthenes, 208
stratêgoi
   Macedonian, 45
   Ptolemaic, 39, 44, 54, 60, 62, 63, 64, 128, 173, 203
Stratonice (d. of Seleucus), 194
Stymphalus, 104
sun-dial, 214
   See gnomon
Syene
   See Aswan
symposium, 137, 138
synoecism, 104
Syracuse, 100
   See Hieron, Hieron II
Syria, 4, 14, 77, 168, 169, 171, 193, 203
   grain from, 101
   kings of, 84, 92
   settlements in, 120
   soldiers from, 116
   trade with, 77
Syrian Wars
   First, 47
   Second, 42, 43, 52, 62, 121
   Third, 42, 89, 101
   Fourth, 82, 85, 86, 93–4, 168
   Fifth, 91
Syros, 35

Tarragona, 203
Tarsus, 185, 186, 193
tax farmers, 71
taxes, 15, 42, 71, 81, 98, 217
   on trade, 14, 71, 77, 167
      See customs dues
   under Rome, 184
temenos, 10, 29, 36, 49, 148, 153
   See sanctuaries, temples
temples, 190
   at Delphi, 153
   at Olympia, 50

Egyptian, 157
   on Cos, 153
   on Rhodes, 66
   on Thera, 9, 146
   See Delos, Samos
Tenos, 35
Teos, 3, 104, 198
Termessos, 34
textiles, 15, 185
   See clothes, cotton, linen, silk, wool
thalassocracy
   Antigonid, 44
   Ptolemaic, 25, 39–64, 82, 133
   See naval power
Thasos, 72
Theangela, 72
Thebaid, 18, 102, 183
   revolt of, 168
Thebes, 102
Theocritus (poet)
   on Ptolemy II, 11, 41, 47, 83, 107, 108, 120, 129
Theodotus (of Aetolia), 87, 89, 90
Theoi Adelphoi, 9, 36, 39, 46, 50, 64
Theoi Euergetai, 169
Theophrastus (of Eresus), 136, 137, 139, 141
Thera, 9, 10, 18, 30, 56, 57, 58, 59, 60, 91, 127, 158, 165, 166
   cults on, 30, 144, 146–7
   garrison on, 56, 58, 163, 164, 169
   statues from, 143, 145
   temenos of Artemidorus, 29, 36
Thermopylae, 209
Thermus, 143, 153
Thessaly, 115, 124, 125
Thmuis, 6
Thoth
   See Hermes
Thrace, 6, 84, 87, 103, 127, 128, 130, 136, 213
   Ptolemies and, 103, 116, 117
   soldiers from, 110
thunderbolt, 10, 11, 12, 144
Tiber, 195
timber, 15, 40, 217
   See wood
Timosthenes (of Rhodes), 17, 45, 207
   and Marinus, 212
   and Ptolemy, 219–20
   geography of, 207–11, 213, 215, 230
   windrose of, 212–13, 217
Tlepolemus (son of Artapates), 168
Tmoienetis, 172
toparchies, 179, 182

trade, 12, 17, 66
  Aegean, 12
  and piracy, 162
  financing of, 77–81
  Mediterranean, 2, 15
  organisation of, 14, 77–81
  Ptolemaic, 12, 16, 103, 159
  Red Sea, 15, 16
  Rhodes–Egypt, 67–9
  with east, 17
  with India, 202, 205
  See commerce, exports, grain, imports,
     networks, slaves, taxes, transaction costs
traders, 14, 15, 71, 78, 106, 171, 173
  See merchants, pedlars
transaction costs, 69–73, 76
travel, 17, 18, 43, 215
  See routes
travellers, 15, 219
treaties, 4, 75, 125, 144, 164
Troglodytes, 18
  land of, 229
troops, 33
  Greek, 116
  light-armed, 127
  on Nile, 177
  Ptolemaic, 30, 51, 61, 95, 120, 146,
    163
  See soldiers
tutor (royal), 17
Tyre, 89, 93, 94
  purple from, 190
  siege of, 21, 25

uraeus, 148, 157

Vasco da Gama, 198, 206
Venice, 7
  Doge of, 189, 190
vivisection, 139

warfare
  changes in, 16
wealth, 12, 193
  agricultural, 14, 15
  Ptolemaic, 12, 15, 131
  royal, 186
wheat, 12, 15, 33, 178, 182
  See grain
winds, 212–13, 214, 215, 223, 226, 229, 230
  See Hippalus, monsoons
wine, 3, 15, 72, 99, 172, 192
  sweet, 15
women, 172
  quarters for, 190, 193
wood, 3, 144, 189, 190
  See ebony, timber
wool, 3, 172

Zanzibar, 199, 230
Zeno (Stoic philosopher), 139, 140, 141
Zenon
  agent of Apollonius, 43
  papyri of, 39, 42, 43, 52, 72, 79, 81
Zenon (commander), 27, 33, 106, 163
Zeus (god), 11, 41, 49, 50, 138
  eagle of, 10